CHAUCER AND HIS READERS

Frontispiece. The poet laureate and aureate:
Geoffrey Chaucer performs for the court.
The frontispiece from Chaucer's *Troilus and Criseyde*.

SETH LERER

Chaucer and His Readers

Imagining the Author
in Late-Medieval
England

PRINCETON UNIVERSITY

PRESS

Copyright © 1993 by Princeton University Press
Published by Princeton University Press, 41 William Street,
Princeton, New Jersey 08540
In the United Kingdom: Princeton University Press,
Chichester, West Sussex

Library of Congress Cataloging-in-Publication Data

Lerer, Seth, 1955–
Chaucer and his readers : imagining the author in late-medieval
England / Seth Lerer.
p.   cm.
Includes bibliographical references and index.
ISBN 0-691-06811-9
1. Chaucer, Geoffrey, d. 1400—Appreciation—England.
2. English poetry—Middle English, 1100–1500—History and criticism—
Theory, etc.   3. Authors and readers—England—History.
4. Books and reading—England—History.
5. Reader-response criticism.   6. Aesthetics, Medieval.   I. Title.
PR1924.L38   1993
821′.1—dc20   92-33454

This book has been composed in Adobe Caslon
Designed by Jan Lilly

Princeton University Press books are printed on
acid-free paper and meet the guidelines for permanence
and durability of the Committee on Production
Guidelines for Book Longevity of the
Council on Library Resources

Printed in the United States of America

2   4   6   8   10   9   7   5   3   1

for Anthony Grafton

———————

CONTENTS

ILLUSTRATIONS

ACKNOWLEDGMENTS

THIS BOOK could not have been completed without the support of many colleagues, friends, and institutions. Professional Chaucerians have been generous with their responses to this work, especially to papers presented at the Conventions of the Modern Language Association (1982, 1985, 1987, 1989, 1991), the New Chaucer Society (1988), the Medieval Association of the Pacific (1992), and at Kalamazoo (1981, 1985). Portions of this book were also delivered as lectures at the Universities of California at Berkeley, Irvine, and Riverside; Caltech; the University of Chicago; Princeton University; Stanford University; and the Warburg Institute. A memorable conference at the University of Rochester organized by Thomas Hahn in 1988 helped focus the direction and broaden the scope of the book. Among those who offered advice and information, I am pleased to thank R. Howard Bloch, John Bowers, David Carlson, Anne Coiro, Rita Copeland, Carolyn Dinshaw, Tony Edwards, John Fleming, Jay Fliegelman, Louise Fradenburg, Anthony Grafton, Ralph Hanna III, Richard Horvath, Steven Justice, Victoria Kahn, Nancy Lerer, Anne Middleton, Lee Patterson, Russell Peck, George W. Pigman III, Thomas Roche, Brian Stock, Paul Strohm, Karla Taylor, and Eugene Vance. I have also learned from the incisive responses of John Ganim; from the adventurous interdisciplinarity of David Wallace and Robert Harrison; and from the healthy skepticism of Joseph Dane. Susan Crane and John Ganim read the final draft for Princeton University Press, and both offered helpful and extensive suggestions for revision. Throughout the preparation of this book, Robert Brown has been a patient and supportive editor. Mary F. Godfrey once again proved an invaluable research assistant.

Funding for the research and writing of this book was provided by the grant of a Bicentennial Preceptorship from Princeton University, a Huntington-Exxon Grant from the Huntington Library, and a Fellowship for University Teachers from the National Endowment for the Humanities. I am also grateful to the staff and librarians of the following institutions, both for welcome assistance during the process of research and for the generosity in allowing me to quote from manuscripts and books in their possession: The Huntington Library, The British Library, Sion College Library, The Bodleian Library, Trinity College Cambridge, The Warburg Institute, Princeton University, Stanford University, The University of

Chicago, The University of California at Berkeley, and UCLA. I am especially grateful to The Huntington Library, Trinity College Cambridge, Corpus Christi College Cambridge, and Stanford University Library for permission to reproduce materials as illustrations for this book.

Special thanks are also due to the following journals and publishers for permission to incorporate material originally published as articles: to *Exemplaria* and the State University of New York Press; to *Viator* and the University of California Press; to *Notes and Queries*; and to *Spenser Studies* and AMS Press. None of the following chapters reprints previously published essays in their entirety, however. All previous publications have been substantially revised, both to bring their arguments into line with the subject of the book and to attempt to correct errors of fact and judgment that I had originally made.

A NOTE ON EDITIONS

UNLESS otherwise noted, all quotations from the works of Geoffrey Chaucer will be from Larry D. Benson, general editor, *The Riverside Chaucer*, third edition (Boston: Houghton Mifflin, 1987). Quotations from the *Canterbury Tales* (abbreviated *CT*) will be cited by Fragment and line number. Quotations from the works of John Lydgate will be from the following: Henry Bergen, ed., *Lydgate's Fall of Princes*, Parts 1– 4, EETS ES 121–24 (London: Oxford University Press, 1924); Henry Noble MacCracken, ed., *The Minor Poems of John Lydgate, Part I*, EETS ES 107 (London: Kegan Paul, Trench, Trübner, 1911); Henry Noble Mac-Cracken, ed., *The Minor Poems of John Lydgate, Part II*, EETS OS 192 (London: Oxford University Press, 1934). All other editions will be cited in full in the notes.

At times I quote directly from manuscripts, at times from published editions. I use standard library abbreviations, shelf marks, catalogue numbers, and foliation. When quoting from manuscripts, I use square brackets to indicate my editorial expansion of scribal abbreviations. When quoting from published editions or transcriptions of manuscript material, I have tried to check their readings against those of the manuscripts. All unattributed translations are my own.

ABBREVIATIONS

EETS OS   *Early English Text Society, Original Series*
EETS ES   *Early English Text Society, Extra Series*
JMRS   *Journal of Medieval and Renaissance Studies*
Manly-Rickert   John M. Manly and Edith Rickert, *The Text of the Canterbury Tales*
                 (Chicago: University of Chicago Press, 1940), eight volumes,
                 cited by volume number and page
Manual   *A Manual of Writings in Middle English*, ed. J. Burke Severs and
                 Albert E. Hartung (New Haven: Yale University Press, 1967–)
MED   *Middle English Dictionary*, ed. Hans Kurath et al. (Ann Arbor:
                 University of Michigan, 1954–)
OED   *Oxford English Dictionary*, ed. James H. A. Murray et al. (Oxford:
                 Oxford Univeristy Press, 1933
SAC   *Studies in the Age of Chaucer*
SP   *Studies in Philology*

CHAUCER AND HIS READERS

The Subject of Chaucerian Reception

THIS IS a book about subjection. It chronicles the self-conscious invention of an author by those apparently least qualified to do so. It also tries to understand the idea of a literary history engendered by that invention, and to confront the makings of a canon by those apparently most qualified to do so. Its central claim, to be specific, is that Chaucer—as author, as "laureate," and as "father" of English poetry—is a construction of his later fifteenth-century scribes, readers, and poetic imitators. Its argument is that the terms of that construction—the vocabulary of literary imitation and the dynamics of reader response—are already present in his poetry. Throughout his major narratives, Chaucer presents a class of readers and writers subjected to the abuse of their audience or subject to the authority of their sources. The Clerk, the Squire, Geffrey himself, even poor Adam Scriveyn, find themselves at the mercy of a range of unquestionable *auctores*. Whether they be dead poets or distant patrons, the men who challenge Chaucer's fictive readers and writers cannot be assailed. Their own authority renders the work of those who follow them inept, dull, or useless. In such examples as the Clerk's obedience to Petrarch and the Host, the Squire's vain attempts to match his father the Knight, and Adam Scriveyn's garblings of the *Troilus* and *Boece*, Chaucer's inheritors found their personae. The poetry of Clanvowe, Hoccleve, Lydgate, Ashby, Hawes, and Skelton; the scribal work of John Shirley; the criticism of Caxton; the anthologies of the gentry—all in their own distinctive ways draw on these figures from Chaucerian fiction to articulate their understanding of authorial and interpretive control. As children to the father, apprentices to the master, or aspirants before the laureate, those who would read and write after the poet share in the shadows of the secondary. It is the purpose of this book to understand the quality of post-Chaucerian writing in these terms: to chart the forms and consequences of the reception and transmission of Chaucer's poetry by those admittedly unworthy of his mantle.

Fifteenth-century English literature is a literature of paradoxes. In its effusive, if not hyperbolic, praise of Chaucer, it establishes a model of lit-

erary imitation who is so deft in technique and so unassailable in his official sanction that he becomes, in effect, inimitable. In their own, equally
effusive protestations of incompetence or dullness, the writers of the century appear to make a poetry so bad that it is virtually unreadable: to make,
in short, a poetry that is not poetry at all and to articulate a vision of the
author not as a creative individual but rather as the mouthpiece for a
"comun vois" or commonplace didacticism. This is the poetry of C. S.
Lewis's "Drab Age," a poetry of nearly opaque aureate vocabulary, crabbed
syntax, and broken meter.[1] It is a period far outside the canons of contemporary academic study; yet it is the period that sets out the canon of
Chaucer's own work and establishes the origins of English literary history.
Much recent work on fifteenth-century literature has begun to open up
these paradoxes for inspection.[2] The poetry of Hoccleve, Lydgate, and
Hawes has come to be seen as complex attempts to refigure a poetic stance
in the face of earlier fourteenth-century example and current fifteenth-
century dynastic patronage.[3] The work of scribes and compilers such as
John Shirley and the artifacts of personal commission such as the Oxford
Group of manuscripts (Bodleian Library MSS Bodley 638, Tanner 346,
and Fairfax 16), together with the work of Caxton and de Worde, has
come to be appreciated as embedding more or less coherent acts of textual
and literary criticism.[4] Studied in tandem, these documents of literary reception have contributed to a new understanding of the fifteenth century
stripped of its old, teleological flavor: as something other than a way sta-
tion between medieval and Renaissance, English and humanist, script and
print.[5]

Much of this recent scholarship, however, still defines its subject as the
province of imitation. Lines of analysis tend to focus on the local derivations of a text in its Chaucerian pre-texts, and for many readers of the
poetry of fifteenth-century England the "meaning" of a work lies in its
parasitic quality: its status *as* imitation, derivation, or ventriloquism.[6] In
contrast, therefore, to this critical inheritance, my book attends less to the
individuated examples of Chauceriana than to the broader contours of
what may be called a "literary system" for the age. Constructing literary
systems entails positing not just a present of performance but a past of
cultural identity. It necessitates the self-conscious invention of a history to
literature and, in turn, a definition of the poet's self-appointed role in mediating that history to a present reading, commissioning, or judging community. As Richard Helgerson delineates it, in the formulation that informs my usage of this category:

> Meaning in the . . . system of literary careers, as in any sign system,
> derives from relations and oppositions between the elements of that
> system. To write in a certain genre or to speak of one's work in a

certain way or to establish a certain relationship with booksellers, stage managers, or patrons, was to associate oneself with one group of poets and to disassociate oneself from another.[7]

What Helgerson defines for Elizabethan literary culture is the self-creation of a "laureate" poetics, a professionalizing of performance that distinguished itself from the amateurism of the well born and well educated. My book might be thought of as a gesture toward a prehistory of the laureate self-fashioning described by Helgerson. What I define for fifteenth-century poetics is the projection rather than enactment of laureate performance—a self-fashioning not of professional or amateur, but of the patronized and the subservient.

The works I study here thus form what I consider a coherent line of influence and critical response, a literary system defined by writing in certain genres, developing a critical vocabulary, and establishing relations between scribes, patrons, and booksellers. I do not include a discussion of the so-called Scottish Chaucerians, a poetic constellation long appreciated for their mastery of form and tone excelling many of their English counterparts, yet one grounded in a distinctive social context and with governing political and patronage concerns far different from those of the south. I also elide reference to other kinds of fifteenth-century expressions of a literary culture: the prose of Malory, the drama of the northern towns, the historiography of court and cloister.[8] Readers of this book may feel that I have displaced the great for the ephemeral, the lasting for the transitory. But as this Introduction hopes to illustrate, and as the following chapters set out to argue, the history of late medieval English literature *is* in large part the history of ephemera: of the remembered fragments of Chaucer's narratives, the lyrics of his public letters, the tag lines of his tellers, the framings of his fictions. This book attempts to understand what "Chaucer" meant to those who used him. His writings, his name, and his example came to be pressed into the service of a variety of social practices, and what follows is therefore less an account of imitation than of appropriation; it seeks the heritage of Chaucer's presence in late medieval visions of authority and authorship.

Mine is a study of the post-Chaucerian literary system as a phenomenon of subjection, and I mean that term to have a double focus, both on Chaucer's poetry and its reception in the texts that transmit and recast it. Although I discuss the ways in which Chaucer's authority subjects his readers, subjugating them into childhood or incompetence, I also argue that the reader *is the subject* for a range of Chaucer's major fictions. Chaucer creates the fictional persona of the subjugated reader/imitator and, in turn, the processes by which the fifteenth century propagates a literature based on versions of that persona. Thus, many fifteenth-century works tell stories of patronage, where poetic narrators reflect on the relationships of power that commission, read, and judge the work in progress. Many fifteenth-century texts, too, present themselves as educational treatises, as their didactic tone and preceptorial structure both imitate and enact the relationship of father to son inscribed into Chaucer's verse. This strain of Chaucerian reception, furthermore, spoke to a larger set of tastes controlling both the verbal and the visual arts in late medieval England, one that has been dubbed a "cult of childhood" in its appreciation for the body of the Christ child and its almost fetishistic fascination with the mutilated boys and girls who populate the saints' lives and doctrinal literature of the age.

I began by stating that Chaucer's creation as an author is the product of those apparently least qualified to do so, and by that I mean that modern readers have traditionally found fifteenth-century scribes and compilers, as well as writers such as Clanvowe, Hoccleve, Lydgate, and Hawes, incapable of understanding Chaucer's literary genius or his cultural milieu. From the late nineteenth century on, such readers have instead entrusted Chaucer's editing and critical interpretation to the academics trained in textual criticism and close reading. A class of professional interpreters, from Skeat, Kittredge, and Robinson, through the editors of the *Variorum* and the *Riverside Chaucer*, has been privileged as those apparently *most* qualified to transmit the poet to his readers.[9] What I would suggest is that we too have constructed ourselves as subjected readers, and our own subjection is a product of the history of textual criticism that empowers academic editors over medieval scribes. Why, we might ask, are modern editors, so willing to accept the fifteenth century's attributions of Chaucer's work, equally willing to dismiss its readings of his lines? Part of my purpose in asking this question will be to restore a critical authority to the early manuscripts of Chaucer's poetry: to see them not just as the garblings of inept or intrusive scribes but to *read* them as, at times, coherent reconstructions of the poet's work after the social, aesthetic, and political needs of a contemporary readership. Part of my purpose, too, will be to question the received authority of those who would attribute Chaucer's poetry: to see late-medieval attributions less as the articulations of knowing biographers or friends and more as ideologically motivated, textual manipulations for specific literary ends. My interest lies in the processes of attribution, and one way of answering the question I have raised is to explore a critical environment in which a deference to literary authority could coexist with a willful manipulation of the texts created after Chaucer's death.

This is, therefore, also a book about canons. The fifteenth century has long been condemned for its omnivorous inclusion of a mass of poetry into Chaucer's oeuvre. The so-called Chaucerian apocrypha has, since the time of Skeat and Brusendorff, been successively pared down to what most scholars would agree to be the unique representatives of Chaucer's art, and some have recently claimed that works of even slightly dubious manuscript authority, such as *Anelida and Arcite* and the *Canon's Yeoman's Tale*, should be excluded as spurious.[10] Such judgments, for the critics of the twentieth as well as for the scribes of the fifteenth century, articulate what Stephen Orgel has called, writing on the authenticity of Shakespeare, "a strategy of definition."[11] If Chaucer or Shakespeare is to be understood as the best or originary poet, then, Orgel notes, we tend to banish "from the canon whatever is considered insufficiently excellent. . . . [T]he authenticity of the text here is not a function of the poet at all; it is a function precisely of *the text*, in the most limited and literal sense: of the manuscript through which the poem is transmitted." The creation of a Chaucer canon, like that for Shakespeare, proceeds through tests for authenticity: the reliability of certain manuscript traditions, the knowledge of individual scribes, the patterns of metrical control and generic affiliation, the use of distinctive vocabulary or syntactic structures. No single poem of an author's can attain canonical status. Rather, as John Guillory argues, "Canonicity is not a property of the work itself but of its transmission, its relation to other works."[12] Including and excluding works from the production of an author are, in these terms, acts not just of literary criticism but of cultural affirmation. They help to define the nature of authorized literary production. They maintain the aesthetic values of a community, values that often are as much the product of political and social structures as they are the result of artistic choices.

The making of the Chaucer canon in the fifteenth century is thus a twofold process. First, it proceeds by authorizing certain works, naming them as Chaucer's, and transmitting them in manuscript assemblies whose thematic coherence or controlling patronage commission augments their authenticity. Second, it proceeds by selecting from the body of Chaucerian production certain narratives and genres that exemplify the poet's social role.[13] For fifteenth-century aristocratic, gentry, and mercantile audiences, that selection would have included the Clerk's story of Griselda and Chaucer's prose *Melibee* from the *Canterbury Tales*—tales valued for their moral didacticism and thus abstracted from the Canterbury frame to be transmitted independently in single manuscripts or large anthologies. This selection would also have included the *Squire's Tale*. Although this *Tale* (unlike the *Melibee* and those of the Clerk, the Prioress, and the Monk) does not survive in individual manuscript selections, it did have a great appeal for fifteenth- and sixteenth-century readers, in particular the gentry, and it did influence a range of Chaucerian imitations, from Clanvowe's *Book of Cupid* through Book IV of Spenser's *Faerie Queene*. Chaucer was also viewed as a great lyric poet by the fifteenth century, and part of my argument will be that it is in the interest of that century's scribes and

imitators to construct a Chaucer of political advice and lyric virtuosity. For
these reasons, many of the shorter ballads are continually copied into manuscript anthologies, and many ballads, now rejected as Chaucerian by
modern scholarship, are named as Chaucer's or conjoined to his works in
those manuscript collections.

The scribes and imitators of the fifteenth century bequeath a specific
canon of Chaucerian productions and, perhaps more significantly, criteria
for judging just what is "Chaucerian" about them. They pose a set of
questions for the modern editor about relationships between fourteenth-
century culture and fifteenth-century taste—indeed, their legacy has often
prompted modern scholars to place "culture" over "taste" in the appreciation of a poet's own milieu and the dismissal of a later generation's judgments. Such questions, and what I take to be their ideologically motivated
answers, are of primary importance for the historical study of Chaucer, for
the simple fact remains that we have nothing of an unassailable Chaucerian authority. We have no literary documents in Chaucer's hand, as we
do, for example, for Hoccleve.[14] We have no evidence that Chaucer super-
vised the production of his work through designated scriptoria or booksellers, as we have for Gower and Lydgate.[15] Nor do we have, except in the
confusing verses of the Prologue to the *Legend of Good Women* and the
oblique codings of the *Book of the Duchess* and the ballads and envoys, any
clear case of Chaucer's responding to specific commissions or recasting his
poetry in the light of changing social experience, in the way that Gower
and Langland are supposed to have done.[16] What we do have is a collection of fifteenth-century manuscripts, some of which have been promoted
as closest to the poet's ambience or as filtered through what we presume to
be his literary circle. Chaucer's poetry, in a quite literal sense, *is* the
product of his fifteenth-century readers and writers, and this fact of its
dissemination leads to some important discriminations on the nature of
the literary text, on the social function of the author, and on the relationship between formalism and historicism in literary study.[17]

Moving away from the idealism of the New Criticism or the critiques
of that idealism in poststructuralist theory, a number of recent studies of
medieval and Renaissance literature have taken the position that "the aim
of literary studies should be, not the interpretation of individual texts, but
the study of the conventions of interpretation, and thus of the production
and reception of texts in different historical periods."[18] The sense of history at work here involves as much the understanding of a system of signs
or a structure of beliefs as it does the chronicle of events, and such an
understanding has been marked by what one critic has discerned as a "sus-
piciousness and self-conscious playfulness" toward the self-representation
of earlier cultures.[19]

The place of such a history in the study of textual criticism has emerged in recent work that sees the nature of literary creation as "social and collaborative" and that concerns itself with charting "the historical forms in which a work was presented to the public."[20] The studies of Jerome McGann exemplify this approach in their investigations of "the dialectic between the historically located individual author and the historically developing institutions of literary production."[21] The literary text, according to this formulation, exists not as some individuated and empirically recoverable "thing" but as one element in the process between author, audience, and publisher. For the maker of a modern edition, the challenge of the text involves the necessary adjudication between the historical identity of the author and the varying identities his or her work takes on. The nexus between textual criticism and literary theory, then, becomes the point of contact between the historicity of the author and the historical moment of his or her readerships. It lies in the relationship between the search for an authorial intention and the recognition that the reader makes a meaning out of texts, and that each subsequent edition or transcription may, potentially, record that meaning in the editing, layout, arrangement, or appearance of the text itself.[22]

This historicizing understanding of literary works as products of their transmission, rather than of their creation, dovetails with a theoretical perspective garnered from the criticism of the last decade. Out of a constellation of works in psychoanalysis, cultural studies, and literary theory, there has emerged a fascination with the idea of the subject in the text, and furthermore with the creation of subjectivity as the primary business of all forms of writing.[23] A "subject" functions in a system of signification or understanding. Such systems may be construed as linguistic, psychological, or social, and the "subject" in each system operates, respectively, according to its grammatical category, interior condition, or institutional role. For literary criticism, an attention to the subject has tended to erase traditional considerations of the personality of author, character, or speaker. It has brought the focus of criticism to bear on the ways in which named individuals enact their functions in a system that controls them. In consequence, the activity of such criticism has often devolved to the descriptions of a cultural milieu that defined both the codes of conduct for an individual and the social or political conditions that made such codes meaningful.

Perhaps one of the earliest of provocations to consider "authorship" in these terms, and perhaps, too, one of the most influential on a generation of American critics, was Michel Foucault's question, "What is an author?" and his overarching answer that an author is not so much the profession of an individual as it is the creation of society.[24] Authorship, since Foucault, has been discussed more as a function than a calling, where the word *author* and the given name of an individual author do not become the marks of biographical existence, but instead work as ciphers for the relationships of power and control articulated by a culture that requires and receives the literary fictions of itself. Authorship, in this view, becomes a strategy, a way of negotiating those relationships among ruler and ruled. Many modern critics who have projected Foucault's theories back to societies historically earlier than ours have addressed this double function of the author as a kind of subject.[25] Louis Montrose, in one of the most elegant of these formulations, writes:

> In claiming the originative status of an "Author," a writer claims the authority to direct and delimit the interpretive activity of that elite community of readers by whom he himself is authorized to write. (If this strategy stakes out the imaginative space of fiction as the writer's domain, it also seems designed to protect him from any imputation of seditious intent: it is, at once, a strategy of power and a defensive tactic).[26]

Such an authorial construction can, as in the case of Montrose's Spenser, take his own self-fashioning as the subject of his work, and it is Montrose's purpose to delineate how the notion of the authorial self *as subject* operates within the environments of political control and social exchange in which the author is the subject of the ruler and the court. This double sense of the word *subject*, then, refracts the mutual self-fashioning of author and patron, ruled and ruler, within a shared language of social relations.

For the study of Chaucer and Chaucerianism, the terms of this definition have an obvious resonance. Throughout his works, Chaucer imagines that community which authorizes him to write, whether it is the court of love as in the Prologue to the *Legend of Good Women* or the Canterbury pilgrims of the *Thopas / Melibee* conjointure. Defining himself as an author necessarily involves finding a strategy to "direct and delimit the interpretive activity" of that community, in other words, to develop a stance or a persona that controls the possibilities of audience response while at the same time posing to invite the range of audience participation. Chaucer's poetics constantly stakes out the imaginative space of fiction as the writer's domain, and through the manipulations, evasions, and pleas for "correccioun" of his narrators, he defends himself against the imputations of seditious criticism. His meditations on the function of the author or the nature of authoritative sources often transpire in the distant worlds of dream or travel. In the early love visions or the *Squire's Tale*, for example, reflections on *auctoritas* remove themselves from the environments of court or city and occur safely tucked away in dreams. In the *Thopas /*

Melibee section of the *Canterbury Tales*, Chaucer can pause to illustrate the range of possibilities to Harry Bailly's question, "What man artow?" only on the byways of the road to Canterbury.

The construction of the author according to a social ideology carries with it, too, a set of implications for all those who would write after his example. As Foucault points out, there is perhaps an unavoidable sense of genealogy to authorship, one that I think may help explain the maintenance of "father Chaucer" for the fifteenth century and one that may serve to explain the infantilization of his followers. Writing about Marx and Freud, Foucault considers as their "distinctive contribution" the fact "that they produced not only their own work, but the possibility and the rules of formation for other texts. . . . They cleared the space for the introduction of elements other than their own, which, nevertheless, remain within the field of discourse they initiated."[27] It may be said that, for Chaucer's imitators, the creation of a literary history proceeded in an analogous fashion. Like the originary authors Marx and Freud, who would produce a discourse and a form of writing for a culture, Chaucer produces in his own work the "rules of formation for other texts." The genres of the dream vision, pilgrimage narrative, and ballad, and the distinctive idioms of dedication, patronage, and correction that fill those works, were taken up by fifteenth-century poets, not simply out of imitative fealty to Chaucer but instead largely because they were the rules of formation for poetry. They defined a literature in English, and anyone who would aspire to be a poet would necessarily have to write according to those rules. Whatever innovations might have been developed in the course of that century—the rise, say, of an advisory poetry or the flourishing of what might be called a secular hagiography—were pendant on Chaucer's own forms, in these cases, such tales as those of the Prioress and the Clerk. Rephrased in Foucault's terms, all fifteenth-century poetry remained "within the field of discourse" Chaucer had initiated. To put it more bluntly, we might say that to be a poet in the fifteenth century was by necessity to be a Chaucerian.

The invention of literary authority after Chaucer may thus be theorized as the invention of a Chaucerian subject that included both a "subject matter" for the poetry and an authorial or reading subject who defined its social purpose. But the invention and later appropriation of this Chaucerian subject is itself a function of distinctive currents in the intellectual and political life of late-medieval England—currents that generated what has been identified as a distinctively medieval literary theory. Broadly speaking, such a theory has been understood as considering the production and reception of texts as part of a shared, communal process. The *auctor*, for scholastic commentary, was not the kind of personality that would be constructed by the post-Renaissance imagination. Rather, he was but one participant in an enterprise shared by *scriptor*, *compilator*, and *commentator*.[28]

Together, these four figures could participate, to varying degrees, in the transmission of canonical documents of learning, and it is this focus on documents themselves, rather than on the personalities who made them, that gives to the term *auctores* the connotation not of persons but of texts.[29] *Auctoritas*, by this account, thus represents the body of material authoritatively transmitted through the institutions of learning. The idea of authority rests with texts, rather than individuals, and it is this distinctive feature of pre-humanist manuscript culture that permits a certain fluidity among the author, scribe, and reader. Characteristic of the medieval habit of reading was, therefore, a kind of rewriting: a way of engaging with the text by commenting, recasting, and in some sense re-inscribing it.[30] Most medieval manuscripts bear witness to these forms of engagement, either in their various encrustings of gloss and commentary or, more problematically, in their apparently willful revisions of "original" literary works. The intrusions of a scribe like Gui de Mori into the *Roman de la Rose*, recently chronicled by David Hult, challenge our more modern preconceptions of the line between the author and the scribe, and his work, as Hult points out, may question the very notion of narrative authority encoded in the naming of an *auctor*.[31] Scribal intrusions, as well as the acts of compilation by the writers and commissioners of manuscripts, decenter the author's function as the maker of the work. They illustrate just how a medieval reader could make meaning out of received texts; how, in the process of rescription and continuation, they replace what Hult calls the "controlling subjects" of author and patron with new fictions of poetic making.[32]

These phenomena have been seen as contributing to the "openness" of manuscript culture, where, in Gerald Bruns's words, the text "opens outwardly rather than inwardly, in the sense that it seems to a later hand to require collaboration, amplification, embellishment, illustration, to disclose the hidden or the as-yet-unthought of."[33] In contrast with the fixity of printed books, the medieval manuscript could circulate in constant stages of rescription. One problem for the historian of authorship is the effect of this circulation on the separation of labor in the making of texts. There is a recognizable gap between the "theory" of authorship presented in Latin treatises and the flexibility of self-presentation and reader response in literary texts. The neatly codified quadripartite system of production outlined above—and classified, most succinctly, by St. Bonaventure in his commentary on the *Sentences* and explained for modern readers by Malcolm Parkes and Alastair Minnis—has come under close scrutiny by those less comfortable with the translation of scholastic theory into vernacular practice.[34] What Hult, for example, identifies in the manuscripts of the *Roman de la Rose*, or what Sylvia Huot finds in lyric compilations from the thirteenth and fourteenth centuries, and what I find in the manuscript revisions and anthologies that transmit Chaucer's verse, are evidences for the blurring of distinctions between author, scribe, compiler, and commentator. They are the evidence for the social and collaborative nature of literary production and, moreover, for the historicity of that production in the moments of reception and transmission that transcribe it. Lee Patterson puts the matter neatly, writing about one fifteenth-century appropriation of the *Troilus*:

> What is special about this material is that it allows us to reconstruct an inescapably individual moment of literary reception, a moment whose specificity is palpable and whose significance, while necessarily open to debate, raises questions that have an immediacy that the modern reader cannot evade. And what is methodologically interesting, I think, is precisely the amount of interpretation that is required to recover the act of interpretation itself: far from bearing its meaning on its face, this instance of medieval reading requires extensive and careful ministrations to reveal its significance.[35]

One of the goals of the following chapters will be to enact such ministrations: to define those moments of reception in which English readers reconceive their literary past and modern scholars justify their critical present.

Defining such moments, however, goes beyond charting literary history in the phenomena of narrative personae and audience response. There are particular conditions in the life of fifteenth-century England that shape writing in the vernacular and foster what I have seen as the infantilization of Chaucer's later readers. Primary among them is the century's volatile political climate, with its dynastic conflicts, the war with France, and its rapidly changing relationships among crown, nobility, and bourgeoisie.[36] From the deposition of Richard II in 1399 to the ascension of Henry VII in 1485, English political life was marked by several features that both influenced and reinforced the literary climate of the age. Much of the pervasive Boethianism of the century's poetry, for example, may be understood as a response to the unpredictability of its patrons' fortunes. To live under the rule of Fortune is to live without "connynge," and from the verse translation of John Walton (1410) through the poetry of Lydgate, Ashby, and Hawes, the role of the writer in society is to offer counsel in a fickle world. As David Lawton puts it, summarizing much of this development, "Poets offer the consolation of philosophy to themselves, their group and their masters in a world ruled by Fortune, a world from which poets are not set apart but in which, on the contrary, they are deeply, often impotently, involved."[37] Lawton's argument is that this Boethianism fosters a literary culture marked by the self-conscious display of dullness and the denial of a "specialized status . . . that poetry might bring." Poets, he claims, represent themselves as writers of the public sphere, who, in the articulations of a "comun vois," deny the special place of individual achievement and create a literary system in "conformity to a cultural pattern."[38]

But if the English fifteenth century was but another *aetas Boethiana*, it was also an *aetas puerorum*. The childishness of the fifteenth-century poet is, only in part, a response to Chaucer's literary fatherhood; it is, too, a response to the childishness of much fifteenth-century politics. "Woe to thee, O land, when the king is a child." Henry Bolingbroke invoked this tag line from *Ecclesiastes* in his claims to depose Richard II, who, for all *his* childishness, was Henry's exact contemporary.[39] But Bolingbroke's words would come to stand as an ironic epigraph to Lancastrian rule. For the better part of the century, England was governed by a series of kings preoccupied with their unsure relationships to dynastic paternity.[40] Henry IV constantly sought justification for his attainment of the throne, not only from his subjects but his son. The tensions generated between Henry IV and V were those not simply of the errancy of the young prince in the model of Shakespeare's Hal but, more pointedly, were focused on the kindness of the late Richard II to the prince and the deposed king's surrogate paternity in the 1390s when Bolingbroke was abroad. It is significant that one of Henry V's first acts as king after his father's death in 1413 was the recovery of Richard II's body and its reinterment in the royal tombs at Westminster.[41] Henry V's own fatherhood, however, was cut short by his death at the age of 34 in 1422. His son, Henry VI, was only a few months old, and though he was officially crowned king in November 1429 at the age of seven, England was governed by an aristocratic council for the fifteen years between the death of Henry V and Henry VI's assertion of his majority in 1436.[42]

Lydgate, who comes off as a vigorous propagandist for the Lancastrian house during these years, makes clear in his poem on the coronation of 1429 that the young king must aspire to the "myrrour of manhede" that was his father.[43] Much of this poem, like most of Lydgate's poetry on Henry VI, stresses the lineage of the Lancastrian line, not only to justify the descent through Henry IV and his assumption of the throne, but also to articulate the idea of paternity in political succession.

> God graunt þee grace for to resemble in al
>   Vn-to þeos noble worthy conquerrours,
> Longe to contynue in þyn estate royal,
>   And to be lyche to þy progenytours . . .
>
> (89–92)

The power of the king comes from his resemblance to those conquerors who were his progenitors, and Lydgate takes great pains, here and elsewhere, to discern in Henry VI some simulacrum of his famous father. Yet there were few like Lydgate who would find that in the king. For the better part of his minority and reign, Henry VI seemed more like the child than the father of his country. To French observers of the early 1430s, he was *un très beau fils* and *ung tres bel enfant*.[44] Though these remarks have been appreciated for their commentary on the physical deportment of the young king, they also affirm the impression of his youth to contemporary observers. Yorkist propaganda of the 1450s and 1460s considered him, perhaps not unfairly, as "simple and lad by couetous counseylle";[45] the chronicler John Harding thought the king morally inept, foolish, or mad;[46] and even in the writings of those who sought his patronage, like John Whethamstede, there remains a fine and at times blurry line between the king's simplicity and his simplemindedness.[47] His fits of willfullness seemed to many as the tantrums of a child, and for much of the 1460s he was probably schizophrenic. Deposed by Richard of York, Henry VI never formally renounced the kingship, and his brief return to the throne in 1470–71 was clearly an embarrassment to his supporters at home and his allies abroad.[48]

One consequence for English literary life of living under a child king is a certain nostalgia for a politically hegemonous and artistically glistening past. The cultivation of a Chaucer cult, and in turn of the literary politics of Ricardian England, is a form of such nostalgia: a fantasy for a past world in which kings govern, courts patronize, and poets live as "laureates" under their munificent rule.[49] The unassailable authority of Chaucer himself gains in power not just in the light of later, fifteenth-century technical ineptitude but in the context of that century's cultural insecurity. There is a world of difference between Chaucer's counseling of Richard II in *Lak of Stedfastnesse* and Lydgate's own pathetic prayer for Henry VI in the Ballad on his coronation. Chaucer's poem, the model for so much of the political verse of the fifteenth century, exhorts a king to "cherish thy folk," "Shew forth thy swerd," "Dred God," "do law," and "wed thy folk agein to stedfastnesse"—all injunctions to a fatherly, adult king who performs as surrogate for a divine *paternitas*.[50] Lydgate's Ballad, by contrast, can only plead:

> And God I prey, of his hye bountee,
> Of fader and moder in þy tendre youþe
> To taake ensaumple, regnyng in þy see,
> And beon in vertu als famous and als kouþe
>
> (109–12)

Chaucer writes as man to man: The father of English poetry writes to the father of his people. In the *Complaint to His Purse*, he addresses Henry IV as the "conquerour of Brutes Albyon," and the fifteenth-century praise of Chaucer as the poet of "Brutes Albyon" was designed precisely to maintain this fiction of a fatherly poet writing to a father-king.[51] Indeed, by stretching the paternity of both poet and royal patron back to Brutus, the eponymous and founding father of the British Isles, the fifteenth-century encomiasts could claim that Chaucer and his kings shared in the power granted by the fatherhood of politics and poetry.

Lydgate, however, only writes to children: to a boy so young that he must pray for the example of a father and a mother, to a son lost in the *loco parentis* of a Duke Humphrey feuding with the barons. His preoccupations with the lineage of Henry VI stand as the political analogue to his literary concerns with the lineage of English poetry. Poems on the king's title and pedigree, on his coronation, his triumphal entry into London, on the new year's gift of an eagle to the king, and on the kings of England since William the Conqueror all seek to establish the genealogical basis for Henry VI's rule.[52] All of them give voice to the great social anxieties of fifteenth-century dynastic politics, and each of them phrases its search for fatherhood and lineage in terms distinctively akin to Lydgate's search for a Chaucerian *paternitas*.

The search for a father Chaucer, much like the search for a father Henry, motivates a poetry desperately seeking to validate both its infantilized author and its childish patron. This search leads to a second historical context that I think frames much fifteenth-century writing: the changing nature of literary patronage and the shifting status of the patron from the central London court to the great magnate houses and, eventually, the bourgeois commissions of the provinces.[53] The dynastic troubles and the foreign wars of Henry IV and V that preoccupied the court, and the long minority and later indifference of Henry VI all contributed to a decentering of literary patronage away from London and the royal household. Only Humphrey, Duke of Gloucester, stands out as a patron of letters, and though recent scholarship has somewhat debunked his exalted image as the fosterer of English humanism and a bibliophile of some sensitivity, he nonetheless remains the primary commissioner at court of major literary and historical activity in the first decades of the century.[54]

A fair amount of research has been devoted to delineating these shifts and, in the process, illustrating how the patronage of literature created and maintained a kind of national identity for a rising bourgeoisie.[55] But in addition to the social contours of late-medieval English patronage, I am concerned with how such patronage is thematized within the literary text, that is, with how poems write fables of commission and reception, and how, by consequence, the making of the literary text becomes the subject of its fiction. Such a development is both a literary and a social project. On the one hand, it is in the interest of Lydgate, Hoccleve, and other writers to imagine themselves patronized by the state and to see in that patronage an elevation, if only implied, to the laureate status of the dead Chaucer and his Italian predecessors, Petrarch, Dante, and Boccaccio. On the other hand, it is in the interest of aristocratic and bourgeois commissioners of manuscripts to construct books that call attention to their own status as patrons of letters. Mid-century manuscripts such as those of the so-called Oxford Group collect a poetry distinctively concerned with royal commission for the courts of love. The fascination with these poems (the amorous dream visions and political ballads of Chaucer, Lydgate, and Hoccleve and the *Book of Cupide* of Clanvowe) and their widespread copying and circulation illustrate an attempt to imitate the structures of courtly patronage by provincial readers. The fantasy of *fin amours* is a fantasy of commissioning *poetry* of *fin amours*, and I intend to read these manuscripts as books designed to educate their readers in the arts of patronage.

Chaucer's own presentations of his patronage relationships, however, are oblique at best, and the fifteenth century's obsession with the patron may also derive from its attempts at decoding Chaucer's debts and nostalgically imagining the ideals of a public poetry at the Ricardian court. Chaucer never confronts the issue of patronage in any direct or unambiguous way. What we may reconstruct of the historical genesis of the *Book of the Duchess* or the *Legend of Good Women*, both presumably commissioned works, comes from our decipherment of naming codes or allegorical conventions. Whatever landmarks he may give us for determining his patronage or audience are only vaguely visible within the space of fiction. Eltham and Sheene, the references to a boy king excised from the *Melibee*, the cluster of topical allusions toward the close of the *Nun's Priest's Tale*—none of these moments has the transparency of Gower's claims to make a book "for King Richard's sake," of Hoccleve's envoys to the kings, or of Lydgate's reflections on Duke Humphrey. Only in the shorter ballads does Chaucer begin to approach the presentation of his patronage and court position in Gower's or in Lydgate's terms. Poems such as *Lak of Stedfastnesse*, *Truth*, and the envoy to Gower and Strode at the close of *Troilus and Criseyde* were among the most popular of Chaucer's texts in the fifteenth century. They addressed directly the later fascination with the workings of court poetry, a fascination fulsomely articulated in the long historical and biographical headnotes John Shirley wrote to his transcriptions of the ballads. These texts also provided later poets with a model for creating what might be considered as the subgenre of the political envoy. Lydgate, Hoccleve, and Stephen Hawes seem to have spent most of their time rewriting Chaucer's exhortations to his kings and the final stanzas of the *Troilus*. In fact, so much of the lyric poetry that fills the manuscript anthologies of the fifteenth and early sixteenth centuries is full of pleas for "correccioun" and versions of the "Go litel bok" phrase, that we might well view such verse as private versions of the public Chaucer propagated by his later imitators.[56]

In these and in the many other ways I hope to illustrate throughout this book, it is central to the fifteenth-century literary system to imagine

Chaucer as a public, and publicly patronized, poet. Chaucer stands not just as the servant of kings but as the advisor to princes, and it is the consideration of this advisory stance that leads me to the third of my historical contexts. Throughout much of the fifteenth and the early sixteenth century, the purpose of vernacular writing—be it historical prose or amorous verse—was didactic. Developing such genres as the mirror for princes, the courtesy book, and the manual of religious instruction, late-medieval writers produced a glut of texts designed to educate the wealthy and the humble, the rulers and the young. One overall effect of this direction in English literary history was, as Derek Pearsall has noticed, to make the purpose of recreational reading primarily instructive and to inculcate in literary narrators the voice of the teacher.[57] But another overall effect was, quite simply, to render readers of such literature children. The paternalistic tone of much of the literature, combined with the growing cult of childhood in the visual and verbal arts, created a kind of writing preoccupied with the child in all his or her aspects. Manuals of table manners were read alongside such narratives of childhood pathos as the *Prioress's Tale*. The precious visual and dramatic portrayals of the Christ child come to straddle "a very narrow line between religious icon and reassuring talisman."[58] This aesthetic fascination with the child, together with the rise of an advisory literature, could only feed the rhetoric of childishness propounded by the infantilized imitators of Chaucer and the poor poets who would praise a child-king Henry VI. Taken in tandem, these historical, social, and literary phenomena created, by the last decades of the fifteenth century, not just a childish persona for literary writers, but a childhood audience for Chaucer. The *Canterbury Tales* came to be read as children's literature, and selected portions of its narratives were scribally recast to bring out the exemplary purposes of what had become a poetry of manners.[59]

The cultivation of this poetry of manners works in tandem with a notion of Chaucerian reception centering on the domestic. Chaucer's readers, inheritors, and scribes often present themselves as sharing in the coteries of Chaucerian making: in what might be thought of as the *familia Chauceriana* inspired by the shorter lyrics to the poet's friends and by the personal, epistolary feel of the appeal to Strode and Gower at the close of *Troilus and Criseyde*. To write after Chaucer is, in a controlling way, to write after the memory of a departed friend or master, and the personal flavor of much of this elegiac reminiscence has led many modern critics to take it at face value and to see in the creation of a Chaucer cult the maintenance, a generation or two later, of the circle of friends that constituted Chaucer's original audience. Hoccleve, Lydgate, Shirley, George Ashby—indeed, virtually all Chaucerians throughout the century seek to establish their relationship to Chaucer by appealing to some kind of personal rela-

tion to the poet. Either by claiming friendship or imagining a sort of tuto-
rial acquaintance, these writers try to sustain Chaucer's presence in their
work. Like his own Clerk, who offers up a version of the story of Griselda
at least partially in homage to the dead Petrarch, Chaucer's heirs claim a
legacy bequeathed by claims to a direct line of inheritance.

Such claims will motivate the subjects of the first four chapters of my
study, as the imitators, scribes, or manuscript anthologists each, in their
own distinctive ways, seek to rehabilitate the literary system that controlled Chaucerian production. But by the century's close, a decisive
change in the conception of the audience for Chaucer's work as well as in
the notions of an English author began to shift the presence of the poet in
the literary system. Politically, Henry VII's victory at Bosworth field and
the birth of Prince Arthur shortly afterward raised hopes of an assured
dynastic succession. Culturally, a new burst of court patronage came with
the king and his Burgundian relations who established places for those
scholars trained in England, Italy, and the Low Countries. Technologi-
cally, the importation of the printing press brought with it the potential
for refiguring relations among those who wrote, disseminated, and read.
Taken together, these developments changed both the nature and the
focus of Chaucerian reception. They transformed the way in which the
poet was used as well as read, challenged the older imaginations of his
laureation and paternity, and fostered the construction of new models of
performance and literary history.

The last two chapters of this book thus argue that the changes in the
culture and technologies of bookmaking rehistoricized the idea of the laureateship and, in so doing, helped transform Chaucer from a remembered
presence guiding literary making to a dead *auctor* valued for his exemplarity. My history of the historicizing of the laureation begins, however, not
with Henry VII and his scholars, but with the appearance in the 1460s and
1470s of a generation of new "poet laureates," graduates of the universities
of Louvain and Cologne in particular, who brought to the English courts
and universities the Latin learning of the Continent and a revived sense of
that synthesis of political sanction and formal education conjured up by
Petrarch and maintained for Chaucer in the imaginations of his encomiasts. The Italian Stephen Surigonus and the English John Skelton are but
the two most familiar of the rising class of self-styled laureates who offered
up their services to European and English courts. They also offered up
their services to England's first printer, and in the course of Caxton's critical prologues and epilogues they come to serve as arbiters of literary judgment and textual authority.

The laureate, for Caxton, is no longer the dead poet but the living
reader, editor, and critic. In Caxton's epilogue to his edition of the *Boece*
of 1478, Surigonus stands as the laureate interpreter of Chaucer's work for

a new, educated adult readership. His long Latin poem on the poet—offered at the close of Caxton's volume as a transcript of the verses found on Chaucer's tomb at Westminster—shows for the first time a new way of reading Chaucer, a way I call "like a laureate." In the university-educated humanist Surigonus we are invited to find the living example of the laureate Chaucer was long imagined to have been. In his elaborately allusive Latin elegiacs, we are invited, too, to find in Chaucer one of the old *auctores* of a classicizing humanist hermeneutic. Caxton's *Boece*, I argue, buries Chaucer and initiates a break with the traditions of Lydgatean obeisance and coterie appropriation.

For Caxton, in the 1483 *Canterbury Tales*, Chaucer "may wel" have the name of a poet laureate, and it lies in this hesitation, this projection of a current practice onto a past writer, that we may find the gradual decentering of the old terms of literary praise. Laureates are readers rather than writers, interpreters rather than originators. In tandem with this shift, the idea of the literary father is displaced from Chaucer onto those who read, bequeath, and commission the book. Thus, in the 1483 *Canterbury Tales* prologue, the father of the book is the man who owns the authoritative copy of the text and who lets his own son offer it to Caxton as the basis of his new edition. In the 1490 *Eneydos* prologue, the father is Henry VII himself, the sire of the newborn Prince of Wales, whose paternity dovetails with the established laureation of John Skelton, now presented as the arbiter of text and language for Caxton's translation. Chaucer nowhere appears in the 1490 *Eneydos* prologue; in fact, by the turn of the sixteenth century, Chaucer's presence in the literary system has itself changed radically. As I propose in Chapter 6, on Hawes and Skelton, Chaucer functions in the invocations of his name rather than the evocations of his style. He is the object of citation rather than quotation, a figure whose works are not to be imitated in any wholesale or controlling way, but rather as a mine for tag lines, clichés, and allusions.

The theme of these final chapters is the disappearance of the laureate and father Chaucer in the poetry of early Tudor England, and in Hawes and Skelton I discern the nature of this disappearance as a function of these poets' differing approaches to literary fame and political patronage. Skelton and Hawes present, respectively, a laureate and anti-laureate conception of the English writer. For the former, poetic authority rests with the continuities of manuscript culture, with the representations of the writing, and rewriting, self and with the ideals of a coterie circulation for individual works. For the latter, poetic authority rests with the new invention of the printing press, with presentations of the viewing self, and with the ideals of a posthumous identity sought in the hard impressions of the printed volume. Both Hawes and Skelton offer what I take to be responses to the literary system after Caxton, to a literary system that has monumentalized the poet in the buried tomb and, in turn, embodied that monument in the printed book. Inscriptions, epitaphs, and graven images possess both writers, as they seek out the varieties of poetic authority in an age of mechanical reproduction and at a time of changing royal patronage.

The trajectory of this book thus traces the changing status of Chaucer's poetry *as* literature: its place in a particular social and political climate; its transmission through the technologies of book production; its discussion in a contemporary critical vocabulary; and its participation in a canon shaped by, and in turn shaping, a distinctive aesthetic climate. This book illustrates the ways in which both Chaucer and his readers sought to answer Harry Bailly's query, "What man artow?" by constructing narrative personae and their audiences. In Chaucer's predecessors, Petrarch and Boccaccio, it finds the models for the presentation of the writing self. In Chaucer's own creations—the Clerk, the Squire, Adam Scriveyn, the teller of the *Thopas* and the *Melibee,* and the public servant of ballads and the envoys—it finds the templates for his later readers and, in turn, a canon of Chaucerian productions against which those readers could judge all poetry as literature. Its primary goal, therefore, is restorative, in that it attempts to restore to manuscripts and scribes a critical authority long masked by the traditions of academic editorship. But its theme, too, is one of restoration, as it charts a century's attempts to elevate a dead poet to a laureate authority and to find a father for its literary children.

CHAPTER ONE

Writing Like the Clerk: Laureate Poets and the Aureate World

ERHAPS the most dazzling of the few surviving pictures of a medieval English author is the frontispiece to Chaucer's *Troilus and Criseyde* in Corpus Christi College Cambridge MS 61 (reproduced in the *Frontispiece*, above). This famous illustration, with its elevated vision of the poet as performer and its panoply of richly attired and presumably royal listeners, has long been the object of scholarly speculation on the nature of Chaucer's original audience and the conventions of performance for his poetry. Its iconography has been linked to Continental religious illumination, to portraits of the preacher in his pulpit, and most recently to the performance of vernacular drama. Some have taken it to represent the facts of literary making at the court of Richard II, finding in its individual portrayals the recognizable faces of Richard, Queen Anne, and their retinue. The place of such a picture in the *Troilus* manuscript has also been the subject of much controversy. Although most scholars now agree that it dates from the second or third decade of the fifteenth century, there remain questions as to the program of illustrations it may have inaugurated and as to the nature of the commission—royal, aristocratic, or commercial—that ordered its production.[1]

Whatever the precise details of this illumination's making, it remains a unique representation of an early English author. Unlike his counterparts in the many presentation portraits that open medieval manuscripts, the poet is not kneeling before a king or patron but is elevated above his audience.[2] He holds no book before him, and he is attired neither as a university clerk nor as an official servant, after the fashion of other author figures in vernacular texts.[3] And although the quality of decoration in the picture marks it as a distinguished piece of work, there are no indications of the workshop that produced it, nor are there any of the signs that, like many other manuscript illustrations, place it in the ambience of an armigerous patron.[4]

The *Troilus* frontispiece may tell us something about the habits of performance at the Ricardian court. But it says more about the later, fifteenth-century imagination of those habits: about what Derek Pearsall has called the "myths" of poetic recitation and royal patronage generated by the narrative of *Troilus and Criseyde* itself. The picture "represents as reality," Pearsall claims, "the myth of delivery that Chaucer cultivates so assiduously in the poem."[5] In many ways, that myth of delivery was similarly cultivated by the later writers who sought to emulate Chaucer's narrative personae and his style. For Lydgate and the members of the Chaucer cult of the first decades of the fifteenth century, such emulation could extend to borrowing Chaucerian material, appropriating his distinctive genres, and even infiltrating themselves into the fiction of his narratives. Their "myths of performance," however, and the creation of the narrative personae who enact them, are a far cry from the sophistications of the *Troilus* narrator or of the many personalities who voice the *Canterbury Tales*. Theirs is the voice of dullness and ineptitude, a voice conditioned by the literary system of a father Chaucer and his children and, moreover, by a patronage system of childish kings and ambitious magnates. Whatever fantasies they might have had of Chaucer and *his* age would have been, in turn, fantasies of power, where the English poet stands as the advisor to his kings and the master of his technique. Lydgate and his heirs construct a Chaucer of political approval and rhetorical finesse, a poet "laureate" and "aureate." They define him as the refiner of language and the English version of the classical *auctor* and the trecento *poeta*. The Chaucer who inhabits their verse is the kin of the performer at the center of the *Troilus* frontispiece: a laureate figure in an aureate world, a poet for a king whose glittering language befits his golden literary age.

The construction of a "laureate" Chaucer forms a distinct chapter in the history of his reception, and my own first chapter is designed to locate this construction in the cultural mythology and literary politics of fifteenth-century England. Appelling Chaucer "poet laureate" is something different from referring to him as a "master" or a "father." Hoccleve, who develops this instructional and paternal vocabulary and who may expend more energy than does anyone else in his abjection before Chaucer, never calls him laureate or crowns him with the laurel leaves.[6] His encomia invariably couch themselves in ways that place him at the center of Chaucerian influence. Hoccleve is, figuratively, a member of the family, the classroom, or the bureaucratic office led by Chaucer. He is, historically, Clerk of the Privy Seal, a scribe, and possibly an editor of Chaucer's texts.[7] Whatever textual or poetic authority he claims grows out of his relationships— personal, professional, and social—to Chaucer himself, and it is the pictured, corporeal self of Chaucer that defines the Hocclevean project. In the illustration that adorns the *Regiment of Princes*, Chaucer appears not as the public orator of the *Troilus* frontispiece but as a clerkly, meditative "master." Hoccleve presents this portrait "to putte othir men in remembraunce / Of his persone," (4994–95) to provoke a meditation on the man, not an understanding of his audience.[8]

Chaucer is in no sense a laureate for Hoccleve, for the impulse to his posthumous crowning comes from the urge to locate writing in the public sphere. Chaucer's laureation goes on by those writers outside the acquaintance of the poet or the privilege of his executorship. In the poetry of Lydgate, the scribal assemblies of John Shirley, and, I will suggest at this chapter's conclusion, James I's *Kingis Quair* and the *Troilus* frontispiece, the invention of a laureate Chaucer and his aureate past are more than forms of praise or voicings of nostalgia. They are part of a complex and historically definable attempt to understand the social place of literature and the obligations of the writer both to an authorizing past and a commissioning present. They voice the fantasies of a political future by evoking a literary past its writers could not know. Lydgate and his heirs construct a poetics pervasively concerned not with themselves in any psychological, Hocclevian sense, but with the social and political institutions and individuals that order, read, and transmit works of literature. Their fascination with the laureateship, and their concomitant uses of an aureate diction, point toward the construction of an ideal literary past and a debased present. In this elaborate Latinate vocabulary, fifteenth-century writers sought an idiom free from the possibility of temporal decay and patronly caprice. Aureation is a golden language from a golden world; it aids in the recovery of what was thought to be Chaucer's own literary language and his age. Together with its sonically resonating word-pair, laureation, it becomes one of the key terms in the critical terminology of the century.

The propagation of this terminology has both a literary history and a historical moment. Chaucer's *Clerk's Tale* depicts a narrator's encounter with the legacy of a glittering poetic past. As one of the most popular of Chaucer's fictions in the fifteenth century, it provided more than story line or character for later imitators.[9] It presented, too, a paradigm for a writer's relationship to a deceased author and a living patron. Its Prologue bequeathed to an English readership a way of understanding poetic authority as forms of political sanction (laureate) and rhetorical finesse (aureate), while its Envoy dramatized the strategies for controlling an audience response. The *Tale* may be read as a story of both imitation and patronage, a fable of how canonical past texts are transformed and transmitted for demanding present readerships. Harry Bailly's authoritarian requests and Petrarch's authoritative presence stand as the two poles of the Clerk's obligation, and to understand the nature of the *Tale* and its reception is to understand how the Clerk adjudicates between them.

The Clerk's dilemma is that of the post-Chaucerian writer, as well, and I argue in what follows that Lydgate appropriates his voice and narrative techniques—indeed, that he at times seems to live out the condition of the

Clerk. He has mined the Clerk's performance for its vocabulary of poetic praise, its subservient narrative stance, and its overall dramatic structure. He builds out of its elements the dullness that articulates that double obligation to aristocratic patron and laureate model. Like the Clerk, Lydgate presents vernacular translations of exemplary texts drawn from a humanist past. Like the Clerk, too, he must translate both over languages and over time. Continental texts find their new readers within English court or court-like settings, as the writings of the poets come under the hands of the makers. While much of Lydgate's career concerns itself with acting out these strategies, it is the *Fall of Princes* that develops fully and explicitly the stance of what I will call "writing like the Clerk." Here, in its specific presentation of a laureate and aureate Petrarch, in its long meditations on the social status of the poet, and in its general narrative organization of miniature prologue, tale, and envoy, Lydgate dramatizes his appropriation of the Clerk's persona.

But writing like the Clerk entails more than the mere ventriloquism of a Chaucerian figure. It involves, too, the expression of a controlling rhetorical position. Throughout Chaucer's major fictions, appeals to clerks and clerkly authority motivate the apologias of his narrators and help define their relations with future readers. The pleas for "correccioun" that close the *Troilus* and the Prologue to the *Parson's Tale* flesh out their narrators' personae as writers to and for the clerk in the audience. This distinctive idiom, together with what I identify as the dramatic condition of the Clerk himself, will constitute the raw materials of Lydgate's public voice and will define much of the relationship of fifteenth-century writing to Chaucer's own clerkly *auctoritas*. Writing like the Clerk defines a complex set of literary relationships among author, source, and audience. It is, to adopt Louis Montrose's Foucauldian vocabulary, both "a strategy of power and a defensive tactic"—that is, a way of figuring the writer as the subject of both political control and literary fiction.[10] Writing like the Clerk, as Chaucer's own Clerk vividly demonstrates, means centering the drama of performance on the speaking self.

Through his elaborate Prologue and Envoy, Chaucer's Clerk defines his own subjected status in relation to his unassailable, laureate source and his capricious, patronizing, and patron-like Host. If, in the process, he provides the personal example for the fifteenth-century public poet, trapped between Chaucerian authority and the whims of commission, he also offers up a generic model. Elaborate prologues and envoys will come to fill the narratives of Lydgate's *Fall of Princes* and those of the many manuscript anthologies that select and assemble works of Chaucer, Lydgate, Hoccleve, Clanvowe, and others into stories of aristocratic patronage and courtly love. Such poetic assemblies, I will argue in Chapter 2, are a species not of writing like the Clerk but "reading like the Squire," as they give voice to the childlike insecurities of fifteenth-century "New Men" attempting to emulate the courtly patronage of their social superiors and to develop a taste for the kinds of literary gestures emblemized in the performance of Chaucer's Squire. In this chapter, however, I seek to identify a literary stance and a critical vocabulary generated out of an engagement with the *Clerk's Tale* and its possible sources. Furthermore, I hope to show how the construction of Chaucer's poetic authority develops out of the conjunction of such literary imitation with the social conditions of writing at the Henrician court.

This chapter, at its close, will thus consider how the shifting patterns of royal patronage, together with the dynastic insecurities raised by the early death of Henry V and the ascendancy of Henry VI, helped foster the nostalgia for a Chaucerian aureate age. It brought to mind the need for poets laureate, and much of Lydgate's work from the late 1420s through the 1440s centers on managing royal spectacle and Lancastrian propaganda. His interests in the aureate Chaucerian past now become preoccupations with creating a laureate present. In his poetic wordplay and in John Shirley's scribal presentations, we find the Chaucer that Lydgate had hoped to be: a writer before kings, a chronicler of royal occasion. The genealogy of laureation that I offer in what follows is, therefore, a history of dehistoricizing and historicizing. It is a narrative of literary appropriation and subjective misreading, a story about making myths and living them.

I

The idea of the laureation began with Petrarch.[11] Though there are records of university conferrals of degrees before the famous coronation ceremony in 1341, it was the bestowal of King Robert of Naples that institutionalized the laureateship as public reward for literary achievement. Much has been made by modern scholars of Petrarch's own role in the construction of the laureation ceremony and in the staging of his crowning as the self-invention of a Renaissance poet along Roman models. Not only through his coronation speech and diploma that he crafted for himself did Petrarch foster his creation as a laureate poet.[12] In the dissemination of his prose and poetry, and in the figure that he cut in later age, Petrarch contributed to what may be perceived as the creation of a mythology of laureation: a set of ideals and key narrative tropes that would define the poet laureate for several generations and that would control the manuscript circulation of his poetry. The manuscripts of the *Seniles* that contain the story of Griselda, for example, often introduce the tale with some remark on Petrarch as *poeta laureato*, to the point where, by the close of the fourteenth century, Petrarch had become the eponymous poet laureate: a literary figure inseparable from his epithet.[13]

The mythologizing of the laureation forms a large part of Boccaccio's agenda in the *Genealogy of the Gentile Gods*.[14] There, in his accounts of both the coronation ceremony in particular and of Petrarch's achievements in general, Boccaccio contributes to the idea of the Petrarchan life as something of an Edenic fantasy, a golden age in which a living man could stand among the ancients, or conversely, in whom modern readers might see one of the *antiqui* uniquely come to life. Petrarch appears at key moments in the final books of the *Genealogy* to vivify the role of the poet in society and to assist in illustrating Boccaccio's methods of reading and writing. Considering the various misuses of the old Platonic banishment of poetry by modern critics, Boccaccio presents a canon of *auctores*, ancient and modern, whose unification of philosophy and poetry would earn them a place in any republic. How could, he asks, Homer, Virgil, or Ennius be banished from the state, for in their works lie teachings of morality, history, and law. Horace, Perseus, and Juvenal, too, could hardly be exiled from civil intercourse, and to reinforce these arguments Boccaccio notes that in addition to these ancients, it is also "my purpose to cite contemporary instances so that they [i.e., the enemies of poetry] cannot repudiate them [i.e., the poets] by any possible tergiversation."[15] He then asks, "Can anyone imagine that Plato would have been mad enough to banish Francis Petrarch?"[16] and he goes on to catalogue the chaste morality and intellectual attainments of the poet.

> His prose, and his more extensive works in verse, are so splendid, so redolent with sweetness, so loaded down with the bright bloom of his eloquence, so honey-sweet with rounded cadence, so pungent with the sap of his wonderful wisdom, that they seem like the creations of a divine and not a human genius. What more could one say? For surely he exceeds human limits and far outstrips the powers of man. Such praise I utter not of an ancient who died centuries ago, rather of one who, please God, is alive and well. . . . I have no fear that he will share the common fate of great men, whose presence, as Claudian says, impairs their fame. So dignified is his bearing, so flowing and delightful his discourse, so gentle his manners, so tranquil his old age, that one may say of him what Seneca writes of Socrates, that his hearers were even more edified by his character than by his words. I pause in my eulogy of this great man to ask these objectors whether such are the poets [*poetas*] Plato would banish from the state.[17]

Two points are central to this passage. First, Boccaccio stresses the sweetness of Petrarchan rhetoric. The organic metaphors of honey, sap, and flowering make Petrarch's poetry into a veritable landscape created, as he implies, by divine and not by human hands. Second, Boccaccio goes out of his way to attend to Petrarch as a modern who could stand among the

ancients. Though he is a *poeta*, Petrarch is also a living man, and Boccaccio
stresses that the qualities of personality and bearing only reinforce the impact of his reputation. Petrarch stands here as the unique exception to the
rule *minuit presentia fama*, and it is in this quality that Boccaccio grounds
the notion of the physical presence of Petrarch so important to his status
as an author.

What Boccaccio does is to historicize Petrarch as a man and dehistori-
cize him as a writer. He presents a poet of living flesh and blood, working
in specific times and places, whose literary production is, conversely, not
limited to era or to nation. He sets out to treat Petrarch as if *he* were one
of the poet's cherished *familiares*, one of the *antiqui* who, in the collapse of
time granted by philological acuity, becomes an intellectual contemporary.
Like Petrarch on Cicero, Boccaccio presents his *auctor* as a man, one of
character and presence, one who is revealed through the study of his
works. As Petrarch had written of his beloved Roman, in terms Boccaccio
transmutes here:

> Though nearly everything pleases me in Cicero—a man who I cher-
> ish beyond all other friends—and though I expressed adoration for
> his golden eloquence and divine intellect, I could not praise the fick-
> leness of his character.[18]

Petrarch's praise of Cicero becomes the model for Boccaccio's account of
Petrarch. The association of rhetorical ornament with profound wisdom,
and the corollary pairing of the naturally beautiful (golden) with the divine
finds its way into Boccaccio's portrait. But unlike Petrarch's letter, Boccaccio finds no fault with *his* hero; in fact, he makes the point that, unlike the
authors of antiquity, Petrarch's living presence can enable one to see the
character within him. We need no sensitivity of philological training to see
the man behind the style here; nor do we need to summon up the powers
of imagination Petrarch had himself used to resurrect dead authors from
their texts. What is central to Boccaccio, and missing from Petrarch's letters, is that this friend is alive. He becomes, in Boccaccio's handling,
uniquely a familiar author who is genuinely familiar. It is as if Boccaccio
had asked what it would be like to converse with a contemporary in the
way that one converses with an ancient. What would it be like to invert the
Petrarchan challenge and make moderns into ancients?

This question is precisely what Boccaccio answers in his portrayal of
Petrarch. In the account of the laureation ceremony (the last extended reference to the poet in the *Genealogy*), Boccaccio makes explicit the complex
relationship among *antiqui* and *moderni* that Petrarch himself defined and
exemplified.

> Not many years ago at Rome, by vote of the senate and approval of
> the famous King Robert of Sicily and Jerusalem, he received the dec-

oration of the laurel crown from the very hands of the senators. He really deserves to be counted not among the moderns, but among the illustrious ancients. His great eminence as a poet has been recognized by—I will not say merely all Italians, for their glory is singular and perennial—but by all France, and Germany, and even that most remote little corner of the world, England.[19]

Here, Petrarch represents the unique blend of public fame and literary eloquence, a figure whose laureation recognizes his status not just as a man of letters but as one of the *poetae*. If, as Boccaccio's earlier passage had suggested, Petrarch could stand as a modern among the ancients, here he is an ancient among the moderns. He is at once "familiar" to Boccaccio and his contemporaries and, as one of the *familiares*, stands among the ancients with whom they can cultivate the "conversation with the voice of the ancient past." Like one of these *antiqui*, Petrarch is unbounded by the borders of nation or tongue. If he is a man of the world who lives in Italy, he is also an Italian who can speak to all of Europe. He writes with the authority of all past poets, and he addresses, with equal authority, all readers of the present. Together with Boccaccio's rich floral and organic imagery, this passage turns Petrarch into nothing less than a walking world: a near Edenic synthesis of old and new, near and far.

Chaucer's Clerk, by contrast, will have none of this. In his hands, Boccaccio's panegyric gestures become forms of social affiliation rather than literary theory. His praise of the poet operates in the dynamic of obedience conditioned by the Host, and his references to Petrarch distill Boccaccio's effusions into a brisk statement of indebtedness. The Clerk's Prologue is an essay in abbreviation, truncating the praise of Petrarch and delimiting the source material for his tale of Griselda. Just as he pares away Boccaccio's organic imagery, so Chaucer's Clerk cuts off the long geographical account with which Petrarch began his story in *Seniles* 17.3. The streams that flow out of the mountains and that figure forth, in Petrarch's version, both the cosmic harmony and moral gist of the Griselda story are eliminated in the Clerk's telling.[20] Their mention is a "thyng impertinent" (*CT* E 54), a long digression only hindering the Clerk's conveyance of his "mateere." But the Petrarchan matter of the tale is, I think, less central to his Prologue than the complex Boccaccian gestures through which he signals his debts. As he elides the pastoral descriptions of the story in Petrarch's *Seniles* or Boccaccio's *Genealogy*, so too he takes the poet out of Boccaccio's imaginary Eden and places him squarely in the world of men.

> I wol yow telle a tale which that I
> Lerned at Padowe of a worthy clerk,
> As preved by his wordes and his werk.
> He is now deed and nayled in his cheste;

I prey to God so yeve his soule reste!
Fraunceys Petrak, the lauriat poete,
Highte this clerk, whos rethorike sweete
Enlumyned al Ytaille of poetrie,
As Lynyan dide of philosophie,
Or lawe, or oother art particuler . . .

(E 26–35)

Many of Boccaccio's emphases in the *Genealogy* are here: There is the sweetness of Petrarch's language and his appellation as a laureate poet. Both men, too, seek to praise Petrarch as part of a larger interest in defining literature generally and locating themselves in a system of poetic production and reception. And both make it clear that the public, official sanction of poetic prowess ("laureation") goes hand in hand with rhetorical finesse, dulcet tone, and a rich vocabulary. Chaucer's English translates a fair amount of Boccaccio's Latin to express these concerns: Petrarch's fame throughout *Ytali omnes* becomes the Clerk's "al Ytaille"; the *laurea insignitum* Petrarch receives becomes his epithet "lauriat poete"; and the phrasing *orator suavis atque facundus* and the references to Petrarch's work as *suavitate redolente* are distilled into the judgment of his "rethorike sweete." As in Boccaccio's account, the Clerk presents the poet as *familiaris*, as a companion with whom he may share what Anne Middleton has called that "sense of companionship with the mighty dead in books."[21]

But strikingly unlike Boccaccio, the Clerk presents no vision of a living poet. *His* Petrarch may be a personal acquaintance, but we know nothing of his physical appearance. Instead of placing him among the ancients, as Boccaccio does, the Clerk compares him only to Lynyan, a fourteenth-century Bolognese lawyer.[22] Instead of the vast stretches of his influence, the Clerk's Petrarch is himself a clerk of Padua whose repute will illuminate only the country of Italy (albeit all of it). What strikes us here is not so much a critical description of the man or of his works but a simple fact. Petrarch is dead. He offers no exemplum of a living laureate, but now, safely and irrevocably nailed in his coffin, shows us most pointedly that to become such a laureate—and in fact to be a poet at all—is to be dead. When he appears within the sequence of the Clerk's description, he is but another clerk, an unnamed friend and apparently undistinguished contemporary. Alive and known, he functions only as another maker for a locally and temporarily defined community. Not until the Clerk announces, "He is now deed," can he receive his name and epithet. "Fraunceys Petrak" can only become "the lauriat poete" once he has passed from Italy as a man and his fame has spread, to appropriate Boccaccio's phrasing, "to that most remote little corner of the world, England."

Poetry, it has been said, is something that goes on only in the perfect tense.[23] Identified as the writings of the classical *poetae* and their trecento inheritors, "poeseye" to Chaucer and his contemporaries was a literary project toward which the living could only aspire. Its goals were the creation of a "transhistorical prospect," not just a vision of a rehabilitated past but a conception of an ongoing literary present: a way of writing freed from the controlling ideologies or codes of conduct that made all forms of commissioned literature acts of performance. In contrast to the autonomy of "poeseye," "making" was perceived of as a socially constructed ritual, a public affirmation of behavior patterns and ideals. It was a form of writing on demand, located in the specificities of commission and attuned to the responses of an audience. It was an action rather than a thing, a verb rather than a noun, a moment in the here and now.

The Prologue to the *Clerk's Tale* raises these familiar gestures in Chaucerian authorial self-definition to display what happens when the writings of the poets are transformed into the tellings of a maker. The Clerk takes both Petrarch and his story and removes them from their ambience in humanist poetics or trecento Italian coterie production. He places them, instead, within a context shaped by the demands of a present and authoritative patron. His tacit appropriations of Boccaccio's praise of Petrarch will provide the model for Lydgate's later synthesis of Boccaccian praise and Clerkly idiom through which he too will try to find a place for the discourses of poetry in the confines of making. At issue in the *Clerk's Tale* and its place in Lydgate's own performance, therefore, is not simply that its tellers cannot aspire to be poets in the humanist sense; nor is it even the acknowledgment that to be a poet is quite simply to be dead. Rather, the effect of the Host's demands and the Clerk's feints is to create the atmosphere of patronized performance: to conjure up a species of making only to query what the place of an inherently poetic model may be in it.

To see the presence of the *Clerk's Tale* in the *Fall of Princes*, I suggest we read it as an allegory of commission, that is, as an exploration of relationships of power and powerlessness that define the quality of patronized literature.[24] To do so, I suggest, too, that we see the Host as Chaucer's patron of the piece, as something of a sovereign of the Canterbury court. His appearance at the beginning of the *Canterbury Tales* as a man whose literary "voirdit" (A 787) is unquestionable, and his presence at the end as having "hadde the wordes for us alle" (I 67) depict a Host whose judgment is inclusive and unquestionable. It depicts a Host whose discourse, to appropriate the language of one strain of modern criticism, is "totalized." Writing on literary figurations of the culture of patronage, Louise Fradenburg identifies the Host's demeaning presence with the powers of aristocratic commission.

The discourse of the sovereign is totalized: it refuses the idea of pluralized discourse, of debate, of personally motivated symbolism. The sovereign's word alone is legally final: his text alone is unanswerable, cannot be replied to. It does not recognize the text of the other as truly different, as radically other. One is all, one speaks for all; and all speak for one.[25]

Harry Bailly cannot recognize the text of the other, of another author separate from himself, for his requests effectively "authorize" the various tales as much as the intentions of their tellers do. The Clerk's dilemma, in these terms, is not only to produce a tale to please the Host; rather, it is to offer up a telling that, in its fidelity to the requirements of the Host's taste (no high style, no preaching, no rhetorical flourishes, no moralizing) can be said to be as much the "Host's Tale" as the Clerk's. The patron/sovereign's "ownership" of literature may thus be said to map itself onto the Host's relationship both to the Clerk and to his *Tale*, and in these terms the verbal exchanges between the two frame the *Clerk's Tale* in a court-like sequence of relationships.

Throughout the Clerk's performance, courtliness and its critiques stand at the heart of Chaucer's definition of the literary act. From the Host's opening challenge to the pilgrim's horsemanship, to the Clerk's own closing enigmatic Envoy, problems in the commission and reception of exemplary texts frame the story of Griselda. "Ye ryde as coy and still as dooth a mayde / Were newe spoused" (E 2–3), Harry provokes, as if to challenge both the *cheval* and the *chevalrie* of this tale-teller.[26] Codes of courtly conduct are defined by title and horsemanship, and the Clerk responds as the subject he has become:

> "Hooste," quod he, "I am under youre yerde:
> Ye han of us as now the governance,
> And therfore wol I do yow obeisance,
> As fer as resoun axeth, hardily."
>
> (E 22–25)

The Clerk speaks with all the legalisms of a man contracted to a service. His subjugation is, here, the condition of a patronized performer; it recognizes a "governance" that can commission and judge literary action as a form of political fealty. Under the *yerde* of the Host, he stands much like the formel eagle at the court of Nature in the *Parlement of Foules*, "evere under youre yerde" (640), waiting for a judgment; or he stands like one of those kneeling makers who, in the frontispieces of the medieval manuscript, submit their words to judging and rewarding patrons.

The drama of the Prologue's opening is a drama of commission, a barbed acting-out of the inversion of court patronage. What Harry wants is less important than what he does not want, and his string of negative injunctions will prepare us, in effect, for the inversions of our literary expectations granted by the Clerk's own telling and by his concluding

Envoy. That Envoy, at first glance, seems to place the *Tale*'s taking in those relationships of power governed by the patronage of the Clerk's audience. In the earlier French narratives and ballads that developed the form of the stanzaic envoy, in Chaucer's own use of the device in his ballads, and in Lydgate's handling of it in the *Fall of Princes*, the envoy presents direct addresses to the patron-prince. It establishes, as Daniel Poirion defines it in an influential account, specific bonds among the patron and the patronized.[27] Its forms of address and repeated moral saws bridge the space between a lyric fiction and the facts of court request. It functions as a genus of advisory rhetoric, designed to refract the poetic story that precedes it through the codes of conduct governing aristocratic taste.

The Clerk's Envoy, however, challenges these conventions.[28] It addresses not the princes who commission literature but the wives and women who, in reading of Griselda, will find not so much a model as a foil for their domestic behavior. At the generic level, one may say that the inclusion of the Envoy here sustains the figurative relationship between the Clerk, the Host, and the pilgrims as a courtly one. The Clerk himself invites this analogy by introducing his concluding section with the multiply charged line, "But o word, lordynges, herkneth er I go" (E 1163). But as a device of courtly literature now focused at a non-courtly audience, the Envoy challenges the rhetorical and generic expectations raised by the *Tale*. It makes an ostensibly exemplary story into an occasion not for understanding but debate. It opens up the *Tale*'s apparent moral for a kind of questioning that can go on only along the byways of the pilgrimage—that is, far from the confines and conventions of advisory court making. But at the same time, it augments the flavor of the *Tale*'s performance as a patronized occasion. It complements the Prologue's rhetoric of request and obedience by giving us the formal closure to a commissioned work. If Harry is the patron of the piece, and if his brusque demands and univocal tastes signal his sovereignty, then the Envoy comes to represent a formal answer to his charge: a challenge to the strictures of commissioned making; in short, an envoy that is not an envoy.

In this brief reading of the framings to the *Clerk's Tale*, I have sought to call attention to the ways in which Chaucer transmutes the idioms of Boccaccian praise and Petrarchan fame into the idioms of court commission. As a parable of patronage, the Prologue and Envoy, taken together, dramatize the condition of the writer who must translate past texts for a present audience. As a literary model, they inform what I consider to be Lydgate's own dilemmas in the *Fall of Princes*. Like the Clerk, Lydgate must conjure up the spirit of Petrarch to assist him in completing a difficult patronage assignment. And like the Clerk, too, Lydgate recognizes that the laureate aegis under which that assignment is fulfilled holds a political sanction far beyond his own patronized position. "Petrak writeth," the

Clerk had noted at the close of his *Tale*, "This storie, which with heigh stile he enditeth" (E 1147–48). Through these words he carefully reminds us of the Host's claims for the high style in the Prologue: "Heigh style, as whan that men to kynges write" (E 18).[29] These phrasings define Petrarch as a poet laureate not only for his rhetorical finesse or illuminating language but for his political approval. To a Clerk who is a maker, who produces a story that "is seyd" (E 1142) for an occasion rather than written for a king, Petrarch's status as a poet is one of both political approval and verbal control. He is, in essence, a poet both laureate and aureate, and it is Lydgate's purpose to explore the implications of this double quality.

For unlike Chaucer, who, in David Wallace's astute formulation, saw "the Petrarchan text as a response to a particular historical and political moment" and who felt, in turn, compelled "to translate Petrarch into his own cultural present,"[30] Lydgate sees the poet, and for that matter all earlier writers, within a mythological rather than historical moment. Lydgate creates a private mythology of writing, one complete with gods and heroes drawn from the trecento past and with a landscape drawn not to the borders of political states but to the contours of the imagination. In this world, poets live harmoniously with their generous patrons and responsive readers. They receive both praise and payment for their service. In a word, theirs is an "aureate" age, and I argue in what follows that Lydgate recasts the Clerk's and Chaucer's understanding of the place of patron and performer from the here and now of making to the mythic then of (l)aureate poetics.[31]

II

The Prologue to Book VIII of the *Fall of Princes* pointedly rewrites the appeals of the Clerk. The poem's narrator—here, the inept Lydgate as figured through a sad, lethargic "Bochas"—now asks himself, "Whi artow now so dul of look & cheere" (12), and the answer is soon forthcoming: The weariness of this great labor overcomes him and he dreads to embark on this eighth book of the *Fall*. He sees himself old and tired, his sight "dirked" (32), looking forward to a time when he, like other men, will be "buried lowe in the erthe doun" (34). Dullness, darkness, and astonishment cloud his vision until Petrarch appears.

> . . . Fraunceis Petrak, the laureat poete,
> Crownid with laurer, grace was his gide,
> Cam and set hym doun bi his beddis side.
>
> (VIII.61–63)

Bochas welcomes his teacher in the terms provided by the *Genealogy* and the Clerk's Prologue and in his long response synthesizes these sources into a statement of the classic Lydgatean personality.

"Wolkome maister, crownid with laureer,
Which han Itaille like a sunne cleer
With poetrie, pleynli to descryue,
Most soueraynli enlumyned bi your lyue, —

. . . .

Ye haue been lanterne, liht and direccioun
Ay to supporte myn ocupacioun,

As in writyng bookis to compile,
Cheeff exaumplaire to my gret auauntage,
To refourme the rudnesse of my stile
With aureat colours of your fressh langage."

(VIII.67–80)

Petrarch is everything Bochas is not: lightness instead of gloom, revived instead of dying, aureate instead of dull, laureate instead of ignored. He counsels Bochas to return to the work, to finish the eighth book and complete the great task of praise and advice he had initiated. "Sum rioal prince shal quyte thi labour" (147), he advises, raising the expectation of payment in the mind of a Bochas who, by this point in the Prologue, is most clearly a fictive stand-in for Lydgate himself. Petrarch enjoins:

Thynk, be writyng auctours did þer peyne
To yiue princis ther komendaciouns,

. . . .

Of prophetis thei wrot the prophecies
And the noblesse of olde Moises,
Of poetis the laureat poesies,

. . . .

Bi ther writyng—bookis sey the same—
Into this day endureth yit the name.

(VIII.148–61)

Writing poetry brings political patronage and lasting fame. The "laureat poesies" of the past enhance the name and reputation of the patron and, by consequence, the "auctor." But at the same time, Petrarch's speech can only call attention to the distance between Bochas's sad world and his own. He exemplifies that aureate age of the trecento humanist: an age flowing with brilliance and beauty, an age of Edenic fecundity. Petrarch's example raises Bochas from his bed and finds him sharpening his pen. So too, Lydgate "fordullid with rudnesse" (190) continues his work—he, however, without the "colours of rethorik" to help him translate from his source (193). His own excuse for rudeness hinges on a biographical account that seems, now, to rewrite the presentation of an ancient Italy rich with flowing streams that had preceded the Clerk's story of Griselda.

> . . . I was born in Lidgate,
> Wher Bachus licour doth ful scarsli fleete,
> My drie soule for to dewe and weete.
>
> (VIII.194–96)

Lydgate's soul is dry, for he has been denied, both by birth and by ability, the fecund streams of poetic inspiration.

In this Prologue, Lydgate literalizes the figurative elaborations of Boccaccian Edenism and Clerkly servitude. The bracketing of Petrarch, as a laurel crowned master and bearer of aureate colors, encloses his appearance in these two sonically resonating, ideologically linked terms. Now, at first glance, a phrase such as "aureate colours" may seem meaningless when construed literally; yet, when read against Lydgate's other combinations, such as "aureate licour" or "baume aureate," it calls attention to the natural processes that inspire poetry. Breezes, rains, rivers, and sunshine all give rise to the flowering of Petrarchan speech. This is the world of Boccaccio's Eden, a world that restores Petrarch to the living stage of literary life. Instead of a dead Petrarch, Lydgate offers up a living one. He shows us a poet not "nailed in his cheste" but walking once again among the fields of the imagination.

Petrarch's "aureate colours," then, are the skillful mastery of the *colores rhetorici* as well as the illuminations of a *saeculum aureum*, a golden age in which the older poets established perfect models for their fallen heirs. During that golden age, relations among governor and governed, merchant and client, patron and poet, were controlled by temperance and equity. It was, as Lydgate puts it elsewhere in the *Fall*, "The world tho daies callid Aureat" (VII.1157), a "golden world" (VII.1188). This is a world in which "sobirnesse and attemperaunce / Hadde in that world hooli the gouernaunce" (VII.1158–59), one far unlike that of Chaucer's Clerk, in which a blunt Host can inspire only "obedience" to a patronizing and abusive "governance."

This cultivation of a golden age distances the poets from the makers. Again and again, Lydgate refers to "writing of old, with lettres aureate" and to the "poetis olde," calling attention to the historical space between the aureate and laureate writers and those of his own time. In the *Mumming for Mercers*, for example, he brings together Petrarch and Boccaccio with Ovid, Virgil, Cicero, and Macrobius as "poets laureate," whose flowerings of wisdom and effusions of rhetoric distinguish them as "aureate."[32] Alert to the historical distance of laureates, John Shirley annotates this passage in his manuscript in an attempt to gloss this list of literary names. Macrobius is an "olde philosofre"; Ovid and Virgil "weren olde poetes . . . afore þe tyme of Cryst"; and Petrarch, Dante, and Boccaccio, he states, were poets of a century past, having written "withinne þis hundreþe yeere." All we know about these writers from such annotations is, quite simply, that they are *old*. To have received the laurel crown is, now almost by definition, to have lived in an earlier age of gold, whether it be a century or a millennium before.

Lydgate deploys these idioms of aureation and laureation to develop what I have considered as a mythology of poetry: a narrative of literary history grounded not in the facts of authorial biography or the details of historical production but in the legends of a golden age and the imaginations of divine inspiration. Lydgate also creates a myth of patronage befitting his aureate poets. What distinguishes the older writers from their fifteenth-century inheritors is not just their skill with words but their success with patrons. Poets of the golden age have more support from representatives of state control than those, Lydgate presumes, of his own time. In his complaints, made *in propria persona*, in Books II and III of the *Fall of Princes* about the patronage of Duke Humphrey, and in his somewhat more veiled insecurities with his poetic project in Book VIII, Lydgate reflects on this condition and constructs a vision of poetics based on patronage.[33] Laureate poets differ from living makers in the quality of their patronage. They write for the state itself, from whose representatives they receive public sanction and monetary reward, and the economics of this idealized community makes poetry a medium of exchange.

Lydgate illustrates the contrast between the equities of the past and the inequities of the present in the "Chapitle of þe gouernance of Poetis" in Book III of the *Fall* (3837–81). Each of the great dead poets is, from their very mention, directly and almost epithetically linked with the political and economic communities that sanction them:

> Daunt in Itaille, Virgile in Rome toun,
> Petrak in Florence hadde al his plesaunce,
> And prudent Chaucer in Brutis Albioun
> Lik his desir fond vertuous suffisance . . .
>
> (III.3858–61)

Each one receives support of princes, where the generosity of the ruler pays them for their work: "Fredam of lordshepe weied in ther ballaunce" (III.3862), or as Petrarch would advise the slothful Bochas in Book VIII, "Sum roial prince shal quyte thi labour" (VIII.147). Lydgate's myth of a poetic past now becomes a myth of payment. Poets receive honor and cash from the state, and in these terms we may effectively redefine the idioms of laureation and aureation as political reward (the laurel) and economic remuneration (gold). The old world of the poets now seems aureate, not only in that it is ancient, beautiful, and ideal; it is aureate because it is a world of payment in coin.

Against this golden age, Lydgate portrays his own debased environment. Here are no living laureates. Here, in a world of makers, one must beg for payment. This living world is something of an anti-aureate community, much in the way that Lydgate's own place of birth or his own study are stripped of Petrarchan fecundity in the Prologue to Book VIII. There, Lydgate had used the mask of a dull Bochas to disguise what may have been his own impatience with his patron and the tedium of his appointed task. In the verse *Letter to Gloucester*, however, these concerns explicitly direct themselves to the request for payment.[34] To express his poverty in the face of Gloucester's recalcitrant patronage, Lydgate systematically inverts the central images governing his praise of the old, laureate poets. Transforming the fecundity of the Petrarchan world, Lydgate shows us a planet unlighted by either the sun or moon.

> Sol and Luna wer clypsyd of ther liht,
> Ther was no cros nor preent of no visage,
> His lynyng dirk, ther wer no platys briht
>
> (29–31)

The sun and moon, or allegorically, the gold and silver of remuneration, are gone; the impressed faces of the coin (with their crosses or human faces) are empty; the plate with which a poet might be paid is missing. Such poverty inhibits the rich flow of eloquence and inspiration; here there is "nouthir licour nor moisture" (34). Instead of the "sugrid" liquor of the aureate poets or the "honey" of their verse, we have here only "sugreplate" (41), a kind of throat lozenge.[35] Life itself is "hard lik to hony out of a marbil stoon" (33). The only gold here is the gold within the cordial of remedy; the only thing aureate in the poem is the *Aurum Potabile* "for folk ferre ronne in age."[36] And finally, in what may be the great controlling wordplay of the poem, Lydgate asks for the "restauracioun" of his commission: not just a restoration of his due, but a re-aureation, a return to payment in the coin of ducal obligation that will once again provoke the poet to deploy his aureate diction within new lines.

Read in the context of the imagery of poetic creation developed in the *Fall of Princes*, and read against its sources in Boccaccio and Chaucer, Lydgate's little poem manipulates the worlds of poetry and patronage. It represents the poet's poverty as, figuratively, the negation of those images that contributed to the praise of poetic creation. It takes us, in its contradictions and inversions, out of the old world of golden poets and official crownings and sets us squarely in the everyday practicalities of making a living. Its images of sickness, dryness, and darkness contrast sharply with the vision of a healthy, growing, flowing, brilliantly illuminated Petrarchan prospect. In the refrain line plea for "plate" and "coignage," the poem shows us that for a living writer there is no gold quite so valuable as cold hard currency.

If the *Letter to Gloucester* tells us something about Lydgate's professional predicaments and the mythologies he had created out of them, it also tells

us much about the focus of his work in general, and in turn about the
changing subject of writing in the fifteenth century. This chapter has, thus
far, traced not only the progress of an idiom but the history of a subject.
Inherent in Boccaccio's depiction of Petrarch are the seeds of his dehistoricizing, the imperative to take the poet out of Italy and make him a
citizen of the world. Chaucer's Clerk proceeds along these lines, widening
the gap between his *auctor* and himself, not just by killing off that *auctor*
but by presenting his own version of Petrarchan *materia* in the subjected
role of patronized, court-like performance. Lydgate, in what might be
called his allegory of annoyance at the start of Book VIII of the *Fall*,
shows us a Petrarch fully laureate and aureate—a sanctioned poet from a
distant, golden era. The progressive dehistoricizing of Petrarchan authority, therefore, makes it possible to focus less and less on the realistic
details of the *poet* and more and more on the daily condition of the *maker*.
The pressing task of writing becomes the narration of the acts of commission and reception that ground the occasion of a poem's making in court
patronage.

The Prologue and Envoy to the *Clerk's Tale* are the models for this
grounding, and what happens is that the narrative fiction they enclose is
progressively subordinated to the social facts of its telling. We might say
that the Prologue and the Envoy swell out of proportion; they become
read as the most salient features of the *Tale*, offering stories of authorial
and patronly subjection and the strategies for praising the source and pla-
cating the public. They form the model for Lydgate's own practice in the
Fall of Princes, as the personal prologues and abject envoys overwhelm the
exemplary fables that they frame. As scholars long ago had noticed,
Lydgate differs fundamentally from his sources in his expansion of these
personal asides.[37] Such sections of the *Fall* as the prologue to Book VIII or
the many "chapitles" on social mores, literary taste, and political history
that punctuate the collection show us a way of writing like the Clerk—not
by appropriating his *mateere* but rather by opening his frame. Lydgate's
fascination with the placing of a story in the contexts of its telling thematizes the act of making. It is as if an entire poetics had been generated out
of strategies of address rather than narrative material; as if Lydgate had
read the *Clerk's Tale* for its drama rather than its moral, where the natural
consequence of writing verse was to spend time addressing patrons at the
expense of telling stories.

In Lydgate's poetics, the business of writing becomes writing about
business. He brings to the fore relationships among author, patron, and
audience in a manner that not only fosters a conception of the writer's task
but also, as I illustrate throughout this book, shapes the reception of
Chaucerian production. The promulgation of the envoy as a genre almost
in itself, and the apparently obsessive rewriting of Chaucer's envoy to the

Troilus by fifteenth-century versemakers, is but one consequence of this reorienting of the purpose and the subject of a public poetry.[38] The primary purpose of making becomes praising an author or patron and excusing the maker. Sublime praise and fulsome apology become, by the first decades of the century, the controlling speech acts of the writer. They determine what a public literature is and furthermore establish that the subject of a text is the writer and his public. To put it simply, we might say that Lydgate's poetry, for all its learning and prolixity, is always about Lydgate.

There are several implications for this reorientation of the literary subject in the fifteenth century. Some of them are generic, and the later chapters of this book will trace the progress of the scribal headnote and the envoy as the forms of praise and blame. Some of them are political, and this chapter's final section illustrates the ways in which the shifting expectations of royal patronage provoke the posthumous crowning of Chaucer as England's poet laureate. One implication is artistic, however, and in closing this discussion of Lydgate's preoccupations with his status as a maker, I wish to call attention to one piece of pictorial evidence for the confusion raised among conceptions of the reader, scribe, and patron in the construction of literary authority. In the illuminations of a mid-fifteenth-century manuscript of the *Fall of Princes*, we may witness one interpretation of Lydgate's authority and in it garner an understanding of *auctoritas* that controls the laureation of Chaucer in the second quarter of the century.

Huntington Library MS HM 268 is one of a small group of manuscripts that adorn Lydgate's narratives with pictures of the poet and his exemplary tales.[39] It may bear witness to an East Anglian center of reading and production of Lydgate's work, and it has recently been affiliated with a set of texts that testify to the great popularity of the *Fall* among aristocratic readers.[40] One of its many pictures appears on folio 18r: A tonsured monk, seated on a stool, presents a clasped book to an older male figure sitting on a high-backed chair (see Figure 1). The picture was identified by Henry Bergen as a portrait of Lydgate presenting his book to Duke Humphrey, an identification apparently discounted by the editors of the Huntington Library manuscript catalogue, yet one affirmed by M. C. Seymour's recent study of Duke Humphrey portraits.[41]

The picture, though, seems strikingly unlike any of the other illustrations of poetic presentation that fill medieval manuscripts, and its portrayed recipient—though highly stylized—looks nothing like the Duke Humphrey of any other surviving portrait. This figure is dressed more as an academic than a noble patron; the chair here seems most similar to those *cathedrae* of the medieval masters in school-text illumination; and, perhaps most strikingly, the poet (if this is Lydgate) is not kneeling but sitting at the same level as is his "patron."[42] The visual affiliations of this

Of hasty synges/moor of entent ful clene
Than cruel pirrus obstich flowysh posliceue

Figure 1. Lydgate presenting his book. *The Fall of Princes.*
Huntington Library, MS HM 268, fol.18r.

picture lie with scenes of scholarship and with the portraits of the other
scholar-poets in this manuscript of the *Fall*. Like the writer in the picture
on folio 79v (see Figure 2), and like the Bochas of folio 153r (see Figure 3),
the recipient of the book here wears a small black cap, identifiable as the
pileum worn by doctors of the Oxford faculties.[43] His robes are similar in
form and color to the academic gowns of Paris and Oxford, and in general
appearance he seems very similar to fifteenth-century portrayals of Boethius in manuscripts of the *Consolation of Philosophy*.[44] He is an older
man, and although the picture on folio 18r is slightly rubbed, I think he
bears the same facial appearance as the older, bearded writer of folio 79v
and of Bochas in the imaginary audience with Petrarch on folio 153r.

This picture conflates the conventions of the dedication portrait with
the iconography of scholarship to show us Lydgate offering his book not
to his patron but his *auctor*. It shows no vision of a kneeling writer set

Figure 2. "Bochas" the writer. *The Fall of Princes*. Huntington Library,
MS HM 268, fol.79v.

Figure 3. Petrarch appears to "Bochas." *The Fall of Princes*. Huntington Library, MS HM 268, fol.153r.

before an elevated aristocrat, but a presentation between two equals. Lydgate performs an act of *translatio* as he returns the bound text of the *Fall of Princes* to its source. He seeks not the pleasure of the patron but the sanction of the poet, and in this image the manuscript's illuminator nicely captures what I see as the confusions generated by Lydgate's poetics of the subject. By replacing an expected picture of Duke Humphrey with a scholarly Bochas, and by setting Lydgate as his equal in a chair, the illuminator changes the relationships between the poet and the maker. In elevating Lydgate in his picture, he elevates his status in the poem. The *Fall of Princes*, in this manuscript, is governed by the images of authors rather than of patrons. It becomes a text about making rather than about dedication, and the manuscript's illuminator captures, too, the salient features of "writing like the Clerk." For what we have here are the pictures of the maker and his author *as clerks*, attired in the habits of the university and the scriptorium. This illustration shows us that the business of *translatio*, and for that matter, the business of making generally, is the province of the clerk. Moreover, by depicting such a clerk here as a degree-holding Bochas, this illuminator laureates that clerk. He makes the author and his translator participants in a specifically university-oriented project. He laureates the enterprise of writing the *Fall of Princes*, making its source and subject, writer and translator, members of a community of arts graduates. If this illumination is in fact from an East Anglian center of Lydgatean admiration—as it has been recently argued—then what better way is there to promulgate the *auctoritas* of the maker than by making him present his book to its laureate inspirer? The manuscript shows Lydgate not as a man "subgit to alle poesye" in any Chaucerian sense, but instead as an equal to his master, perhaps worthy of the laurel for himself.

III

To this point, I have illustrated the construction of a laureate authority through the elaborate wordplays and the cultivations of a mythic sense of literary history controlling Lydgate's writing in the *Fall of Princes*. Mine has, thus far, been primarily a story of the dehistoricizing of a literary category, a story of a set of tropes and narrative personae pressed into the service of a fantasy of public poetry. For all of his attentions to the moment of commission or the act of writing, Lydgate's notion of the laureateship is a profoundly ahistorical one. It ignores the social history of university affiliation and political approval to participate, instead, in a conception of the literary performance as a species of praise. In addition, the conception of an "aureate" poetics I have chronicled has less to do with the specifics of developing a Romance or Latinate vocabulary than it has with a similar propagation of a myth. For all his usage of that rich, at times opaque, vocabulary, Lydgate's uses of the term *aureate* itself are designed to conjure up a vision of a past world, what I have seen as the Edenic fantasy of the Petrarchan prospect.

If Lydgate is a fashioner of myth, he is also a creature of wordplay, and the historical devolves to the merely verbal in his conjurings of the great poets. Scholars have long been sensitive to Lydgate's taste for pun and sonic effect;[45] one might well claim that the very image of his dried-up literary sensibilities in Book VII of the *Fall*, "Where Bacus licour doth ful scarsli fleete" (VIII.195), hinges on a controlling pun between the present, dullard "Bochas" and this absent and inspiring "Bachus." So, too, his usages *laureate* and *aureate* often rely on sound rather than sense for their impact, and they may also have informed the later scribal applications of these terms to Chaucer's authorship itself. The words come to function in Lydgate's own poetry as encomiastic terms lacking any specific connotations whatever. The possibilities for rhyme and wordplay on these words are nearly endless, and to read Lydgate is, again and again, to find these words chiming in the ear. In the *Mumming for Mercers*, for example, he makes the equation:

> Thoroughe þat sugred bawme aureate
> Þey called weren poetes laureate.
>
> (34–35)

In the *Fall of Princes*, he again associates them in a rhyming pair:

> Writyng of old, with lettres aureat,
> Labour of poetis doth hihli magnefie,
> Record on Petrak, in Rome laureat.
>
> (IV.106–8)

In the Envoy to Book II of the *Fall*, he avers, stressing the importance of poets to sovereigns through internal rhyme:

> Poetis olde thi tryumphes rehersyng,
> Thi laureat knyhtis, most statli ther ridyng,
> Thyn aureat glorie, thy nobless tenlumyne.
>
> (II.4470–72)

And, in what may be his last, commissioned poem, the *Life of St. Albon and St. Amphibalus*, Lydgate begins by once again invoking Petrarch as an inimitable model of style and sanction. How can he, he asks,

> . . . folwe the steppis aureat
> Of Franceis Petrak, the poete laureat?
>
> (I.13–14)[46]

Nowhere in these lines, or in the many other pairings of the terms in Lydgate's poetry, do we find mention of a coronation ceremony or a specific university degree. Poets come to be laureates, here, *because* they are aureate—that is, because of their facility with rhetoric or their engagement with or evocation of past glory.

When Chaucer enters this literary system, it is apparently as but one more laureate and aureate past writer. Most readers of the poetry of Lydgate and his heirs have understood this transformation as a simple mapping of the terms of Petrarchan praise onto the English writer, and to a certain extent the Clerk's praise of Petrarch does provide Lydgate with the ways of praising a recently dead national poet.[47] But what is at stake in the early decades of the fifteenth century is, I think, a complex set of relations among poets and patrons, writers and kings. Chaucer is elevated to the laureateship as part of a program of political appeal. He stands, in one sense, as the model for Lydgate's own aspirations to official sanction and royal compensation. But, in another sense, his appellation as the laureate or aureate poet works only on the page. It forms part of a set of scribal confusions and collocations that may partly respond to political realities but that are also generated out of orthographic jumbles. Chaucer's construction as the (l)aureate poet is thus a function of the dehistoricizing of these terms as well as an event in the historicizable relations between poet and patron.

Perhaps the figure most responsible for many of these confusions is John Shirley. Maintaining Chaucer's reputation as the laureate and aureate poet seems almost an obsession with him. His elaborate headnotes to the poetry he transcribes tell stories of political commission and bibliographical response so detailed that generations of modern critics have accepted them as fact. His headnote to *Lak of Stedfastness*, for example, places the composition of that poem in a quite specific place and time:[48] "Balade Royal made by oure laureal poete of albyoun in hees laste yeers" (TCC R.3.20). In the copy of the poem preserved in BL Harley MS 7333, most likely a Shirley-derived production, the description of its composition is expanded: "This balade made Geffrey Chaunciers the Laureall Poete of Albion and sent it to his souerain lorde Kynge Richarde the secounde þane being in his Castell of Windesore." What is at stake in such headnotes is less their accuracy as to Chaucer's composition and more their critical presuppositions about what constitutes Chaucerian production and, more generally, what defines public poetry. Shirley's manuscripts, and those that derive from his influence, develop the Lydgatean imagination of a laureate Chaucer by situating his poetry in kinds of patronage environments that Lydgate himself had detailed in the *Fall of Princes* or the *Troy Book*. But they also maintain the ideal of an aureate Chaucer: of a poet of rhetorical finesse and rich vocabulary. The headnote to the poem now known as the *Complaint Unto Pity* in Shirley's manuscript reads: "And nowe here filowing begynneþe a complaint of pitee by Geffrey Chaucier þe aureat poete þat euer was fonde in oure vulgare to fore hees dayes" (BL MS Harley 78, fol. 80r).[49] Chaucer is here the poet not of political commission but of linguistic facility; a poet of the "vulgare" whose command of English makes him "aureat."

Shirley's double encomia to Chaucer led, however, to confusions in the manuscripts that imitate or copy his examples. In the headnote to the *Canterbury Tales* from Harley 7333, Chaucer is called "þe laureal and most famous poete þat euer was to-fore him as in þemvelisshing of our rude moders englisshe tonge." Here, he is not "laureal" because of any commission or royal request; nor is he "aureat" because of the embellishing of the vernacular. Rather, the laureate is the aureate, the political is the rhetorical; one term can just as well suffice as another. Chaucer is the laureate *because* of his finesse with words, and it would seem that by the later fifteenth century *laureate* and *aureate* have become virtually interchangeable terms. When Shirley's text of *Pity*, for example, was copied into BL MS Additional 34360, the language of the headnote was preserved (with some slight variation); yet, at the conclusion to the poem, another scribe has written under the words "Explicit Pyte," the appellation, "dan chaucer laurere" (fol.53r).[50]

The Additional Manuscript brackets its text of the *Complaint Unto Pity* with references to a Chaucer both aureate and laureate. It scribally enacts the kind of verbal framing that presented Petrarch in Book VIII of Lydgate's *Fall*. Moreover, it sustains, perhaps, what had become by the end of the century an orthographic confusion between the two words. The tradition of Lydgate's rhyming pairs, together with the influence of French orthography in manuscripts of the century, could very well have shaped the various confusions of these terms. The habit of spelling *Envoy* as *Lenvoy* together with the redundant English definite article before it, points to a tendency of writing French proclitic articles before vowels. It exemplifies, too, the overall confusions in late medieval written French and English, where issues in spelling, syntax, and pronunciation codified by modern grammarians were not rigorously separated in the study and use of the languages. Such confusions have recently been seen, however, for their literary creativity instead of for their scribal failure, and in this linguistic and interpretive context I suggest that the word *laureate* could at times be little more (or little less) than *l'aureate*. In a climate of sonic and orthographic leveling, aureation and laureation fall together as formulaic epithets.[51]

There may also be problems of dittography in certain manuscripts, as for example, when Shirley writes in his copy of Lydgate's *Procession of Corpus Christi*:

> Ambrosius, with sugerd elloquence,
> Wryteþe with his penne and langage laureate[52]
>
> (193–94)

Surely the wording should be "langage aureate," in keeping with his "su-gerd elloquence"; or perhaps, to give Shirley more credit, the two terms had so fallen together by mid-century that "langage" can indeed be "laure-ate." Neither *laureate* nor *aureate* has by this time the historical specificity or mythological resonance governing its earlier uses. Both words operate only at the level of sound and spelling, giving a flexibility to the scribes and contributing to the radically dehistoricized climate of literary praise.

For all this literary wordplay and scribal confusion, there is a histori-cal reality to the construction of a laureate authority for Chaucer. Texts datable to the first twenty years of the fifteenth century seem hardly con-cerned with crowning the poet. There is, of course, the paean to Chaucer in the *Floure of Courtesye*, perhaps one of the first of Lydgate's poems (dated by Schirmer 1400–1402);[53] yet the vague affiliation of the poet with the laurel is not so much a political as a rhetorical phenomenon.

> Chaucer is deed, that had suche a name
> Of fayre makyng, that, without[en] wene
> Fayrest in our tonge, as the laurer grene.
>
> (236–38)

Though he is dead, Chaucer remains here one of the makers. Unlike the Petrarch of the Clerk's Prologue, he is no "laureat poete" but one whose making is as verdant as the "laurer grene." The simile is grounded in the familiar metaphors of literary inspiration as a kind of well—that liquid poetics that Lydgate would exploit much later in the *Fall of Princes*—and Chaucer's death, Lydgate continues, dries up that source whose "lycour swete" sprang from the muses Clio and Calliope (239–42).

Not until the *Lyfe of Oure Lady*, written a decade or two later, does Lydgate label Chaucer as a poet and grant him the right to wear the laurel crown.

> And eke my master Chauceris nowe is graue
> The noble rethor Poete of breteine
> That worthy was the laurer to haue.[54]

Though he is still primarily a writer of rhetorical finesse, Chaucer becomes here a political poet: one whose identity depends both on the nation of his origin and the political rewards for his service. His worthiness to have received the laurel crown is thus a recognition of that service, and the phrasing in these lines looks forward to the arguments of Lydgate's *Fall of Princes* and the string of poets (Dante, Virgil, Petrarch) who had shared with Chaucer an affiliation as official writer of the state.

Something quite specific has occurred between the early references to Chaucer and his laureation in the work of Lydgate and Shirley in the second quarter of the fifteenth century. Beginning with Henry V's restoration of Richard II's bones to Westminster in 1413 and his triumphal return from Agincourt in 1415, the court had reaffirmed itself as the locus of both political control and literary patronage.[55] The commissioning of the deluxe manuscript of Chaucer's *Troilus and Criseyde* (now known as the Campsall Manuscript) when Henry was Prince of Wales, the request for Lydgate's *Troy Book*, and the range of his book collecting all speak to the assertions of a confident English ruler seeking a literary context for the affirmations of dynastic legitimacy.[56] That context, as has long been understood, was a distinctively vernacular one, for the years between the victory at Agincourt and Henry V's death marked a new interest in the possibilities of English as the medium of official communication.[57] The king's addresses to the citizens of London in 1416, his letters to his chancellor Henry Beaufort in 1417, and his correspondence with the Chancery throughout the later years of his reign were all in English. Several historians of the language have found in this political revival of the vernacular a corresponding interest in the work of Chaucer, and in turn, the efforts to promote the poet as the literary analogue to Henry V himself. Associations between Chaucer and Henry pepper the *Troy Book*, commissioned when he was Prince of Wales in 1412. As Lydgate puts it, Henry V's ascendancy would restore a new *aureate* age for English politics and by implication would renew the call for those laureate poets to record and celebrate that restoration.

> And þanne I hope þe tyme fortunat,
> Of þe olde worlde called aureat
> Restore shal, . . .
>
> (*Troy Book* V.3399–3401)

The poetry that Lydgate wrote during this period is filled with possibilities and promise. It seeks to give voice to an ideal of poetic patronage by investing in that fantasy of an Edenic world and furthermore, by imagining a current royal patronage along the models of an imagined Chaucerian laureateship. Such poems as *Lak of Stedfastnesse* and the *Complaint to His Purse* formed the templates for Lydgate's own public makings, as they fit the pattern of an English poet writing to his king. Both the dead Chaucer and the young Henry V become citizens of that "Brutes Albion" that had been conquered, in the *Complaint to His Purse*, by Henry IV. Lydgate's investment in Chaucerian authority, at this time, is a function of his own aspirations to royal patronage. His claims for the social function of the poet are, in turn, wrapped up in his own pleas for laureate office.[58] As he argued in the Prologue to the then Prince Henry in the *Troy Book*, poets preserved the memory of their patrons' great deeds. Without them, he states,

> For-dirked age elles wolde haue slayn
> By lenthe of ȝeris þe noble worthi fame
> Of conquerors, and pleynly of her name
> For-dymmed eke the lettris aureat,
> And diffaced the palmed laureat,
> Which þat þei wan by knyȝthod in her dayes,
> Whos fretyng rust newe and newe assayes
> For to eclipse the honour and the glorie
> Of hiȝe prowes, which clerkis in memorie
> Han trewly set thoruȝ diligent labour,
> And enlumyned with many corious flour
> Of rethorik, to make vs comprehende
> The trouthe of al, as it was in kende . . .
>
> (Prol. 208–20)

All the machinery of Lydgate's writing is at work here. The contrasts between illumination and darkness, the aureate and the dim, the laureate and the forgotten—all look back to the traditions of Petrarchan praise and look forward to an English royal patronage for poetry. Chaucerian allusions fill the later portions of this Prologue—its appeals to the "key of remembraunce" (224), its reference to "Lollius" (309), and its use of the *Troilus* tag line "as men in bokys fynde" (326). By Book III, associations between earlier poet and present patron are made explicit, when Lydgate acknowledges the precedence of Chaucer in the making of an English Troy poem.

> The hool story Chaucer kan yow telle
> Yif that ye liste, no man bet alyve,
> Nor the processe halfe so wel discryve,
> For he owre englishe gilt with his sawes,
> Rude and boistous first be olde dawes
> That was ful fer from al perfeccioun
> And but of litel reputaticoun
> Til that he cam & thorug his poetrie
> Gan oure tonge firste to magnifie,
> And adourne it with his elloquence.
> To whom honour laude & reverence
> Thorug-oute this londe yove be & songe
> So that the laurer of oure englishe tonge
> Be to hym yove for his excellence
> Rigt a whilom by ful hige sentence
> Perpetuelly for a memorial.
>
> (III.4234–49)

Here is a political agenda told as a story of the "tonge." Through praise of Chaucer's English, Lydgate can evoke both a literary past and a political future, an aureate age and a laureate control that both operate through the appropriations of "oure englishe tonge." Lydgate's claims, here and throughout the poetry of the period of Henry V as king and Prince of Wales, are for a laureation grounded in the language of the court and poet.

Within a decade, however, all this had changed. The death of Henry V in 1422 left England in the hands of an infant Henry VI and a protectorate of royal relations headed by the Duke of Gloucester. The London court progressively lost interest in supporting purely literary efforts, and Lydgate began to cast a wide net among regional aristocrats and commercial patrons.[59] Humphrey himself became one of the primary commissioners, though as the work of Lydgate and others testify, not a terribly responsible one.[60] The images of brilliance and control give way, now, to the rhetoric of darkness and despair. The coronation of Henry VI in 1429 and his entry into London in 1432 thus raised the expectations for a restored royal patronage for literature.

Lydgate clearly spent much of this period writing propaganda for the young king. His poems on the coronation and the entry, together with his genealogical texts and mummings, are at one level designed as public proclamations of the legitimacy of Henry's rule. But at another level, they are pleas for the creation of a laureateship. Lydgate fills these works with the same kinds of Edenic fantasies that had informed his visions of a literary past and his hopes for a Henrician present.[61] Again and again, Henry VI brings a new paradise to the English court; again and again, he participates in pageants filled with staged representations of an artificial Eden. The public Lydgate is, in these terms, the propagandist not just for a king but for a literary office. The possibilities of a new aureate England so preoccupy him that by 1445, in his pageant verses for the entry of Margaret of Anjou into London, he confusingly and perhaps unwittingly addresses her as "Emprise queene and ladie laureate" (151).[62] He projects onto Margaret's coronation his own aspirations for a literary crowning, and the prayer to the Virgin may be read as a plea for the right governance not only of a people but of poets.

> Praie for our queene that crist will here gouerne
> Longe here on lyue in hire noble astate
> Aftirward Crowne here in blisse eterne
>
> (152–54)

But these are not perhaps the lines or the original pageant script; in the surviving manuscript the word *crist* in line 152 has been inserted interlinearly in a different hand.[63] If we read the line, "Praie for our queene that will here gouerne," we may now see Margaret herself as an ideal of literary rulership. Her "governance," as Lydgate would have put it in the *Fall of Princes*, will confer just payment on her poets, and her reign will be in need of writers to sustain her praise. Her status as a "ladie laureate" is thus something of a transferred epithet, or perhaps an example of the revealing dittography of a poet with the laureation on his mind. In a manner far different from the bold securities of the Prologue to the *Troy Book*, Lydgate here obliquely and insecurely voices his pleas to a queen who, although she may herself be crowned "in blisse eterne," is beseeched to crown her poet.

England during the first decades of Henry VI's reign was in need of a laureate poet, much as it was in need of royal patrons to confer that title. Lydgate's own propaganda and his pleas for patronage during this period articulate the fantasies of a writer needing to be that laureate, and it is in this environment that Chaucer becomes what Shirley would call England's "laureall poete." Lydgate's narratives and Shirley's headnotes both construct and sustain Chaucer as the poet of "Brutes Albyon," the poet who, in service to his kings, wrote verses of praise and counsel. They also imagine a Chaucer of a literary coterie: a writer who, among such friends as Bukton and Scogan, Gower and Strode, could offer personal advice while at the same time seeking the responses of an informed, sympathetic readership. These visions of a Chaucer are maintained by writers out of power—writers who may plead for preferment, as Lydgate did, or commercial success, as Shirley would. They are the fantasies of writers who have made themselves the subject of their work and who, in turn, would find in Chaucer's narratives embedded stories of commission, friendship, and reader response. The fascination with the laureateship, therefore, is almost inseparable from the cultivation of the literary envoy: that moment when the writer sends his text out for judgment and rescription, when the business of the poem, be it plea for money, office, or literary criticism, is conducted.

It is significant, therefore, that the first poetic reference to Chaucer as specifically the "poet laureate" comes from precisely this moment of English dynastic insecurity, from the pen of a writer stripped of his power and his home, and in the form of an envoy modeled on the coterie submission of the *Troilus*. The Scottish king James I, writing in England in the early 1420s in anticipation of his return to Scotland, gives voice to the fantasy of literary patronage, now from the perspective of the patron rather than the poet.[64] His *Kingis Quair* may be read as a response to the Lydgatean constructions of Chaucerian authority in explicitly royal terms— a poem that draws not just on the tropes and matter of late-medieval English vision, but also on the stance of the alienated dreamer-poet and on the rhetoric of dullness fostered by the first generation of Chaucerians. A

pawn in English courtly politics since his capture in 1406, James was variously a court ward, prisoner, ambassador, and diplomatic shuttlecock until
his release in 1424. During this time, he received an education at the hands
of court tutors and most likely became acquainted with such canonical
texts of courtly learning as the *Consolation of Philosophy* and the works of
Chaucer, Gower, and Lydgate. At the conclusion of the poem, synthesiz-
ing the inheritance of literary envoys from Chaucer's *Troilus* and Lydgate's
Temple of Glas, James commends his work:

> Vnto [th']inpnis of my maisteris dere,
> Gowere and Chaucere, that on the steppis satt
> Of rethorike quhill thai were lyvand here,
> Superlatiue as poetis laureate
> In moralitee and eloquence ornate,
> I recommend my buk in lynis sevin—
> And eke thair saulis vnto the blisse of hevin.

> (1373–79)

James's act of laureation is both a political and a literary response to the
authority of England's fourteenth-century vernacular poets. It is a literary
response, in that it sustains the burgeoning encomia of Chaucer through
the first two decades of the fifteenth century and, more precisely, makes
explicit the associations between Chaucer and the laurel promoted by
Lydgate. It is a political response, in that first and foremost James is writing as a king himself. He can, without the periphrases of a Lydgate, name
the poets as *his* laureates now: as his imaginary readers who may be
uniquely qualified to judge the writings not just of an imitator but a king.
The drama of release at the close of the *Kingis Quair* is the dream of release not just from the prison of the Henrys but the confines of the subject.
James has carefully rewritten Chaucer's *Troilus* Envoy to remove all sense
of literary *and* political subjection. His poets do not kiss the steps in subjugation to the ancient *poetae* but sit on the steps of rhetoric. They are not
"subgit to alle poesye" but instead are "superlatiue," quite literally raised
above (*super latus*) as direct antithesis to the experience of lying below (*sub
iacet*, and hence subject).

James's imagination of a court poetics is analogous to that imagined in
the aureate past of Lydgate's fantasies of patronage and pictorially envi-
sioned by the East Anglian artist who had illustrated Lydgate and his
Bochas. It is a world not of master and subjects, but of literary equals; a
world in which political patronage does not subject the maker but en-
nobles the poet; a world in which that poet need not kneel upon the
ground but sit beside his *auctor*. That world is what is represented in the
Troilus frontispiece (reproduced in the *Frontispiece*, above), and we may
now consider this illumination in the contexts of the laureate and aureate

imaginings of Lydgatean poetics and Henrician politics. It shows the poet not as subject but as center, elevated among his presumably royal audience. With his golden hair and rich brocade, Chaucer is himself an aureate figure, and the gold trimmings and bright colors of his audience make this into what Lydgate would have recognized as a "world tho daies callid Aureat." Like the Petrarch of the Clerk's Prologue, Chaucer illumines all his realm with poetry, or as Lydgate would put it in his Petrarchan fantasy of Book VIII of the *Fall of Princes*, "with aureat colours of [his] fressh langage."

But if the Chaucer of the *Troilus* frontispiece embodies the Lydgatean fantasies of a literary past, he also represents the aspirations of a political present. Chaucer is here, like Lydgate, not just the orator to a king but the manager of a spectacle. He does not read before his courtly audience as much as he appears to greet them, and perhaps the narrative displayed within this picture—with its double portrait of a static listenership and an active processional—is, in itself, the story of a pageant. Lydgate's professions to a laureateship of some sort had taken shape in the creation of such courtly spectacles, and there is much in this picture that may reflect the artifice of glittering castles and fantastic forests constructed for the royal entries of the Henrys. There is, specifically moreover, much that may reflect the spectacle of Ricardian pageant. If Chaucer stands here as an archetype of the Lydgatean manager of spectacle, then the model for that spectacle is the triumphal entry of King Richard into London in 1392: a historical event recalled in Henry V's return of Richard's bones to Westminster and preserved in the Latin poetry and vernacular chronicle of the early fifteenth century.[65]

The Pageant of 1392 celebrated the king's reconciliation with the mercantile and civic authorities of the city of London. The celebrations organized for his return to the city set a tone of popular renewal couched in the images of an Edenic fantasy. Richard Maydiston's Latin poem on the pageant places its events, from the start, in the paradise (*in coelis*) of Ciceronian friendship, where the poet and the king may be thought of as *amici*.[66] The king enters his city bedecked in a golden cloak (*auro vestis*), while his queen is covered in brocade and gems. In the course of their procession through the city, they marvel at a magnificent artificial castle, suspended on cords and towering to the sky, and they witness a tableau of a forest populated by all the beasts of creation.

The story of this pageant may be thought of as providing a master narrative of laureate responsibility: one written in the scripts of Lydgate's later celebrations for Henry VI and Margaret of Anjou and visualized in the *Troilus* frontispiece. With its royal processional through wilderness to castle and its noble audience before a welcoming orator, the frontispiece stands as a visual reminder of the royal return as restoration of an Eden in the wilderness. It stands, too, as a quite specific recollection of King Richard himself, who, as Maydison had put it, entered his city "beautiful as Troilus" ("Iste velut Troilus . . . decorus") and conferred upon a London now renamed as *Nova Troja* and as *Troynovant* a new era of political control. Here, on the first leaf of Chaucer's own Troy poem, we have the associations of a Troilus and his poet: of a king who stands as figure for the poem's hero and a London that may stand as figure for his city. The *Troilus* frontispiece may thus be read as the representation of the poet's place in the remembered vision of a triumphal Ricardian return. It is a fantasy both laureate and aureate, one whose details and overall effect contribute to the cultural need for the poet and his royal patron.

In the limnings of the *Troilus* frontispiece and the last stanzas of the *Kingis Quair*, we may find contemporary responses to the Lydgatean fantasy of literary politics. If, as I have suggested, Lydgate cobbled his persona out of the abjections of Chaucer's Clerk, then these two presentations show us ways of getting out from underneath the "yerde" of patronage and old *auctoritas*. The frontispiece presents the poet as the organizer of royal spectacle rather than the servant of an aristocracy; the envoy to the *Quair* imagines writers who may fittingly respond to kingly making. In both we see a Chaucer at the center of a royally sanctioned coterie of poets and readers, a figure now "superlatiue" rather than "subgit." They make the occasions of commission or composition central to the readers' understanding of their texts and in so doing enact the functions of the prologue and the envoy I have found at the heart of Lydgate's "writing like the Clerk." What is visually represented in the *Troilus* frontispiece is the same kind of information offered in the Lydgatean prologue or the Shirleyan headnote: information about time and place, author and audience. As the pictorial equivalent to Lydgate's verse or Shirley's prose, the frontispiece reveals a drama of commission and response. It prepares the reader of the *Troilus* for a poem that is laureate in authorship and aureate in origin—a poem bracketed, within its manuscript, by the prologue and envoy that take as their subjects the making and sending out of the literary work.

The effect of the *Troilus* frontispiece may thus be appreciated as reshaping Chaucer's poem in its manuscript according to the generic expectations of a Lydgatean poetics. But if, in the process, it looks back to a golden age, it also looks ahead to transformations in the fifteenth-century literary system. It anticipates, for example, the idea of the *orator regius* as the office into which the laureateship would mutate by the century's end.[67] Moreover, because the Corpus Christi manuscript was at one time in the possession of John Shirley himself, its portraiture may have fostered the maintenance of Chaucer as a laureate and aureate poet well into the century's second half.[68] But also, the *Troilus* frontispiece may stand as frontispiece to my own study. Its subsequent chapters on poetic anthologies as coded narratives of patronage, on Shirley's construction of the Chaucer canon, on the development of Chaucer's poetry as children's literature, and on the restoration of the laureateship and its implications for an early Tudor literary history are designed to trace out the developments of the critical idiom and literary subjectivity whose genealogy I have explored here. The following studies of developments in literary personae, in technologies of book production, and in the social history and thematics of the patronage process illustrate the centrality of Chaucer and his texts, not only to the presentations of authorial control or fantasies of power for a later generation of his imitators, but to the ongoing invention and narration of English literary history itself.

CHAPTER TWO

Reading Like the Squire: Chaucer,
Lydgate, Clanvowe, and the
Fifteenth-Century Anthology

AMONG THE many Canterbury pilgrims who purport to "sey some-what of love," few do so with the blend of self-effacement and ineptitude of the Squire. The Host's initial confidence in his re-quest—"for certes ye / Konnen theron as muche as any man" (F 2–3)—derives from what he and Chaucer's audience know of the Squire from the *General Prologue.* As "A lovyere and a lusty bacheler" (A 80), with his curled locks, his fashionable dress, and his lyric aspirations, the Squire seems the ideal candidate to tell a tale of amorous desire. Embodying a new generation of chivalric taste, he may be charged with offering a change from the epic effusions of his father the Knight; certainly his ac-count of Cambuskyan's Tartary, complete with magic steeds and talking birds, is a far cry from the stateliness of Theseus's Athens. It soon becomes apparent, however, that the Squire fails both the requests of Harry Bailly and his own ambitions as a literary son. The amplifications of his father give way to mere dilatoriness; the philosophical promise of the *Squire's Tale*'s avian lecture yields to bathos; and, just perhaps, the possibility of an extended story of Canacee and her brother, previously condemned by the Man of Law, provokes suspicions of a major breach of politesse in this most desperately polite tale-teller.[1]

It comes as little wonder, therefore, that the Franklin interrupts these ramblings. Aptly focusing on the Squire's skills at "spekyng felyngly," he pinpoints what, for many modern critics, are the chief features of the boy's performance, notably his inability to get beyond the emotive response to his own fictional exotica. Readers of the Franklin's stripe may also take some comfort in what they may think of as a "medieval reading" of the *Squire's Tale* in Jean of Angoulême's dismissive annotation in his manu-script: "Ista fabula est valde absurda in terminis et ideo ad presens preter-mittatur nec ulterius de ea procedatur."[2]

Jean and the Franklin notwithstanding, many of Chaucer's readers clearly appreciated the *Squire's Tale* in the first three centuries of its circulation. For a contemporary audience, the *Tale* may have appealed to what Paul Strohm identifies as the late-fourteenth-century taste for narratives that "tend towards deliberate frustration of generic expectations" and that had "the potential to stimulate, to challenge, to annoy."[3] Though outpaced by the stories of the Clerk, the Prioress, and Chaucer's own *Melibee* among tales popular with fifteenth-century audiences, the story of Canacee and the falcon had an obvious hold on Lydgate, who includes it prominently in his lists of Chaucer's works, and perhaps on Hoccleve, whose own topoi of humility are founded on the Squire's idiom.[4] And for readers of the sixteenth, seventeenth, and eighteenth centuries, the *Squire's Tale* exemplified that predilection for fantastic romance which, from Spenser through Milton to Thomas Wharton, was seen as a quintessentially "medieval" quality in Chaucer's work.[5]

The literary history of the Squire and his *Tale* has been admirably traced by David Lawton, and my purpose here is not to chronicle anew the specifics of their reception or rewriting. Instead, I hope to illustrate the ways in which the Squire's persona and performance shaped the literary values of the fifteenth century, conditioning the dissemination of one portion of the Chaucer canon and one strain of imitation written in its wake. The Squire provided a new generation of Chaucer's readers with a way of conceiving literary history as genealogical, that is, as a relationship between father and son analogous to the Knight's fatherhood of the Squire. The drama of his predicament—being trapped between the desire to emulate the fatherly *auctoritas* of the Knight and to live up to the paternalistic critical expectations of the Franklin—offered Chaucer's imitators a model for articulating their relationship to their master.

Traditional, critical accounts of Chaucer's literary fatherhood begin, however, not with the embedded dramas of paternity behind the Squire and the Knight but with the post-Chaucerian obeisances of Hoccleve. The well-known gestures in the *Regiment of Princes* to Chaucer as "fader reverent" and "universal fadir in science" have long been seen as the initiations of what A. C. Spearing (in a sensitive analysis of this tradition) calls "the constitutive idea of the English poetic tradition."[6] Spearing recognizes that notions of paternity have shaped much of Western literary history from Lucretius to Harold Bloom, and he locates a double sense of "father Chaucer" in the critical reception and the fictional creations of his tales of parents and children. More recently, the fatherhood of Chaucer has been understood through models more psychological than critical, where Hoccleve's Oedipalized insecurities project onto a "culturally powerful literary father Chaucer" the political and corporeal powers of the ruler.[7] Whether we see the "father Chaucer" Hoccleve makes as the product of literary trope or psychological dysfunction, this appellation has its hold on modern readers precisely in its ambiguous relationship to both: Neither wholly conventional nor wholly autobiographical, Hoccleve's responses to Chaucerian authority feed our understandings of reception and response as problems in the personal adjudication of the troped.

These critical attentions to the personalization of the Chaucerian inheritance, I think, have obscured the idea of a literary fatherhood established in the fiction of the *Canterbury Tales* itself, and my purpose in this chapter will be to find in the responses of the individual imitator and in a class of readers the workings out of a relationship embedded in the *Tales*. For the first of these categories, I argue that John Clanvowe's *Book of Cupid* figures its relationship to Chaucer through a Squire-like appropriation of materials from his authoritative fictions. With its authoritative opening lines drawn from Theseus's lecture in the *Knight's Tale* and its oddly abbreviated avian debate pendant on that of the *Squire's Tale*, the *Book of Cupid* plays out the dramatic tensions inherent between the two tale-tellers. It gives us a reading, and a rewriting, of Chaucerian paternity by playfully adopting the voice of the rhetorically insecure and dilatory son of the *Canterbury Tales*.

For the second category, the Squire may be taken to encapsulate the literary tastes of that new class of readers who commissioned those collections that transmitted Clanvowe's poem along with the minor works of Chaucer: anthologies filled with the love visions of the *Legend of Good Women*, the *Parlement of Foules*, and the *Book of the Duchess*; with the mythological *Complaints* of *Mars* and *Venus*; and with the courtly imitations of Lydgate and Hoccleve. These readers are the heirs to Chaucer's Squire, members of a rising gentry who, much like Chaucer's fictional son, share a taste for courtly making in the service of the god of love. They enact, in their manuscript commissions, many of the literary values found not only in the Squire's portrait and performance but in Chaucer's Prologue to the *Legend of Good Women* and in the critiques of the Prologue to the *Man of Law's Tale*. Anne Middleton has defined this complex of literary attitudes as a "gallant" style associated with what she labels the "New Men" among the Canterbury narrators. As she puts it, such new men "agree that the pleasure and the use of literature are one thing, and are realized in worldly performance."[8] Theirs is a taste for the "contemporary, stylish, and polite," where the telling of a tale becomes "a way of reaffirming one's possession of the tastes and qualities that assure one's membership in polite society."[9] This is the poetry, and the poetic stance, voiced in the Prologue to the *Legend of Good Women*, where the god of love charges Chaucer with the socially affirming rituals of courtly making. It is the poetry of the Squire, where the "small skirmishes rather than a 'gret emprise' in the service of love" distinguish him from his father the Knight.[10] And it is also, I argue in this chapter, the poetry of fifteenth-century gentry readers seeking to reimagine the courtly worlds of patronage and making dramatized in Chaucer's fictions.

In addition to considering the fictional new men of Chaucer's poetry (what might be called the models for his implied readers), I address the social new men of the fifteenth century (his historical readers) and their understanding of a "gallant" Chaucer and the imitative poetry he sparked.[11] My primary evidence in recovering their literary values will be the first of a set of manuscript anthologies containing Clanvowe's *Book of Cupid* and the Chaucerian dream-debate texts, Bodleian Library MS Tanner 346.[12] Probably dating from the 1440s, Tanner 346 is a manuscript that clearly shows the signs of a controlling critical intelligence.[13] Its three scribes produced its four separate booklets in a coordinated way that strongly suggests a guiding commission from a patron.[14] Its provenance has been traced to the Greystoke family in Yorkshire at the end of the fifteenth century, one of the rising Northern baronetcies whose members saw distinguished service at the level of the county and the royal court. This likely ambience, together with the manuscript's selection of texts, plan of decoration, and high quality of workmanship, mark it as the product of a magnate literary culture.[15] Its making and reception participate in the mid-century movement to "consolidate a sense of national identity" through the reading of vernacular literature and history and in the process testify to a new attitude toward books, their authors, and their social function.[16]

The rise in literacy among the gentry, whether through a greater access to the schools or as a consequence of widespread use of documents in mercantile and political affairs, fostered a social need for works of literature that edified and entertained.[17] Richard II, Henry IV, and Henry V and his brother Humphrey Duke of Gloucester had set the standard for the kind of patronage deemed necessary to produce such literary works, and for the rising gentry and the regional aristocracy of the fifteenth century these earlier royal courts were seen as objects of imitation in the pursuit of social self-definition through literary patronage.[18] Magnates imitated the courts, and the lesser gentry, in turn, imitated the magnates in desiring books that would affirm their social status. Compendia of moral instruction, historical narratives by Lydgate, advisory poetry by Hoccleve, and above all, the courtly texts of Chaucer became the central documents in fifteenth-century commissions. As Derek Pearsall put it, "It is as if for the first time a traditional body of knowledge on the conduct of life is being committed to English for the benefit of a new generation."[19] Aristocrats such as John Stanley of Hooton, aspiring gentry such as Robert Thornton, and members of a rising commercial class such as the Pastons all contributed to the dissemination not just of the texts of that body of knowledge, but of the *idea* of patronage itself.[20]

Chapter 1 of this book claimed that Lydgate refigured his relationship to Chaucer, and to English literary history generally, through a reconstruction of the idea of literary patronage encoded in Chaucer's fictions. His own obsessions with detailing the genesis of his works in commissions by Humphrey and Henry V, and his construction of an "aureate" past peopled by "laureate" poets, suggested that the definition of a poet is to be found, in part, in the nature of his patron, and further, that the ideal patron for a poet is the state itself. In these terms, we may read both the narratives of Lydgate and the sources for those narratives in Chaucer's *Clerk's Tale* as what I called fables of patronage: fictional accounts of power relationships that, in allegorical or figurative ways, tell stories of the commission and reception of literature. Such fables of patronage, I will argue here, become the central narrative for Tanner 346, as the sequence of its poems illustrates for fifteenth-century readers the conventions of Ricardian literary sponsorship and thematizes the problems of commission and production of the manuscript anthology. Tanner 346 is a book that educates its readers in the standards of a "gallant" taste and in the conventions of court patronage that form the model for fifteenth-century gentry commission. The Tanner manuscript, too, is itself a product of such a commission, and my reading of the manuscript as a whole and of what I take to be its thematically and narratively central poems is designed to illustrate the self-reflexiveness of this anthology—in other words, its concern with the principles and social structures that condition its own making.

To these ends I consider Clanvowe's *Book of Cupid* and the Tanner manuscript in differing, yet complementary ways, as products of "reading like the Squire." They show us ways of reading like a lover, attending to the worlds of dream and vision, to the courtly patterns of rhetorical behavior, and to the structures of disputation that frame the *débats d'amour* of the vernacular inheritance. They also illustrate the ways of reading like a son, defining oneself as a member of a new generation faced with adapting older philosophical *materia* for a new audience attuned to the gallant style. What the Squire represents, therefore, is the nexus of social and aesthetic problems facing fifteenth-century Chaucerians. How is it possible, his performance seems to ask, to tell a tale after the authoritative first telling of his father the Knight? How is it possible, too, to adjust the philosophical agendas of an older generation to a teller's taste for fancy?

These distinctions between father and son will inform the shape of Tanner 346, and if that manuscript encompasses both ways of reading— that is, reading like the Knight as well as like the Squire—then it must also contain the foil for Clanvowe's poem. It must offer up a text that reads its Chaucer like the Knight. That text is Lydgate's *Temple of Glas*, prominently centered in the Tanner manuscript and prominently apposing material from the *Knight's Tale* and the *Squire's Tale* in its list of legendary lovers. In this poem and in Clanvowe's, the appositions between Knight and Squire come together to define the nature of Chaucerian *auctoritas* and the boundaries of vernacular love poetry. They give us, both in their own narrations and in their juxtaposition in the Tanner manuscript, the two poles of vernacular love poetry, and in consequence two ways of reading the Chaucerian inheritance.

In characterizing the coherence of the Tanner manuscript and the interpretive place of its constituent poems, I draw on a set of distinctions developed by Sylvia Huot in her study of Old French poetic anthologies.[21] What she calls "thematically" organized manuscripts are those whose texts share an overarching intellectual or authorial concern. This type of manuscript may organize itself around a single major work placed in the center of the compilation, where the details of surrounding texts refract the meaning of the central work to provide a richer understanding of its author's oeuvre. In such a manuscript, as Huot puts it, "each text contributes to the structure of the whole, and each in turn contributes to the others. We can begin to see the intimate relationship between poetic and scribal practices, between the microstructure of the individual text and the macrostructure of the anthology codex."[22] In manuscripts organized "narratively," however, the component works may best be read as a linear sequence, with each succeeding poem sustaining and augmenting the formal or dramatic features of its predecessors. Narrative collections are designed to be read from beginning to end, and the experience of reading such a compilation is that of participating in a longer, interlocking story. Manuscripts narratively organized conjoin their poems in ways that seem to blur the demarcations of their beginnings and endings. As Huot states, "the personages, themes, and motifs shared among works [offer] the possibility for a poetic conjointure that transcends the boundaries of individual texts."[23]

I propose to read the Tanner manuscript in both these ways, from beginning to end and from the center outward, in order to discern the conceptions of vernacular authorship and reader response governing the assembly as a whole. Tanner 346 brings together poems that themselves thematize the workings of literary patronage and the problems of defining social taste. It assembles texts preeminently focused on authority, be it the authorizing power of Chaucer or the commissioning control of royal or mythic patrons. More than a manuscript concerned with the "sophisticated morality and the trials and tribulations of *fin amours*" appealing to a "lettered chivalry,"[24] Tanner specifically addresses the problems of reading and writing the texts central to creating such a lettered chivalry. Its poems give voice to the tensions generated between author and audience in literary service to the god of love. It is also narratively sensitive to the structures of vision and debate that characterize many of its individual components. Read in sequence, its poems sustain one long visionary disputation on the nature of love and love poetry. Read from the center outward, its texts try to come to terms with Chaucer as the progenitor of vernacular love verse. The F-Prologue to the *Legend of Good Women*, which begins the anthology, and Lydgate's *Temple of Glas*, which forms its center, are thus the two poles of my reading, and Clanvowe's *Book of Cupid* may be understood as a playful, if not self-ironizing, account of the problems of authorship and patronage raised by both. Tanner, one might say, is in itself a "book of Cupid," in that it forms a chronicle of lovers as writers and readers and reveals a god of love as a commissioning patron for the production and the proper reception of its poems. The fictional personae of the Tanner poems are themselves interpreters of love's texts, and they may be taken as the models for the reader of the manuscript itself.

But the Ricardian and mythic patrons of the poems may also be models for the manuscript's reader, for Tanner is an education in the arts of patronage as well as in the canons of those English texts worthy of commission. This is a manuscript about the forms of literary emulation: about regional aristocracy or gentry imitating the literary styles of an earlier generation of royalty, and about fifteenth-century writers imitating the authoritative patterns of Chaucerian versemaking. To say that Tanner 346 and some of its poems are, therefore, versions of "reading like the Squire" is to find in this collection the persona of that anxious son looking in, seeking both to read and emulate the matter and the manner of a literature from a noble past.

I

Central to both the narrative and thematic concerns of the Tanner manuscript is the idea of the anthology itself, an idea coded in the actions of the lover-readers of its poems. Most heroes of the Middle English vision are themselves anthologists of a sort, often confronting the pictorial assemblies of past lovers that adorn the architectural constructions that so frequently enclose them. Their recollections bring together stories from classical and medieval texts, and their recitations are often designed to "set in order" exemplary fictions into compilations of didactic value. This impulse to confront and disentangle groups of texts or stories motivates Chaucer's narrators from the beginning of his career. From his earliest forays in the *Book of the Duchess*, through the *Canterbury Tales* and the *Legend of Good Women*, Chaucer presents acts of reading and writing as confrontations with the anthology. The dreamer-narrator of his first poem reads himself to sleep with a collection encompassing "fables" and histories, stories of both the great and of "thinges smale," and the works of both "clerkes" and of "other poets." His exercise, here, of what Alastair Minnis has identified as *lectoris arbitrium* (the freedom of the reader to pick and choose among a compilation's contents) also motivates the famous Prologue to the *Miller's*

Tale, where Chaucer enjoins his discontented readers to "Turne over the leef and chese another tale."[25] The restrictions on the writer, by contrast, form the drama of the Prologue to the *Legend of Good Women*, where the god of love delineates a program of translation, adaptation, and collection controlled by courtly taste and political decorum. At moments such as these, Chaucer's poetry simultaneously affirms and queries the distinct roles played by *auctor*, *compilator*, and *lector* in the construction of literary meaning, and in the process it invites later poets, scribes, and imitators to participate in the creation of that meaning.[26]

Tanner 346 responds to such an invitation, as its narrative coherence grows out of the literary and dramatic problems raised by the F-Prologue to the *Legend*. Its catalogue of Chaucer's works provides a guide to reading the entire manuscript collection, for all the subjects and dramatic forms of Tanner's contents may be found mentioned in the Prologue. The "Deeth of Blaunche the Duchesse" and the "Parlement of Foules," prominently announced by Alceste at the beginning of her catalogue, conclude the Tanner manuscript, and between them and the *Legend* lies the range of lyric pieces classified as "balades, roundels, virelayes." Alceste's allusion to the *Knight's Tale* ("al the love of Palamon and Arcite / Of Thebes" F 420–21) is picked up in Tanner by Lydgate's *precis* of the story in the *Temple of Glas* and by the familiar Thesean maxim that opens Clanvowe's *Book of Cupid*, while *Anelida and Arcite* presents a poem linked in texture and ambiance with the Theban evocations of the *Tale*. Alceste's claims that the poet's works make up for what he had "mysseyde" in his translation of the *Romance of the Rose* find their analogue in Hoccleve's *Letter of Cupid*, the poem following the *Legend* in Tanner. With its playful defense of Jean de Meun and the Ovidian traditions, Hoccleve's poem offers a rejoinder to Cupid's protestations in the F-Prologue and effectively sustains Alceste's defense of Chaucer. The Prologue, too, contains within it catalogues of ancient lovers, notably in the "Balade to Absolon," whose details would provide the raw materials for Lydgate's visions in the *Temple of Glas*.

Such catalogues, both of the poet's work and of his sources, make the Prologue to the *Legend of Good Women* an ideal text with which to begin a manuscript anthology. They identify the details of Chaucerian production, and for a compilation such as Tanner 346—with its apparent disregard for scribal attributions, running heads, or titles—they function as a kind of table of contents: a set of attributions that bequeath Chaucer's authority on certain texts and educate their readers in the habits of the quintessentially Chaucerian. They also illustrate the technical and social contexts for producing an anthology, and toward the end of the F-Prologue, Chaucer problematizes the conventions of commission and compilation that produce it. Cupid states clearly that the basis for the *Legend*'s subjects will be in his reading: "And in thy bookes all thou shalt hem fynde" (F 556). But, as the god avers, there is no limit to the number of such literary women who could be included.

> Have hem now in thy legende al in mynde;
> I mene of hem that ben in thy knowynge.
> For here ben twenty thousand moo sittynge
> Than thou knowest, goode wommen alle,
> And trewe of love for oght that may byfalle.
> Make the metres of hem as the lest—
>
> (F 557–62)

In these lines, missing from the G-revision of the Prologue, Cupid enjoins the poet to rely on his own judgment in selecting women for the compilation. Given the vast number of eligible subjects, the poet must rely on those with whom he is familiar. "Make the metres of hem as the lest," the god commands, as if to say that the selection from the poet's reading—*his* exercise of *lectoris arbitrium*—will determine the shape of the anthology about to be created. In fact, Cupid seems to care little for the details of that anthology. Only Cleopatra is named as the subject of the first text, and the god is vague about what follows: "At Cleopatre I wol that thou beginne / And so forth" (F 566–67). There is no sense of plan or purpose here, no "ordre" into which the legendary lives are set. All that appears to matter is the opening, and Cupid seems aware that such a collection could go on without end. Instead, he wishes only a selective compilation, one that will please the reader without being far too long:

> I wot wel that thou maist nat al yt ryme,
> That swiche lovers diden in hire tyme;
> It were to long to reden and to here.
> Suffiseth me thou make in this manere:
> That thou reherce of al hir lyf the grete,
> After thise olde auctours lysten for to trete.
>
> (F 570–75)

The god of love's words constitute a lesson not just to Chaucer, but to the maker of any anthology, and the compiler of Tanner 346 seems to have taken him at his word. Each of the manuscript's first two booklets begins with a major, authorizing text, amatory in concern, catenulate in structure, and antique in its sources. Following these texts, the scribes have added works of successively shorter length and greater anonymity—works that respond to or develop the Chaucerian allusions and narrative stances featured in the longer texts.

The principles of compilation articulated by the god of love and apparently followed by the Tanner manuscript, are quite specifically the general principles of what has been identified as "fascicular assembly," the way of

building a long manuscript out of individually composed booklets or fasci-
cles of varying length. Such booklets will frequently begin "with a substantial and important work," often a major vernacular text by an identifiable
author.[27] They will proceed, then, more or less according to the wishes of
the compiler or patron, until the booklet is filled and a new section may be
started. Ralph Hanna describes the process and its implications:

> A fundamental purpose of fascicularity is to postpone, so far as possi-
> ble, decisions about the ultimate shape of the codex in production.
> Such a goal is furthered by opening booklets with extensive texts and
> building up the manuscript out of sequences introduced by such sub-
> stantial works. The last questions the compiler will settle, probably
> only at the time of binding, is the actual order of these "top-heavy"
> units.[28]

We may profitably read Cupid's compilatory injunctions in this spirit. Instead of detailing the precise shape of the forthcoming *Legend of Good
Women*, he (or Chaucer through him) only announces the beginning of
the work, enabling decisions about contents and conclusions to be put off,
or postponed, until some later time. The collection, in this version, is an
open-ended one, whose ultimate appearance will conform to only a small
fraction of the "twenty thousand" possibilities available.

This impression of the open-endedness of both the *Legend* and the
Tanner anthology as a whole contributes to the generic affiliations of the
manuscript's component poems and sustains the narrative coherence of
the assembly. The disputative structure of the F-Prologue, with its irresolutions carried over to the world of waking courts, is played out, for example, as the cuckoo and the nightingale of Clanvowe's poem argue for the
relative merits of different kinds of love and, by implication, love poetry.
In an analogous manner, the avian disputants of the *Parlement of Foules*
describe their plaints before a mythical judge, only to defer the final arbitration to the following year. The knightly lover and the narrator of the
Book of the Duchess, and their counterparts in Lydgate's *Complaint of a
Lover's Life*, parry the pros and cons of amatory service and its costs. In
each of these works, resolutions are deferred to judges, rulers, or authorities outside the poems' fictions. The coded references to the "Queen at
Wodestock" (*Book of Cupid*, 284–85), Eltham and Sheene (F-Prologue,
496–97), and the "long castel with walles white" (*Book of the Duchess*, 1318),
are all designed to take the poems' visionary disputations into the lived
realm of human courts. Together with the elaborate and politically
charged Envoys that conclude Lydgate's poems and the possible coterie
references embedded in the *Complaints* of *Mars* and *Venus*, these features
of the Tanner texts bring them together into one long patronage anthol-

ogy. If there is a single patron for these poems, it may be neither king nor queen but Cupid himself.

As a literary patron, the god of love is, in Anne Middleton's apt characterization, "arbitrary and capricious." The playful bonhommie that defines Harry Bailly's literary invitations is absent from Cupid's, for his injunctions make him into an impatient patron ordering a volume. "I charge the," he proclaims twice (F 548, 551), and Middleton succinctly describes the nature of his charge:

> The God of Love, it seems, keeps his devoted servants on a rather short tether; placating him requires the writer to renounce epic subjects and their complex narrative sweep, and the broadly human rather than the cultic ethical questions that attend them.[29]

The poetry produced under this aegis will, Middleton continues, be characterized by its restraint in the use of traditional rhetorical forms. It will hold back from the full-throated forensics and philosophical reflections of the great Chaucerian ballads. As Cupid himself puts it, such a poetry should be brief and to the point:

> For whoso shal so many a storye telle,
> Sey shortly, or he shal to longe dwelle.
>
> (F 576–77)

Readers will recognize the spirit of this directive elsewhere in Chaucer, for example, the criticism that interrupts the *Tale of Sir Thopas* and the *Monk's Tale*. But in the F-Prologue this claim for concision links itself to a generic and a tonal quality. It commissions a poetry and produces a poet more at home with gallantry than epic, with "small skirmishes rather than a 'gret emprise' in the service of love."[30]

This "gallant Chaucer" is, for Middleton, the figure that the F-Prologue creates for Chaucer and the figure that the Man of Law considers his poetic foil. *His* Chaucer is a maker of love stories, a performer in a social context bounded by the cultic practices of court and the rhetorical demands of current style. Tales are told, in this context, not to prescribe a moral code but to display the teller's skill. Making of this sort is "contemporary, stylish, and polite"; verses fit for the "games and rituals of [Cupid's] court."[31] It is a practice circumscribed by the demands of Cupid, and what the Man of Law makes clear is that the *Legend of Good Women* in particular is Cupid's poetry. For him, the poem is that "large volume ... / Cleped the Seintes Legende of Cupide" (II 60–61), and Lydgate picks up this retitling in the *Fall of Princes*. There, he commends Chaucer as the poet of "the legend of martyrs of Cupyde" and notes again his authorship of "the legende of Cupyde."[32]

Chaucer's self-presentations in the F-Prologue and in the Prologue to the *Man of Law's Tale* redefine his status as a maker for the fifteenth century. Their lists of Chaucer's works and their titling of those works define a class of amorous poetry and a context for its understanding. To call the *Legend of Good Women* a "legend of Cupid" is to realign its focus toward the contexts of cultic production and commission that produced it: to make it, in other words, not a book of women but a book of Cupid. It is, further, to provide a paradigm for the appreciation of performances constructed out of similar obediences, to foster a taste for the "contemporary, stylish, and polite"—that is, for the poetry of the Squire. Chaucer, as both the Man of Law and Middleton aver, can thus be read in two ways: as a poet of the epic and the classical and as a maker of the courtly and contemporary. The contrast between the great and the gallant exemplifies itself in the dramatic differences between the *Knight's* and *Squire's Tales*, and Lydgate's apposition of material from these two tales affirms this dual approach and informs the thematic coherence of the Tanner manuscript.

The search for thematic coherence moves from the collection's center outward. Appearing at the opening of the anthology's second booklet, nearly at the dead center of the manuscript's foliation, and standing as one of only two texts in Tanner with a scribal title in English, Lydgate's *Temple of Glas* is the kernel of the collection.[33] Much like the F-Prologue to the *Legend of Good Women*, it presents an anthology of Chaucer's production. But here, its central figure is a reader rather than a writer. Its collections of Chaucerian allusion are designed, unlike those of the *Legend*'s Prologue, to refract the conditions of Chaucer's reception rather than to reflect the worlds of his commissions. For if the F-Prologue presents a parable of writing an anthology, then Lydgate's *Temple* offers us an allegory of reading an anthology. It tells a tale of trying to explain the many texts collected and transmitted by Chaucerian authority.

Lydgate's opening catalogue of lovers is as bookish as anything Chaucer could have concocted. Each of its images is "Isette in ordre" (47), ranged more like the contents of a volume than a set of pictures on a wall. Lydgate's phrase resonates with the descriptions of anthologies in a range of fourteenth- and fifteenth-century Middle English texts, and it prepares his reader for confronting a contemporary *compilatio* of lovers.[34] One follows another much as a collection of stories would follow in a bound book, and the imaginary text one might construct out of this catalogue would embrace nearly all of Chaucer's amatory verse. It is made up of borrowings from the *Legend of Good Women*, the *Complaints*, the *Canterbury Tales*, and *Troilus and Criseyde*.[35] The individual descriptions are so close to Chaucer's that it is easy to dismiss this portion of the poem as an otiose pastiche. But the derivative phrasings that fill the catalogue are precisely what is interesting about Lydgate's lines, for they transform his narrator from dreamer into reader. This is, in short, a catalogue not so much of what Lydgate's dreamer sees as of what Lydgate himself has read, and the two texts prominent among those readings are the *Knight's Tale* and the *Squire's Tale*.

Midway through the narrator's vision, the dreamer comes upon the tale of Palamon and Arcite:

> There saugh I also þe sorov of Palamoun,
> That he in prison felt, and al þe smert,
> And hov þat he, þurugh vnto his hert,
> Was hurt vnwarli þurugh casting of an eyʒe
> Of faire fressh, þe ʒung[e] Emelie,
> And al þe strife bitwene him and his broþir,
> And hou þat one fauʒt eke with þat oþir
> Wiþin þe groue, til þei bi Theseus
> Acordid were, as Chaucer telliþ us.
>
> (102–10)

This is the longest single description of any of the stories pictured on the wall and the only one that cites an author for its telling. Chaucer's is the only writer's name to appear in the course of the entire poem, and this single attribution occurs in the center of the catalogue of lovers. Lydgate's list has become, so to speak, a compilation with thematic coherence: a list of texts and stories spun out from the work of the single authoritative vernacular author, himself mentioned at the center of the compilation.[36]

As if to frame this compilation as a Chaucerian collection, Lydgate concludes his list with reference to the *Squire's Tale*:

> And vppermore depeint men myʒt[e] se,
> Hov with hir ring, goodli Canace
> Of euere foule þe ledne and þe song
> Coud vndirstond, as she welk hem among;
> And hou hir broþir so oft holpen was
> In his myschefe bi þe stede of bras.
>
> (137–42)

By offering a list of legendary lovers bounded by the *Knight's Tale* at its center and the *Squire's* at its end, Lydgate presents the range of possibilities for understanding the Chaucerian canon. All the classical heroes and heroines that Lydgate's dreamer sees are drawn from Chaucer's texts, and Chaucer's name right in the middle of the list stands like a central authorizing figure in a manuscript anthology. By centering the ultimate authority in the most classicizing and authoritative of his fictions, Lydgate presents a double layer of Chaucerian *auctoritas*. If we were to read Lydgate's list as we would read the Tanner manuscript—for its thematic coherence and from its centerpiece outward—then we would find its structure and its meaning in the central reference to the *Knight's Tale* and its Chaucerian authorship. This is a list about the possibilities of the Chaucerian encounter with the classics, a list that begins with the great myths of the originary literary experience—the story of Dido, with its resonances to the *House of Fame* and the *Legend of Good Women*—and ends with the least finished of the tales of love. If we began with the great cities of the past, Rome and Carthage, and moved through the central point of Thebes, then we end only in the realm of Tartary. If we began with the great stories of the falls of kings and conflicts among men and gods, we close with a tale of talking birds and brother-sister play.

The list of lovers introduces the materials and methods out of which the *Temple of Glas* is built. Lydgate has presented his narrator-lover as a reader, faced with the scope of Chaucer's amatory texts, their classical sources, and the strategies of their interpretation. To educate that reader and to illustrate the ways of understanding the set texts that fix the canon of vernacular literature, Lydgate devotes the remainder of his poem to his hero's, and his own, encounters with the making and reception of interpretable documents. Immediately after his long list of lovers, Lydgate's narrator confronts an explicitly written text.

> Enbrouded was (as men my3t[e] se):
> DE MIEULX EN MIEULX with stones and perre.
>
> (309–10)

Lydgate then clarifies the meaning of this inscription, much in the way that Chaucer would define an odd word or an aphorism in his narrative ("This is to sein . . ." 311), before displaying Venus and the "litel bil" she will present as part of her case to the other gods. The contents of this document will form the matter of the first stanzaic section of the poem, and the soliloquy of Venus thus, in Lydgate's handling, becomes not so much the felt effusions of, say, the goddess of the *Knight's Tale* as the read-out performance of a courtly text. The Black Knight of this poem, too, speaks in the language of complaint transformed into a written text, for although his speech appears unread, it is Lydgate's persona who, scribe-like, transcribes it. "My penne I fele quaken as I write" (947), he avers after the Knight's stanzas. Punning on the double meaning of literary style and the instrument of the stylus, he states, "Wherfor þei nyl directe as nov my stile" (956), and his subsequent prayer to the muses is not so much full of inspiration as of ink and paper:

> Nou lete 3oure teris into myn inke reyne,
> With woful woordis my pauper forto blot,
> This woful mater to peint[e] not but spotte.
>
> (961–63)

Finally, at the poem's end, Lydgate reminds his audience that they are not just listeners but readers, too, and that his poem is not a performance but a text. On waking from the dream, his narrator proposes to transcribe its events into a "litil tretise" (1380), a "simple tretis" (1387) on which his lady may "loke" (1392). This is, as the Envoy states, a "litel rude boke" (1393), and the rhetoric of Lydgate's closing lines (clearly borrowed from Chaucer's Envoy to the *Troilus*, Hoccleve's Envoys to his political poems, and recalling "L'envoye de quare" that ends his own *Complaint of a Lover's Life*) calls attention to the problems of misinterpretation and correction that, in many ways, preoccupied the speakers of most of the poems of the Tanner manuscript.

> Nou go þi wai, þou litel rude boke,
> To hir presence, as I þe commaund,
> And first of al þou me recomavnd
> Vnto hir and to hir excellence
> And prai to hir þat it be noon offence
> If eny woorde in þe be myssaide,
> Biseching hir she be not euel apaied;
> For as hir list I wil þe efte correcte
> Whan þat hir likeþ againward þe directe:
> I mene þat benygne and goodli of hir face.
> Nou go þi way and put þe in hir grace.
>
> (1393–1403)

It is this documentary quality of the *Temple of Glas*, its status as a *compilatio* of visionary narratives and insecure narrators, that contributes to its centrality in the Tanner collection. The self-consciousness of the F-Prologue's grounding in books and reading is matched by the specifically documentary status of Hoccleve's poem: a *littera* directed to its readers. The *Envoy to Alison* that closes the manuscript's second booklet refers to the "lewede book" it sends off. And the concerns of writing down the visionary narrative at the conclusion of the *Book of the Duchess* and the opening of the *Temple of Glas* make it clear that Tanner's interests center not just on the experience of *fin amours* but on the problems of its textual transmission and reception.

These interests in the textually governed quality of love and love literature have a special focus in the catalogue of lovers at the opening of the *Temple*. Each one of these portrayals has a reference to a poem of Chaucer's; each myth, each hero, and each woman can be found in one of Chaucer's writings, whether it be the extended treatments of the *Legend of Good Women* or the *Canterbury Tales* or in the allusive asides of the *Troilus*. Lydgate's dreamer is again a reader, for he evidences a command of Chaucerian material that encompasses virtually everything the poet wrote.

How one reads that material, as I have suggested, is encoded in the list itself. One may read like the Knight, with his attentions to *auctoritas* in both the literary and political arenas; or one may read like the Squire, with his attentions to "felyng" in both the psychological and social arenas. Both ways of reading reinforce each other in the manuscript, giving to Tanner 346 a complex and interlocking set of self-references and allusions.

This opposition between Knight and Squire, and between the two styles of interpretation and categories of taste each figure generates, is further played out in the juxtaposition of the *Temple of Glas* and the *Book of Cupid* in the Tanner manuscript's second booklet.[37] The schematic presentation in the *Temple*—with its clear emphasis on the Chaucerian *auctoritas* behind the tale of Palamon and Arcite—is both dramatized and inverted in Clanvowe's poem, for there we find the words of Theseus subverted in a dilatory catalogue. We find the irresolutions of the Chaucerian dream texts further unresolved. And we find, throughout the poem, all appeals to reason and authority undermined by "felyng" and responses of the moment. Clanvowe's *Book of Cupid* reads the Chaucerian inheritance "like the Squire," and in the analysis that follows, we may find all of that pilgrim's tropes and turns deployed to challenge (playfully, I think) the governing authority of Chaucer as the father of vernacular literary history, and further, to counterpoint the authorizing impulse of the kind of poetry that precedes it in the Tanner manuscript.[38]

I I

Clanvowe begins with Theseus and with what may be one of the most neatly aphoristic of his pronouncements in the *Knight's Tale*:

> The god of love, a! benedicite,
> How myghty and how grete a lorde is he!
>
> *(BC 1-2)*

The speech on love that contains these lines is frequently distinguished in the early manuscripts of the *Canterbury Tales*, and this couplet in particular is often scribally set off by a paragraph marker or a large capital.[39] It would appear that, very early in the textual transmission of the *Knight's Tale*, the couplet assumed the status of a Chaucerian maxim all its own. Clanvowe takes these lines, virtually emblematic of Thesean and Chaucerian authority, and undermines their power through rhetorical dilation. Theseus's assertions of what the god "can maken" (*CT*, A 1789) becomes, in the *Book of Cupid*, a long litany of just what precisely "he can make" (*BC* 3, 6). Rhetorically, this narrator is nearly out of control, as the pattern of anaphora that structures his speech—the initial word *And* repeated fifteen times in thirty-five lines—takes nearly to the extremes of parody Theseus's use of the device (see *CT*, A 1793–96). Our confidence in Clanvowe's narrative skills wanes as he apologizes for his shortcomings. His "wit may not suffice" (*BC* 11) to describe the god's might; and yet he proceeds to enumerate what he can do. He tries to be brief ("Shortely, . . ." *BC* 16) yet winds up only being fulsome. He offers a detailed description of the month of May, only to denature the details with an intrusive phrase "as thynkes me" (*BC* 25). These are, even at first glance, the strategies of the Squire, and a close look at the language of the *Book of Cupid* and the duke's speech from the *Knight's Tale* brings out the disparities between the literary father and the son.

Theseus's speech explores the nature of the god of love's power, as the duke meditates on the actions of the warring Palamon and Arcite. He debates with himself on the pains and benefits of love. Although a lover is a fool and Palamon and Arcite bleed, those who serve love are nevertheless considered wise (A 1798–1805). Theseus then reflects on his own life as a lover:

> But all moot ben assayed, hoot and coold;
> A man moot ben a fool, or yong or oold—
> I woot it by myself ful yore agon,
> For in my tyme a servant was I oon.
> And therfore, syn I knowe of loves peyne . . .
> (*CT*, A 1811–15)

But although Theseus has outgrown love's pain, Clanvowe remains mired in it:

> I speke this of felyng trewely,
> For al thogh I be olde and vnlusty,
> Yet haue I felt of that sekenes in May
> Bothe hote and colde, an accesse euery day,
> How sore ywis ther wot no wight but I.
> (*BC* 36–40)

Theseus's confident voice offers a foil for the unsure complaint of Clanvowe's persona. He had opened with an axiomatic couplet behind which stood the figure of one of Chaucer's most authoritative literary creations. But the narrator's inept rhetoric undercuts this *auctoritas*, and his personal statement fails to mediate contrasting positions with the assured manner of the duke. Although Theseus has the power to turn experience into authority, Clanvowe's narrator cannot use his own experience either to confirm or deny the view of love gleaned from Chaucer's text. Instead, he offers only his "feelings"—experiences and reactions colored by the expressions of an insufficient wit and the subjectivity of such phrases as "as thynkes me." This opening subjectivity will characterize the narrator's progress throughout the poem, and his habit of indecisiveness will establish a controlling structure of ambiguity for the ensuing vision. When he goes "forthe allone priuely" (*BC* 59) to listen in on the debate between the cuckoo and the nightingale within his dream, he enters the traditional *locus amoenus* of the vision. Yet this, too, is clouded with ambiguities:

> And for delyte therof, I note ner how,
> I fel in such a slombre and a swowe—
> Not al on slepe, ne fully wakynge—
> And in that swowe me thoght I herde singe
> That sory bridde, the lewede cukkowe.
>
> (*BC* 86–90)

Unlike the Chaucerian dreamer, Clanvowe's narrator is neither fully asleep nor fully awake; yet this is not to reduce his dream, as A. C. Spearing implies, to a meaningless Macrobian *phantasma*.[40] The narrator's experiences cannot so easily be pegged into the familiar medieval classifications. Despite his half-sleeping/half-waking state, the things he will see and hear will not necessarily be devoid of interpretable meaning. Instead, this detail shows that problems of interpretation itself will become the motivating subject of the poem. We move more deeply into the world of personal impressions. The subjunctive mood predominates, with the phrases "I thought" and "me thought" punctuating descriptions of events. "I note ner how," his narrator states, defining this world of experience in terms of what it is *not*, rather than for what it is. This is an arena of unsure knowledge, subjective feelings, and unclear facts, an arena in which the narrator's opening insecurity about the value of love transforms itself into an insecurity about the meaning of love poetry.

If Clanvowe has borrowed the unsure voice of the Squire, he has also drawn on the fantasies of his plot. His narrator's visionary activities, and in particular his withdrawal from the confusions of the "comune tale" into the *locus amoenus* of talking birds, finds its parallel in Canacee's actions in the *Squire's Tale*. Its *prima pars* displays the noisy, pointless debate over the magic gifts brought by the visiting knight. Within this "Greet . . . prees" (*CT*, F 189) the onlookers babble not as humans but as bees (*CT*, F 204), and the Squire remarks: "Of sondry doutes thus they jangle and trete, / As lewed peple demeth *comunly*" (*CT*, F 220–21, emphasis mine). Such "comune" disputation offers only the public display of misjudgment from which Canacee seeks to escape. In the *pars secunda* of the *Tale*, Cambyuskan and his revelers wander off to bed and sleep through until morning. This section opens with a long meditation on sleep and dreams, and in keeping with his philosophical vocabulary, Chaucer characterizes Canacee's private experiences of that night. Out of womanly moderation, she had retired earlier in the evening "And slepte hire firste sleep, and thanne awook" (*CT*, F 367). Excited by her new presents, the magic mirror and ring, she dreams about their powers: "And in hire sleep, right for impressioun / Of hire mirour, she hadde a visioun" (*CT*, F 371–72). The status of her vision is, of course, in doubt for the reader, as Chaucer sustains the ambiguities inherent in his scene. Canacee's vision leads her to wake early in the predawn, leave her protesting chambermaids, and wander into a beautiful park. Even though a pervasive vapor clouds the scene (*CT*, F 313–14), Canacee can understand clearly the birds she encounters. By virtue of her magic ring,

> For right anon she wiste what they mente
> Right by hir song, and knew al hire entente.
> (*CT*, F 399–400)

So too, Clanvowe can understand the language of the birds in his half-waking vision:

> But now I wil yow tel a wonder thinge;
> As longe as I lay in that swonynge,
> Me thoght I wist al that the briddes ment,
> And what they seyde, and what was her entent,
> And of her speche I had good knovynge.
> (*BC* 106–10)

The suddenness and wonder of this moment in the *Book of Cupid* aptly recreates the immediacy of Canacee's knowledge in the *Squire's Tale*. Both passages hinge on the ability to know not only what the birds say but what they mean, and the shared rhyme on *ment* and *entent* reifies the momentary unity, and the potential split, between intention and expression. Canacee's apparent waking in the middle of the night and her physical removal from public squabble to private landscape place her in a hazy existence between day and night, dream and consciousness. Similarly, Clanvowe's conflation of dream and waking life casts into doubt the ordinary perceptions of reality that are made possible only when we can surely distinguish between being awake and being asleep. Canacee and Clanvowe enter a private world stripped of commonplaces where everyday hermeneutic laws do not apply. Their acquisition of knowledge here is designed to bypass the familiar techniques of perception or reflection, happening immediately and with awe. Both figures dismiss the experience and authorities gained in waking life as the mind itself gains access into thoughts unmediated by the foibles of human language.

But if Canacee and Clanvowe's dreamer hope to find the key to new understanding by leaving the world of "comune" speech, they will be disappointed. Within the embedded bird debate reported by the falcon, the clarity of meaning and intention apparently once granted to Canacee is mocked by the vision of the tercel's hypocrisy. He conceals rather than reveals, and the identical rhyme on *entente* and *mente* heightens the shift:[41]

> And in this wise he served his entente
> That, save the feend, noon wiste what he mente.
>
> (*CT*, F 521–22)

The tercel's speech is "ful of doublenesse" (*CT*, F 543); he employs "sophymes" (*CT*, F 554); he revels in the ambiguities of rhetoric (*CT*, F 560–61). His verbal performance is a far cry from the perspicacity that governed the speech of the strange knight who entered at the *Squire's Tale*'s beginning. "Accordant to his wordes was his cheere" (*CT*, F 103), and the unity of intention and expression he embodies becomes a measure for the verbal performances not only of the tale's characters but of its teller as well. The Squire himself stands in apologetic awe of his own fictional creation:

> Yet seye I this, as to commune entente:
> This muche amounteth al that evere he mente.
>
> (*CT*, F 107–8)

He tries in vain to reproduce the words and the intentions of this knight, and his attempts and failures parallel the problems of understanding Canacee and her falcon confront.

In both the *Squire's Tale* and the *Book of Cupid*, these patterns of rhyme and emphases on the distinction between communal and private knowledge signal a thematic interest in the fit between one's words and will, and they point to a broader set of structural and tonal filiations between the two poems. If Canacee and the dreamer share an apparent insight into avian language, then the narrators of both poems, as well, voice an acute awareness of their inabilities to convey the marvels or the majesty of their subject. The Squire's protestations ("Myn Englissh eek is insufficient," *CT*, F 37) find an echo in Clanvowe's apology before the god of love ("To telle his myght my wit may not suffice," *BC* 11). Their shared reliance on the clichés of pleasance poetics is evident in their descriptions of the force of springtime, though Clanvowe darkens the Squire's meteorology ("Ful lusty was the weder and benigne," *CT*, F 52) into a somewhat more ambiguous psychological landscape filled with "lusty thoghtes ful of grete longynge" (*BC* 30).

Within their avian disputes, the accusations of sophistry and duplicity that the falcon levels at the tercel anticipate the mutual condemnations of the cuckoo and the nightingale. In Clanvowe's text, debate hinges on the relationship of meaning to intention. Thus, the cuckoo claims its song to be "bothe trewe and pleyn," (*BC* 118), that is, both expressively clear and honest in intention. To the nightingale, he states that the nonsensical "ocy, ocy" of her cry renders her both foolish and obscure: "nyse" and "qyente" instead of "trewe" and "pleyn" (*BC* 123–24). "Euery wight may vnderstonde me" (*BC* 121), the cuckoo avers, and the nightingale must counter with an explanation of her own:

> When that I sey "ocy! ocy!" iwisse,
> Then *mene* I that I wolde wonder fayne
> That alle tho wer shamefully slayne,
> That *menen* oght ayen love amys.
> (*BC* 126–30, emphases mine)

Her argument relies on a notion of intention as it applies both to her words and to others' intents. She *means* "kill, kill" to those who would intent (*menen*) ill of love. Moreover, she predicates her own future actions according to the thoughts of others: "I *wold* alle tho were dede, / That *thenke* not her lyve in love to lede" (*BC* 131–32, emphases mine).[42] She sees herself engaged in a battle of wills against the foes of love, and the cuckoo takes up the challenge when she replies to the nightingale's injunction to love or die:

> ffor myn *entent* is neyther for to dye,
> Ne, while I lyve, in loves yoke to drawe.
> (*BC* 139–40, emphasis mine)

By using the word *entent*, the cuckoo speaks directly to the nightingale's claims for meaning, and the linkage of these two terms vivifies the philosophical issues posed at the poem's beginning. Meaning and intention now become issues in action as well as speech, as the birds skirt the obvious issue of bilingual confusion to focus insistently on mental states and social contexts. Clanvowe, too, seems less interested in exploiting the obvious Babel of bird talk than in exploring the interior processes that motivate communication. If neither bird can make sense out of the other, it may have less to do with the absolute "truth" or "plainness" of their speech than with the ways in which their wills impede the successful apprehension of their words.

Much like the *Squire's Tale*, the *Book of Cupid* spins out a drama of misunderstanding generated by a signal rhyming pair. Its visionary characters together with its narrator seem overcome by the desire to express themselves both faithfully and clearly. The problem of the will is a concern for their avian subjects as well as their human storytellers, and it seems that in the end both Clanvowe's dreamer-poet and the Squire are left to rely on feelings rather than reason. Intelligent and intelligible discourse

breaks down in both poems. Canacee's falcon stops her reminiscences with
an emotional outburst: "Word" becomes "crie," and she swoons inarticu-
lately into Canacee's lap. So, too, the human-sounding discourse of the
birds in Clanvowe's poem dissipates into nonverbal pain. The nightingale,
much like the falcon of the *Squire's Tale*, can speak no more:

> She kest a sighe out of her herte depe,
> And seyde, "Alas, that euer I was bore!
> I can for tene sey not oon worde more."
> And ryght with that she brast on forto wepe.
>
> (*BC* 207–10)

Her anger seems infectious here, as the narrator, caught up in the nightingale's pain, sees himself attack the cuckoo in the dream:

> Me thoghte then that I stert vp anone,
> And to the broke I ran and gatte a stone,
> And at the cukkow *hertely* I cast,
> And he for drede flyed away ful fast,
> And *glad* was I when that he was agone.
>
> (*BC* 216–20)

Once again, the intrusive "me thoghte" pinpoints the dreamer's inability
to distinguish rational comprehension from subjective impression. The
nightingale's frustration at being unable to speak finds expression in the
dreamer's delight in being unable to reason, as he attacks the cuckoo
heartily and gladly.

   Both the *Squire's Tale* and the *Book of Cupid* move toward their endings
with the breakdown of intelligent debate, but they differ in their respective
attempts to restore some authority to their fictions. Although the Squire
does not physically break into the imagined world of his exotica, his, too,
is a performance gone out of control, and it takes the Franklin, in the form
of his surrogate father, to break in and stop a near interminable *pars tercia*
before it begins. In an analogous manner, the *Book of Cupid* seeks an authority outside its fiction for the resolution of its avian debate and ultimately for assurances of its literary—and political—reception. Here, the
poem brings together the conclusions from the *Parlement of Foules* and the
Prologue to the *Legend of Good Women* to sustain its playful challenge not
just to the authority of Chaucer's work but to the social structures of commission that produced it. Clanvowe's poem ends, it might be said, with a
Squire-like reading of the Chaucerian dream texts. All the strategies of
judgment brought together in the *Parlement* are subtly twisted here. The
nightingale returns to offer an appeal to her peers, an appeal based not on
her review of the debate with the cuckoo, but instead on the familiar assumptions governing a popular approach to both birds.

Yee knowe wel, hit is not fro yow hidde,
How that the cukkow and y fast haue chidde
Euer sithe hit was dayes lyght.

(BC 266–68)

It is enough that we "knowe wel" what has gone on between the two birds, not only in Clanvowe's poem but throughout the whole tradition of beast poetry. The birds, and the poem's readers, are invited to rely on just that body of "comune tale" which had motivated Clanvowe's narrator at the beginning and which cannot admit to a specially empowered judge to arbitrate it. For, unlike the *Parlement of Foules*, there can be no goddess Nature here, no unassailable authority to "commaunde" (*Parlement* 617), to "judge" (629), and offer "my conclusioun" (620). Instead of the univocality of the group at the *Parlement*'s conclusion, Clanvowe's poem offers only one bird, speaking for all, and his penultimate stanzas neatly recast the idiom of Chaucer's poem into an unsure pattern of deferrals and excuses.

Then spake oon brid for alle by oune assent:
"This mater asketh good avysement,
ffor we be fewe briddes her in fere,
And soth hit is the cukkow is not here,
Therfore we wol haue a parlement.

. . . .

Ther shal be yeven the iugement,
Or elles we shul fynalli make acorde.

(BC 271–80, from Tanner)

Clanvowe's assembly of few birds contrasts with Chaucer's audience composed of "the briddes alle" (527). Each of the classes of the birds in Chaucer's poem discusses their decision, and Clanvowe's language seems most clearly taken from the consultation among the water fowls in the *Parlement*:

The water-foules han here hedes leid
Togedere, and of a short avysement,
Whan everych hadde his large golee seyd,
They seyden sothly, al by oon assent, . . .

(Parl. 554–56)

Clanvowe has given a remarkably pared-down version of the *Parlement*'s conclusion, one that strips away the forensic drama of avian discussion in favor of a single decision not to decide. I have quoted from the Tanner version of the poem here because its wording subtly enhances the deferring strategies at the poem's end. In Tanner, there is the birds' resistance to make not just "summe acorde" but "fynalli make acorde." Even the avian day of judgment itself, St. Valentine's Day, toward which the *Parlement* points, will not suffice for the Tanner text. There, the poem's decision will transpire "The morowe *after* Seynt Valentynes day" (282, emphasis mine), a detail that serves further to dilate the birds' expectations and heighten the poem's sense of irresolution.[43] Not even the literary bearings of the *Parlement* survive here, for instead of the concluding, celebratory rondel that "imaked was in Fraunce" (*Parl.* 677), we get here one of the narrator's "songes newe" (*BC* 247), and an allusion to a popular lyric (*BC* 289).

Finally, as the birds and perhaps the poet submit their words to "the Quene / At Wodestok" (*BC* 284–85), we realize that outside the poem's fiction lies a living judge whose social and political authority grant the power to make dialectical and aesthetic judgments. Clanvowe now hearkens back to the contexts of royal commission that inform the F-Prologue of the *Legend of Good Women*, but it should not, I think, be assumed that they present transparent sources for the patronage commission of his own work. Clanvowe has not only appropriated the topical language of the Prologue; he has imitated the *idea* of topicality to give his poem the aura of a commissioned work. Clanvowe does not avow to return to the books that had generated his verse (as in the *Parlement*), nor does he promise to write down his poem (as in the Prologues to the *Legend* or the ending of the *Book of the Duchess*). His allusions to the court of Richard II do not involve intruding on the court itself—as in the case of actually giving the book to the Queen, for example, in the *Legend*. Rather, his is a poetry that goes on just outside the walls of royal purview. His birds will present their arguments again "before the chambre wyndow of the Quene" (284), that is, outside the court interiors where the commands of patronage transpire.

This final detail, read in tandem with the strategies of dilation and deferral I have outlined here, affirm the *Book of Cupid* as what I would figuratively label a poem of the Squire. It is a poem constructed out of the rhetorical protestations of the literary son, seeking to imitate the genres of his fatherly *auctor* and to participate in the environments that validated him. The Queen at Woodstock is, in Clanvowe's poem, as much of a fiction as his birds, and the promise of royal patronage may be as much a fantasy as Clanvowe's dream. This is a poem, too, full of the "felyng" of the Squire, where emotions get the better of reason and where things are felt or seem to be. Anne Middleton's version of the Squire's busy mind nicely defines the world of Clanvowe's poem:

This "felyng" mind enriches the present moment by averting the immediate assimilation of new wonders to the familiar and present, by keeping them slightly alien and surrounding them with likeness to the storied past. By such means, it is not the far-off exotic "then" of the story, but the "now" of seeing, hearing, and feeling that is made into art.[44]

This focus on the "now," moreover, links the poetics of the Squire with the *Book of Cupid* at another level. For unlike Lydgate, or for that matter unlike Chaucer's Knight, Clanvowe nowhere mentions his *auctor* or attributes his allusions. One might justifiably argue that as a member of the Chaucer circle, Clanvowe would not need to mention Chaucer's name; his own texts would have participated in that coterie environment that, it has been presumed, formed the first audience for Chaucer's works. But Clanvowe's poem, with its climate of interpretive ambiguity and its deferrals of authoritative judgment, need not admit to such a narrowly biographical reading. What we have here, I suggest, is a complex form of literary suppression. By refusing to refer to Chaucer by name, Clanvowe provides no stable ground for judging his own efforts or the birds' debate, no prospect of a resolution either to the postponed parliament or to his own literary debts. This is a truly open-ended poem, one whose irresolutions and rhetorical insecurities so precisely mime the Chaucerian persona on which it is modeled that the *Book of Cupid* is no longer an imitation. It is an impersonation. Clanvowe's work so apes the literary gestures of its source that no need for acknowledgment is necessary. In fact, such an acknowledgment would break what I think is the poem's overarching fiction: that it is a Chaucerian poem. Chaucer's name does not enter into the poem's texture because it is a seamless impersonation of Chaucer's work.

If Clanvowe's poem is, as I have argued, an attempt to read the philosophico-amorous conundrums of the *Knight's Tale* through the avian fantasies of the Squire, then its refusal to acknowledge its own literary father is a strategy fully in keeping with the anonymities of Chaucer's *Squire's Tale* itself. For there, in a tale that offers no named source, that baffles scholars intent on precisely locating its poet's debts to learned texts, the Squire has achieved his literary task.[45] In contrast to his father, he has told a tale ungrounded in the texts of a canonical antiquity. Though he defers, at one point, to what "the storie telleth us" (*CT* F 655), we know that such a story exists not in some compendium of ancient writings but in the jumble of the Squire's mind. His tale may have no named textual source because it represents a different attitude toward textual authority than that of his father. It represents, as the performance of one of Chaucer's "New Men," what Middleton refers to as "a way of reaffirming one's possession of the tastes and qualities that assure one's membership in polite society"—an act of telling "efficacious chiefly for the teller."[46] We read the *Squire's Tale* not for its transformation of familiar, attributed material, but for the drama of its telling and the humor of its display. Its suppression or neglect of named *auctores* makes it a tale whose governing effect lies, then, in the context of its commission and reception.

III

Reading and writing like the Squire now take on a new edge. They imply no longer participating in those elaborate gestures of authorial obedience that characterize the Knight and in turn fill so much of Lydgate's poetry. There is a world of difference between the citational precision of the *Temple of Glas* and the suppression of Chaucer's name in the *Book of Cupid*, and these two paired texts exemplify two ways of understanding the Chaucerian inheritance. What they may also help explain is the apparent anonymity of the Tanner manuscript's own texts. Unlike its cousins Bodley 638 and Fairfax 16, and unlike, too, the later Sinclair manuscript, no poem in the Tanner manuscript bears attribution to its author by the scribe. There is little sense of what Louise Fradenburg, commenting on the Scottish compilation, calls a "manuscript as historical discourse," where Chaucer's named works are brought together to attest to the centrality of the Chaucerian text to the aspirations of a culture.[47] The concerns of Tanner lie less with Chaucerian authority or problems of authorship than they do with issues of patronage. The poet's name does not appear because its poems come to be concerned less with their origin than with their use: that is, less with their genesis in authorial imagination than with their generation out of royal commission and their transmission through courtly patronage. Stripped of Chaucer's and their other author's names and for the most part stripped of titles, Tanner's poems become texts pressed into the service of the "now" of telling—texts servicing the performative structures of the social practice of courtly making. The poems are thus simultaneously de-authorized and dehistoricized, made products of the charges of the god of love, dead kings and queens, or absent noble ladies. These poems come together, therefore, to give voice to the literary aspirations of a readership, rather than to ground that readership in the named authority of authors.

In the end, Tanner 346 is a dream book. It gives us poems that are not simply texts of visionary lovers. It gives us poems that, taken together, articulate the dreams of a mid-century gentry. Tanner focuses on the poetry of court commission—the fictions of the F-Prologue, the codings of the *Book of the Duchess*, and the topical allegories of the *Parlement of Foules*, of the *Complaint of Mars* and the *Complaint of Venus*, and of the Envoys to the poetry of Lydgate, Hoccleve, and Clanvowe. It is a manuscript that, in its various rewritings, juxtapositions, and controlling *ordinatio*, constructs a set of poems made for specific consequences. Even the odd little *Envoy to Alison* may be read as just such a strategy. The *Envoy* here is not an appendage to the *Book of Cupid*, as some have thought.[48] Instead, it is a conclusion to the entire second booklet as a unit: a poem that brings these texts together into a miniature compilation of love visions for a single, named addressee. Its stanzas synthesize the forms of Lydgate's rhyme-royal with the idioms of Hoccleve's submissions, in that much of its language appears pendant on the kinds of obeisances Hoccleve offers to Henry, Prince of Wales, in the Envoy to his *Regiment of Princes*.[49]

As in the envoys on which it is modeled, the *Envoy to Alison* directs its attentions away from the author to the reader; yet it does so not by addressing the reader but by anagrammatically inscribing her name. Its final six-line stanza spells out in its initial letters the name Alison, a familiar strategy of coded naming for late Middle English literature. In her account of signatory authorizing in the work of Langland, Anne Middleton argues that, for late-medieval literature in general, the force of an acrostic signature lies in the way it "foregrounds and celebrates the 'writtenness' of writing: in the acrostic the author becomes entirely and literally a man *of letters*." She continues:

> But if the acrostic is an efficient little Derridean postulate, unambiv-alently proclaiming the absence of the author, the anagrammatic sig-nature pointedly raises and repeatedly worries the possibility of au-thorial presence in the work. . . . Anagrammatic naming implies that "menyng" is always *someone's* meaning; it resides in, and represents, persons and their 'intentes.'[50]

But, of course, *The Envoy to Alison*, like Tanner 346 itself, has little inter-est in authors; the absence of names and titles, as I have suggested, re-inforces the collection's thematic concern with patronage, commission, and response—with those who read rather than write the poetry. Alison's name does not "worry," in Middleton's sense, "the possibility of authorial presence" in the manuscript. It affirms, rather, the abiding presence of the audience. It reinforces the appellative impulse of Tanner 346 away from naming those who make its texts and toward those who use them.

In these thematizings of the poet-patron dialogue, Tanner 346 refracts the interests of a gentry seeking to develop its commissioning voice, its status as a class capable of ordering the making of verse for social purposes. The manuscript thus documents those projects of "self-legitimation" for the gentry, as its members find their place in the production of literature and the definitions of acceptable verse.[51] Like the Prologue to the *Man of Law's Tale* or the god of love's demands in the F-Prologue to the *Legend*, Tanner gives us the parameters for social verse and the outlines of a Chaucerian canon. Like those texts, Tanner does not so much voice a preexisting literary taste; instead, it helps create it, shaping both the narrowly textual and the broadly thematic features of a generation of popular reading.

The "courtliness" of Tanner's poems may be as much a fiction as its dreams. Tanner is a text that does not reflect social practice as much as it imagines it. For a gentry readership, far from the ambiences of a London court and far removed in time from the golden age of Ricardian patronage, the poems of the Tanner manuscript contribute to a fantasy about the social function of literature. To define themselves as members of a class, the individuals who ordered and read Tanner 346 sought to emulate the habits of patronage that defined the aristocracy. They sought to imitate a pattern of behavior that distinguished their social superiors. To aspire to the magnate culture, gentry readers sought to mime the structures of commission that granted authority to the patron.

If Tanner is a dream book, then it needs to be assessed in retrospect by waking readers in the world, and when we come upon its end, we will be greeted by the Chaucerian dreamer waking from his vision of the noisy birds. The emphasis on reading in the *Parlement*'s final stanza (with the word *read* repeated four times in as many lines) recalls the narrative and thematic coherence of the volume as a whole. Now, the resolve to turn to other books becomes not simply the fictive persona's resolution to continue working; it becomes in addition a directive to Tanner's readers to continue searching the anthologies for poetry that will both stimulate and educate them in the tropes of love and the gestures of courtesy. This is an education in the literary history of England, an education read through the eyes of squires of a later day. Much like their fictive ancestor, these squires may be said to have recast the poetry of an earlier time for current tastes. But if, unlike that dilatory son, they are successful in creating something of a gallant Chaucer, then the measure of their success lies in the creation of anthologies and the later, scribal manipulations of Chaucer's own texts that will sustain a way of reading like the Squire.

CHAPTER THREE

*Reading Like a Child: Advisory Aesthetics
and Scribal Revision in the*
Canterbury Tales

MIDWAY THROUGH the late-fifteenth-century didactic poem known as the *Book of Curtesye*, its paternal narrator advises his young audience to "Exersise your self . . . in redynge" (309).[1] In tandem with the mastery of table manners and the codes of formal discourse, the accomplishments of the young user of this manual would also have included some familiarity with works of religious doctrine and vernacular literature. The English writers singled out for study, therefore, are those noted for their blend of virtue and entertainment: Gower for his moral fables, Hoccleve for his public lessons, and Lydgate for his classical learning and spiritual instruction. Chaucer, too, has a place in this pantheon as the "fader and founder of ornate eloquence" (330), and the *Book of Curtesye* enjoins its student reader:

> Redith his werkis / ful of plesaunce
> Clere in sentence / in langage excellent
> Briefly to wryte / such was his suffysance
> What euer to saye / he toke in his entente
> His langage was so fayr and pertynente
> It semeth vnto mannys heerynge
> Not only the worde / but verely the thynge.
>
> (337–43)

Like many panegyrists of the fifteenth century, the father-narrator of this poem promotes a Chaucer famous for his "langage," for that "welle of eloquence" (350) from which all later writers draw. Chaucer's verbal finesse had "enlumened . . . alle our bretayne" with his "laureate scyence," (331, 332) and in this melding of the aureate and laureate, the author of the *Book of Curtesye* looks back to such encomiastic moments as the praise of Petrarch in the Prologue to the *Clerk's Tale* and to the Lydgatean praise of Chaucer it had generated. But unlike Chaucer's Clerk, and for that matter unlike many of the century's Chaucerians, this writer gives us little sense of either the rhetorical sophistication or political sanction of a "fader Chaucer." The clarity and brevity he stresses contrast sharply with the Latinate prolixity of Lydgate's imitation, and his overriding concern with social performance may, for medieval as for modern readers, elide much of that "philosophy" for which Chaucer had been studied.

For this particular poem, Chaucer is now a children's writer. His *cleere sentence* and thematic concern with the *entente* of public speech serve here not to father a tradition of vernacular poetics but to augment the authority of a fatherly narrator. Chaucer himself, of course, had taken on such an advisory role in his *Treatise on the Astrolabe*, a work whose educational directives and opening address to "Lyte Lowys my sone" had, already by the early fifteenth century, fostered an impression of the poet as a teacher of children. Several of its fifteenth-century manuscripts call it "Brede and milke for children," and much of the paternalistic idiom of Lydgate's advisory verses, as well as that of the *Book of Curtesye* itself, derives from the verbal condescensions of the *Astrolabe*'s prologue.[2]

This sense of Chaucer's fatherly authority develops, too, in Lydgate's catalogue of Chaucer's canon in the *Fall of Princes*, where we see the poet progress from the youthful makings of love poetry to the mature advice for children. Reading Lydgate's list we may see a progress from the "translacioun" of the *Troilus* made "In youthe" (I:283–87), through the translation of the *Consolation of Philosophy*, to the *Astrolabe* itself: "And to his sone, that callid was Lowis / He made a tretis, ful noble & off gret pris" (I:293–94). By introducing Chaucer's works in this way, Lydgate gives not only the generic range of his productions but implies a personal chronology to those productions: a sense of growth that brings the poet from his own youth to fatherhood, one that affirms his status as a "maistir." By the time of the *Book of Curtesye*, this notion of a father Chaucer thus comes to have less to do with the global concerns of English literary history or public politics than with the experience of social education. It provokes the creation of a domesticated Chaucer, tamed in his complexities for childish readers and reserved for the indoctrination of domestic values.

The construction of a children's Chaucer is the natural development of literary habits at work throughout the fifteenth century.[3] As the *Canterbury Tales* came to provide its later readers with the critical personae through which they could confront Chaucer's work, the image of a father Chaucer transformed later audiences into children modeled on his fictional figures: inept Squires before his unassailable Knight, or hesitant Clerks before his laureate Petrarch. The propagation of this image infantilized those who succeeded him, whether psychologically as with Hoccleve or rhetorically as with Lydgate. Such infantilization worked in tandem with a growing sense of literature's primarily advisory function to create an audience of children for the poet's teachings—indeed, to construct the Chaucerian audience generally as childish. Along with the handbooks of manners proliferating in the commercial bookshops and the early printing houses, much earlier poetry was reread and at times rewritten with practical didacticism in mind. The works of Chaucer, Lydgate, Hoccleve, and a range of other writers were mined as guides for public and private conduct, and the many manuscripts and house anthologies surviving from the later fifteenth century testify to the kind of audience addressed by the *Book of Curtesye*. "Redith my chylde," that book advised, and to assess just what it meant to read the poet like a child necessitates our understanding of a social fact as well as of a literary trope. The scribes, compilers, and potential patrons who constructed Chaucer as a children's writer recast not just his complexities of style but, in a fundamental way, transformed the status of his work as literature and the cultural importance of his authorial role.

A children's Chaucer is a poet socially appropriated for specific educative and commercial goals, and certain of the *Canterbury Tales* that figured forth the plight of children both as literary subjects and as literary makers became the most popular of his stories and the places where a childhood readership could find itself inscribed. More than simply directives for good manners or essays on social decorum, these tales came to be read as fables of reading like a child. In the case of the *Thopas / Melibee* section and the *Clerk's Tale* in particular, fifteenth-century readers would have found the dramatic exposition of the guides to governance exemplified by such works as the *Book of Curtesye*. What is especially intriguing for the study of these tales and their reception is how such readers had occasion to recast them as texts specifically addressing the condition of the reading child. These poems are rewritten with an advisory aesthetics in mind. Those rewritings, moreover, have the effect of de-authorizing the Chaucerian text, first by framing it in manuscripts or compilations without heading, name, or attribution, and second by realigning the thematic foci of their narratives. Instead of queries on authorial identity, we get affirmations of reader response; instead of rhetorically self-conscious and revealingly discursive performances, we find fast-paced lines of action. Reading like a child is therefore reading *for* the child: in one sense, reading for the fictive children who enact the reader's interests; in another, reading for the benefit of those whom it is now the purpose of the text of father Chaucer to teach.

Two manuscripts, roughly contemporary with the *Book of Curtesye* and likely products of individual commission and response, will constitute the evidence for my recovery of these ways of reading Chaucer and of the attendant consequences of his de-authorization and his changing status as a literary writer. One is the Helmingham manuscript of the *Canterbury Tales*, a paper assembly reconstructing a text around an older, parchment core, whose scribe has rewritten portions of the *Pardoner's Prologue and Tale*, the *Thopas / Melibee* Link, and the *Melibee* itself.[4] The other is Huntington Library MS HM 140, an anthology of Middle English verse that contains an unattributed copy of the *Clerk's Tale*, pared of its opening Prologue, denuded of its references to the *Canterbury Tales*, and concluding with the lines of Chaucer's ballad *Truth*.[5] The former reduces some of Chaucer's most rhetorically complex and theoretically discursive passages into quickly paced dramatic episodes. The latter strips one of the fifteenth century's most popular tales of its Chaucerian authorization and literary context. Both of them challenge modern critical and editorial presuppositions about the integrity of Chaucer's fictions and the transmission of his text. Both seem to transmute original reflections into banal moralisms. And both contain—in marginalia, additions, and in their physical appearances—the evidence of personal responses to the genres, themes, and social purposes of vernacular poetry during the first half century or so of their use.

If we find in these manuscripts a kind of negative alchemy—a reduction, in David Lawton's phrasing, of Chaucerian gold into Lydgatean lead[6]—we may also find in them the evidence, both physical and interpretive, for removing their poems from the autonomy of "literature" and grounding them and their once self-conscious narrators in the anonymities of moral compilation. What these manuscripts exemplify are individual attempts to read and reconstruct a poetry both of and for social occasion. Their uniqueness as witnesses to editorial revision or as repositories of otherwise untranscribed verses may make them seem merely idiosyncratic, "bad" texts that may pique scholarly curiosity and little more.[7] Yet what I hope to show at this chapter's conclusion is that such uniquely bad texts say something about childish writing as well as childish reading. They illustrate a form of amateur versification stimulated by the literary contents of the manuscripts themselves. They offer cases of what might be called apprentice poetry for their apprentice readers, a poetry domesticated in all senses of that word, that shows the possibilities of taking Chaucer's philosophical fictions as fables for the home and of presenting these new fables in the unassuming forms of homemade compilations.

I

Much recent scholarship has illustrated how the social pressures of a rising bourgeois class, together with the rapid changes in the habits of personal and commercial bookmaking, stimulated the production of advisory literature in fifteenth-century England.[8] Manuals of good behavior had been flourishing since the twelfth and thirteenth centuries and had derived their dicta from a blend of Ciceronian example, folk belief, and political theory.

The literary influence of these manuals may be seen in the range of vernacular poetry from the *Roman de la Rose* to *Sir Gawain and the Green Knight*, and the making and transmission of this "courtly" literature clearly geared itself to the establishment of social values for the European aristocracy.[9] In the course of the fifteenth century, however, gentry and mercantile readers adapted these traditions of a courtly ethos into a poetry of manners. In ways similar to their appropriations of the tropes of patronage and the *débats d'amour*, this new readership used books of courtesy as part of the consolidation of a social as well as a national identity. Merchants and gentry who had learned to read for business reasons turned their skills to works of edification and entertainment, while at the same time paper came to replace parchment as a more affordable medium for such works.[10] Commodity bookmaking fostered the dissemination of those class values identified as a "commitment to the family as a locus of privacy in the public world, its investment in its future in the form of its children, and its habits of child rearing—all [of which] entail a privileged position for childhood."[11]

In general, the growth of advisory literature may be attributed to this conjunction of class and commercial opportunity. But the verbal texture of that literature owes so much to the details of Chaucer's own poetry of social decorum, that we might well think of it as yet another form of Chaucerian reception. Such sections of the *Canterbury Tales* as the *General Prologue* portraits of the Squire and the Prioress came to be studied for their depictions of idealized behavior and their allegories of the moral life. Though many modern critics may find the description of the Prioress's table manners colored by a knowledge of its source in Jean de Meun's Vielle and by critical presuppositions about Chaucer's ironizing use of such material, fifteenth-century readers clearly saw in these lines a succinct guide to good manners.[12] Judging by their repeated and augmented appearance in such works as the *Babees Book*, *Urbanitatis*, *Stans Puer ad Mensam*, *The Book of Curtesye*, and many others, the Prioress at table set a standard for several generations of young eaters.[13] In an analogous way, the Squire's "servysable" qualities, his musical and literary tastes, and his ability to "carf biforn his fader at the table" (*CT*, A 99–100) mapped out the expected habits of a new generation of aspiring squires. Many of the courtesy handbooks latch on to the word *servysable* to distill ideal conduct.[14] Many, too, like the *Book of Curtesye*, advise their children to disport themselves like Chaucer's Squire, "To harpe or lute / or lustely to synge / Or in the prees right manerly to daunce" (304–5). And although Chaucer no doubt drew on the traditions of aristocratic courtesy in mentioning the Squire's carving, the prominence he gave that skill as the last line of the *General Prologue* portrait provoked many fifteenth-century advisors—from John Russell in his *Book of Nurture* to the author of the *Book of Keruynge* printed by de Worde—to a near obsession with good carving as the mark of social achievement.[15]

Chaucer's influence on the making and dissemination of advisory poetry, however, went beyond providing set pieces of domestic decorum. It fostered the development of an advisory poetics: a conjunction of themes, images, and narrative personae that made pedagogy both the form and purpose of poetic making and that argued for the centrality of verbal performance to social accountability. Those issues that in Lydgate and Hoccleve were problems of literary inheritance or philosophical speculation became, in their transformations in the manuals of courtesy, the province of family life. Thus, "father Chaucer" speaks not as the founder of a literary system but as the familiar preceptorial persona of the wisdom traditions. The concern with the relationship of meaning and intention that had operated as a philosophical conundrum throughout Chaucer's fictions now becomes a problem in good manners. And the dramas of the subjugated child—so central to the voicings of that Chaucerian "consciousness" of writing—became in the manuals of conduct exempla for the proprieties of family life.

Chaucer's own verse, on occasion, seeks to rephrase problems of philosophy as dilemmas of social decorum, and the *Squire's Tale* in particular anticipates many of the dramatic strategies constructed by his later, pedagogically minded readers. For the narrator of that *Tale*, perhaps as much as for the audience of the *Book of Curtesye*, literary success and social approval hinge on speaking "Withouten vice of silable or of lettre" (*CT*, F 101). In its mysterious intruding knight, the *Tale* distills those ideals of personal and verbal decorum that it is the Squire's own task to embody.

> Accordant to his wordes was his cheere,
> As techeth art of speche hem that it leere.
> Al be that I kan nat sowne his stile,
> Ne kan nat clymben over so heigh a style,
> Yet seye I this, as to commune entente:
> This muche amounteth al that evere he mente,
> If it be so that I have it in mynde.
>
> (*CT*, F 103–8)

Chaucer himself exemplifies this union of intention and expression that may "techeth art of speche hem that it leere." In the *Book of Curtesye*, his proficiency in words bespeaks a mastery of social forms. Much like the Squire's alien knight, who could teach courtliness even to Gawain, the Chaucer of this manual deploys his verbal prowess as a way of generating social harmony. His skill with language goes beyond the surfaces of style or the decorums of occasion to enact that philosophical identity of word and object. Everything that could be said, the poem states, "he toke in his entente" (340), and what it labels as the fairness and the pertinence of his "langage" makes it appear that, when he speaks, he utters "Not only the worde / but verely the thynge" (343). Chaucer's instructive value, therefore, lies in his ability to match private interest with public expectation. As the Squire seeks a teacher in his fictional knight, so the author of the *Book of Curtesye* presents a Chaucer who can teach the young.

> Redeth my chylde / redeth his bookes alle
> Refuseth none / they ben expedyente
> Sentence or langage / or bothe fynde ye shalle
> Ful delectable / *for that good fader mente*
> Of al his purpose / *and his hole entente*
> How to plese in euery audyence
> And in our tunge / was welle of eloquence
>
> (344–350, emphases mine)

Meaning and intention come together in this well of eloquence, and the product of that union is the pleasure and instruction of his audience. Chaucer is now a "fader" who can speak to children but who also can provide the model for the author of the *Book of Curtesye*. For now, unlike the Squire's foreign knight, this father Chaucer is part of the heritage of English verse, a true paternal figure whose conspicuous presence in the poem validates both the authority of its narrator and the legitimacy of its pedagogic agenda.

The *Book of Curtesye*, much like the *Squire's Tale*, finds few to match the unassailable authority of these paternal figures, and both occupy their verse with chronicling the failures of that union of intention and expression— that is, with the breakdown of polite discourse and the mistaking of the public voice. The search for *mente* and *entente* in the *Tale* finds its fulfillment not in the waking world of courtly life, but in the half-dreamed workings of the magical technology of Canacee's ring. It finds its breakdown not in the tensions between human interlocutors, but in the duplicities of the sophistical tercel ("And in this wise he served his entente / That, save the feend, noon wiste what he mente," F 521–22). The Squire's is in many ways a meditation on the aspirations of the verbally *in*decorous, and the dramatic context of the *Tale* articulates the delicacies necessary in a good audience. In the Franklin's gentle interruption, with its paternalistic comparisons of the Squire to his own son who "to vertu listeth nat entende" (F 689), readers would see exemplified the touchy problems of intrusion and response—problems addressed explicitly in the *Book of Curtesye*.

> And whan another man / spekith atte table
> Beware ye enterrupte not / his langage

For that is a thinge discomendable
Ande it is no signe of folkes sage
To be of langage / besy ande outrage
For the wyse man saide / in his sentence
He sholde be wyse / that gyueth audience

Vnderstonde therfore or than ye speke
Prynte in your mynde / clerly the sentence
Who that vsith / a mannes tale to breke
Letteth vncurteysly / all the audyence
Ande hurteth hym self / for lack of science
He may no gyue answere conuenyente
That herith not fynally / what is mente.

(274–87)

With his elaborate protestations of gentility, the Franklin may be seen as trying to negotiate between the public condemnation of his possibly uncourteous interruption of the Squire and his private impatience with the ramblings of this literary son. Though he has given audience to much of what the Squire has performed, his protestations indicate that, one presumes, he has heard finally that *nothing* has been meant here, and the one with "lack of science" is the teller, not the interrupter.

No such elaborate explanation, though, is needed for the Host, who most discourteously breaks in with his "Straw for youre gentillesse." In an apparent reversal of priorities, it is he who challenges both the decorum and the contract of the Franklin. But Harry's notion of decorum limits itself, here as always, to his own narrow demands of contract and occasion, and *his* interruption of the Franklin anticipates his later eruption at the *Tale of Sir Thopas*. His stinting of Chaucer's performance, together with his preceding salutation to the poet and his later fulsome praise of *Melibee*, precisely dramatize the polemics of the *Book of Curtesye*. From the aggressive call, "What man artow?" (*CT*, VII 695), through his demeaning appellation of the narrator as a "popet" and as "elvyssh," to his infamously scatological interruption of the *Thopas* and his mindlessly self-referential response to the *Melibee*, the Host exemplifies the rudeness of the man who, in the *Book of Curtesye*'s terms, speaks "Auauntparler / in euery mannys tale" (459). He embodies both the inattentions and the "lack of science" that the *Book of Curtesye* discerns in the man "That herith not fynally / what is mente" (287). At least one fifteenth-century reader understood Harry's interruption in this way, and he has reconstructed it to conform to the paradigms of the courtesy book. The Helmingham manuscript's version of the *Thopas / Melibee* Link, together with its editing of other portions of the *Canterbury Tales*, brings Chaucer's poetry in line with an advisory literature for children. Read in the context of the manuscript's own physical appearance, and of what may be recovered of its making and initial use, these large-scale reworkings of the *Tales* present what I will illustrate as, quite specifically, a children's Chaucer: one executed for the interests of a boyish reader.

II

With its infantile marginalia and in its tattered shape, the Helmingham manuscript may well appear to be the volume of a child. Manly and Rickert imagined it as a disused family heirloom, suitable by the mid-sixteenth century only for the playful annotations of a puerile Lionel Tollemache III and his friends.[16] But there is much to argue for its making as a manuscript for general family use, one utilitarian in function whose contents would be read and heard by both children and adults. The physical construction of the manuscript—with its paper quires of the late fifteenth century surrounding a vellum core of several decades earlier—implies that what we have here is a once-damaged volume, reconstructed quickly and inexpensively for domestic use.[17]

Its domesticity affirms itself, too, in the appearance of one of its opening flyleaves: a piece of paper from the last quarter of the fifteenth century on which a contemporary hand has written out a table of the times of sunrise and sunset for January to June.[18] Its first line reads:

> Here ys a generall reule to knowe by / þᵉ rysyng [and] þᵉ goyng doun of þᵉ sonne throwgh oute þᵉ yeer

> (flyleaf iii)

Such observations reflect what has been seen as the growing lay concern in late-medieval England with astronomy for both practical and abstract purposes.[19] This list may have served a variety of purposes; but one such purpose would have been as a collection of the very data necessary to the operation of an astrolabe. It is as if the writer of this page had followed Chaucer's own injunctions in the *Treatise on the Astrolabe* to record "the spryng of the dawening and the end of the evenyng" (*RC* 671), and certainly the "generall reule" presented here fits with the pedagogical directions of a work that the fifteenth century appreciated as Chaucer's "brede and milke for children."

This flyleaf, too, received its share of childish annotations—from the kinds of alphabets and pen trials that litter the rest of the manuscript, to the scraps of the opening line of the *General Prologue* written in at least three different hands that, by all appearances, date from the early to the mid-sixteenth century. Manly and Rickert do not notice these scribbles, for they are interested only in those annotations that reveal a name, a place, or provenance. Thus, they miss the various writings of the word *father* upside down on folio 6r in a hand displaying early sixteenth-century secretary features. They miss, as well, the kinds of doodles that respond to Chaucer's text, repeating his words or attempting to imitate the hand of the original scribe. These doodles scatter themselves throughout the manuscript, occasionally concentrating on a few leaves here and there where the book or the poem caught the eye of childish readers. One such concentration appears on folios 160v–162r, the portion of the manuscript containing the end of *Sir Thopas*, the *Thopas / Melibee* Link, and the opening of the *Melibee*. Here, several hands in differing inks have marked the pages. In one, a childish hand has written *hornchild* followed by some letters after the line in the *Thopas* "Of hornchilde and of ipotise" (fol.160v); on the page of the *Thopas / Melibee* Link (fol.161r), a set of doodles ranging from infantile squares, to Latin abbreviations, to secretary-style engrossed letters, charts a range of readerships.[20]

I have recorded these details of Helmingham's annotation because I want to emphasize, in contrast to received descriptions, the many years in which the manuscript was handled in this manner. Rather than find its childish doodles in the single moment of appropriation by the Tollemache children in the 1540s, as Manly and Rickert do, I find in its attached flyleaf, in its many different markings, and most importantly in its revised text, the evidence for a late-medieval conception of the manuscript as a household volume—one that from its earliest years of ownership was accoutred with directives and responses for a childish readership. Helmingham, I posit, was a book for everyday enjoyment and household utility, and the children of its audience would have found themselves addressed, if not, so to speak, inscribed in the romance adventures of Sir Thopas and the story of the narrator in the revised *Thopas / Melibee* Link.

Indeed, in the conjunction of the *Thopas* and the *Melibee*, Chaucer's fifteenth-century readers would have found the ideal site for meditating on the issues central to instruction of the young—issues such as the cultivation of verbal decorum and the public presentation of the private self. It may be difficult for us, still faced with several generations of an ironizing Chaucer, to take anything as bad, indeed as childish, as the *Tale of Sir Thopas* seriously.[21] Though we may find the *Melibee* not to our tastes— and much critical commentary on the *Melibee* hinges on just that historical distance and topical context that makes it so hard to appreciate now—we can explain and understand with ease its great popularity throughout the fifteenth century.[22] Yet the *Tale of Sir Thopas*, like the equally fragmentary *Squire's Tale*, has mostly been subjected to a criticism that can only claim it as a case of Chaucer's "unimpersonated artistry," that is, as an example of the poet demonstrating his control by writing verse out of control.[23] Like the *Squire's Tale*, the *Thopas* must be seen, it would appear, as little more than an extended joke: a literary text whose meaning inheres not in the details of its narrative or characterizations but instead in the simple fact of its existence. Whether we see it as Chaucer's parody of the tale-rhyme romance or as the pilgrim's joke on the Host, we make its meaning pendant on the externals of literary drama or generic environment. Even among those critics sensitive to the verbal and thematic function of the *Tale*, the seriousness of their criticism focuses on what it tells us of the poet's self-conception or his understanding of his literary project as a whole.

But, like the *Squire's Tale* as well, the *Tale of Sir Thopas* was clearly read and enjoyed on its own terms during the first two centuries of Chaucer's reception. John Burrow has recently chronicled the impact of the *Thopas* on verse from Dunbar and Skelton to Spenser and Shakespeare, and he notes how readers and writers at the turn of the sixteenth century would have recognized affiliations between the *Thopas* and the "rymes of Robin Hood" that circulated as one strain of popular ballad.[24] As an example of these ballad narratives it may have sought to parody, this *Tale* would have been associated with the many stories of adventure, combat, and fantasy that appealed to boyish readers.[25] Such stories had become the staple of a younger generation's reading: *Guy of Warwick, Havelok the Dane*, and many other Middle English romances had served as entertainment for the late-medieval household.[26] So associated were these texts with family or childish reading that the early Tudor educators who sought to reform the education of the young were almost universal in their condemnation of this poetry as "childish follye."[27]

What would have made the *Thopas* so appealing to those childish readers would have been just those features that made it so condemnable both to Renaissance and modern scholars: its fast, almost manic pace; its violent drama of the giant and his threats; and, most pointedly, its presentation of its hero as a kind of child. This "child Thopas," as Chaucer calls him (VII 830), lives out those encounters with the monstrous that have been the staple of much boyhood fantasy. In the following Link to the *Melibee*, the Host's special brand of rudeness distinguishes this moment from his careful attentions to rank and occupation in his other intrusions, and it augments the thematic concerns of the fictions Chaucer tells on this occasion. If the *Thopas* tells a story of an elfin knight tilting against nightmare giants, the *Melibee* dictates an allegory of the social nightmare of invasion. Both fictions seek to come to terms with aggressive challenges to proper speech and action. Thopas himself, initially presented as a model of chivalric ethics on the pattern of the old romances, answers his stone-throwing monster only with words. Melibeus, whose first response to the attack on his wife and daughter is blunt action, finds eventual counsel in the verbal directives of his wife Prudence and by the end of the treatise mollifies his stance to offer "sentence and judgement" against his transgressors. Both these stories share with the *Thopas / Melibee* Link a focus on the challenges to socialized behavior: challenges that demand verbal decorum in the face of physical provocation; but challenges, too, that place the figure of the child at the nexus of proper speech and improper behavior.

The Helmingham manuscript's revisions of the Link enable our interpretation of the sequence of these tales (and, perhaps, even beginning with the previous *Prioress's Tale*) as a drama of the threatened child.[28] From little Hugh of Lincoln, through the elfin Thopas and the battered Sophie, these tales tell stories of children menaced by the monsters of a child's imagination.[29] The evil Jews of the *Prioress's Tale*, the giant Olifaunt of *Thopas*, and the housebreakers of the *Melibee* all threaten the domestic, spiritual, and imaginative norms of children's life. Writing on this sequence, Lee Patterson has recently claimed that such threats and dramas serve "to articulate a form of consciousness that is at the center of Chaucer's kind of poetry"; that they use "childhood to stage a problematic central to the act of writing."[30] But the occasion of these poems in the Helmingham manuscript, I believe, uses these representations of childhood to stage problems in the act of reading rather than writing. It draws out, here and throughout its editings, the figure of the child as reader and in consequence addresses Chaucer's fictions to the reading child.

In Helmingham, Chaucer's Host comes off as little different from Sir Thopas's Olifaunt, as the childish hero of the romance and the infantilized narrator of the Link confront similarly abusive monsters. "Child, by Termagaunt," the giant begins his threat to Sir Thopas (VII 810), and this child manages to escape both the verbal and the stony assaults made on his "sydes smale" (VII 836). Not so the narrator. In spite of his appeal to "holde youre mouth, *par charitee*" (891)—a line that echoes in its macaronic idiom Thopas's own response to Olifaunt, "And yet I hope, *par ma fay*" (820)—the Host breaks in with his now-famous "Namoore of this, for Goddes dignitee" (919). In the full, original Chaucerian version of the Link, this drama of abuse and its attendant associations between Thopas and the narrator, the Host and the giant, fades behind the discursive meditations on literary theory that distinguish the passage for modern readers.[31] In Helmingham, all references to such a theory and its terms have been excised so as not to occlude this drama. Chaucer's long excursus on the relationship between *sentence* and literary authority is gone (VII 939–60); so is Harry's apparently offhand remark on "som murthe or som doctryne" and the narrator's answer (VII 935–36), as well as the accusation that Chaucer simply "despendest tyme" (VII 931–32). By eliminating any mention of theory or any reference to its terms, the scribe transforms a scene of reflection and argument into a fast-paced dramatic episode.[32] Like the scribes of *Troilus and Criseyde* who, as Barry Windeatt has shown, revised their text to make "direction and movement in the narrative more explicit than Chaucer leaves them in his own style," the Helmingham scribe-reviser breezes past the complex relationship of author to audience and source established in the received text of the passage.[33]

But, as I am proposing, his revisions have at their heart something more than the desire for narrative simplicity of the *Troilus* scribes. They have a thematic agenda. When the Chaucerian narrator excuses himself for the forthcoming *Melibee*, we see little of the meditation on authority and textual transmission that distinguishes the full version of the Link. Instead, we get a brief reflection on literary taste.

> I wol ʒowe tel alitil thing in prose
> That oght to like ʒowe as I suppose
> Blamyth me nat for as in my centence
> Shul yee no wher fynd dyference
> Ffro the centence of this tretise lite
>
> (fol.161r)

In the complete text of this passage, the narrator had asked not to be blamed if the version of his tale differed from familiar ones. He argued that, even though the Evangelists differ in their accounts of the life of Jesus, the *sentence*—the gist, moral meaning, or generally narrative lines—of their account remained the same. The force of his excuse confronts the audience's expectations of a certain plot and stylistic manner. In the revised text, however, his words have the effect of asking, simply, not to be blamed if the audience does not like the tale. As he implies, they do not expect the specific words of a familiar story but rather look forward to an overall pleasure in his performance. We are not told, as in the full text of the Link, of the possible reasons for *not* liking the story.

> I wol yow telle a litel thyng in prose
> That oghte liken yow, as I suppose,
> Or elles, certes, ye been to daungerous.
>
> (VII 937–39)

If the audience does not enjoy the tale, the reason is that they are too *daungerous*: too hard to please, or arrogant.[34] In the Helmingham manuscript, however, Chaucer is not passing judgment on his audience's potential response. The effect of the abridgment is to alter the tone as well as the substance of the excuse. Missing is the implicit contrast between the ideal audience that should both like and profit from the *Tale* and those who will not.

The effect of this abridgment also alters our perception of the Host.

Unlike the several other *Canterbury Tales* manuscripts that bowdlerize his response here,[35] the Helmingham text lets Harry Bailly's vulgarisms shine through unimpeded:

> By God quod he ful pleynly at o word
> Thy drasty rymyng is nat worth a tord
>
> (fol.161r)

His brusque demand for something told "in prose" now provokes the Chaucerian narrator's response in the following line to tell "alitil thing in prose." We have nothing of the deliberative reflection that intercedes between the Host's demands and the narrator's decision. What we do have is the drama of interruption and capitulation: a drama whose near comic-book fast pace is now fully in keeping with the childish narrative line of the *Tale of Sir Thopas*. We have, in Helmingham, a version of the frightened child's retreat before a bully. The manuscript's revisions shift Chaucer's emphases away from private, authorial speculation and toward public social response. They create, I believe, a drama grounded in the kinds of behavioral injunctions voiced by the *Book of Curtesye* against discourteous interruption. In the process, they bring the Link's narrations firmly into line with the longer narrative of a poetry directed at the child: a poetry that brings to life the fantasies of boyish readers while at the same time driving home the need for good public behavior. Moreover, by eliding the excurses on literary theory that distinguish the original version of the Link, the Helmingham manuscript brings the poem as a whole more into line with the aesthetic expectations of the *Book of Curtesye*. It is a verse, now, "clere in sentence," written "briefly" to articulate as directly as possible the unity of meaning and intention prized as the accomplishment of Chaucer's "langage."

This emphasis on brevity and clarity also guides Helmingham's revisions to the *Melibee* and *Pardoner's Tale*. By abbreviating the prose treatise, the Helmingham scribe reads the tale more for its narrative line than its advisory *copia*. He has cut down much of the technical argument and has eliminated many of its philosophical references. He even summarizes Chaucer's text in his own words, as this example illustrates:[36]

> Mellebeus answerid and seid he wold nat werk by her counsel for
> mony resons þat is affermyd by so many wys pepil and men wold sey
> that I had ʒev þe mastery / / for I sey thy counsel is noght.
>
> (fol. 162v)

The scribe's primary goal is concision and narrative pace, and to this end he abbreviates the Aristotelian classification of causes that stand behind Prudence's understanding of her husband's grief. Instead of five "resons," the scribe offers only one. The long advocate's speech is pared down to a third of its original length, and the following description of the young people's response to the speech appears simply: "Then up sterte than al these ʒong folk attonys 7 skornyd þis wise man and crydyn werr." The characteristic plethora of quotations and citations that punctuate the *Tale* and that appear in many of its Latin and French analogues is similarly reduced by the scribe, even though he adopts the marginal annotation of authoritative names present in the earlier, parchment portion of the manuscript.

In his handling of the *Pardoner's Prologue and Tale*, the scribe does with rhetorical digression what his *Melibee* does with philosophical allusion. The similes and asides in the prologue are pared down, as are the Pardoner's ironically self-revealing remarks on preaching technique.[37] Within the *Tale* itself, the scribe successively eliminates examples supporting the Pardoner's points, and his editorial actions reveal more than mere impatience with the tale-teller's prolixity.[38] They effectively realign the narrative force and conception of character that modern critics have grasped as governing the shape of Chaucer's poem. The Pardoner's use of *occupatio* to delay action and reveal ironically his rhetorical motives is less obvious in the Helmingham version. Nowhere do we find the undermining power of the Pardoner's phrase "it oghte ynogh suffise" and its variants that conclude his long lists of historical or literary examples.[39] The scribe even goes so far as to strip the *Tale* of its final challenging interchange between the Pardoner and the Host. Here, tensions between teller and tale and teller and audience vanish—along with much of the humor and violence of the moment—as the *Pardoner's Tale* ends simply with the death of the rioters. But the scribe's elisions here need not be thought of as mere censorship, though certainly for younger readers such a scene of implied castration and coprophilia would express a violence far different in kind from Harry's later and more jocular equation of the *Thopas* with a turd.

What is at work in Helmingham's revision of the *Pardoner's Tale* is an approach to character and authorial interest akin to the manuscript's revisions elsewhere. This version of the *Tale* creates a poem strikingly different from the one twentieth-century critics have come to know. This new poem cannot support the psychologizing interpretations of the Pardoner that have marked criticism of the *Tale* from, say, George Lyman Kittredge through Donald Howard and H. Marshall Leicester, Jr.[40] The many rhetorical sleights, confidential asides, and revealing admissions out of which modern critics have constructed their vision of the character are, for the most part, missing in Helmingham.[41] What we find, instead, is an apparently more coarsely tuned version of the poem: one whose narrative may move more quickly but without the defining nuances that mark this episode as one of Chaucer's most psychologically adept achievements.

The Helmingham revisions to the *Pardoner's Tale*, much like its editing of the *Thopas / Melibee* section, shift our attentions from the problem of authorial self-presentation to more narrowly definable issues in reader response. These are stories about readers rather than tellers, stories for childish audiences rather than adult critics. What we have in these cut-down versions is, ultimately, a quite different version of the *Canterbury Tales* as "literature." The stories have been, one might say, de-authorized. The details of form and narrative that create psychologically motivated or critically preoccupied tellers have been effaced in the manuscript's revisions. "Chaucer" or "The Pardoner" are no longer the subjects of these performances. Instead, as I am arguing, their subject is the childish reader—the audience for whom these tales have been recast as exempla of moral action. We can, I think, quite effectively read the Helmingham version of the Pardoner's story of the three rioters as the straightforward narrative it purports to be. Whatever modern, ironizing frames we may place around it are impossible in Helmingham's unframed versions. Similarly, whatever theoretical abstractions we may cull from the *Thopas / Melibee* Link are absent from this drama of simple abuse. Helmingham stands, in short, not as a testimony to the literary autonomy of Chaucerian fiction but rather as a document for the lived world of social responsibilities.

III

By rewriting scenes of rhetorical self-presentation and critical speculation, the Helmingham manuscript transforms essays in authorship into fables of decorum for a gentry readership. In an analogous way, the version of the *Clerk's Tale* anthologized in Huntington Library MS HM 140 reworks Chaucer's complex reflections on authority into unironic ethical exempla. Without its Prologue and its references to the Canterbury frame, this manuscript's *Clerk's Tale* draws out those aspects of generic stability and moral theme that made it one of the most popular of Chaucer's fictions in the fifteenth century. With the lines from Chaucer's *Truth* now appended to its end, the *Tale* fits neatly into the anthology's Lydgatean patterns of stanzaic, exemplary stories. Beginning with Lydgate's *Life of St. Albon and St. Amphibalus*, moving through the *Clerk's Tale*, a selection of Lydgate's didactic ballads, the Complaint from Chaucer's *Anelida and Arcite*, and concluding with an anonymous Middle English Life of Job, the first portion of HM 140 stands as a thematically and formally coherent assembly. English saints, an Italian wife, a mythological lover, Jesus, Job, and Lydgate himself all function as ideals of faith and patience within the structures of human and divine authority. They offer models of behavior for a readership reared on the didactic, as they mutually refract the codes of patience and obedience to institutional authority that mark the fitting conduct of the child.[42]

This first part of HM 140 has long been studied as an originally separate manuscript. Manly and Rickert identified it with the book bequeathed in the will of Thomas Chaworth of Wiverton, Northamptonshire, in 1459: "A newe boke of Inglise ye which beginnyth with ye lyffe of Seynt Albon and Amphiabell and many other dyvers lyfez and thinges in ye same boke."[43] Certainly, HM 140's first portion begins this way, and its subsequent collection of "lyfez" fits neatly into the kind of moral, exemplary narratives of fable and hagiography connoted by that Middle English term.[44] In the absence of competing evidence, Manly and Rickert's identification has been accepted by virtually all later scholars of the manuscript; yet the physical evidence does not rule out a later origin. If watermarks are anything to go by, the paper stocks of the first part of the manuscript are datable to two decades after Chaworth's will; and although the many hands that wrote those pages cannot be identified with certainty, they reflect scribal practices at work anywhere from 1450 to 1480.[45] The manuscript's second section, a long, single paper quire, is more easily definable as a late-fifteenth-, early-sixteenth-century assembly from the orbit of a courtly and commercial London readership. It has the look more of a commonplace book than a commissioned production, and it too has been generally assumed to have been a separate manuscript originally, bound at a later date (possibly in the 1520s) with the first section.[46]

Part of my purpose in what follows will be to suggest an alternative to these received scholarly interpretations of HM 140 and its contexts. There is much in the manuscript's first section to appeal directly to a civic and commercial readership, although it is also possible to read the final quire as an originally added blank book, filled in as the occasion rose with texts addressing the concerns of the first part. Rather than relying on the serendipity of the coincidence of HM 140 with the description of a book in the external evidence of Chaworth's bequest, I will try to read its compilations for their internal evidence of a formal and thematic coherence to the commission. My goal is to recover both the historical and the implied readerships for the assembly as a whole. In its attentions to ideals of social conduct and relations among parents and children, HM 140's first section inscribes the figure of the child as its implied reader. In its amateur verses on apprentices, the leaves of the second section testify to a critical response to those thematic interests, and they serve as a direct address to a socially definable young audience for the collection. In an approach that parallels my reading of the Helmingham manuscript, I seek an understanding of those intersections between "real" and "fictive" readerships for HM 140 to argue, in the end, that the assembly narrates stories of the patience necessary to the childhood apprentice, and more specifically that it presents a Lydgateanized version of the *Clerk's Tale* for a young readership schooled in the advisory literature of the century. Like Helmingham, HM 140 decenters Chaucer's authority by effacing his poems' reflections on authorial responsibility to source and patron. But unlike Helmingham, it affirms a new authorial control and offers evidence for understanding readerly responsibility as forms of both social and literary apprenticeships.

Among the many, interrelated criteria for assessing the anthology's guiding principles, one may be found in the writings of John Shirley. In his headnote to the copy of the Complaint from *Anelida and Arcite* in his manuscript (Trinity College Cambridge MS R.3.20), Shirley offers a critical terminology that may be helpful in assessing the place of Chaucer's poems in the HM 140 collection.

> Takeþe heed sirs I prey yowe of þis compleynt of Anelyda Qweene of Cartage. Roote of trouthe and stedfastnesse þat pytously compleyneþe vpon þe varyance of Daun Arcyte lord borne of þe blood Royal of Thebes . englisshed by Geffrey Chaucier in þe best wyse . and moost Rettoricyous þe moost vnkouþe metre . coloures and Rymes þat euer was sayde . tofore þis day—redeþe and preveþe þe sooþe.[47]

Two features of this criticism stand out. First, Shirley finds in the Complaint the themes of "trouthe and stedfastnesse" that characterize Anelida herself. Second, he attends to those features of form and diction that the fifteenth century found so "curious" about Chaucer's work.[48] The poem appears in "þe best wyse and moost Rettoricyous," that is, in the most highly controlled and ornate diction. By stressing the "vnkouþe metre coloures and rymes," Shirley further calls attention to the elaborate structure of the Complaint: its control of the decasyllabic line (*metre*); its heightened use of rhetorical tropes and figures (*coloures*); and its elaborate stanzaic structure (*Rymes*). The formal and thematic qualities that Shirley notices in the Complaint can characterize the other poetry of HM 140. Virtuosity in metrical and stanzaic form marks the *Clerk's Tale* and *Truth* and remains the ideal to which Lydgate had aspired in the ballads. The rhetorical addresses throughout the Complaint find their analogue in the exhortations that motivate *Truth* and the Lydgatean lyrics, while Shirley's interest in the theme of "trouthe and stedfastnesse" applies equally well to all of the characters of the manuscript's narratives.

It is this emphasis on rhetorical control and moral example that distinguishes *Truth* as a conclusion to the HM 140 version of the *Clerk's Tale*. The ballad's lines sustain the narrator's addresses to the reader that bring Chaucer's poem to its close. *Truth* continues in the hortatory injunctions "folweth Ekko" (E 1189), "stondeth at defense" (E 1195), and the others that shape the stanzas of the *Tale's* conclusion. "Flee from the prees," the ballad begins, continuing through a sequence of rhetorical markers addressed to the reader:[49] "Suffise the thyne owne"; "Ffavor nomore"; "Rewle well thyself"; "Tempest the not"; "Be ware therfore"; "Stryv not"; and they continue, culminating in the great Boethian injunction, "Fforth pylgrime forth!" Taken in tandem, these patterns of advice reaffirm the theme of patience in the story of Griselda. They enjoin the reader to recognize the authority of an ordered world and not to challenge it.[50] But these words of advice also resonate with the Clerk's words to his own readers. *Truth*'s appeals to "sothfastnesse" and to "Rewle well thyself" harmonize with the Clerk's advice for wives to "sharply taak on yow the governaille" (E 1192). Self-control and personal resolve are important to both poems. And yet, while the *Clerk's Tale* ends with a word to wives, *Truth* speaks to human-kind generally. From the specifically domestic context of marriage we move to a more abstract sense of living in the world at large. "Maistrie" over a spouse becomes mastery over the self, as the ballad removes its read-ers from the details of domestic life and leaves them looking toward heaven.

There is a precedent for appending *Truth* to the *Clerk's Tale*, one that speaks more generally to the relationship of Chaucer and Lydgate implicit in the manuscript's assembly. As a conclusion to the *Tale*, *Truth* operates after the manner of the refrain line stanzas that close Lydgate's *Life of St. Albon and St. Amphibalus*: an Envoy designed to explain the general appli-cability of the narrative to the reader. It comes to stand as a set piece of morality concluding a poem that, for its fifteenth-century readers, would have been apprehended as what one modern critic calls "a secular saint's life."[51] Other manuscripts perform similar acts of synthesis. Stanzas of the *Monk's Tale* are yoked together with those from the *Fall of Princes*; on occasion, the *Fall of Princes* joins together pieces from *Troilus and Cri-seyde*.[52] More specifically, the Naples manuscript of the *Clerk's Tale* ends with the concluding stanza from Lydgate's *Doubleness*, and in so doing, it explicitly provides a Lydgatean moral interpretation to the tale. From this and other evidence, A. S. G. Edwards has argued that fifteenth-century compilers of Lydgate's poetry showed, in their selections from his texts, a concerted interest in the "sententious didactic content of the Envoys he added to his work, his reduction of human tragedies to generalities or gnomic wordplay."[53] This is, in essence, what I take to be one effect of HM 140's action. At issue is not whether *Truth* succeeds unambiguously as a conclusion to the *Clerk's Tale*, or whether its rhetorical exhortations and Boethian imagery form a critically intelligent commentary on the story of Griselda. Instead, it is how the scribe's version of the *Tale* reflects a climate of literary taste in which Chaucer's moral stories came to be read through Lydgate's, reducing both to the repetitive compendia of lore that formed the spine of the advisory anthologies of the mid-fifteenth century.

If the scribes of HM 140 have offered an implicit reading of the *Tale* by combining two poems, they have also reinforced that reading by acts of excision. All references to the Canterbury collection have been removed, enabling the poem to stand on its own in the anthology. While many manuscripts of the *Tale*—whether presented alone in an anthology or as part of the *Canterbury Tales*—cut the stanza on the Wife of Bath (E 1170–76), HM 140 uniquely eliminates both it and the preceding stanza (E 1163–69).[54] It strips the poem's conclusion of its refreshing ironies, avoiding the witty comparisons between Griselda and modern women, or between the Clerk and the Wife of Bath as moralizing narrators. By ending the *Tale* proper at line 1162, HM 140 presents a reading that implies an almost fatalistic acquiescence to authoritative rule. The implicit association between Griselda's fidelity to Walter and our faith in God is heightened in this pared-down telling. The "sharpe scourges of adversitee" (E 1157) and a life of "vertuous suffraunce" (E 1162) are what concerns this version of the poem, and the scribe of this part of the manuscript pointedly underlines this moral with a conspicuous *amen*, written in the margin after the latter phrase. In the received Chaucerian text, the shift in tone signaled by the following line—"But o word, lordynges, herkneth er I go" (E 1163)—relieves something of the tension building at the poem's end. In this full version, the Clerk progressively distances himself from confronting the moral implications of his story. He shifts the burden of interpretation and application onto the reader, and instead of offering a *moralitas* to conclude his narrative, he announces:

> I wol with lusty herte, fressh and grene,
> Seyn yow a song to glade yow, I wene;
> And lat us stynte of ernestful matere.
>
> (E 1173–75)

In his shift from earnest to play, the Clerk seems to avoid explicit comment on the *Tale*. His announcement of the forthcoming Envoy shifts radically the verbal environment in which his performance transpires: He moves from an attention to writing (in the tale Petrarch "writeth," E 1147) to a concern with singing. He turns his audience into listeners rather than readers, just as he turns himself from a reader into a composer. One effect of these stanzas is thus to call attention to the audience's responsibility away from moral interpretation and toward aesthetic pleasure. In its complete version, the *Clerk's Tale* offers a built-in release from the burden of moral interpretation—a shift from learning to enjoying, from *sentence* to *solaas*. But for the readership of HM 140, there is no stinting of this "ernestful matere." By stripping away all possible emotional release or interpretive debate, the manuscript presents a critical interpretation of the *Tale*, to borrow Shirley's words on Anelida's Complaint, as one of "trouthe and stedfastnesse." By adding on the stanzas from the ballad *Truth*, it augments that moralism and generic stability that so many fifteenth-century readers found at the heart of this and other popular Chaucerian productions.

These generic and formal alterations to the *Clerk's Tale* have the effect of transforming the conception of authority behind the poem and changing its identifiable voice. All possible *auctoritates*, real and fictional, have been effaced here. The loss of the *Tale's* Prologue does more than free it from the Canterbury frame. It removes Petrarch and the Host as authorizing agents for its telling. The drama of commission that had generated the Clerk's performance—indeed, the whole feeling of performance in the *Tale*—is gone here, as is the laureate example of the poet from whom he had learned the tale. It might even be unclear, from the garbled appellation at its end (the claim to follow what "patrik writeth"), whether this scribe even knew who Petrarch was, let alone how to spell his name.[55] Read in this light, the absence of the Wife of Bath and of the "lordyngs" who had been invited into the *Tale's* audience now eliminate from this new narrative any outside, critical authority. Without the scribal denotations of a "Lenvoy de Chaucer," without even a title, this transcript of the tale may seem but a free-floating exemplary story: one that deploys its anonymity only to augment its application to all comers.

The effect of this anonymity, however, is not to render it a separable story but to ground it firmly in the one explicitly announced and authorizing figure for the manuscript assembly as a whole. Not only have the HM 140 scribes recast Chaucer's verse into Lydgatean form; they have decentered its locus of authorial control onto Lydgate himself. They have made it participate in a sequence of verses governed by the manuscript's opening set of authorizing gestures. HM 140's first section is, by all appearances, a book of Lydgatean rather than Chaucerian production. It is a book controlled by Lydgate's authority established in its opening selection, for here, all the accoutrements of official production cluster to affirm the name, the time, and the occasion of authorship.

> Here endith the glorious lyf and passyoun of the
> blessid martir Seint Albone and seint Amphiaball
> which glorious livis were translatid oute of Frenssh
> and latyn by dane John lydgate Monke of Bury at þe
> request and prayer of Master John Whethamstede the yere
> of oure lord M^l CCCC xxxix and of the said Master
> John Whethamstede of his Abisse xix
>
> (fol.67r)[56]

And if Lydgate is granted the commission of this poem, so too, within the manuscript's assembly, he is granted the right to invoke outside, laureate example for his work. Here, in the writing of a scribe who clearly knows who Petrarch was, Lydgate can raise the name later effaced from the following *Clerk's Tale*. In the second stanza of *Albon and Amphibalus* he protests:

> I nat acqueyntid with musis of Maro,
> Nor with metris of Lucan nor Virgile,
> Nor sugrid ditees of Tullius Chithero,
> Nor of Omerus to folwe the fressh stile,
> Crokid to clymb ouer so high a stile,
> Or for to folwe the steppis aureat
> Of Franceis Petrak, the poete laureat?
>
> (I:8–14)

This collection of humility *topoi*, drawn from the *Franklin's* and the *Squire's Tales*, as well as from the *Troilus* and the Prologue to the *Clerk's Tale*, synthesizes the inheritance of Chaucer's rhetorical protestations into quintessential Lydgatean "dullness." As the opening salvo to what may be Lydgate's final, major poem, this stanza reviews a lifetime of appropriating Chaucer's idiom. But, as the opening abjection of a manuscript anthology thematically concerned with patience and humility, this stanza neatly serves to construct the controlling authorial voice for the poetry. Lydgate himself, again, is but the follower before the laureate and aureate authority of past poets. Rather than leave it to the Clerk to stand humbled before his own commissioner or literary model, the assembly of HM 140 locates this particular obedience—and, for that matter, all possible protestations of literary indebtedness—in Lydgate's opening lines. "Meeke suffraunce" is the model now not only for social behavior but for literary practice, and in the opening description of St. Albon we may find Lydgate's own idea of his achievement, as well as a guideline for the anthology's characters and readers.

> Thorugh meeke suffraunce he gat the victorie,
> A palme of conquest to be put in memorie,
> A laureat crowne, bi triumphis manyfold
> For his meritis set on his hed, of gold.
>
> (I:88–92)

Suffering brings its rewards, and Albon, much like Griselda, Job, or Anelida, figures forth the governing conception of literary authorship that begins the manuscript. The crown and the gold, laureation and aureation, come together here as a reward for a subservient apprenticeship both to the will of God and the example of the poets.

But that example needed to be taught as well as shown, and in the course of HM 140's assembly, Lydgate's poetry becomes progressively less exemplary and more explicitly pedagogic. Its overriding interest in the steadfastness essential to life in this mutable, material world comes to be

voiced by a variety of teaching figures, and the sequence of the manuscript's assembly creates in the reader's mind the focus of this pedagogic
telos. The *Prayer Upon the Cross* that follows the *Clerk's Tale / Truth* com-
bination in the manuscript rephrases the ideals of suffering in the mouth
of a Jesus who is not just a savior but a teacher.

> Thinke ageyn pride on myn humylyte;
> > Kom to scole, recorde weell this lessoun;
>
> . . . .
>
> Afforn thyn herte hang this lytel table,
> Swetter than bawme geyn al goostly poisoun, —
> > Be thow nat froward, sith I am mercyable.
>
> > > > (*Prayer*, 25–32)

Jesus now speaks in the paternal idioms of advisory verse. His tone comes
as the compassionate father facing a recalcitrant child: "Sith I am kynde,
why artow so onstable?" (22). In fact, by the end of this brief poem, the
reader has been transformed into a child, one pushed to "kom to scole" and
write the lesson on the schoolboy's tablet.[57] The "thee" of this poem is
the reading child, and HM 140's unique extra stanza on the story on Cain
and Abel only reinforces Jesus's message as an object lesson to aberrant
children.[58]

The next of Lydgate's poems in the manuscript, *As a Midsomer Rose*,
takes a somewhat different tack, questioning the absolute value of education in a mutable world. "Al stant on chaung," the poem iterates in its
refrain line; even the "wisdam" and "elloquence" (7) of the learned cannot
stop it.[59] "Lat no man booste of konnyng nor vertue" (1), he begins, while
one of his final stanzas laments the passing of all the "aureat ditees that be
red and songe" (83). But, as if to answer this lament, the following *Song of
Vertue* reaffirms the relationship of virtuous practice and ethical instruction. "Who sueth vertu, vertu he shal leere," it states again and again in its
refrains.[60]

> Reede in bookys of antiquyte,
> Of oold stooryes be glad good thyng to heere,
> > And it shal tourne to gret comodite, —
> Sewe aftir vertu, and vertu thu shalt leere.
>
> > > > (*Song*, 77–80)

Having worked through the steadfastness of St. Albon, the patience of
Griselda, and the suffering of Anelida, a reader of this compilation would
approach, in these lines, the controlling pedagogical imperative behind the
whole of HM 140. Reading the books of antiquity bound together in this
volume, the audience would take these "oold stooryes" and turn them to a
"gret comodite"—the practical wisdom that leads to a virtuous life.

This notion of literature as something to be used—as a program for living or a guide to everyday behavior—would have been familiar from the many didactic assemblies that had filled the shelves of late-fifteenth-century book buyers. To a certain extent, then, Lydgate's injunctions in the *Song of Vertue* dovetail with those of the later *Book of Curtesye* and with the Helmingham revisions of the *Thopas / Melibee* section I had traced earlier. Here in HM 140, however, they look forward to the personal responses of the poet himself, and the last of the manuscript's selections from Lydgate is an abbreviated version of his *Testament*. On the surviving leaves of the collection, the first fourteen of the poem's one hundred and eighteen stanzas appear. The editors of the Huntington Library *Guide* note that, with only one leaf missing from this quire, "the text was probably never complete in this manuscript."[61] This proposed missing leaf (following folio 92 of the current compilation) is the sixteenth and final leaf of the sixth quire. A new quire then begins with the Middle English Life of Job. I think it highly likely that what is missing here is not just a single page but a whole quire, and that the manuscript as it was originally compiled contained a substantial portion of the *Testament*, if not the whole poem. This missing quire may have been lost when the manuscript was erroneously and damagingly bound in the late-fifteenth or early-sixteenth century (quires three and four are reversed in the binding, and several leaves from other quires are lost, as well).[62]

Such codicological speculation has a thematic import for the reading and reception of the manuscript. Lydgate's *Testament* would have been the natural component in a volume of instruction in the ideals of patience and virtue. As its tone becomes more pedagogic, its audience becomes, in effect, more childish: more in need of direct instruction, but also more pointedly inscribed through the child-figures of the texts. The *Testament* is a poem of the poet's childhood. From its meditations on his "tender youthe" (241), through its catalogue of the poet's own childish mischiefs, the poem addresses pointedly the codes of conduct for the young boy in commercial, social, and religious spheres of action. It tells stories of neglect of schoolwork, petty thefts, and the disrespect of elders with such vigor and detail that many of the poem's modern readers have taken its autobiographical content as unadulterated truth and have relied on its descriptions to construct a history of childhood education at the close of the Middle Ages.[63]

One of this poem's fifteenth-century readers, however, clearly recognized the *Testament* as raw material for his own essay in advice. In the verses now known as the "Poem to Apprentices" inscribed into HM 140's second section, a user of this manuscript recognized the emphases on childhood education stressed in the first section, and he attempted to apply the ideas of patience under stress learned from those previous poems to the specifics of young life in the commercial world. This poem may be taken as a personal response to the experience of reading, in Lydgate's words, the "bookys of antiquite" compiled in HM 140. This writer's verses are so clearly modeled on the order and the idiom of Lydgate's *Testament* that they may well be construed as a directive for the childish reader to review those "oold stooryes" he has just finished.

The poem begins as a fatherly instruction to those children entering service in the city.[64]

> Children[n] and yonge men[n] that co[m]me to this citee
> And purpose your[e] self app[re]ntices to be
> To lerne crafte or connyng
> I counsaill[e] yow all[e] doo after me
> And than ye shall[e] not reprovid be
> Yf ye use my doctryne sikerly
>
> > ("Apprentices" 1–6)

What follows is a string of specific injunctions on timely rising, responsible work, good service at the table, moral virtues generally, and a range of other lessons modeled on Lydgate's own stories of his youthful indiscretions. Its counsel reads as a pointed rewriting of Lydgate's admissions of his bad behavior in the *Testament*.

> Ffyrst that ye rise in the mornyng erly
> And that ye s[er]ve god devoutly
> With pater noster Ave and crede
> Arraye your self lightly
> Be with your maister in the mornyng tymely
> And doo that he you bidde
>
> > ("Apprentices" 7–12)

> Loth to ryse, lother to bedde at eve,
> > With vnwasshe hondes redy to dyner,
> My pater noster, my crede, or my beleve,
> > Cast atte cok, lo, this was my maner!
> > Wawed with eche wynd, as doth a reedspere,
> Snybbed of my frendes, sucche tecches tamende,
> Mad deef ere, list not to them attende.
>
> > (*Testament* 649–55)

All of Lydgate's confessions of disobedience, discourtesy, impatience, irreverence, and immodesty catalogued in the *Testament* (see lines 698–718) are answered in the "Poem to Apprentices":

> Speke to your maister rev[er]ently
> And answere hym ev[er] curteisly
> See your arraye be clene
> Suffer maister and maistresse paciently
> And doo their biddyng obediently
> And loke noo pride in yow be sene
>
> ("Apprentices" 13–18)

Writing almost with Lydgate at his shoulder, or at the very least with Lydgate's poetry before his eyes, the author of these lines reviews the range of advice in HM 140. From the specifics of the *Testament* he turns, at his close, to the injunctions of the *Song of Vertue*. Lydgate's refrain "Who sueth vertue, vertue he shal leere" becomes in his hands the prayer for god to "Sende these app[re]ntices goode lernyng" ("Apprentices" 44) so that they may "alwey goode vertues to sue" ("Apprentices" 48).

The "Poem to Apprentices" may be appreciated, as I have suggested here, as an amateur recasting of the saws and maxims of Lydgatean advice that fill the first part of HM 140.[65] But it may also tell us something of the audience for the assembly, one occupied with the relationship of literary learning to commercial life. As Lydgate put it in the *Song of Vertue*, reading "oold stooryes" can turn one "to gret comodite"—where we may take "comodite" as quite specifically the "useful products" or "material advantages" that the *OED* identifies as the range of new fifteenth-century associations of the word.[66] The place of learning in the holding of commodities is, at least in part, the subject of the *Song of Vertue* itself, with its counsel, "In prosperite be nat to proud of cheere, / In aduersite be pacient with meekness" (70–71). But it is also, I believe, the subject of the Middle English Life of Job that closes the first part of HM 140 and that controls in retrospect the literary and the social understandings of its verse.

HM 140 is, in many ways, a book directed at the interests of commercial, civic readers. The story of Albon and Amphibalus, for example, draws on the legends of establishing a city in order, at the poem's end, to make St. Albon himself into a kind of patron saint for daily political and commercial pursuits. At the conclusion of the poem, Lydgate asks the saint, "To the citee be patron, prince, and guyde" (*Albon and Amphibalus* III.1548); he begs him to pray for "the syxt Henry, of thes roealmes kyng" (III.1564) and for the princes to "gouerne" (III.1569) and the Church to "guye" (III.1572). In the last of the poem's exhortative stanzas, Albon himself becomes the patron of commercial interests, as his moral guidance now directs mercantile behavior.

> Pray for marchauntis and artificers
> To encrese by vertu in their businesse,
> That ther be founde no fraude in their desires,

So that falce lucre haue noone entresse.
Bit thi prayer do all-so represse
All tyranny and all facle extorcioun,
O prothomartir of Brutis Albioun

(III.1576–82)

Such lines would have spoken directly to the members of the merchant class who read this volume: individuals who had valued books and education as the mark not just of learning generally but as passages of entry into a successful commercial life. Whatever instructional value Lydgate's poem may have held for such a readership, its closing lines may have affirmed the moral basis many sought for economic success.

The conflation of moral directives and economic direction at the close of Lydgate's poem may exemplify the broader reading interests of a London mercantile community. What Mervyn James calls the late-fifteenth-century city fascination with "a moralized and providentialist history" found its expression in the commissions and bequests of a range of hagiographic, biblical, and prophetic narratives.[67] Special among these various productions was a new interest in the story of Job.[68] The evidence that this biblical book was read and copied separately, together with the presentations in the visual and plastic arts of the time, suggests that Job had come to represent a constellation of new, cultural concerns—ones that may help us understand the critical trajectory of HM 140's assembly. By the close of the fifteenth century, literary and artistic representations of the Job story had shifted away from the old, figural readings of the moral exegetes and toward newer, social concerns. In a survey of these shifts, F. Harth defines the relevance of Job to northern European culture in terms that precisely match those of the Middle English Life of Job. By the end of the century, he writes:

A quite different idea of the significance of Job emerges along with the rise of the bourgeois class in northern Europe. The intricate, symmetrical symbolic systems of the thirteenth and fourteenth centuries have begun to give way, and Job represents not so much the prefigurement of the Passion of Christ as an example of patience under suffering and continued faith in God after the loss of all one's possessions. The representations of him in art and in mystery plays relate these sufferings, but omit any reference to the symbolic and prophetic aspects so dear to the Middle Ages.[69]

It is this patience in the face of the "loss of all one's possessions" that may bring together the sustained narratives of HM 140. Completing what we might call the poetic bracketing of the manuscript's first part is the anonymous Life of Job, a work that, for all its resonances to anterior sources, is a unique vernacular account, perhaps deliberately constructed to reflect the interests of the compilation's other poems. Instead of drawing lines of figural relationship, this poem focuses on exemplarity for living audiences; instead of doctrinal reflection, it attends to social response. The poem is, in the words of its opening stanzas, an instruction in how "wysely to lyve," and at its end, we see Job restored as the master of his house, offering a "ryall feest" to family and friends. He celebrates the "Greeter hospytalite" that he enjoys and, in the poem's penultimate stanza, Job is described as fathering more children and living long enough to see "the fourthe degree of his generacion."

   Job's sorrow and success, his lesson and his moral, circumscribe the life of man in the community of family and children. The lesson that he teaches is, in Harth's words, a lesson about possessions and their value, a lesson carefully directed to a readership whose status in the world was deeply invested (in all senses of that word) in the responsibilities of child rearing and the education of a "generacion." To be Job-like in adversity is an injunction to fathers and sons together, and it is significant that at the poem's opening much is made of Job's role as an example to his children. He is as much a teacher as a sufferer:

> Here, lo, holy Iob his children doth sanctifie,
> And techith his sonnes with-oute presumpcion
> To kepe theire festes, and ever God to magnifie,
> And wysely to lyve with-oute any detraccion.
> And to his doughtres, with-outen pryde or ellacion
> Of their native beaute, he bad them have respect
> Hough bryght Lucyfer for his pryde from heven was deiect.

> And by cause in grete festynges is ofte tymes sayn
> Voluptuose fraylte and ydell loquacite,
> This holy Iob for all his children, certeyn,
> Lest they therin shuld synn or offende of symplicite,
> Here offreth to God and prayth unto his deyte
> That his oblacio and holocaust myght habond
> Ayenst theire synnes, if any in them were fownd.

> (15–28)

   The exemplary quality of Job extends here to an audience of children. Job "techith his sonnes," and in this enactment of a pedagogic imperative, the Middle English Life of Job returns us to the paternal, instructive idioms of the *Book of Curtesye* and the reception of a fatherly Chaucer and a didactic Lydgate. Job and his children function as another inscribed audience for this collection. They stand for a readership who should both teach and be taught and who may find themselves in various ways refracted through the patient suffering of HM 140's many childlike and parental figures.

Among those many figures would, of course, have been Griselda and her father and Walter and his children, and we may return now to the *Clerk's Tale* to explore, in retrospect, the range of critical and social meanings that it would have held for the late-medieval readers of HM 140. With its theme of steadfastness in a mutable, material world, the *Clerk's Tale* functions as a fable for apprentice readers. It is a tale of patience in the face of adverse father figures, a story of the loss of children to the demands of the state, and a lesson in the acquiescence to authoritative control.[70] It is a tale of "gouernance" in the Lydgatean sense, a story of control both of the self and by authority. It is a narrative of *sadness*, not just in the sense of an emotion felt by Griselda or her emotionally responsive readers, but in the broader, Middle English connotations of resolve, ethical certitude, and socially motivated patience.[71] It is a legend, too, that hinges on the many meanings of *array*—on the outward trappings of that governance and the essential link between personal decorousness and social decorum.[72]

These emphases on *sadness* and *array* would have caught the eye of a fifteenth-century reader reared on the advisory literature of social decorum. They seem, certainly, to have caught the eye of the writer of the "Poem to Apprentices," for they become the key terms of his advice. To "Walke by the wey verry sadly" (31), to watch one's own "array" (10, 15) become the hallmarks of appropriate apprentice behavior. What they also become, however, are the hallmarks of a way of reading Chaucer's poem like a child. For what I have addressed throughout this chapter are the ways in which a children's Chaucer is a literature of surfaces. It picks up on the late-fifteenth-century concern with patterns of public behavior, forms of speech, and habits of dress to transform Chaucer's reflections on meaning and intention, morality and poetics, into dramas of social occasion. In this way, as I had suggested, the Helmingham revisions of the *Thopas / Melibee* section write a narrative of such occasion—a story that no longer takes the reader into Chaucer's mind or workshop but that draws that reader into the dynamics of narrative and pace. The Helmingham version of the *Thopas / Melibee* Link is thus more superficial than its full, original text not just because it seems less critically sophisticated or more narratively blunt; it is more superficial because, thematically, it concerns itself with surfaces. Its focus is the fast-paced exchange of insult and excuse, the swift and unreflective moments of a plot on a par with the rapid, childish jauntings of Sir Thopas.

In a similar way, the version of the *Clerk's Tale* in HM 140 works in tandem with the other poems of the collection to present a story about surfaces. In one sense, it gives us a superficial, Lydgateanized version of one of Chaucer's most subtle performances, one stripped of the ironies and complexities of the *Tale*'s appearance in the Canterbury collection and, further, one framed formally by the generic and metrical patterns that make it conform to Lydgate's moral ballad-narratives. But in another sense, it moves beyond the superficial to present a story about surface appearance. Griselda's "array" is a lesson in personal appearance. The lesson that it teaches is the lesson of the manuals of good behavior: to attend to personal dress and appearance, to recognize the virtues of modest demeanor, and to value the moral self beneath the trappings of commercial success or aristocratic "richesse." In these terms, the *Tale*'s emphasis on "sadness" similarly focuses on surface presentation. It concerns the public face put on in private grief, the relation between intention and expression formed now, not as a problem in words but as an issue in self-presentation. It is, in short, as much a feature of "array" as clothes or hair: something one puts on to confront with decorum a potentially judgmental world.

This thematizing of the surface in the revised narratives of Helmingham and HM 140 may extend, as well, to a conception of the narrative authority that stands behind them. What these revisers have done, at the most basic level, is to make the poetry of Chaucer *look like* something else, whether it be the exemplary fables of the courtesy book or the moral tales of Lydgate. They have recast their poetry in what may seem to us mechanical or superficial ways; yet it is precisely that superficiality that is of concern to them. If HM 140 presents, in some sense, poetry for the apprentice, it also offers us poetry by the apprentice. It codifies a kind of literary servitude to the example of Lydgatean authority with which it had begun and to which each of its poems has done homage. HM 140 is a compilation of apprentice works, in that unique poems like the Middle English Life of Job and the "Poem to Apprentices," as well as received texts such as the *Clerk's Tale* have been cast and recast as explicitly derivative works, pendant on Lydgate's model. What is at stake in the revisions of the *Clerk's Tale*, in the end, is not so much the ways in which it has been reshaped to conform to a Lydgatean poetics, though that certainly defines the contours of its narrative and the controlling principles of augmentation and excision that construct its present version. The *Clerk's Tale* has been highly simplified for simple readers *and* for simple writers. It stands here as an example of the kind of writing done by literary amateurs: a writing that announces not its authorial control but its readerly servitude; a writing that may be appreciated as self-consciously homemade, domestic, and familiar.

The condition of "reading like a child" may now extend to the practice of writing like a child. If one potential audience for HM 140 was the young apprentice, then one kind of writer represented in its texts is the apprentice, too, cowed not by the specificities of Chaucerian authority but by the idea of authority itself. As a book controlled by the authorship of Lydgate, HM 140 shapes its poems to the confines of the didactic stanzas he had written. The formal and thematic unity of the collection now extends to an idea of authorship that revels in its anonymity and deliberately erases or unwittingly garbles all its named *auctoritates* to construct a volume of unnamed, apprentice verse.[73]

The notion of apprentice versemaking may help explain not just the function of these manuscripts in the fifteenth century but also their reputation in the twentieth. Helmingham and HM 140 have long been dismissed by editors as "bad" texts, corrupt in their individual readings and damaged in their physical appearance. In contrast to such elaborate productions as the Ellesmere manuscript or such visually unappealing yet editorially controlled compilations as Hengwrt, Helmingham seems little more than makeshift in its assembly. In contrast, too, to the great house anthologies of the mid-fifteenth century, such as the Oxford Group, HM 140 also seems nothing if not personally idiosyncratic. These manuscripts have, to a large degree, been neglected because they tell us little of the contexts of Chaucerian production in the fourteenth century and because their revisions and editions seem to have been made by misunderstanding scribes or dull compilers.

Although I have tried to reconstruct the critical approaches and the personal "readings" embedded in these revisions, I do not wish to claim a greater value than has been assumed for them in establishing Chaucer's own texts. These manuscripts *are* idiosyncratic, personal productions that broadly reflect current tastes but also constitute important witnesses to individual response. Their value lies in how they illustrate a notion of the utilitarian function of Chaucer's poetry in the late fifteenth century. As homemade works they exemplify what it means to make books for, and perhaps *as*, children. They present attempts by individual scribes, compilers, or commissioners to become "writers." The uniqueness of the *Thopas / Melibee* Link in Helmingham, and the singularity of its elisions to the *Pardoner's Tale* and the *Melibee*, illustrate how Chaucer's texts could be recast in ways that augment our appreciation of this manuscript's personal, amateur quality.

The distinctiveness of the constellation of texts in HM 140, moreover, and the uniqueness of its poems on the Job and the apprentices—although representative of currents in late-fifteenth-century bookmaking—illustrate how individuals could respond to the models of Chaucerian and Lydgatean writing and in the process construct interpretations of these authors' works. Neither the Middle English Life of Job nor the "Poem to Apprentices" confronts the literary authority of its models with the directness or the complexity of the more well known Chaucerian impersonators of the century. Nor does either aspire to the verbal competence of even the most self-possessedly dull of those writers. What both accomplish is the domestication of the idioms, forms, and thematic interests of the canon of vernacular verse. They give us poetry so simple and so unprepossessing that we might at first glance simply think it bad. It is bad poetry, by any stretch of the imagination; yet its badness is a function of its purpose and its audience.

Throughout this book, I have attended to the ways in which Chaucer's authority infantilized, diminished, or dulled the self-presentations of those writers who would follow him or of those readers who would bring his works together into compilations of didactic or exemplary value. One consequence of this development had been the effacement of named authorship itself. For a literature concerned with readers rather than writers, for a form of versemaking self-consciously allied with "making" rather than "poetry," the urge to attribute would be subsumed beneath the need to teach. What I suggest is that the anonymous impulse extends to those amateur writers who would write in the wake of Lydgatean imitation— indeed, that it fosters the conception of writing as an amateur pursuit: as something to be done not in the confrontation with the *auctores* but in the communication with the young. Anonymity, apprenticeship, amateurity: All these come together to construct a form of writing that is fundamentally "childish" not just because it is jejune, but because it is unnamed.

Yet in tandem with the various traditions I have traced here was the urge to name the poet and the impulse to ascribe his poems and construct the history behind their making. Lydgate's canon of Chaucer's works had provided one context for these new interests in appellation, as did his preoccupations with detailing the occasions of commission and reception that produced his own texts. In the work of the scribe and bibliophile John Shirley, I find this impulse to name and date. Shirley's headnotes construct, in miniature, the histories of Chaucer's poems and the biography of the poet in ways so apparently precise that most modern critics have taken Shirley's appellations at face value and have willingly believed his pose as personal acquaintance of Lydgate and the first generation of the Chaucer circle. Whether or not Shirley's claims have historical validity, they do have a critical purpose, and it will be the concern of the following chapter to trace out the ideological presuppositions that enable Shirley to construct a Chaucer as a public, lyric, and occasional poet and that have lead modern scholars to accept his attributions in the making of the Chaucer canon.

The Complaints of Adam Scriveyn: John Shirley and the Canonicity of Chaucer's Short Poems

I N T H E six centuries of Chaucer's critical reception, the status of his lyric poetry has invariably seemed in doubt. Alceste's commendation, in the Prologue to the *Legend of Good Women*, of the poet's service in composing many "balades, roundels, [and] vyrelayes" (F 423) for courtly entertainment is tempered, in the *Canterbury Tales' Retraction*, by the self-condemnations of the "many a song and many a leccherous lay" for which Chaucer seeks forgiveness. Although Henry Scogan, in what may be one of the earliest independent attestations of Chaucer's authorship, incorporates the poem *Gentillesse* in his own moral ballad addressed to Henry IV's sons, he qualifies his view of Chaucer's lyric gifts by fixing on the "curious" quality of his "langage" and by presenting the poet, in this context, as a pedagogue for royal children.[1] Lydgate apparently adored the lyric Chaucer, modeling his own political and moral ballads on such poems as *Lak of Stedfastnesse*, *Truth*, and the various envoys to his friends. In terms derived from Alceste's bibliography, he too commends his master for the making of

> ful many a fressh dite,
> Compleyntis, baladis roundelis, virelaies
> Ful delectable to heryn and to see.
> *(Fall of Princes*, I.352–54)

As if to fill in the outlines of this making, many manuscript anthologists throughout the fifteenth century transmitted a host of political and amorous short poems under Chaucer's name or in the ambience of his authority.[2] Yet, for all the popularity of such verse, Chaucer's early printers seemed somewhat ambivalent about its publication. Caxton printed hardly any of the lyric pieces, and de Worde and Pynson appear to have confined themselves to publishing the major, narrative works of the poet (though the latter did include a collection of amatory and proverbial verses in a 1526 publication centered on the *House of Fame*).[3] With William Thynne's editions of the poet (1532, 1542), however, the collection of short poems grew to nearly thirty pieces, and in later sixteenth-century editions of John Stowe (1561) and Thomas Speght (1598) the editorial impulse was to expand the range of works that could be printed under Chaucer's name. Thynne's phrasing in his Preface, touting his publication of the "dyuers other [works] neuer tyll nowe imprinted," exemplifies the omnivorous character of sixteenth-century Chaucerian editing.[4]

If it had been the task of late-medieval and Renaissance compilers to inflate the canon of Chaucer's work, it soon became the purpose of the post-Romantic critics to deflate it. The concern with the originary and the unique, the philological perspective that selected the few genuine productions out of many derivative ones—and that, in turn, fostered the development of stemmatic textual criticism, with its primacy of the authorial over the scribal, the *lectio difficilior* over the commonplace—informed late-nineteenth-century attitudes toward the making of the Chaucer canon.[5] The publications of the Early English Text Society, the project of the *Oxford English Dictionary*, and the establishment of the Chaucer Society all fostered that positivistic historicism that, in the editing of Chaucer's work, found its apogee in Skeat's *Oxford Chaucer*.[6] In his *Chaucerian and Other Pieces*, published as the final volume of his edition, and his essay *The Chaucer Canon*, Skeat established both the formal and historical parameters for defining a work as Chaucer's, parameters still circumscribing the editions of F. N. Robinson and the recent *Riverside Chaucer*.[7]

The remaining twenty-odd pieces, now classed generically as the "Short Poems," some identified as the "Boethian Ballads," represent a different side of Chaucer than the one imagined by the readers of the *Troilus* or the *Canterbury Tales*. These poems frequently are taken to present the poet in his public mode. As works commissioned by political expedience or personal request, they may be stripped of the familiar ironies and distancings that characterize the personae of the longer narratives. They have been used, variously, to gloss the sentiments of Chaucer's fictional narrators or to illuminate the byways of his professional life. Chaucer the courtier poet, Chaucer the king's servant, Chaucer the friend—all these supposedly historical persons can be, and have been, extracted from the corpus of the short poems. For most modern critics, they serve not so much as subjects of literary study as the objects of historical and biographical speculation. They are, perhaps, the most historicizable of Chaucer's writings; yet, as a consequence, they are the least valued. They stand apart from the appreciation of a Chaucer as a poet of ideas and a topographer of character developed by twentieth-century criticism. For a writer who has come to be enjoyed for his aspirations to be one of the *poetae*, these ballads and verse epistles serve, almost embarrassingly, to recall his job as "maker." They are to be explained, if not explained away, as the remaining legacy of Chaucer as he had to be, not as he wished to become.[8]

The critical history of Chaucer as a lyric poet is intimately linked to the textual history of the poems themselves. The body of this poetry does not come with the assurances of attribution, internal or external, that accompany the *Canterbury Tales*, the *Troilus*, and the longer dream poems. What we know of their authorship derives from the annotations of fifteenth-century scribes and compilers who transmitted them. They stand side by side with works variously attributed to Lydgate, Hoccleve, Clanvowe, Richard Roos, and other named and unnamed late-medieval poetasters. Within the contexts of these manuscript productions, the ascription of a poem to Chaucer and the compilation of a text itself were often due to circumstances more commercial or political than literary. Some poems carry Chaucer's authorship simply to make a manuscript more attractive to a potential buyer. Some poems also carry his name because he was one of the few named authors in the vernacular.

But many of these shorter poems appear as Chaucer's because of the efforts of one productive, highly influential scribe and bibliophile. It is to John Shirley that we owe attributions of a half dozen of Chaucer's shorter poems and to Shirley that we owe the information on the circumstances of the composition of these and many others.[9] In his elaborate headnotes to the poems in his manuscripts, and in those that derive from his texts or are modeled on his scribal example, modern scholars have found evidence of Chaucer's authorship in poems ranging from the private *Adam Scriveyn* to the public *Lak of Stedfastnesse*, from the coded courtly allegories of the *Complaints* of *Mars* and *Venus* to the amorous obscurities of *Womanly Noblesse*.[10] Some scholars have lauded Shirley as a reliable witness to Chaucerian and Lydgatean making; others have questioned his memory (he was over eighty when some of his manuscripts were written) and his motives (he may have been a commercial bookseller). Whatever we may think of his accomplishments or of the motives of those modern scholars who assess them, the fact remains that in the work of Shirley and the critical debates it spawns we find not just the details but the controlling idea of a lyric, public Chaucer. What is invented in the fifteenth century and maintained in the twentieth is the conception of what Paul Strohm has called a "social Chaucer": a poet of occasion and request, a writer of coterie verse not for the distant future of imagined readers but for the present known recipients of court and city.[11]

By claiming that this Chaucer is "invented," I do not, of course, deny that he did function as a social poet for much of his life; nor, by querying the motivations of both medieval and modern editors, do I wish to revise radically the canon of his shorter verse. What interests me here is the larger, critical concept of attribution and the aesthetic, if not ideological, motives for maintaining certain works as Chaucer's. Shirley's attributions, together with the long biographical narratives that head his copies of Chaucer's and Lydgate's work in his manuscripts, may be construed as acts of canonization. They offer up a special kind of poetry for special readers, as they maintain the imaginations of a Lydgatean nostalgia for an earlier time. Shirley's Chaucer is both a laureate and an aureate poet: an advisor to kings and a master of rhetorical design. He is an author of a near-ency-clopaedic scope, an author whose productions range from philosophical prose translation through political verse, from private devotions to public counsel. Sustaining the encomiastic rhetoric of Lydgate and perhaps con-tributing to its formation as well, Shirley helps foster the notion of a poet of all things and kinds; yet, also in keeping with the Lydgatean strategies of self-presentation, he grounds Chaucer's works in the specifics of their composition. Much as Lydgate himself would occupy his lines with chronicles of patronage, commission, and response, so Shirley in his head-notes places Chaucer's poetry in the biographical contexts of production. Shirley's annotations function in the manner of Lydgate's self-narratives, for both seek to personalize and historicize the act of writing and reveal the living maker behind the poet.

Throughout this book, I have used Shirley piecemeal as a source for much of the late-medieval critical vocabulary at work in the Lydgatean traditions of reading and writing. In this chapter I hope to reassess more systematically Shirley's contribution to the making of the Chaucer canon from a variety of historical and theoretical perspectives. Central to my ar-gument has been the claim that Chaucer's later readers modeled them-selves on the various subjected figures deployed in his fictions of recep-tion and retelling. The abused Clerk, the boyish Squire, or the childlike Chaucer himself became representatives of the inscribed or implied read-ers for the poetry, and fifteenth-century writers of various sorts appropri-ated their voices or stances to articulate relations to a Chaucer who was father, master, or laureate poet. In the case of Shirley, I find that model in the figures of those errant scribes who, at the close of *Troilus and Criseyde* and in *Adam Scriveyn*, are charged with copying his texts.

"So prey I God that non myswrite the, / Ne the mysmetre for defaute of tonge" (*TC* V.1795–96), Chaucer had appealed, and for generations *Adam Scriveyn* has been appreciated as the autobiographical complement to these fictive fears of the *Troilus* narrator. In these two moments, modern critics have found a concern on a par with Petrarch's recorded complaints to his scribes and *topos* of authorial complaint that spans literature in man-uscript culture from Martial to Jan Gerson.[12] Some have searched for a real, fourteenth-century Adam to fit these laments, while others have found in the stanza to the scribe an allegorical *clericus Adam* or a type of first man condemned by a jealous writing God.[13] What John Shirley had found, however, was the literary figuration of his own condition: that of the scribe whose mutilating labors are rewarded only with a curse. Shirley presents himself as this laboring Adam to Chaucer's near-divine authority, as someone who had transcribed the whole of the *Boece* and who had, throughout his life, copied the bits and pieces of the *Troilus* as they struck his fancy.[14]

Shirley may have responded to many familiar things in *Adam Scriveyn*; but he just might have created them, as well. For this brief poem survives only in his hand, in a unique manuscript appearance toward the end of his compilation, now Trinity College Cambridge MS R.3.20, where he titles it, "Chauciers wordes . a Geffrey vn to Adame his owen scryveyne." The poem stands at the close of a series of short verse epistles, dialogues, and bits of moralizing all centering on the relationship of writing to desire and knowledge. Shirley's inclusion of the *Adam Scriveyn* stanza at this point in his collection has both a thematic and dramatic purpose, functioning as a reflection on the author/scribe relationship akin to that which closes *Troilus and Criseyde*. But *Adam Scriveyn* also has what might be thought of as a personal, if not a psychological, purpose in Shirley's larger enterprise. It testifies to his controlling fascination with authority both literary and political, while at the same time giving voice to his tastes for the envoyistic, the epistolary, and the romance narrative of writing itself.

Adam Scriveyn may serve as a touchstone for recovering those processes by which Shirley preserves, attributes, and hence canonizes Chaucer's shorter poetry. And yet the canonicity of *Adam Scriveyn*, or for that matter of any of the individual short poems published now as Chaucer's, does not inhere in any single attribute of form or meter or in any recoverable fact of composition. Chaucer's poems are Chaucer's because they fit into a critically constructed notion of just what his poetry was, what features it shared, and how it functioned (and continues to function) in the systems of literary performance, teaching, and study. The canonicity of Chaucer's shorter poems may be thought of as a problem in the history of their transmission. Determining whether or not a poem is by Chaucer requires an attention to the climates of fifteenth-century manuscript making and an appreciation of how certain of his poems, much like Lydgate's, could become part of daily educated speech and writing: memorized texts deployed as maxims to illuminate a moral problem or to buttress a personal claim. It requires, too, attentions to the popularity of certain forms and the sense that the construction of the authentically Chaucerian proceeds through a generic consciousness among fifteenth-century readers.

Chaucer's reception, as I have implied throughout this book, is the reception not just of individual poems but of types and tropes, of stances and personae. The dynamic between poet and patron thematized in Lydgate's verse is, to a certain extent, projected back onto Chaucer's models. Imagining Chaucer as a patronized writer entails finding a poetry that can be located at the nexus of political request and authorial response. It provokes the creation of a canon of verse that is not just political in outline, content, or contexts but that articulates relations of subjection and authority between the patron and the poet. The canon of Chaucer's shorter poetry is constructed along these generic and rhetorical lines established by Lydgate and Shirley. It is a poetry of bill and complaint, a poetry that enacts the fiction of submission whereby writers present documents to readers in the hope of praise, approval, or correction. The Chaucer found on Shirley's pages, like the Chaucer largely found in Lydgate's lines, is a poet of political approval and personal request—in short, an epistolary Chaucer, one whose shorter ballads and longer courtly poems present letters from the writer and, consequently, offer up that writer as a lover, servant, and a scribe.

This chapter sets out to define the contours of this amatory and epistolary Chaucer for the fifteenth century. Its telos will be *Adam Scriveyn* and the many scribal, generic, and scholarly contexts that have framed this little poem as the epitome of authorial self-reflection. But to clarify those contexts, it is necessary to expose the habits of the scribe, the reader, and the editor in fifteenth- and sixteenth-century Chaucerian production. The appellative history of Chaucer's *Lak of Stedfastnesse* exemplifies how political and social interests control the attribution of his verse. In a similar manner, the manuscript traditions of the poems now known as the *Complaint Unto Pity* and the *Complaint to a Lady* illustrate the workings of a fifteenth-century readership seeking to imagine Chaucer as a laureate envoyist to sovereigns and an aureate belletrist to lovers. In each of these cases, John Shirley is the nexus of scribal production and critical reception, the place where we may understand how late-medieval readers and modern scholars construe the canon of Chaucer's shorter poetry and judge its literary merit.

I

Central to the modern scholarly perception of Shirley's reliability is the presumption of his personal familiarity with the authors he transcribes.[15] Historical research paints him as a figure intimately conversant with the literary giants of the late fourteenth and early fifteenth centuries, and his bizarre personal marginalia to his manuscripts of Chaucer and Lydgate have led many to imagine him sustaining some internal dialogue with his dead or distant friends. In lieu of such speculation are the recoverable literary tastes and conceptions of authorship that govern much of the poetic response of Shirley's day. As Julia Boffey has convincingly shown, the attributions of individual poems, both by Shirley and others, may hinge on a variety of circumstances unrelated to the text's presumed original creation.

> The mention of an author's name in a heading or colophon must denote some attempt on the part of the manuscript-compiler to "place" the piece with which it is associated, and to supply background or context.[16]

In Shirley's case in particular, "the interest of the rubrics to the lyrics . . . rivals that of the poems themselves," and Shirley may have, on occasion, "cooked up the attributions himself as a means of enhancing the prestigious literary-aristocratic connections of his anthology."[17] The apparent deviations from accepted manuscript readings, and the insistent desire to attribute literary works that fall under Shirley's pen, may thus find their motivations less in the transcriptions of autobiography than in the structures of a critical perspective. In turn, the preservation of the canon of Chaucer's poetry, and of the shorter poems in particular, may be more properly construed as a *creation* of that canon.

At the heart of Shirley's enterprise is the attribution of literary texts and his own, insistent separation of his actions as a "writer" from the status of his "author." Authors, to Shirley, are to be praised and thanked, for theirs is the responsibility for whatever pleasure or instruction their works provide. The naming of the author is of prime importance to the scribal act, for each work must be matched with an identifiable creator. Shirley's insistence on attribution is so great that, when he is unable to match work and man, it causes him no small consternation, as when he states in the Kalendar that opens BL MS Add. 16165:[18]

> Regula sacerdotalis men clepen hit
> God helpe me so as þat I not
> Who first hit made ne hit wrot
> þer fore noon Auctour I allegge.
>
> (66–69)

For Shirley, works have authors and authors have names, and it is the task of the compiler to attribute ("allegge") texts to authors. There is a difference, too, as he implies here, between a work whose title is the gift of common consent ("men clepen hit") and one whose name is an authorial bequest. What we might call a cult of authorship informs the nature of the blame and praise that will redound to scribe or writer. As Shirley puts it later in his other Kalendar, now preserved in Stowe's transcription in BL MS Add. 29729:[19]

I aske of you no other dett
bot wher defaute is or y^e blame
y^t it nenpayr y^e auctors name.

$$(66–68)$$

Unlike the Chaucerian narrators on whom this plea is modeled, Shirley does not appeal to narrative fidelity or fictional response. He himself is to be blamed for any errors of transmission: errors "of y^e scripture / of y^e meter or ortagrafyure" which he vouchsafes his reader "to correcte" (MS Add.29729, lines 69–71). All of these are scribal rather than authorial responsibilities, and the notion of correction here differs markedly from the pleas that close the *Troilus* or the Prologue to the *Parson's Tale*. In the former, Gower and Strode are not textual but moral and philosophical critics, and their presumed acts of "correccioun" involve a realigning of the poem's narrative or intellectual details within a predetermined interpretive agenda. In the latter, it is the Parson who protests that he is not "textuell," submitting his tale to "correccioun" by clerks more familiar with the theological sources and written commentaries that form the basis of his sermon. In contrast to these more problematic notions of correction, Shirley limits himself to scribal variation: "writing," as such, measured against the expectations of professional scriptorial practice.

Part of the problem, therefore, in assessing Shirley's work is the critical desire to trust his attributions coupled with the editorial desire to dismiss his incorrect transcriptions. Perhaps the best place to begin the exploration of this paradox is in the appellative history of *Lak of Stedfastnesse*.[20] Almost from its first appearance in manuscript, this poem became one of Chaucer's most popular lyrics. It survives in fifteen manuscript copies, second only to *Truth* in frequency of transcription. Like *Truth*, its blend of the proverbial and the political appealed to the taste for a public and advisory Chaucer that was shaped by the pervasive Boethianism of philosophically minded readers and by the fascination with his courtiership by his socially attuned audience.[21] Like certain passages from *Troilus and Criseyde* and the *Canterbury Tales*, the poem came to form part of the verbal inheritance of late-medieval English literary culture. Some of its transcriptions clearly indicate that it was written down from memory; one shows how certain lines were singled out for aphoristic quotation; for the scribe of another manuscript, it was clearly so well liked or apposite to the collection that its Envoy was copied twice in different places.[22] For all its medieval popularity and for all its modern scholarly acceptance, the poem bears Chaucer's name in only one manuscript, the Shirley-derived BL MS Harley 7333. Shirley had attributed it in his own copy, now Trinity College Cambridge MS R.3.20, to "oure laureal poet of Albyoun"; and while the Cotton Otho text may have included in the title the author's name " . . . Poetecall Chaucyer a Gaufrede," this appellation survives only in the eighteenth-century copy of the manuscript burned in the Cotton Library fire.[23]

Lak of Stedfastnesse may have a recoverable, historical meaning in the contexts of late-fourteenth-century literary politics.[24] But it also has a recoverable meaning in its fifteenth-century manuscript environments, one that may vary in accordance with the purposes of those manuscripts themselves. Shirley and his successor situate the making of *Lak of Stedfastnesse* in specific moments of Chaucer's biography and English history. In Harley 7333, it appears with the following introduction:

> This balade made Geffrey Chaunciers the Laureall Poete Of Albion and sent it to his souerain lorde Kynge Richarde the secounde þane being / in his Castell / of Windesore.
>
> (fol.147b)

Shirley's own TCC R.3.20 introduces it as follows:

> Balade Royal made by · oure laureal poete of Albyoun · in hees laste yeeres.
>
> (p. 356)

Though superficially similar, these headings differ markedly in their conception of the poem's composition and its literary meaning, and these differences reflect the larger purposes of the anthologies in which they appear. Harley 7333 is a public text. It offers a capsule library of canonical vernacular poetry for a religious community (the house of Austin canons at Leicester).[25] In contrast with the convenient quarto size of Trinity, Harley is a large folio volume; unlike the paper quirings of the former, the latter is on vellum; while Trinity is the sustained work of a single writer, Harley is a communal product of many scribes, working over several decades. Although Harley does contain a range of short poetry, its bulk is made up of long documents of political instruction and narrative complexity: Hoccleve's *Regiment of Princes*, Chaucer's *Canterbury Tales*, the English *Brut*, the *Gesta Romanorum* in an English prose translation, and such basic didactic texts as Burgh's *Cato* and Lydgate's history of the English kings.

Harley 7333 might well be thought of as a book of secular instruction for the canons who commissioned it, a book designed to tell as much about the outside world of courtly politics and royal diplomacy as about the inner world of the literary imagination and moral behavior. Though written over many years by many hands, the manuscript betrays the evidence of institutional control—both in its editings of texts and its identifying marginalia—and such control has been identified with the political and literary interests of the Austin canons of the third quarter of the fifteenth century. Manly and Rickert find this evidence so secure that its implications, they claim, "need not be argued" (I:216); and, although their primary concern is identifying the textual traditions of the manuscript, they also note that Leicester at this time had vital contacts with the London book trade and the court.

> During the last years of Henry VI's reign—the very years in which [Harley 7333] seems to have been begun—London, in a sense, went to Leicester. It was several times the place of meeting for Parliament and the Council, and Henry VI spent Christmas in 1459–60 in the Abbey.
>
>   (I:216)

At least two of its identifiable scribes, William Stoughton and John Peny, had access to royal power such that the day after Henry VII's victory at Bosworth Field in 1485, they could approach him in Leicester "to ask leave to elect a new abbot" (M-R I:215).

The political connections and instructional interests shared by the makers and the readers of Harley 7333 would have informed their interests in the manuscript's elaborate headnotes. Though they may be Shirlean in origin or inspiration (as their length, detail, and occasional idiosyncratic spellings suggest), they differ both in tone and focus from those of the TCC R.3.20 manuscript. Harley's headnote to *Lak of Stedfastnesse* is fully in keeping with the extended annotations that explain many of its other poems' origins in primarily political terms. Its account of the *Complaint to His Purse* ("A supplication to King Richard by Chaucier"), the remarks on the unattributed *Complaint D'Amours* ("an amourouse complainte made at wyndesore in the laste May tofore November"), the comments on the lineage of Henry VI and the patronage of Warwick that introduce the Lydgate selections, and the detailed instructions that preface the *Canterbury Tales*—all these illustrate the nature of a manuscript prepared for an audience interested in the profiles of patronage, the effects of reading, and the political consequences of authorship. Indeed, these headnotes say as much about these poems and their authors as about the kinds of readers they inscribe.[26]

The well-known headnote to the *Canterbury Tales* is representative of Harley 7333's attempt to recover a historical audience for Chaucer's poetry.[27] It speaks to those "noble and worthi pryncis and princesse, oþer estatis or degrees" who will receive instruction and delight from Chaucer's work. But this is not a manuscript made for the aristocracy; its readers would not have been those "gentile of birthe or of condicions"; and its appellation of Chaucer as the "laureal and moste famous poete" would have little impact on an audience ensconced in a religious house. The purpose of this kind of diction and of these headnotes in general was to delineate the royal and courtly audiences for Chaucer's work. It is not so much that these headnotes address the manuscript's actual readers in any hortatory way. Rather, they contribute to those readers' imaginations of who would have read the poetry: aristocrats around the *Canterbury Tales*, or, as in the example of the headnote to its *Anelida and Arcite*, the "lordis and ladyes" who would find in Anelida an example of "oon of þe trewest gentilwomen that bere lyf" (fol.134r). These headnotes are an education in the kind of poetry that Chaucer wrote and in the kind of audience for whom he wrote it. In keeping with its critical construction of a courtly, "laureate" poet, Harley 7333 appends an extra stanza to the *Parlement of Foules*.

> Maister geffrey Chauucers þat now lith graue
> þe noble Rethor poete . of grete bretayne
> þat worthi . was the laurer to haue
> Of poyetry . And þe palme atain
> þat furst made to still & to rain
> þe gold dew Dropes . of speche in eloquence
> In english tonge / þorow his excellens.[28]

These lines, adapted from Lydgate's *Lyfe of Oure Lady*, differ widely in their critical importance from their composition a half century before. In Lydgate's poem, they initiate the making of a Chaucer laureate and aureate, a poet dead and buried like the Petrarch after whose Clerkly praise these phrases are constructed. But for Harley 7333, these lines would only reaffirm the link between the two poets. The same scribe (Manly and Rickert's scribe 1) wrote the portions of the manuscript that include the *Clerk's Tale*, the *Parlement of Foules*, and *Lak of Stedfastnesse*;[29] under his hand, these Lydgatean lines shift from propagandizing in the century's first decades to educating readers in its last. They remind the reader (or at the very least remind the scribe) of the "laureal" embellishings of the *Canterbury Tales* headnote a hundred folios before. Taken together, the conclusion to the *Parlement* and the introduction to the *Tales* inform the reader of the aesthetic and political terms of value for assessing Chaucer's work. Whether the origins of these texts are with Shirley and his manuscripts or Lydgate and his verses, both have been appropriated here to tell stories about poems, rather than identify those poems per se. Their social and educative function differs from their purely informational content; what they do is different from what they say.

In these environments, the appellation of *Lak of Stedfastnesse* to Chaucer in particular, or to his epithetical authority as "laureal poete of Albyoun," tells us something about how Chaucerian authority may be invoked to write out narratives of literary history from personal or institutional perspectives. The headnotes of Harley 7333 define the historical and biographical parameters of English vernacular versemaking in order to establish who Chaucer and his contemporaries were. By contrast, Shirley in R.3.20 can entitle *Lak of Stedfastnesse* as by "oure laureal poete of Albyoun" because *he* knows its author. Chaucer is the "laureal poete" much as Petrarch a half a century before was the *poeta laureatus*. It is enough simply to refer to him by his epithet. But the goal of Harley 7333 is to teach its audience that Chaucer is the "laureal poete," that he wrote for Richard II, and that his poetry was focused at a certain audience. Unlike the later, socially directed prologues and epilogues of Caxton—with their appeals to a "gentle" audience who would be purchasing his books—these headnotes do not seek to flatter their prospective readers by attending to their worthiness. And also unlike Lydgate's effusive praises, the force of these phrases cannot be to humble a religious readership further. What these headnotes do is define the range of vernacular literature *as literature*. They present a canon of named authors together with their most representative, canonical productions.

If Harley 7333 is a public volume, Trinity R.3.20 is a private assembly. Its headnotes seem primarily directed toward the personally circumstantial rather than the nationally historical or the political. This compilation, most likely part of a once-larger anthology Shirley constructed, ranges widely over works by Chaucer, Lydgate, and others and offers everything from French ballads and English lyrics to Latin medical recipes.[30] Though it contains some highly elaborate headnotes, most of its introductions are brief and to the point. Among its non-Chaucerian items, Lydgate's *Gaude Virgo Mater Christi* was composed, Shirley states, "by Daun Iohan þe munke Lydegate by night as he lay in his bedde at Londoun."[31] The bilingual introduction to the French lyrics of the manuscript attribute them to William de la Pole, Duke of Suffolk, made "whyles he was prisonier in ffraunce" (in French, "quant il estoit prysonier en ffraunce").[32] What Julia Boffey calls the "piquant suggestions about the situation in which [these lyrics] were composed" extend to the notes to the poems Shirley calls the *Broche of Thebes* and the *Complaint of Venus*.[33] In these, perhaps the most elaborate and detailed of the headnotes in the manuscript, Shirley provides the background information for discerning these as poems of intrigue—love-allegories grounded in the facts of royal biography.[34] Together with the many other headnotes that attend to the personal lives of the poets, they give a meaning to their poems as articulations of a personal condition. They provide the reader of the manuscript with information for assessing them as pieces of a verse biography. Though they convey the contexts of the poem's patronage, these headnotes privilege the personal over the political. Though its Envoy is headed "Lenvoye to kyng Richard," *Lak of Stedfastnesse* appears in Trinity first and foremost as a poem of Chaucer's old age, a poem written "in hees laste yeeres." As with his transcript of the poet's *Truth* in the same manuscript—titled "Balade þat Chaucier made on his deeth bedde"[35]—Shirley's primary concerns are with the places of the poetry in the chronology of his authors' lives. The appellations in his headnotes here thus do not convey information of the sort interpreted by modern editors. They do not name the poems to construct a canon of their poets' works, nor do they necessarily privilege the poet in order to make the volume in itself more worthy to the prospective reader or buyer. Rather, they identify their contents to construct a narrative of personal biography—a narrative into which Shirley has inscribed himself.

In a volume of his translations, copied by a later scribe, Shirley identifies his work as composed "by youre symple subget John Shirley in his laste age"; and twice more, Shirley refers to his "last age" and to his work "in the last dayes of his grete Age."[36] In the Kalendars that prefaced his manuscript assemblies, too, Shirley remarks on his "feblesse," that is, on his feebleness of age. All of these works are datable products of Shirley's last decades: the translations, work of the 1440s; the Kalendars and TCC R.3.20, probably work of the mid-1430s. Shirley was anywhere from sixty-five to eighty when these texts were written, and it has long been assumed that he began his scribal enterprises as an old man. To read the personal in Shirley's volume, therefore, is to find the person thus inscribed; that is, to see how Shirley has projected his own self-consciousness of writing as an aged scribe onto the dating of Chaucer's lyric works. His fascinations with the lives of his authors mirrors his own preoccupations with the circumstances of his life; the attentions to the biographical reflects the autobiographical. Shirley's assemblies in general, and R.3.20 in particular, are personalized collections, not only in their reflections of a scribe's private tastes but in their overall assumptions that the personal includes his authors and himself. Shirley has made himself as much a figure in his texts as his own writers, and his apparent dating of *Truth* and *Lak of Stedfastnesse* makes Chaucer's work, much like his own, the product of his final years.

II

Such prepossessions with the personal are but one of the concerns that control Shirley's manuscript assemblies. His other major focus is generic. Throughout his writings, Shirley evinces an abiding interest in the patterns of romance. Scribal and compilatory tasks present themselves as quests of textual recovery, where the persona of the compiler or even the figure of the book is seen participating in romance-like narrative of loss, journey, discovery, and restoration. In the two Kalendars designed to preface his major collections, Shirley articulates the scribal project as this romance quest, as he claims to restore to convenient and readable form the works of distant and dead authors.

The story of compilation is the story of the journey. As he puts it in the verses that open BL MS Add. 16165, he sought his "copie in many a place" (line 15), and as he phrases it in his other Kalendar, now surviving in the version copied by John Stowe: "In sondry place haue I them soughte /on this hallfe and beyonde yᵉ see" (BL MS Add.29729, lines 18–19). Whether from England or Europe, these texts come together in "Þis litell booke with myn hande" (16165.13), as they are ranged "by ordre" into compilations of both educational and entertaining value. Shirley binds these works together: the "gret" with the "commune," the "right kynde with þe crooked." So, too, his reader is expected to bind fast within the mind the moral lessons recalled from this reading, as the physicality of Shirley's bookmaking becomes the controlling didactic metaphor for Shirley's audience. Finally, when these books have been made, bound, and sent off to a discerning readership, the audience is asked to send them back to Shirley: to correct them where they are in error, or more generally, to appreciate the work that has gone into their collection.

> Right godely looke and ye may seon
> And whane ye haue þis booke ouerloked
> Þe right kynde with þe crooked
> And þe sentence vnderstonden
> With Inne youre mynde hit fast ebounden
> Thankeþe þAuctoures þat þees storyes
> Renoueld haue to youre memoryes
> And þe wryter for his distresse
> Whiche besechiþe youre gentylesse
> Þat ye sende þis booke ageyne
> Hoome to *Shirley* þat is right feyne
> If hit haþe beon to yowe plesaunce
> As in þe Reedyng of þe Romaunce
> And alle þat beon in þis companye
> God sende hem Ioye of hir ladye
> And euery womman of hir loue
> Prey I to god þat sitteþe aboue
>
> (MS Add.16165, lines 88–104)

Shirley's invitation, here and elsewhere in his manuscripts, to read and to return his volumes sustains the controlling imagery of travel and recovery that made them. Texts circulate in Shirley's world, and Shirley himself, as scribe, traveler, and compiler, acts now as a kind of romance hero, reading and recording, setting in order the authors he transcribes. Much like the lover-narrators of the Lydgatean romances, Shirley is an anthologist of the imagination. Acts of travel dovetail with the processes of compilation. The quest for copies, as he puts it, is indeed a kind of romance quest, and the subsequent circulation of those manuscripts invites the reader to participate, as well, in what we might call the romance construction of authorized meaning.

> . . . sendeth this boke to me agayne
> Shirley I meane wch is right feyne
> if ye ther of haue had plesaunce
> as in ye weddinge of ye romance
> than am I glad by god onlyue
> as I were lorde of tonnes fyue
> and so at your commaundement
> It shall bene eft when you list send
> w^t all ye saruice y^t I can
> as he y^t is your oune man
> and all y^t in this company
> ben knight squyer or lady
> or other estat what euer they be
> (MS Add.29729, lines 81–93)

This is the language not of bibliographic but of knightly service. Shirley explicitly likens the reader's pleasure of his texts with the pleasure felt "as in ye weddinge of ye romance," that is, with the same kind of joy felt at the resolution of a romance plot, with its successful return of the hero, his repatriation into the community, and his wedding of the beloved. The rhetoric of lordship and service here aristocratizes the dynamic of scribal work and audience judgment—not necessarily because Shirley was working for commissioning aristocrats, but rather because Shirley constructs an aristocratic romance narrative out of the processes of edition and transcription, reading and response. The books themselves, within this master narrative, also become romance figures of a sort, as their return home completes the cycle of loss, recovery, restoration, and correction that produced them.

Shirley's attentions to the idea of romance production go beyond adherence to the contours of the genre's plot. They center, too, on names and naming. Throughout the various traditions of the medieval romance, authors and narrators present themselves as named performers and preservers of the stories that we read or hear. The tellings of the hero dovetail with the writings of the poet to make of the text itself a kind of quest, a reader's search for the identity of actor, writer, and performer. Patricia Parker, working from the arguments of Frederic Jameson, states that romance "necessitates the projection of an Other, a *project* which comes to an end when that Other reveals his identity or 'name.'"[37] Deferrals and announcements of the name delineate what Parker calls the "process of discovery" behind the affirmations of heroic and authorial identity, and that delineation may embrace the scribal role as well.

In these terms, David Hult has recently assessed the critical intrusiveness of one of the scribes of the *Roman de la Rose*.[38] In the recastings and self-attributions of the late-thirteenth-century scribe Gui de Mori, Hult finds a test case for understanding how writing personae are inserted, fictionalized, and historicized in romance texts. Unlike Shirley, Gui writes himself into the verse of the *Roman*, deleting passages from the original and adding lines of his own, as he states, to make the poem "more accessible and more enjoyable to listen to."[39] But like Shirley, Gui is concerned with narrating his own scribal and editorial engagements: He records how the *Roman* came to his hands; he dates his work with reference to the various transmissions of his texts; and he recognizes the role of his later readers in the correction of his writing. Much like Shirley, Gui stands midway between the slavish praise of his *auctores* and the glib announcements of his own manipulations. Hult finds in these manipulations Gui's "midway position, marking a struggle between scribal passivity and authorial aggressivity."[40] They illustrate the centrality of the scribe in the construction both of authorized texts and authorial identity; and Hult's textual analyses, together with Parker's theoretical reflections, can provide a matrix for assessing what I think of as the romance of Shirley's *Adam Scriveyn*.

Both Gui de Mori and Shirley place themselves within the processes of literary composition by their various, attention-getting acts of naming. Within the atmospheres created by their romance and romance-like narratives, they live as heroes of a sort, as figures on quests textual rather than amorous or moral who have as their goal the teaching and delight of the discerning reader. Shirley's position may not be so much a "struggle between scribal passivity and authorial aggressivity"—though one may well read *Adam Scriveyn* as expressing these anxieties—as it is an attempt to reverse the categories of the author's stance. Throughout the work of Chaucer, Hoccleve, and Lydgate, the poet figures himself as a scribe, recording the events he sees or the emotions that he feels. Though offered up with varying degrees of literary and autobiographical specificity—Chaucer, perhaps, appropriating the stance from Dante, Hoccleve fictionalizing his profession in the office of the Privy Seal, Lydgate reflecting on the sheer physical labor of writing itself—each of these authors would have given Shirley an appreciation of the blurry line between authorial and scribal work. Moreover, in their many poems of amorous servitude, fictive lovers take on scribal stances, offering ballads and complaints self-consciously written down as "bills" or documents for submission. Taken together with the romance patterns of Shirley's textual enterprise, this notion of the lover/scribe contributes to the characteristic epistolary flavor of his invitations for correction. Shirley's manuscripts become, in some sense, letters written to a readership expected to respond by emending the text or commending the writer.

In the TCC R.3.20 manuscript, these generic and narrative concerns control the selection and ordering of texts beginning on page 361 and frame the contexts in which *Adam Scriveyn* was transcribed.[41] Starting with a stanza of personal address, Shirley describes the nature of his volume and the various social and professional contexts that give it meaning.

> Yee þat desyre in herte and haue plesaunce
> Olde storyes in bokis for to rede
> Gode matiers putte hem in remembraunce
> And of oþer ne take ye none hede.
> Besechyng yowe of youre godely hede
> Whane yee þis boke haue over redde and seyne
> To Johan Shirley restore yee it ageyne.[42]

These lines recall the invitations of the Kalendars for Shirley's audience to read, review, and return the book in their hands. They focus on the powers of written documents to foster the "remembraunce" of "Gode matiers" and affirm both the moral and the pleasurable lessons of the "olde storyes in bokis." Shirley's stanzaic address to his reader is immediately followed on the same page by the whetstone stanza of *Troilus and Criseyde* (I.631–37). Headed "Pandare to Trojlus," it sustains the dialogic impulse Shirley brings to the assembly of his texts, while at the same time offering a piece of well-worn maximal advice about the possibility of the inept teaching the great. "Eschuw thow that, for swich thing to the scole is; / Thus often wise men ben war by foolys" (*TC*, I.634–35). Within the allegory of reception Shirley has begun to write, Shirley's own book is the whetstone to the honing of his reader's minds. Stripped of its ironies within the *Troilus*, Pandarus's words here seem to speak for Shirley himself, one of the "foolys" who would teach his readers. After the following proverbial Latin couplet, those readers would encounter Lydgate's *Verbum Caro Factum Est*.[43] Taken in isolation, it is a bluntly doctrinal meditation on the kissing of the tokens of the faith in church. Yet, read in this manuscript context, its attentions to the incisions of texts, the interpretation of signs, and the documentary quality of scripture all catch the eye. "Graue all these sygnes depe in thy memory" (14), it commands, as if to bring together all the idioms of remembrance, texts, and the "kervyng instrument" from Pandarus's speech.

In the immediately following copy of Lydgate's *Complaint for My Lady of Gloucester and Holland* and the *Adam Scriveyn* itself, these various generic and thematic interests coalesce. The *Complaint* clearly had appealed to Shirley for a variety of reasons.[44] Its thinly veiled political narrative of Humphrey, Duke of Gloucester, and his wife spoke to the kinds of fascinations Shirley voiced in the Kalendar that prefaced what may have been the original, large compilation of this manuscript. It exemplifies what he identifies as Lydgate's "ympnes . . . of loue and lawe and of pleyinges / of lordes of ladyes of qwenes of kynges" (BL MS Add.29729, lines 28–30).

But the *Complaint* must also have intrigued Shirley for its presentations of the lover as a writer. Lydgate's visionary preoccupies himself with the problems of transcribing his dream: with taking the pen in hand, remembering the words, and finding cause and audience to compose. Toward the poem's conclusion, Lydgate describes the lover's amorous desire as scriptorial anxiety.

> And so as he coude vnderstande,
>   He gane to do his besy cure,
> Tooke towardes morowe his penne on hande,
>   And thought remembre it by scripture,
>   Þey song lyche to þe Chaunteplure,
> Þe peoples menynge for tacquyte,
> Was cause why þat he did it wryte.
>
>   (92–98)

These are the Shirlean concerns about remembering and writing down; indeed, the poem's argument, like that of so much of the poetry on which it is modeled, is that writing fosters remembrance. As at the close of Chaucer's *Book of the Duchess*, or as at the beginning of the Prologue to the *Legend of Good Women*, the authorized transcription of a vision grants public meaning to private experience. Books are, as Chaucer put it in the latter poem, the keys of remembrance (F 25–26). That Shirley took this maxim to heart is evident from his transcription of his personalized stanza on page 361 of this manuscript and from his interests in this *Complaint* of Lydgate. He copied it again into the manuscript now preserved as Bodleian Library Ashmole 59, even while his own memory of its lines was clearly failing.

Appearing on the heels of such a poem, and after the string of individuated stanzas on books and their makers and readers, "Chauciers wordes . a Geffrey vn to Adame his owen scryveyne" now takes on the status of a miniature drama of writing and remembrance (Figure 4).

> Adam · scryveyne / if euer it þee byfalle
> Boece or Troylus / for to wryten nuwe /
> Vnder þy long lokkes / þowe most haue þe scalle
> But affter my makyng / þowe wryte more truwe
> So offt adaye · I mot þy werk renuwe /
> It to · corect / and eke to rubbe and scrape /
> And al is thorugh · þy necglygence and rape /[45]

The stanza constitutes a dialogue on the construction of texts and the possibilities of their reception. The iterated interest in the "remembrance" fostered by books becomes a blunt condemnation of the scribe's lack of attention, of the mutilations wrought by those incapable of taking, in

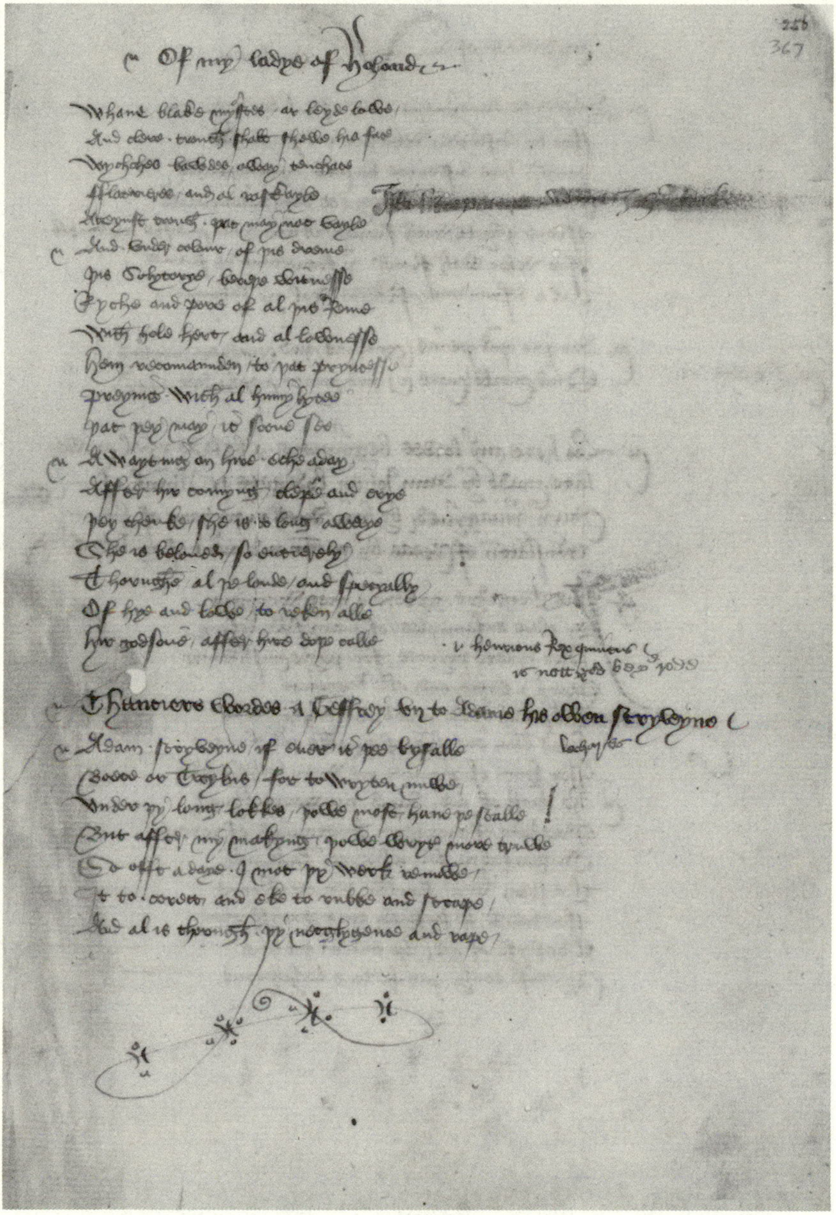

Figure 4. The poem as afterthought: John Shirley's copy of
Chaucer's *Adam Scriveyn*.
Trinity College Cambridge, MS R.3.20, page 367.

Lydgate's words, "penne on hande." And although the figurative whetstone of Pandarus's proverb is "no kerving instrument," the knife in
Chaucer's hand through which he must "rubbe and scrape" imaginatively
sharpens the texts that Adam dulled. Like Pandarus who sends his Troilus
"to the scole," Chaucer disparagingly offers education to a scribe whose
handling of a text is marked by "necglygence and rape." This last line ends
the page on which it stands, and a large flourish fills the space between the
poem and the bottom of the paper. *Adam Scriveyn* is set apart here, though
its moral may have been clearly on his mind when he began a new page
with a proverbial stanza drawn from Lydgate's *Fall of Princes*: "Disceyte
deceyueþe and shal bee deceyued."

The final leaves of R.3.20, with their selections from Lydgate, their list
of members of the Order of the Garter, and their Latin maxims contain
what must have been familiar material to Shirley. Much of it in the same
order appears in his Ashmole 59 collection, though without the *Adam
Scriveyn*, and it seems that R.3.20 at its close becomes more like a personalized commonplace book than a public commission.[46] These closing
leaves become dramatically self-referential, as Shirley transforms the dialogues of his own headnotes into appropriated verse dialogues between
fictive or historical personae. Such invitations from the headnotes as the
appeal to the readers of the *Anelida* to "redeþe and preveþe þe sooþe," or
the appeal to "my frendes" at the beginning of the Lydgate's *Gloriosa Dicta
Sunt* that opens the collection as it now stands, present a colloquy between
the scribe and audience. So, too, his annotations to the texts of Lydgate's
poems preserved here and elsewhere in his work bespeak the intimate fa-
miliarities of scribe and poet. Such marginal remarks as those in R.3.20
("A daun Johan est yvray"), Additional 16165 ("be stille daun Johan · suche
is youre fortune"), and the many personal *notae* transcribed into the copies
of John Stowe (Harley 2251 and Additional 29729) display the colloquies
between the poet and his copyist not in the condemnations of the *Adam
Scriveyn* but as playful jibes between aging friends.[47]

The brief selections that close R.3.20 show themselves as colloquies,
too: "Pandare to Trojlus" heads the whetstone stanza; a selection from the
Fall of Princes appears as Lydgate's work "by the commandement of my
lord of Gloucestre" (p.368); a prayer on page 372 is "made by a devoute
recluse to be sayde anone affter þe levacion of þe sacrament · whane þe
preste is at masse"; and the final selection of the volume is a medical recipe
"proved by þe nobul duc of lancastre Johan for þe maladye of þe stone"
(p.373). Each of these final texts is "voiced" in some sense. Each carries
with it the name of not just the writer but of the speaking authority, and
the references to addressee, to context, to commission, or to personage
make these last entries into bits of conversation among known and knowing individuals. In this environment, the "Johan Shirley" of the stanza on

page 361 is but another speaker offering his volume to a reading audience. And *Adam Scriveyn* stands as more than "Chauciers wordes," but as those of Geffrey, too: the words "a Geffrey vn to Adam" that vent the complaints of writers about love and lore and offer, in the language of advice or condemnation, individuated, named, and voiced reflections on the arts of the scriptorium.

III

The last few pages of TCC R.3.20 are the nexus of the personal and the conventional in Shirley's work. Although products of a literary taste and a professional self-absorbtion, the order and selection of its entries reflects a broader, late-medieval English fashion for the poem of complaint and for the narrative self-presentation of the poet as a lover *and* a scribe.[48] Such poems as the *Troilus* and the verse epistles of Chaucer, the *Letter of Cupid* by Hoccleve, and the range of Lydgate's visions and political ballads brought to the form of the complaint a generic stability. The rhetoric of submission governs both the narrative personae and the formal qualities of much late-fourteenth- and fifteenth-century verse, and Shirley's fascination with that rhetoric—and his various attempts to inscribe himself within it—motivates what I see as his making of another piece of Chaucer's poetry.

In a surviving fragment in his hand, two poems recognized today as separate works are linked together in a narrative conforming to the patterns of the lover/scribe complaints that fill his other manuscripts. The poems known now as *The Complaint Unto Pity* and the *Complaint to a Lady* join in sequence to produce a new piece of Chauceriana.[49] Named and titled, marked with running heads that insist on its authorship and unity, this double poem clearly stands, at least for Shirley, as another version of such braced texts as the *Broche of Thebes* and *Anelida and Arcite*. Yet, unlike those verses, Shirley's version of the Pity poems has evaporated from editions of the poet's works and from the critical discussion of Chaucerian lyric. What I propose, therefore, is to restore this text to its environments of genre and convention: to find its place, if not in the Chaucer canon, then at least in the canonical discourses of its criticism.

Shirley's poem survives on four leaves bound together as fols.80–83 in British Library MS Harley 78, a mid-sixteenth-century assembly possibly made by John Stowe out of a variety of different pages and sections from earlier manuscripts.[50] These leaves are recognizably in Shirley's hand, contain familiar Shirlean extended headnotes and running heads, and are written on a paper stock identifiably the same as that used in his other manuscripts. It has been argued that they, in fact, may have formed part of a once larger assembly composed of what are now Sion College Manuscript Arc.L.40.2/E.44 (Lydgate's translation of de Guilleville's *Pilgrimage of the Life of Man*, with Chaucer's *ABC* inserted and attributed) and TCC R.3.20.[51] Before this manuscript's disassembly in the sixteenth century, a late-fifteenth-century scribe copied out its version of the *Complaint Unto Pity* and the *Complaint to a Lady* into the compilation now preserved as BL MS Add.34360.[52] This later manuscript contains an extra, final stanza to the poem Shirley wrote out, together with a final "Explicit Pity," and a following annotation, in a different hand, "dan Chaucer laurere."

What is preserved in these texts, then, is the seventeen-stanza poem (the *Complaint Unto Pity*), together with the stanzas of what is now called the *Complaint to a Lady* (thirteen stanzas in Harley 78, fourteen in Add.34360). Modern editions speak of the final stanza in the Additional copy as an "added" stanza;[53] yet I think it clear from the condition of the Harley 78 leaves that this final stanza must have appeared on another following leaf of Shirley's text, cut off when the anthology of Harley 78 was made.[54] It is this second poem that is uniquely preserved in these two manuscripts. The *Complaint Unto Pity* appears independently in seven other manuscripts, and although none of these attributes the poem to Chaucer, modern scholars have accepted Shirley's attribution of the poem, while universally printing the succeeding text as a separate poem.

The poem that has been preserved in these Shirlean texts opens with the poet's complaint to a personified Pity, a figure who soon appears as a kind of female lover figure, now dead. He comes to Pity's funeral to offer his complaint, presented as he states, "writen in myn hond, / For to have put to Pite as a bille" (*Pity* 43–44). Lamenting that the intended recipient of this bill now is dead, the narrator presents "Th'effect" of the bille, and the remaining nine stanzas of the poem present the document as a direct address to the Lady. At this point, modern editions of the poem end. In Shirley's copy, the following two stanzas sustain the seven-line rhyme royal of the previous poem. They shift from the direct address to Pity to reflections on the sleeplessness and pain that beset the bereft lover. What follows is a set of metrically diverse stanzas reflecting on the loss of love, on the various allegorical names granted to the lover, and concluding with a set of stanzas, often seen as Chaucer's imitation of Dantean terza rima, mourning the loss and praying for the departed lover.

Shirley's construction conforms to contemporary expectations for the poetry of bill and complaint. As developed out of the epistolary gestures at the close of *Troilus and Criseyde* and the Hocclevean and Lydgatean productions written after their example, such poetry used the devices of submission and request to bring amorous billets into the flow of personal fictions and, as a consequence, to blur the line between the author and the lover, the reader and the addressee. Those little "bills" that pepper Lydgate's poetry—in particular, the *Complaint of a Lover's Life*, the *Temple of*

Glas, and the *Verbum Caro Factum Est* and *Complaint for My Lady of Gloucester and Holland* that Shirley himself had copied—together with the frequent closing envoys, foster what might be considered as the dialectic of the complaint poem. The sequence of first-person narrative, transcription of the bill, and concluding voiced complaint becomes the pattern for the bulk of fifteenth-century amorous poetry: a poetry, as Derek Pearsall describes it, where "[t]here is no movement, no action, only the lover and his mistress forever frozen into ritual gestures of beseeching and disdain."[55]

These frozen gestures have been long sought, too, in the most courtly of Chaucer's own works, notably the *Complaints* of *Mars* and *Venus* and *Anelida and Arcite*. Shirley himself had recognized their origins and popularity in the displays of play and courtiership after French literary models, and his copies of these poems, I believe, reflect the same generic and dramatic preoccupations as does his construction of the double poem on Pity. For *Anelida and Arcite*, it seems clear that the two constituent sections had circulated as separate poems in the fifteenth century, one known as the "Complaint" of Anelida, the other as the "Ballad." Recent scholarship has shown that Shirley's copies of the freestanding "Ballad" and "Complaint" sections indicate that he considered them two separate poems, both not necessarily by Chaucer.[56] It also appears that, in the course of the fifteenth century, a variety of scribes experimented with ways of ordering and joining them to make a poem that conformed to certain expectations of Chaucerian authorship and literary form. The order of the stanzas accepted by modern editions is the one that seems to have been shaken out, as it were, by the late fifteenth century in the Shirley-derived text of Harley 7333. There, *Anelida and Arcite* presents a bill framed in a ballad narrative. The complaint section explicitly appears as a written text, as the narrator of the poem announces:

> And of her owne hond she gan hit write,
> And sente hit to her Theban knyght, Arcite.
>
> (209–10)

The final stanza of the poem, the start of a truncated continuation of the this text that she "Hath of her hand ywriten" (352) and moves us back into the narrative form of the first section. The structure of *Anelida and Arcite* that seems most "Chaucerian" to modern editors thus may have been the one that seemed to work best for the later fifteenth century: a poem that, however fragmentary it appears, roughly conforms to the contours of complaint poetry.

The two poems known now as the *Complaint of Mars* and the *Complaint of Venus* are paired together in six fifteenth-century manuscripts. Although there is, as Julia Boffey notes, "nothing in the text of either poem [that] suggests it should be linked with the other," it remains clear that for many readers of the century these two texts seemed almost naturally to make up a familiar narrative/complaint structure.[57] Boffey characterizes this juxta-position, as it appears in the Bodleian MS Fairfax 16, as producing "a for-mal complaint whose function as 'speech' within a framing story gives it more in common with Troilus's songs and complaints, and turns it into an intercalated lyric."[58] But, as I have suggested throughout my discussion, the model for this genre is not "speech" but "text." What is intercalated is the document of the complaint; the literary template is not the lyric but the epistolary Troilus. John Shirley may have been responsible for the original conflation of the poems, and Boffey reports F. N. Robinson's original suggestion that Shirley's biographical headnotes connected them into a broad, topical allegory of late-fourteenth-century courtly life.[59] Shirley's text of the poems in his TCC R.3.20 manuscript does, in essence, do that; but it also affirms what I am considering as the generic qualities of the two texts. He writes out first the *Complaint of Mars*, which he calls "Þallyaunce betwene Mars and Venus" (p.130) and which he concludes with the note, "Þus eondethe here þis *complaint* . . ." (p.139). Then he adds the *Complaint of Venus*, headed as "A *balade* translated out of frenshe . . ." (p.139), and that too concludes, "hit is sayde þat graunsomme made þis last *balade* . . ." (p.142; all emphases mine).

Shirley distinguishes between "complaint" and "balade," the former re-ferring to the consciously presented written bill within the poem, the latter referring to the narrative account of the lover's condition. His headnotes to the *Anelida*, in its various forms, similarly distinguish between "com-plaint" and "ballad" sections, and when we return to the Pity poems of Harley 78, it becomes clear that these two terms define two parts of a sin-gle poem, rather than two different works. Shirley's headnote introduces the poem as follows:

> And nowe here filowing begynneþe a complaint of pitee by Geffrey Chaucier þe aureat poete þat euer was fonde in oure vulgare to fore hees dayes.
>
> (fol.80r)

In his running heads, however, he refers to the poem as a "ballad": fol.80v–81r, "Balade of piete / By Chaucier"; fols. 81v–82r, "Þe balade / Of pitee"; fols 82v–83r, "Þe balade of pitee / By Chauciers"; fol.83v, "Þe balade of pitee." And in the text of the poem itself, Shirley makes a large cross in the margin and draws a line across the page separating stanzas 17 and 18 of the poem. This mark and line, thus, do not signal what Shirley thought to be two separate poems of Chaucerian authorship but rather demarcate the break between the "complaint" and the "ballade" sections of one longer work. The differences in terminology between headnote and running heads similarly differentiate the "complaint" and the "ballad" sections of a single work. That the scribe who copied Shirley's text into BL Add.34360 concluded it with "Explicit Pity" and that another reader added the "dan Chaucer laurere" affirms the late-fifteenth-century response to this text as a single poem of assumed Chaucerian authorship.

IV

That Shirley and at least two later fifteenth-century readers thought that this poetry was by Chaucer and considered it as one long poem need not, of course, persuade us that we do as well. Not even John Stowe, in most things a slave to Shirley's editorial authority, printed both together. In his *Chaucer's Works* of 1561, he published the second of the poems with the following heading: "These verses next folowing were compiled by Geffray Chauser and in the writen copies foloweth at the end of the complainte of petee" (sig.Qqq, fols.1r–1v). As Stowe's remark makes clear, the textual tradition of a separately circulating *Complaint Unto Pity* challenges the integrity of the collocation Shirley had created. Modern critics, too, are quick to affirm the separation of the two texts. Compared with the stanzaic regularities of the *Complaint Unto Pity*, the metrical oddities of the *Complaint to a Lady* distinguish it as a distinct work, in the words of one critic, "a series of unfinished metrical innovations, showing Chaucer experimenting and practicing his art."[60] And though John Norton-Smith acknowledges the "verbal polish" of the poem, he notes that "there is little literary evidence in terms of structure, argumentation and imagery to support Chaucerian authenticity."[61]

It is this question of "Chaucerian authenticity" that motivates considerations of the canonicity of Chaucer's shorter poetry, and in the case of these two *Complaints*, that generates their literary valuation as well. On the one hand, the very regularities of *Pity* are believed to mark it as an early work. According to the *Riverside Chaucer*, "it is artificial and therefore must have been written when Chaucer was still learning his craft."[62] On the other hand, the *irregularities* of *Lady* brand it as a product of experiment and practice: a text tried out, revised, and possibly rejected by an author capable of writing poetry like *Troilus and Criseyde*. Familiar notions of authorial development presuppose that the experimental and conventional coexist within the province of the "early work." Indeed, it is the fact of such a coexistence that defines, for biographically oriented criticism, what is "early." For Chaucer studies, the progression of the author's work moves inexorably from the lyric to the narrative, from the topical to the timeless, from the conventional to the original.[63] One only need turn to Chaucer's contemporary, Gower, to see the antiquity of this view.

> And gret wel Chaucer whan ye mete,
> As mi disciple and mi poete:
> For in the floures of his youthe
> In sondri wise, as he wel couthe,
> Of Ditees and of songes glade,
> The whiche he for mi sake made,
> The lond fulfild is overal.
>
> (*CA*, VIII.*2941–47)[64]

The "Ditees" are the works of the "disciple," not the master, works of his "youthe" rather than of what Gower would call, several lines later, "hise daies olde" (VIII.*2950). They are products made for someone's "sake," that is, works of commission or assignment and designed to please. What I would argue, therefore, is not just that Chaucer's lyrics but the *idea* of a lyric Chaucer is inexorably linked to biographical approaches to the work. What makes these poems part of the canon, what makes it possible to praise, transcribe, print, and discuss them is their "place," the locus for their writing and reception in the personal development and critical appreciation of the poet.

I began this chapter by considering the nature of that critical appreciation, and in turn by seeking to continue this book's interest in the status of Chaucer's work as "literature." What has been called "institutional construction" of that literature and of the canons that contribute to it goes on in the processes of transmitting and reading Chaucer's poetry.[65] Stanley Fish defines this issue with characteristic flair in the first pages of his influential *Is There a Text in this Class?*

> Literature . . . is a conventional category. What will, at any time, be recognized as literature is a function of a communal decision as to what will count as literature. All texts have the potential of so counting, in that it is possible to regard any stretch of language in such a way that it will display those properties presently understood to be literary. In other words it is not that literature exhibits certain formal properties that compel a certain kind of attention; rather, paying a certain kind of attention (as defined by what literature is understood to be) results in the emergence into noticeability of the properties we know in advance to be literary. The conclusion is that while literature is still a category, it is an open category, not definable by fictionality, or by a predominance of tropes and figures, but simply by what we decide to put into it. And the conclusion to that conclusion is that it is the reader who "makes" literature.[66]

What readers such as Lydgate, Shirley, and their various contemporaries recognized "as literature" were forms of writing that conformed to certain narrative, generic, or thematic interests. What they constructed as Chaucer's was thus predicated on how Chaucer's writing authorized those interests, both in the sense that he wrote in these forms himself and in the sense that he sanctioned them, made them authoritative forms for writing poetry. The Chaucer fostered by this "communal decision" is, in his lyric modes, an epistolarist of the social and the amatory. *Truth, Steadfastnesse,* and *Gentillesse*—the triad of Chaucer's public poems often linked together in their manuscripts—present a laureate envoyist to kings and princes: a writer of letters of specific occasion and to specific addressees. Such poems as those known now as the *Envoy to Bukton* and the *Envoy to Scogan*, and the unique fifth stanza to Vache in the Additional Manuscript of *Truth*, appear canonical to modern editors and medieval scribes in that they fill in the details of this epistolary Chaucer. They exemplify the kind of poetry that fifteenth-century writers were writing and fifteenth-century readers were reading. They also provide something of a political foil for the Chaucer of philosophical reflection and psychological insight constructed by the various traditions of twentieth-century criticism. What links them all together, beyond their metrical similarities, Boethian materia, and courtly context, is their self-conscious quality as documents: as letters, bills, submissions, or accounts. With the exception of *The Former Age* and *An ABC*—which medieval scribes recognized as versified parts of longer prose works[67]—virtually all the works currently accepted as Chaucer's "Short Poems," together with *Anelida and Arcite*, present themselves as independent or embedded letters to a reader. They offer up the poet and his lovers in the personae of scribes, and Shirley formed his own professional persona and controlled his selection of Chaucer's texts out of these scribal fictions and their sustained imitation in the writings of the fifteenth century.

For John Shirley, then, the canonicity of *Adam Scriveyn* lies in its participation in a system of transmission—indeed, the preoccupations of the poem are the very systems of transmission that confer a canonicity on authorized production. Form and genre, voice and drama, all contribute to what I have understood to be this scribe's appreciation of the poem and its place in the most personal of his collections. For modern readers, though, the canonicity of *Adam Scriveyn* lies in its *unvoiced* participation in a system. It stands not as an offhand, scribal entry but as the epitome of Chaucerian making. It enters our canon not in the transcriptions of a hand but in the printings of a bound edition. It has meaning not as a familiar piece of writing but as testimony to the very unfamiliarity of Chaucer's world: to the alterities of manuscript production in an age of print. If Chaucer's verse is, in some sense, "made" by his readers, then we can add that his verse is constantly "remade" by those who transcribe, reprint, and reauthorize it.

John Stowe was the first to print the *Adam Scriveyn* stanza, on the last page of his edition of Chaucer's works published in 1561. As the collector of Shirley's manuscripts, he may have even been the first to read it in the hundred years since Shirley had written it down.[68] He was, as I have mentioned, the first to print the poem now known as the *Complaint to a Lady* and to recognize its textual distinctions from the previous *Pity* in Shirley's manuscript. Stowe also separates the *Adam Scriveyn* from its manuscript environment, but in so doing he makes something different from the *Complaint*. He presents a poem central, not appended, to the Chaucerian project, makes it "literature" by taking it from personal transcription and granting it the autonomy of authorship.

Stowe's *Adam Scriveyn* is a summary of Chaucer's work, a retrospective of the poet looking back over the range of his productions and reflecting on the foibles of his culture (see Figure 5). These now are very much Chaucer's words, and the author's name erases Adam's in Stowe's title: "Chaucers woordes vnto his owne Scriuener." The poet takes both writerly and typographic pride of place here, with the large black-letter format of his name now standing as the heading to the poem. And it is Chaucer's name that brackets these words, as the reader's eye moves from the boldly printed "Chaucer" at the top, through the text of the poem, to its concluding, italic "Et sic finis" and its black-letter "Thus endeth," and to the final italic "the workes of Geffray Chaucer." That final Chaucer, set at the center of its line, centers the poem firmly in the corpus of the poet's work. What has been finished here is not just the collection of that work within the printed book, but Chaucer's literary life itself. "Et sic est finis," and thus is the end, for on the next column of this last page Stowe prints the Latin epitaph supposedly inscribed on Chaucer's tomb. Here, in the clear-cut Roman typeface of its lines, we see the last page of the works of Chaucer as a monument to his accomplishments. And we see, as well, in the virtual encyclopaedism of the typographer's art, the range of fonts and figures that transmit the works of England's poet. *Adam Scriveyn* has a place in Stowe's book far removed from Shirley's manuscript. No longer the remembered stanza of complaint and verse epistle, no longer the scribe's entry in a string of poems on the writing self, "Chaucers woordes" are now an author's work, a monumentalized conclusion to a printed canon.

Stowe leaves his reader with a dead and buried Chaucer. Set side by side, the *Adam Scriveyn* and the Latin verses from the tomb effectively present two forms of epitaphic writing: one, the words of the English writer briefly looking back over the scope and nature of his works; the other, the words of a European humanist, reviewing literary history from Socrates and Virgil to the present. Stowe's final page displays the personal against the public, the vernacular against the learned. But it also juxtaposes

Chaucers woor-
des vnto his o'wne

Scriuener.

Adam Scriuener yf euer it
the be falle
Boece or Troilus for to
write new
vnder thy longe lockes þ
must haue the scalle
But after my mockynge
thou write more true
So ofte adaye I mote thy werke renew
It to correcte and eke to rubbe and scrape
And al is thorow thy negligence and rape.

Et sic est finis.

Thus endeth

the workes of Geffray

Chaucer

Figure 5. The poem as epitaph: Chaucer's *Adam Scriveyn*.
The Works of Geoffrey Chaucer,
edited by John Stowe (1561), Sig. Rrriiiv.

manuscript against print. *Adam Scriveyn*, placed here against the monu-
mentalisms of the tomb poem and at the close of this printed volume,
stands as a lament not just for scribal manglings but for manuscript culture
itself. It looks back from the fixities of type to a previous time, when the
hands of Adam or John Shirley could impede the reader's understanding
of the poet and the scholarly recovery of texts.

Adam Scriveyn and the poem from the tomb appose the two technologies of literary production that preserve and transmit Chaucer's poetry.
But the triumphs of the printed book signaled by Stowe—and, for that
matter, by the range of other, sixteenth-century editions of the English
poet and his classical forebears—are in themselves something of a critical
illusion. Book and manuscript would coexist for decades after the importation of movable type to England, and the literary system of both "laureate"
and "amateur" in Tudor England was, in fact, largely controlled by private
circulation of handwritten pages.[69] Chaucer's place in early English print
culture thus needs to be assessed against its legacy in manuscript, and furthermore against the various competing strategies of authorial self-presentation in both technologies.

The following two chapters are designed to fill the space between the
Adam Scriveyn and the poem on the tomb. The differences Stowe adum-
brates between script and print, scribe and publisher, English writer and
European humanist may be exposed in Chaucer's earliest appearances in
printed books and in the cultural poetics generated out of the affinities
between the court and university at the close of the fifteenth century. My
book closes, then, with a study of the buried Chaucer and with the creations of authorial and critical personae who no longer need to share in the
remembrances of "Geffrey" or the fictions of his "wordes" to friends or
scribes.

CHAPTER FIVE

At Chaucer's Tomb: Laureation and
Paternity in Caxton's Criticism

SOMETIME during the year 1478, perhaps at the same time as he was printing his first edition of the *Canterbury Tales*, William Caxton published Chaucer's translation of the *Consolation of Philosophy*. In the extended epilogue to that volume, Caxton offered his first critical assessment of Chaucer—not, however, as a vernacular poet, but as a translator.

> Therfore the worshipful fader 7 first foundeur 7 enbelissher of ornate eloquence in our englissh. I mene Maister Geffrey Chaucer hath translated this sayd werke oute of latyn in to oure vsual and moder tonge.
>
> (*Caxton*, 37)[1]

At first glance, Caxton's praise seems little different from the laudatory idioms of Chaucer's fifteenth-century imitators and from Caxton's own characterizations of the poet's craft elsewhere in his editions. In the prologues to the 1483 *Canterbury Tales* and the *House of Fame* of about the same year, as well as in the versified *Book of Curtesye* that Caxton published in 1477, Chaucer's initial appearances in printed books seem of a piece with the familiar assessments of rhetorical finesse, aureate diction, laureate status, and educative value that marked his reception from the time of Lydgate.[2] But, if we continue reading Caxton's *Boece* epilogue, we come to something quite distinctive in the century's representation of the poet.

> And furthermore I desire 7 requi.re you that of your charite ye wold praye for the soule of the sayd worshipful mann Geffrey Chaucer first translatour of this sayde boke into englissh 7 enbelissher in making the sayd langage ornate 7 fayr. whiche shal endure perpetuelly. and therfore he ought eternelly to be remembrid. of whom the body and the corps lieth buried in thabbay of Westmestre beside london to fore the chapele of seynte benet. by whos sepulture is wreton on a table

hongyng on a pylere his Epitaphye maad by a poete laureat whereof
the copye foloweth 7c.

(Caxton, 37)

What follows is a Latin elegy on Chaucer, purporting to be his tomb inscription, written by a certain Stephen Surigonus, poet laureate from
Milan; and at the end of this elegy, Caxton himself has appended four
Latin lines noting how his imprinting of the volume and the tomb poem
preserve the memory of Chaucer's work and secure his fame for future
readers.

Chaucer is dead. This simple fact, no news for readers of the 1470s,
comes at the close of the *Boece* for purposes far different from those of the
lamentations of the poets who had imitated him throughout the fifteenth
century. Caxton presents the buried body of the poet and the monumentality of his tomb to distance present readers from the past and to maintain
that in the reproduction of his works his fame should live perpetually. This
strategy differs in kind from the remembrances—real or affected—that
distinguish the obeisances to Chaucer by Hoccleve or Lydgate or that
frame John Shirley's scribal dialogues with those whose works he copied.
Throughout the fifteenth century, it was the idea of a personal acquain-
tanceship with Chaucer and his followers that placed the writer in the
genealogy of English letters. As student to the master or child to the father, the fifteenth-century writer was simultaneously enabled as a maker
and disabled as a poet. The paradox of seeking to imitate the inimitable,
the paradox of fifteenth-century poetics, sustained itself in the traditions
of remembrance that kept the dead Chaucer present before all.

Caxton's *Boece* presents for the first time a Chaucer not of the remembered legacy of English coterie making but of the dead *auctores* of the
Continental humanist tradition. He is the subject of a learned elegy, the
object of historical recovery, a figure in the origins of literary history from
ancient times to the present. The first critical discussion of Chaucer in a
printed book focuses on an author who survives not in the memories of
medieval readers but in the performances of humanist laureates. If this
appearance seems to close a chapter in the history of his reception, it inaugurates a reconsideration of the English literary past in which a new role
may be found for the vernacular poet in the political present.

Throughout this book I have sought to detail the ways in which
Chaucer's authority infantilized his later readers, scribes, and imitators.
The impositions of a father Chaucer construct an implied audience of
children, one that on occasion had been socialized into the gentry audiences or young students for whom Chaucer's works were reproduced. In
this and the following chapter, I wish to consider how this audience for
Chaucer changes from the self-imagined childhood of Lydgatean abnega-

tion to the laureate adulthood of humanist scholarship. Caxton initiates a way of reading Chaucer and of vernacular literature generally "like a laureate," that is, as if one were the living version of the politically sanctioned poet Chaucer was long imagined to have been. Entombing Chaucer elevates him to the status of an *auctor* on the classical or the Petrarchan model, and in consequence it signals a series of redefinitions of the idea of the laureate itself and of relations among writers and readers, critics and editors.

These two chapters seek the place of Chaucer in the various constructions of a laureate poetics at the close of the fifteenth century. Their argument will be that the creations of an English literary history and the self-presentations of new English writers distance Chaucer and his work from current literary practice. They remove the poet to the past—historicize him, in effect—while in the process rehistoricizing the conceptions of a critical authority that mediate that past. No longer can the "poet laureate" stand as a cipher for the wishes of Lydgatean preferment or the fantasies of Shirlean nostalgia; no longer can the fictions of a literary "father" be projected onto an advisory and entertaining Chaucer. What happens at the close of the fifteenth century is a new grounding of the ideas of paternity and laureation in the social practices of university and courtly education and the political environments of royal patronage. To read Chaucer like a laureate is to read him as an exemplar of ancient practice, as a model for the pursuit of poetic fame, as a monument of literature. It is, in short, to read him in a humanist manner, and my concerns throughout these chapters center on the multiple relations between Continental scholarship, court culture, and print technology that align the poet in a changing literary system.

Central to these concerns will be the narrative of textual recovery that forms what might be thought of as the masterplot of humanist interpretation.[3] The hermeneutics of discovery—articulated in the great Petrarchan projects of historical imagination and reconstructive philology and extended in the fifteenth-century invention of the methodology of textual criticism—has long been seen as framing Renaissance conceptions of the literary past. For many, it defines the shape of Renaissance culture itself: a culture of what Thomas Greene calls, in an influential formulation, metaphoric intertextuality.[4] In Greene's account, and its extensions in a range of later criticism, Renaissance reading is inherently historicizing. It displaces past texts onto an antiquity that must be textually recovered, where the actions of that scholarly recovery are, in themselves, the subject for new narratives of reading and response. In contrast to the "metonymic" quality of medieval intertextuality—with its ahistoricizing allegories, its simultaneities of figural typology, and its sense of sharing in an ongoing literary present—Renaissance uses of the past are exemplary, focusing on the historical distance of the early narrative and consciously recovering such narratives for application in the present world.

In these terms, the reflections of the fifteenth-century Chaucerians I have discussed maintain the metonymic quality of medieval intertextuality, what Greene identifies, working from the studies of Gerald Bruns, as the "tacitly unfinished" status of the inherited text. "What the later hand writes fills in, lengthens, deepens, clarifies, without any strain of disjuncture. . . . [Medieval] intertextuality is metonymic because the later text touches, connects with, grows out of the earlier one. All writing enjoys a neighborly community."[5] It is the fiction of this "neighborly community" that fosters the extensions of a Chaucer cult throughout the century and that requires of the poet's imitators, scribes, and encomiasts a sense of personal engagement with the author and his work.

What happens at the close of the century, however, and what is initiated in the prologues and the epilogues of Caxton's volumes, is the distancing of author and reader. Caxton defines the texts he prints not in the open-endedness of medieval imitation or rescription but in the teleologies of humanist discovery. His criticism presents, in highly personalized narrative form, stories of the individual recovery of early texts. He tells of finding rare translations, supplanting old editions, and returning to the past for exempla of learning and behavior. Caxton presents his published volumes as the products of recovery: products now offered for a readership defined as learned and erudite, a readership not limited by birth or class (though Caxton is acutely aware of the role of both in securing his patronage) but opened up to those qualified by education.

To say that Caxton's work is somehow "humanistic" in these terms is, of course, not to deny the powerful conservatism of his literary tastes or, by contrast, to elide the various commercial or political motives for the selection of his volumes and their publication.[6] Whatever "literary theory" we might derive from the various productions of his press might seem to fit assuredly in the conceptions of that education and entertainment—that Chaucerian blend of "sentence" and "solaas"—that motivated so much of the century's literary energies.[7] And, though Caxton seems at various times sensitive to the relationship of his texts to those of the manuscript exemplars he had used, it would be difficult to abstract from his practice any editorial self-consciousness on a par with that of his contemporaries on the Continent.[8] Nonetheless, there is what I would call a formal quality to Caxton's humanism in his criticism. His construction of a narrative persona and his cultivation of a few key tropes effectively emplot the reading of the past as the recovery, reception, and reediting of texts. Within each of his critical accounts of publishing lies the humanist impulse to narrativize the personal encounter with the past as one of textual discovery and recovery: to tell a story of the book as a story of the self.[9]

My purpose will thus be to read the prologues and the epilogues *as criticism* and to find in Caxton's three discussions of paternity and laureation the controlled displacement of authority from writer onto reader, from the originator of a text to those who transmit and interpret it.[10] The *Boece* epilogue of 1478 presents a buried father Chaucer, whose discovery is guided by a living poet laureate. The prologue to the 1483 *Canterbury Tales* qualifies the popular impression of Chaucer as a poet laureate by socializing the production of his work in the environments of commercial bookmaking, while in the process shifting the fatherhood of his texts onto the father of the reader who bequeaths his manuscript for Caxton's press. Finally, the 1490 *Eneydos* prologue narrates a retrospective of Caxton's career as printer and translator to present John Skelton as the new English laureate, while the fatherhood controlling this production is that of Henry VII as enacted in his siring of Arthur, Prince of Wales.

Caxton's writings may be read in sequence as delineating a story of their own, a story of burial and birth, of genealogies both textual and political. Their personal reflections charge the reader with the task of retrospection, too, and the *Eneydos* prologue in particular looks back over a publishing career that began with another Troy book and another language. The personal and the patronized, the laureate poet and a new aureate age, combine here to rewrite the tropes of fifteenth-century nostalgia and realign the patterns of the literary system. Chaucer, however, is nowhere to be found in that system, neither as a foil for Skelton nor as an English analogue to the classical traditions he commands. His disappearance from the discourse of literary commentary, and his subsequent yet altered appearance in the poetry of Hawes and Skelton, signal basic shifts in the conception of the poet laureate and the ideals of literary fatherhood controlling vernacular authorship.

The Chaucer at the close of the fifteenth century progressively appears and disappears from narratives of literary history. From the *Boece* to the *Eneydos*, from Hawes's *Pastime of Pleasure* to Skelton's *Garlande of Laurell*, Chaucer's authority shifts between a remembered presence and a buried absence, from that of a "maker" in the constantly rescripted manuscripts of entertainment and instruction to that of a "poet" in the printed volumes of the library. Chaucerian citation thus moves from evocation to invocation. The listing of his works or the appeals to his verbal mastery are no longer designed to evoke his presence on the page or conjure his discerning visage over the impersonator's shoulder. Rather, such references move toward establishing the distance of the poet and his world from the contemporanities of courtly life or typographical production. Chaucer becomes, in Hawes's later term, "antique" as he begins to share with Virgil and the classics a deep past recoverable not by the memories of cult or coterie but by the work of individual readers. Each of the following accounts tells a story of the personal engagement with the author where the reader is a traveler among the texts and contexts of vernacular production, whose goal is the presentation of a critical self sharing in the making of a literary history.

I

That history begins and ends with epitaphs. For Chaucer's Clerk, the "lauriat poete" is neatly dead and buried in his country. "Nayled in his cheste" (*CT* E 29), Petrarch is both a legacy and artifact, a writer outlived by his texts, but more decisively a writer who, entombed in Italy, becomes an object of veneration. This status of the poet as entombed creator stands for the Clerk as well as for Caxton as the mark of change in literary history. Both use the veneration of the dead as ways of introducing new translations for new audiences, and both focus on the physical encryptment of the poet to distinguish their presented projects as recovered texts.[11] As I have traced it throughout this book, the Clerk's encomium on Petrarch became a model for the range of fifteenth-century Chaucerian praise, and one might go so far as to say that various traditions of that praise may be classed together as varieties of mourning. To a certain extent, all fifteenth-century Chauceriana is elegiac in this sense, as it stresses the remembered presence of the dead Chaucer much as the Clerk calls attention to his personal acquaintance with the "clerk" of Padua.[12] But unlike Chaucer's Clerk, Caxton does not claim personal knowlege of Chaucer; nor does he at this point crown Chaucer as the poet laureate. Instead, he places both that title and the burden of panegyric on a contemporary—one who, in his education and his charge, would have made a career out of encomium.

Caxton's reliance on Surigonus for the elegy on Chaucer, together with his placement of that elegy at the close of the *Boece* epilogue, speaks not to the traditions of obeisance generated by the Clerk but rather draws on the contemporary practices of Continental humanism. The encryptment of the praised poet takes on a specific quality beyond the status of a literary trope; it becomes part of an obsession with the actual crypts of famous poets. From the late fourteenth through the early sixteenth century, the poet's tomb served as the locus of the literary enterprise, the physical locale where one could bury the past and celebrate the present.[13] The tombs of Virgil, Ovid, and Livy became objects of much Continental fascination. Motivated, in part, by interest in the lives of classical *auctores*, and stimulated by Petrarch's own project of rhetorical resuscitation in the *Familiares*, European scholars sought the poets' tombs from Italy to Romania. The personality, or better yet the "person-hood," of classical *auctores* had become the mainstay of a growing, critical approach that separated out the writer from the text, splitting apart the medieval identification of *auctor* with textualized *auctoritas*.

But there were more narrowly scholarly or philological motives for searching out the poets' tombs. The humanists were modeling their Latin, both grammatically and orthographically, on presumed classical examples. The interests in the history of Latin scripts and verbal forms led scholars to the epitaphs found on old Roman tombs. This fascination, together with the social practice of the public eulogy, led to a reassessment of the value of the tombs.[14] Many orators and poets imitated the forms of the old inscriptions, as the funeral oration, elegy, and literary epitaph became the genres that affirmed the cultural poetics of a classical revival.[15]

The humanist funeral elegy, it has been argued, helped "to create and propagate historical myths" about the definition of the past and its recovery in the present.[16] Primary among these myths was that of a cultural renewal, a rebirth of the past through the discovery, transmission, and rereading of its texts. The bibliophilic journeys of Poggio Bracciolini and Niccolo Niccoli at the beginning of the fifteenth century had, by its end, attained the status of a legend, such that even Caxton could appeal to their ideals of book collecting in his vision of a gentlemanly readership.[17]

The hunt for books found its equivalent in this search for ruins—for the epigraphic remains of the Greek and Roman world and for the tombs of the famous ancient dead. As Joseph Trapp has told it, the hunt for the tombs of Virgil, Livy, and in particular Ovid had become a near obsession for the humanists. Stories circulated of discovering the tombs of the great poets, with their marmoreal inscriptions telling not just of the poet's death, but also in themselves exemplifying the orthographic purity of classical writing. Accounts of Ovid's tomb in the 1490s, Trapp shows, found their models in the search for Livy's tomb made in the 1410s.[18] One of the details of these stories, and what I will illustrate to be the central image of Chaucer's epitaph, was encoded in the legends of the author's book found undecayed within his tomb. The medieval life of Ovid prefixed to the pseudo-Ovidian *De Vetula* offers this account:

> Recently there was discovered in a suburb of the city of Dioscori, capital of the kingdom of Colchis, when certain ancient pagan tombs were being removed from the public cemetary which is beside Tomis, one tomb among the rest, with an epitaph engraved on it in Armenian characters, of which the interpretation goes like this: "Hic iacet Ovidius ingeniosissimus poetarum." At the head of this tomb an ivory casket was found. In it unconsumed by the ages, was a book. The local inhabitants unable to read what was in it, sent it to Constantinople, where there were many "Latins."[19]

This story, widely circulated in the fourteenth century, formed by the fifteenth a significant part of the apparently veracious narratives about finding Ovid's tomb. So many literary accounts of these searches survive, with so many of them pressed into the service of authorial reflection and cultural commentary, that we might think of the trip to the tomb as something of a topos for the humanist self-definition: a blend of the historical and the legendary designed to illustrate the discovery of a usable, classical past. But that discovery, as Trapp points out, is one that must be mediated by a "metropolitan scholarship," that is, by translators ensconced in seats of institutional control whose acts of understanding may unclose, for sanctioned readers, the volumes of the distant and the dead.[20]

Such narratives of textual discovery, though they inform the projects of the humanist philologists in general, control in detail the plot lines of their funeral elegies. Enacting a form of recovered classical discourse in its own language, such elegies rehearse the very story of burial and fame in terms of textual discovery. They show the drama of mourning as a drama of reading, as the living poet and the audience confront the body and the character of the deceased in an incised, memorial text—an artifact whose interpretation is deferred until the close of the poetic drama.[21] In Politian's great elegy on Albiera degli Albizzi, for example, the sequence of panegyric moves through physical descriptions of the deceased and imagined dialogues among divinities and the dead and concludes with the text of the epitaph. "And finally the tomb of elaborately worked marble shuts in the icy limbs, and has on it a short verse."[22] The poem moves from the spoken to the written, from the publicly addressed to the privately read. From the familial house, now dark and empty (lines 8–9), through the memories of the dead woman, through the mythic heavens and the cold earth, we come to the final resting place in the marble tomb. Politian closes the poem "finally" (*tandem*), as if we have shared with him the travels from the home to the grave in search of an incised and monumental text whose discovery and interpretation grant us insight into the deceased's spirit.

In a more abbreviated fashion, many of the elegies collected in Pontanus's *De tumulis* volumes tell stories of encountering the tomb.[23] Travelers speak with the gods and fates, the parents of the dead lament, and on occasion the funery urn itself gives voice to the story of the dead. These poems function, in effect, as epitaphs themselves, as texts incised on stone that tell the passing traveler just who is buried there and why.

This drama of incision is so central to the elegiac narrative that critical discussions of the genre return to it again and again. Summarizing a history of such generic analysis, Puttenham at the close of the sixteenth century defines the elegy precisely in these terms.

> An Epitaph is but a kind of Epigram only applied to the report of the dead persons estate and degree, or of his other good or bad partes, to his commendation or reproch, and is an inscription such as a man may commodiously write or engrave upon a tombe in a few verses, pithie, quicke, and sententious, for the passer-by to peruse and judge upon without long tariaunce.[24]

Central to Puttenham's description is the narrative of reading that the elegy engenders. Its purpose is to catch the casual eye, to appear briefly but memorably to the passer-by. It is, in short, a text to be discovered, one that stimulates the reading (perusal) and the criticism (judgment) of the discoverer.

Stephen Surigonus's epitaph on Chaucer tells such a story of discovery. It invites us to find the entombed poet, not just in the abbey but in the poem, as it figuratively and structurally enacts the narrowing of focus that will situate his body.

> Pyerides muse, si possunt numina fletus
>   Fundere . diuinas atque rigare genas,
> Galfridi vatis chaucer crudelia fata
>   Plangite . sit lacrimis abstinuisse nephas
> Vos coluit viuens . at vos celebrate sepultum
>   Reddatur merito gracia digna viro
> Grande decus vobis . est docti musa maronis
>   Qua didicit melius lingua latina loqui
> Grande nouumque decus Chaucer . famamque parauit
>   Heu quantum fuerat prisca britanna rudis
> Reddidit insignem maternis versibus . vt iam
>   Aurea splendescat . ferrea facta prius
> Hunc latuisse virum nil . si tot opuscula vertes
>   Dixeris . egregiis que decorata modis
> Socratis ingenium . vel fontes philosophie
>   Quitquid & archani dogmata sacra ferunt
> Et quascunque velis tenuit dignissimus artes
>   Hic vates . paruo conditus hoc tumulo
> Ah laudis quantum preclara britannia perdis
>   Dum rapuit tantum mors odiosa virum
> Crudeles parce . crudelia fila sorores
>   Non tamen extincto corpore . fama perit
> Viuet ineternum . viuent dum scripta poete
>   Viuant eterno tot monimenta die
> Si qua bonos tangit pietas . si carmine dignus
>   Carmina qui cecinit tot cumulata modis
> Hec sibi marmoreo scribantur verba sepulchro
>   Hec maneat laudis sarcina summa sue
> Galfridus Chaucer vates : et fama poesis
>   Materne . hac sacra sum tumulatus humo
>
> Post obitum Caxton voluit te viuere cura
>   Willelmi. Chaucer clare poeta tuj
> Nam tua non solum compressit opuscula formis
>   Has quoque sed laudes . iussit hic esse tuas

Pierian Muses, if heavenly powers can pour forth tears and moisten their divine cheeks, lament the cruel fate of the bard Geoffrey Chaucer. Let it be a crime to refrain from weeping. He worshipped you in his lifetime, but [I bid you] honour him now that he is buried. Let a worthy reward be paid to a deserving man. The Muse [or Music] of learned Maro is a great honour to you, the Muse through whose agency the Latin tongue learned to speak better. A great new honour and fame has Chaucer provided for you. By the verses [that he has composed] in his [British] mother tongue he made it [as] illustrious as, alas, it had once been uncouth, so that now it takes on a golden splendour where formerly it was iron.

One will affirm that there was nothing in which this man was not distinguished if he turns the pages of so many works which [are] embellished with excellent measures. The genius of Socrates or the springs of philosophy, and all the secrets which holy doctrine contains and all the arts that you could wish for—these were in the possession of this most worthy bard [who is] buried in this tiny grave.

Ah, how much renown you lose, famed Britannia, now that hateful death has snatched away so great a man! Cruel [are the] Fates, cruel their threads, O Sisters! Yet even when the body is dead fame does not perish. It will live forever, as long as the poets' writings live. May all these monuments live in everlasting day. If the good are touched by any piety and if the man who sang songs amassed in so many measures is [himself] worthy of a song, let these words as spoken on his own behalf, be inscribed upon his marble tomb, let this remain the crowning burden to his own praise:

"I, Geoffrey Chaucer the bard, glory of my native
poesy, am buried in this sacred ground."

It was the eager wish of your admirer William Caxton that you should live, illustrious poet Chaucer. For not only has he printed your works but he has also ordered this eulogy of you to be here.[25]

From the cosmic meditations on the Muses and the Fates, we move to local habitations in the church; from the deep past and foreign tongues of Socrates and Virgil, we progress to the mother tongue of Britain. The poem's reader walks through its allusions and its verbal intricacies to discern, as at the center of a maze, the buried poet. Bracketed by the ancient and the modern, by the *numina* of heaven and the *hic* of Westminster, lies Chaucer himself, *hunc virum*, buried both in earth and in the text. At the dead center of these lines we find him and his book.

Hunc latuisse virum nil . si tot opuscula vertes
Dixeris . egregiis que decorata modis

(13–14)

The published modern translation I have offered here construes these lines, "One will affirm that there was nothing in which this man was not distinguished if he turns the pages of so many works which are embellished with excellent measures."[26] But I think we may take the Latin far more literally:

> You might say that this man does not lie hidden at all, if you will turn over the pages of so many little works embellished in such beautiful ways.[27]

Though the tomb may hide him, the book does not conceal him; though the covers of that book may enclose him, the discerning reader may peruse and judge. The key verb here is *latere*, to lie hidden, be concealed, and Surigonus's own poem, like the books of Chaucer and the tomb we have approached, conceals him too. Complex patterns of echo and repetition verbally enclose these two lines: The name of Geoffrey Chaucer at lines 3 and 29 encases the poem's story much as it closes the tomb; the appellation *vates* at lines 3, 18, and 29 punctuates our entry into and our exit from the text and crypt; the *tumulus* encountered at the poem's middle reappears in Chaucer's own words at its end. These patterns, I suggest, enact the very quiring of pages and the binding of the book that hold the poet's writings. Their interlacements place before our eyes no transcript of a funeral oration but the written, indeed printed, document of praise.

Surigonus's poem is as crafted as the tomb it represents, and these verbal complexities make it as much a work of visual appeal as the made tomb or Chaucer's books themselves, embellished—as I take the phrase *decorata modis*—with adornments of the bookmaker's art: finely written lines, visible illuminations, cunningly worked covers. The story of the epitaph is the story of humanist textual recovery. But the object of the epitaph, its status as a created thing, embodies the equation of the poet and the book, the *vir* and the *opus*, stated at its center. Discerning Chaucer in the book is, in these terms, as much an act of *translatio* as Chaucer himself had performed in the *Boece*: a *translatio*, now, of physically moving Chaucer's bones from place to place. But *translatio*, too, is the process of readerly movement through the elegy, and more generally through Caxton's whole epilogue. We have come to Chaucer here not by wandering among the graves but by reading in the book: by seeing a translation of a text, the *Consolation of Philosophy*, as part of a sequence of *translationes studii*. Caxton's epilogue dwells on the multiple translations that generate the book we hold, from Boethius's Latin renderings of the classics, through Chaucer's Englishings, to Caxton's own recovery of Chaucer's "rare" volume.

By the time we get to the conclusion of this Latin elegy, we find ourselves led through the byways of a literary history to the precise location of the poet's body: "in thabbay of Westmestre beside london to fore the chapele of seynte benet." And having found that body, and the tomb, we are directed further to appreciate the nature of the journey we have taken. Caxton has added four lines of his own, establishing his role in the transmission of this text. "For not only has he printed your works (*compressit opuscula formis*) but he has also ordered this eulogy of you to be here." Now, it is unclear whether Caxton seeks to take the credit for the printing of the poem or the raising of the tomb, and some have argued that the final *hic* in his lines does indeed refer to Westminster itself.[28] But I think this confusion is, if not deliberate, at least critically creative, for what Caxton has done in these verbal ambiguities is to equate the book and the tomb. The *opuscula* we were invited to open in line 13 are now the *opuscula* we hold in our hands. The *monimenta* are not just, metaphorically, the poet's writings but the printed book itself, a palpable monument to his fame. The *archana* of dogma are not just the secrets of learning but the knowledge secreted away, in the *arcae* of the study or the library. And in the little tomb, the *paruo tumulo*, lies not the body of the poet but the corpus of his works. If the central image of the poem is enclosure and release, then when we come to Caxton's final lines we see that his claim, *compressit opuscula formis*, means, quite literally, that he has brought Chaucer's works back together, compressed them in the bound volumes of the book we hold in our hands.

Read in the ways I am suggesting, the *Boece* epilogue enacts the narrative of textual recovery emerging from that nexus of epideictic performance and bibliographical self-consciousness that distinguishes the humanist hermeneutic. At the formal level, Caxton's story fits the paradigms of poetic discovery drawn from the Ovid legends. Finding the poet means uncovering the book, for what is found within the tomb is not the relic of the writer's body but the uncorrupted work. In the decipherments of metropolitan scholarship—its rephrasings into the language of the city and the learning of the institutions of political control—the author's work becomes appropriated for a new appreciative social order. Yet Caxton's narrative inverts this paradigm as well. In the *Boece*, the journey ends not by finding the book in the tomb, but by recognizing the tomb in the book. Here, the epitaph incises itself not upon the face of marble but upon the sheet of paper (see Figure 6). The monumentalism of the epitaph is captured in typography; for those who cannot go to Westminster, it is reduced for readers in the shop or study. The final printed leaf of Caxton's book begins afresh, and at the top of folio 94r the break in his account is both linguistic and typographic:

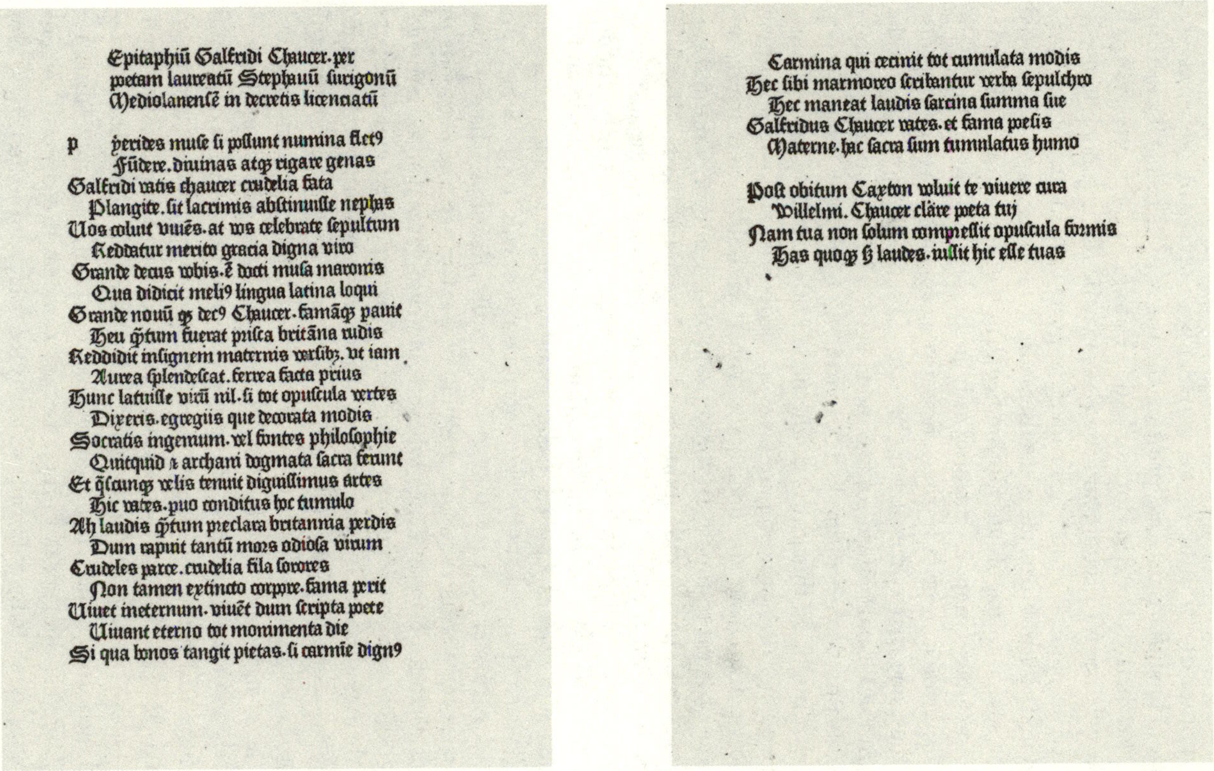

Epitaphiū Galfridi Chaucer. per poetam laureatū Stephanū surigonū Mediolanenše in decretis licenciatū

Pierides muse si possunt numina fletus
Fundere. diuinas atqʒ rigare genas
Galfridi vates ducere cuncta fata
Plangite. sit lacrimis abstinuisse nephas
Vos coluit viuens. at vos celebrate sepulcrum
Reddatur merito gracia digna viro
Grande decus vobis. ē docti musa maronis
Qua didicit meliꝰ lingua latina loqui
Grande nouū q decꝰ Chaucer. famaqʒ pauit
Heu qntum fuerat prisca britāna rudis
Reddidit insignem maternis versibʒ. ut iam
Aurea splendescat. ferrea facta prius
Hunc latuisse virū nil. si tot opuscula vertes
Dixeris. egregiis que decorata modis
Socratis ingenium. vel fontes philosophie
Quicquid & archani dogmata sacra ferunt
Et ꝗscunqʒ velis tenuit dignissimus artes
Hic vates. ꝓuo conditus hoc tumulo
Ah laudis qntum preclara britannia perdis
Dum rapuit tantū mors odiosa virum
Crudeles parce. crudelia fila sorores
Non tamen extincto corpore. fama perit
Viuet ineternum. viuet dum scripta poete
Viuant eterno tot monumenta die
Si qua bonos tangit pietas. si carmine dign9

Carmina qui cecinit tot cumulata modis
Hec sibi marmoreo scribantur verba sepulchro
Hec maneat laudis sarcina summa sue
Galfridus Chaucer vates. et fama poesis
Materne. hac sacra sum tumulatus humo

Post obitum Caxton voluit te viuere cura
Willelmi. Chaucer clare poeta tui
Nam tua non solum compressit opuscula formis
Has quoqʒ ꝗ laudes. iussit hic esse tuas

Figure 6. The epitaph as poem: Stephen Surigonus's epitaph on Chaucer. Geoffrey Chaucer, *Boece*, printed by William Caxton (1478), fols.90v–91r.

Epitaphium Galfridi Chaucer. per
poetam laureatum Stephanum Surigonum
Mediolanensem in decretis licenciatum.

The printer captures the impression—in both senses of the word—on
the page. He shifts typefaces, printing the inscription in his Type 3, reserved elsewhere in the *Boece* for the Latin headings to the *Consolation*.[29] It
is a new typeface for Caxton, and the *Boece* may be the first book to use it.
Elsewhere in publications at this time, it appears only in the *Sarum Ordi-
nal* and in its Latin broadside advertisement.[30] It is a display type, derived
from the square forms of late Gothic bookhand, differing markedly from
his two previous typefaces cut originally in Bruges and modeled on the
batard hands of Europe.[31] In these first uses it appears as something of a
public font, one that evokes if not the heft of the inscription, then at the
very least the formal patterns of the monument. There is nothing following in Caxton's book—no marked "explicit," no excrescent colophon—to
break what might be thought of as the fiction of epigraphic reading here.
All we are left with at the end are Caxton's Latin lines and two remaining
blank leaves filling out the final quire. What we hold in our hands becomes the physical testimony to the recovery of the author, a printed volume that is both handy and monumental, both text and tomb.

Emerging from the close of the *Boece* is an awareness of the historicity
of Chaucer and perhaps of literary history itself. The poet is positioned
both within the story of *translatio* told in Caxton's English prose and in
the canon of *auctores* catalogued in Surigonus's Latin verse. Such a historicized Chaucer cannot share in the remembrances of cult or circle. He cannot serve as master to a reverent class of pupils. Reading Chaucer now
necessitates recovering him, and the bulk of Caxton's epilogue attends to
the construction of an audience whose "erudicion" and whose "lernyng"
privileges them as recovering readers. What Caxton's *Boece* epilogue performs, then, is an act of making readers while remaking authors. It defines
the qualities essential to an audience for the *Boece*: an audience both erudite and learned, one skilled in the nuances of humanist Latin and the
intricacies of native prose—an audience, in short, of English laureates.

The vision of these laureates, however, does not necessarily correspond
to the historical realities of laureation. No Englishman, as far as we can
tell, received a "laureation" by the time the *Boece* had been published; and,
as Surigonus's own poem demonstrates, the discourse of the laureate remained the Latin of the schools rather than the English of the courts. Yet
Caxton's project does speak to the nascent awareness in Edward IV's England of the potentially political, as well as the social or the literary, role of
laureates, and it is in those political roles that Caxton seeks to fashion his
ideal, adult readership for an English literature.

II

Petrarch's crowning in 1341 had not immediately spurred a rush of laureations in the European courts.[32] It was not until well after his death that universities began to grant the title "laureate" with any degree of regularity, and not until the 1460s that a group of European institutions, notably the universities of Louvain and Cologne, record their graduates or faculties as having "poet laureates." Such *laureati* often traveled from school to school and court to court seeking further commendations and employment. One of the earliest was the Florentine James Publicius Rufus; though by profession a physician, he was a professor of rhetoric at Louvain in 1464 and called himself *poeta laureatus*.[33] Throughout the next decade, he traveled to Brabant, Leipzig, Cologne, and most of the major university towns of Europe, reflecting a pattern of itinerant teaching that would be followed by many of the university graduates of the 1470s and 1480s. Surigonus came out of Milan with a bachelor's degree in canon law, may have taught at Oxford in the 1460s, studied at Cologne sometime in 1471, and in 1472 matriculated at the University of Louvain, whose records call him "Mgr stephanus de suroi[n]bus qui dicit se poetam laureatum" (Master Stephen Surigonus who calls himself poet laureate).[34] His stay in the Low Countries was marked by his various attempts to interest Charles the Bold, Duke of Burgundy, in his services as panegyrist and court orator, after the fashion of the other local and imported scholars used to propagate what Gordon Kipling has reconstructed as that special brand of courtly humanism central to the Burgundian patronage of arts and letters.[35] Surigonus was apparently unsuccessful in obtaining a position at the court; yet there is evidence that he made contact with several important Louvain humanists, and the evidence of his surviving Latin poetry, together with his epitaph on Chaucer, suggests a panegyrist of at least some formal competence, if not flair.

Traditional accounts of Surigonus's relationship to Caxton seek to reconstruct a biographical encounter from the details of the *Boece* epilogue.[36] Both men were in Cologne in 1471, though their stays may have overlapped by only a few months; and though Surigonus may have been teaching at Oxford sometime before that, it remains unclear whether the two had met and whether Caxton had commissioned Chaucer's epitaph from the Italian or simply found it on the tomb in Westminster. But Surigonus's place in Caxton's epilogue has less to do with the specifics of biography than with the polemics of reading—with an attempt to construct rhetorically an ideal readership for Chaucer's work and furthermore to establish an outside critical authority for Caxton's project of textual recovery and printing. Caxton's first round of printings, it has long been known, were tailored to Burgundian taste.[37] The *History of Troy*, the *Game and*

Play of Chess, and *Jason* were prepared as French books for a courtly readership. As governor of the English Nation at Bruges, Caxton would have come in contact with the coterie around Edward IV, who had spent his brief exile of 1470–71 at the court of his sister's husband, Charles the Bold.[38] The patronage of the Edwardian court, and in particular of Edward's sister, Margaret of Burgundy, may have led him to Westminster in 1474. Broadly speaking, the climate of their literary taste during the decade was vernacular and edifying, centering on those works of "learned chivalry" befitting the instruction of a Burgundian courtier. The patronage of letters extended to products not just of the jousting field but of the university as well, as the Burgundian dukes began to solicit the advice of scholars for diplomacy, education, and entertainment. Surigonus's attempts at Valois patronage clearly had been motivated by the example of other scholars in courtly service, and what seems to be emerging from the 1470s is a conception of the laureate as someone with a university degree in public service.

In this environment, Surigonus and his Latin encomium on Chaucer would appeal to an audience reared on the courtly patronage and university education of the various humanist traditions coalescing at the Burgundian courts and brought to England in the circle around Edward IV. Surigonus stands for a kind of readership for Chaucer; but, more pointedly for Caxton, he enacts a critical arbitration of the work of textual recovery. Throughout Caxton's writings, outside readers—some named, some anonymous—mediate the discovery and printing of the texts at hand. The Earl Rivers, the Bishop of Westminster, William Pratt, Skelton, and a range of unnamed "freends" share in the autobiographical narrations through which Caxton frames his work. They select texts for publication, provide commentary on their value, or correct and edit Caxton's versions of them. Surigonus stands as the first in this line of critical judges. His scholarly training and contacts with the Valois dukes make him the ideal voice for a new, humanist-inspired panegyric on Chaucer. Schooled in the *auctores*, he can appreciate Chaucer's verbal artistry, rightly grouping him with Virgil and with Socrates. Having served at court (or at the very least, publically aspired to court service), he can present the poet as a fitting writer for aristocratic readers.

Chaucer's status as the "lauriat poete" could not but be affected by this changing value of the epithet. In the years after Surigonus received his various degrees, many teachers began to appear with the title.[39] In 1478 a course of lectures on poetry was delivered at Louvain by Lodewic Bruyn, described as poet laureate; so too, his successor at Louvain, Franciscus de Crementis, is recorded with the title as of 1492. John Kay, known only for his translation of Caoursin's *Siege of Rhodes*, presents his work in 1482 to Edward IV as the king's "poet laureate," and Bernard André had received in 1486 what may be the first royal annuity, now from Henry VII, as poet laureate. And, of course, Skelton would receive his laureations, first from Oxford in 1488, and later from Louvain and Cambridge in the early 1490s.[40] These laureations represented confirmation of an educational achievement. Although in itself the title did not confirm office for the state or court, it had become the habit of the Valois dukes to employ university-educated men as tutors, advisors, and ambassadors. Their roles were mediative, for as translators, transmitters, and interpreters of culture they brought texts to bear on the instruction of the politically controlling and their young.

This understanding of the laureate informs Caxton's use of the term and his relations with the early humanists. Poet laureates for Caxton are readers rather than writers. As editors, emenders, and critics, they mediate a distant literary past to present audiences. Their purpose in a court or in a printshop is to bring classical learning to bear on the interpretation or display of politics and power. Such was the function of the various Italians who had passed through England after Surigonus in the 1470s and 1480s: figures such as Lorenzo Traversagni, who secured a teaching post at Cambridge, and Pietro Carmeliano who, after a stint at Oxford, secured employment with the Keeper of the Rolls and rose to the position of Henry VII's Latin secretary. Caxton had printed Latin works by both men, and in 1483 he published Carmeliano's *Sex Epistole*, a collection of exchanges between Pope Sixtus IV and the doge of Venice. The colophon describes the text as "printed by William Caxton and diligently emended by Petrus Carmelianus Poet Laureate."[41] Caxton's biographer, George Painter, has argued that the publishing of the *Sex Epistole* was a politically motivated action, the making public of "a Venetian White Paper" arguing the Venetian cause in the hope of influencing English policy.[42]

Whatever the precise circumstances of this publication, however, its presentation of Carmeliano as a poet laureate is perfectly consistent with the role of Surigonus at the close of the *Boece*. Both men embody an imported humanist philology brought to bear on the constructions of an English literary or political program. Though they write in Latin, they may well be thought of as "translators" in the root sense of that term: as those who bring across from time or place a textual inheritance. Chaucer's accomplishments cannot fit those of living laureates. Without a university degree, without the sanctions of a foreign court or culture, and without that emendatory role of the scholar, Chaucer cannot function as a laureate in Caxton's critical program. When he thus appears with his old epithet in the 1484 *Canterbury Tales*, it is in a cultural environment that makes his laureation an act of historical projection. Caxton crowns Chaucer only by analogy and in the process alters not just the perceptions of the laureateship but the narrative of literary fatherhood that had controlled the poet's afterlife for the preceding eighty years.

Much has been made of Caxton's decision to reprint the *Canterbury Tales*, and most scholars take at face value the claims made in the prologue for offering a new, textually improved edition of the poem.[43] Certainly there are broad differences between the first and second printings, notably in their ordering of the *Tales* themselves. Caxton's 1478 edition fits securely in what Manly and Rickert identified as the *b*-version of the *Tales*, an ordering in fairly wide circulation in the fifteenth century (three manuscripts survive with this arrangement, among which is the Helmingham Manuscript). Yet the edition Caxton offered in 1483 does not correspond, as does his first, with any known textual tradition of the poem. Its ordering of the *Tales* is unique, and many of its individual readings seem to have originated with Caxton himself. It is generally presumed, therefore, that Caxton's second edition of the *Tales* is a reedited version of his first edition, using new manuscript evidence for its reorderings and corrections, rather than a printing from a wholly new copy-text.[44]

Caxton's reprinting of the *Canterbury Tales* thus offers something of an editorial paradox: although it aspires to correct its errors and produce a book "for to satysfye thauctour" (*Caxton*, 91), it remains a highly idiosyncratic volume, universally dismissed by modern editors in the establishment of Chaucer's text and valued today largely for the pleasures of its illustrative woodcuts of the Canterbury pilgrims. To read the prologue to this second printing as a story of editorial correction is, in these narrow terms, misleading, for Caxton's narrative is not so much an account of textual fidelity as it is a story of literary paternity and the social function of vernacular literature. Caxton's prologue redefines the traditional epithets "laureate" and "father" used for Chaucer, while it also develops the narratives of textual discovery characteristic of the range of Caxton's critical writing.

Caxton moves from the general to the specific. Modeling his opening on his earlier prologue to the *Polychronicon*, he begins with praise for the "clerkes / poetes / and historiographs that haue wreton many noble bokes of wysedom," for their work preserves the histories of holy actions and noble events "sith the begynnyng of the creacion of the world / vnto thys present tyme" (*Caxton*, 90). These are the makers of the "monumentis" that preserve the past, and Chaucer enters this edition as one of the writers of such monuments: not as the foremost poet of English life but as a "noble 7 grete philosopher." Chaucer's place in this panorama of writing rests on his ability to reproduce all the literary and historical genres Caxton defines as the range of human writing. In keeping with the opening encylopaedism of Caxton's literary history, Chaucer has made "many bokes and treatyces of many a noble historye as wel in metre as in ryme and prose." The *Canterbury Tales* presents histories "of euery astate and degre" and contains tales of "noblesse / wysedom / gentylesse / Myrthe /

and also of veray holynesse and vertue" (*Caxton*, 90). Though a certain amount of this critical prolixity may be attributed to the habitual iterations of late-medieval English prose, it is a critical prolixity pressed into the service of defining Chaucer's range. Though Caxton offers up a Chaucer who contains quite nearly everything, we are neither in the world of Dryden's vision of "God's plenty" nor in that of the post-Kittredgean appreciation of his literary imitation of the scope of social or psychological reality.[45] Nor are we wholly in the age of Lydgate and Shirley, whose need to codify the vast productions of the poet gave a voracity to literary making or manuscript compilation. Caxton's Chaucer is a writer of all forms and genres. His work encompasses the range of human *literary* experience. His is a book, in essence, full of other books, a work presented as the microcosm of the literary history that stands behind it.

Caxton's presentation of his editoral revisions has less to do with corruption at the level of the word or line than with abridgment, ordering, and expansion. His fear is that he might have misrepresented Chaucer's range of verbal artistry. The question here is just what Chaucer "made" or "sette in hys booke," and Caxton's sense of error lies "in settyng in somme thynges that he neuer sayd ne made / and leuyng out many thynges that he made whyche ben requysite to be sette in it" (*Caxton*, 91). The goal of editorial revision, therefore, is to produce a volume full of everything that Chaucer did. It is to make a book that represents the scope of Chaucerian poetry, that prints a *Canterbury Tales* corresponding to the generic encyclopaedism of what Caxton sees as Chaucer's achievement.

To that generic encyclopaedism Caxton adds a professional omnivorousness. Poets, historians, philosophers, and clerks all stand within the prologue as embodiments of that verbal control and command of historical material that prefigure Chaucer. To this collection of affiliations, Caxton adds that of the laureate, and his crowning of the poet also works as an analogy to past and current literary practice. Caxton writes of

> that noble 7 grete philosopher Gefferey chaucer the whiche for his ornate wrytyng in our tongue may wel haue the name of a laureate poete / For to fore that he by hys labour enbelysshyd / ornated / and made faire our englisshe.
>
> (*Caxton*, 90)

The key words in this passage are not those that praise Chaucer but those that qualify him. The relationship between the poet's eloquence and his laureate status is but a congruence, a loose association of past performance, rather than the absolute equation of the earlier fifteenth century. Chaucer here is not, as he is, for example, in the Harley 7333 headnote to the *Canterbury Tales*, "þe laureal and moste famous poete þat euer was to-fore him as in þemvelisshing of oure rude moders englisshe tonge."

Rather, as Caxton puts it, he "may wel haue the name of a laureate poete"—that is, Chaucer *may well* be imagined as being the historical equivalent of present poets laureate. His status as the laureate is a function of his place in the history of literature rather than his place at court or university. Nowhere does Caxton cultivate the vision of a Chaucer as the poet to King Richard II or Henry IV; nowhere does he invest in the elaborations of a poet of "Brutes Albyon" that had become the mainstay of the myth of Chaucer's laureate position. The only "laureates" in Caxton's world are those with university degrees, just as the only "historiographs"— a word Caxton uses for the first time in English—are those appointed historiographers by the Burgundian dukes or the English king.[46]

The point is that the place of Chaucer as a poet laureate is now quite markedly a product of the critical imagination; it is a projection of a present practice onto a past authority—not, as in the case of Lydgate or Shirley, the imagination of a previous model (i.e., Petrarch) onto an English equivalent. Caxton rehistoricizes the idea and office of the laureate to remove Chaucer from their operation and to fill those roles with his contemporaries. He recuperates the title from nostalgic fantasy and situates its function squarely in the lived world of rhetorical achievement and political sanction.

Changing the notion of the laureation also changes notions of paternity. In the *Boece* epilogue, Caxton displaced the laureateship from his author to his critic, while at the same time maintaining the inherited epithet of "fader" for his Chaucer. In the prologue to the 1483 *Canterbury Tales*, though, paternity shifts from Chaucer—here "first auctour" (*Caxton*, 91) but nowhere a father—to the owner of the book's exemplar. Caxton tells a story of what modern scholars would call textual criticism. He reports how his first edition of the *Canterbury Tales* was somehow deficient, "not accordyng in many places vnto the book that Gefferey chaucer had made," as one reader reports to him (*Caxton*, 91). But when Caxton rejoins that he had neither added to nor subtracted from the copy-text used for this first edition, this reader responds:

> Thenne he sayd he knewe a book whyche hys fader had and moche louyd / that was very trewe / and accordyng vnto his owen first book by hym [i.e., Chaucer] made / and sayd more yf I wold enprynte it agayn he wold gete me the same book for a copye / how be it he wyst wel / that hys fader wold not gladly departe fro it. . . . And thus we fyll at accord / And he ful gentylly gate of hys fader the said book / and delyuerd it to me / by whiche I haue corrected my book. /
>
> (*Caxton*, 91)

This is a story of editorial revision told as a tale of fathers and sons. It represents a notion of textual fidelity as genealogical, where the original text of the *Canterbury Tales* becomes an heirloom to be passed on. The authority of the text, and by consequence of Caxton's new edition, is thus inherently paternal. The father's book is copied from Chaucer's "owen first book," and the son's protestation that it "was very trewe" is as much a statement of filial pride as it is an assertion of textual integrity.

The genealogies of Caxton's story of republication resonate with what had come to be a new sense, in European scholarship, of genetic relations among texts and of textual history itself as a form of familial relations. What Anthony Grafton has shown as the rise of a genealogical method in the work of Politian and his contemporaries in the 1480s figures itself forth in Caxton's prologue: attentions to the archetypic status of the author's copy, to the privileging of manuscripts that descend from that copy, and to the reliability of ownership and provenance gave rise to the methods of collation and edition that would form the basis of modern textual criticism.[47] Certainly, Caxton's quick pragmatic operations on the *Canterbury Tales* that made his new edition are a far cry from the systematic principles of a Politian; yet Caxton's story of recovery and reproduction bears comparison with one published by Politian only six years later.

> I have obtained a very old volume of Cicero's *Epistolae Familiares* . . .
> and another one copied from it, as some think, by the hand of Francesco Petrarca. There is much evidence, which I shall now omit, that the one is copied from the other. But the latter manuscript . . . was bound in such a way by a careless bookbinder that we can see from the numbers of the gatherings that one gathering has clearly been transposed. . . . Now the book is in the public library of the Medici family. From this one, then, so far as I can tell, are derived all the extant manuscripts of these letters, as if from a spring or fountainhead. And all of them have the text in that ridiculous and confused order which I must now put into proper form and, as it were, restore.[48]

Politian's story shows considerable similarities to Caxton's in its broad outlines. Both phrase the act of editing in terms of personal discovery; both note the errors of a previous copy and locate those errors in the shop of the bookmaker (in Caxton's case, his own; in Politian's, that of a bookbinder). Both also invest in the image of a family that owns a true, originary document of authorial making. But in the details of their narratives lies all the difference. Politian's is an account of names and owners, of authoritative writers and transmitters who confer onto the text the power of their claim. From Petrarch to the Medici, from the personal hand of the poet laureate of Europe to the public library of the greatest of its patrons, this "fountainhead" of Cicero's texts owes its authority. The "I" of Politian's account moves through these various landmarks of literary power and control to restore Cicero's work to its proper form.

By contrast, Caxton dwells on the anonymous. We are not told who owned the text, nor are we given any information about just who this emending son might be. Nor are there any other names in Caxton's prologue. We find none of the familiar writers specified among its "clerkes / poetes / and historiographs," none of the various patrons addressed for Caxton's work. It has been argued that the anonymities of this prologue are due to the political circumstances in which Caxton reprinted Chaucer: The instabilities of the brief reign of Richard III, the recent death of the Earl Rivers and the loss of the Woodvilles as old patrons, and the shifting alliances among the city and the court may have left Caxton with an insecure sense of who his prospective patrons could have been.[49] The absence of named readers, patrons, or commissioners from this book has been thus explained as Caxton's way of steering among these uncertainties, of effectively playing it safe without committing to a faction. But these anonymities have a thematic, and I think commercial, purpose in the prologue. They grant a public readership for Chaucer, one not limited to coterie or class. They take the poet's legacy out of the possessions of named or armigerous readers and display it for whoever may decide to buy it. To make the book a sellable commodity, it must appeal to all potential readers, without recognition of specific genealogy or patronly faction.[50]

By offering a narrative of paternal bequeathal and commercial reproduction, Caxton effaces the fatherhood of Chaucer. He displaces the authority of this edition from the "first auctor" onto the later, yet unnamed, reader, transforming the processes of correction from those of coterie manuscript rescription to those of commercial return. The "father" in this story is the owner of a better manuscript, and what he sires is not just the new edition but a new audience: one critically astute enough to recognize the need for textual correction and the charge of commercial exchange. The reading son takes Chaucer's poetry out of the environments of family legacy and brings it into the public marketplace. Chaucer's work is "translated" here, moved from the manor to the bookshop, from the genealogies of family bequeathal to the narratives of literary history. What is "paternal," in the end, is the paternity of text and ownership, not composition. And what matters, too, is less the specificity of Chaucer's own inheritance than the generic patterns of his writing. Placing the *Canterbury Tales* in genealogies of literary history entails a generality of literary forms. The poem measures itself against *kinds* of writing, rather than specific writers, and its new edition need not seek approval from the patron or the laureate but from the buyer.

But if the anonymities of this essay appear to contradict its nascent genealogical approach to textual criticism and in consequence provide the foil for the articulations of Politian's method, they provide the foil, too, for the later versions of recovery told in the 1490 *Eneydos*. Its prologue revels in the name. Throughout, we find the specificities of readers, sailors, merchants, laureates, and kings. We find the details of a canon of classical literature, with Virgil and Ovid, Dares and Dictys, appealed to as the progenitors of a literary history. The *Eneydos* prologue is, in a profound way, about naming—about redefining, for a new political and critical hegemony, the proper texts, readers, and patrons for vernacular bookmaking. Within this plethora of proper names, though, one is conspicuously absent. Nowhere is Chaucer mentioned, nowhere is he the father or the laureate. Its English figures are the newly born, John Skelton and Prince Arthur, not the dead and buried. It is a story of the here and now, and its controlled evocations of the immediate have led many modern critics to value it for its facts rather than its tropes: for its reliable account of history instead of its creative control of fiction. In what follows, I read the *Eneydos* prologue as a deeply retrospective essay, one that looks back over a career in printing to place the recovery of texts amid the personal travels of Caxton himself. This is an autobiography of the imagination, an account of finding books in the emplotting of a reader's life.

III

Sitting alone, Caxton discovers the book of the *Eneydos* lying among the piles of books and manuscripts that clutter his shop. He tries to translate from its French yet is unsure about the dialect and diction into which the book should go. The Abbot of Westminster is invoked as an authority on the English language, for in his possession are documents in what Caxton calls "olde englysshe," so alien as to be unreadable: "it was more lyke to dutche than englysshe" (*Caxton*, 108). Caxton's ensuing reflections on diachronic change lead to a story of synchronic variation, and we get the now famous account of the mercers who try to buy eggs in Kent, only to discover that the London "eggys" should be Kentish "eyren." Into what dialect should Caxton's book be translated, and for whom should it be produced and sold? he muses. In the end, it is John Skelton, "late created poete laureate in the vnyuersite of oxenforde," who is the arbiter of Caxton's critical decisions (*Caxton*, 109). He calls on Skelton "to ouersee and correcte this sayd booke," and after much praise of his abilities, the prologue closes with a commendation to the newly born Prince Arthur, Prince of Wales, and to King Henry VII himself (*Caxton*, 109–10).

The work is done, the printed books have all been made, and Caxton sits surveying the past records of his life when a new book appears. The story told here is a story that begins at the beginning of all literary history, with Virgil and the classics, and takes us to the present moment of a living laureate. We move, in the course of the narrative, from the city to the country, from the church to the court, from the printshop to the university, from Kent to Oxford. But the *Eneydos* prologue also recapitulates the life of its own printer. Caxton began and ended his career with the story of Troy. His first translation was from Raoul le Fevre's *Recueil des Histoires de Troyes*, made between 1469 and 1471 and printed as his first book sometime in 1474 or 1475. What he calls, in the epilogue to that book, "the generall destruccion of that noble cyte of Troye" (*Caxton*, 8) reappears, at the close of his life, with the book of "the generall destruccyon of the grete Troye" (*Caxton*, 107). Caxton's reflections on linguistic change may be as personal as they are factual. Certainly, English had changed greatly in the sixty-odd years of Caxton's life, and historians of language have often relied on the *Eneydos* prologue to confirm the impact of such philological phenomena as the Great Vowel Shift and the growth of the vernacular vocabulary in the fifteenth century.[51] But Caxton's phrasing takes us back again and again to his own life. Behind his apparently offhand remark that the Abbot of Westminster's early English documents look like "dutche" lie Caxton's sojourns in Cologne and the Low Countries: what he refers to in his first book as his ".xxx. yere for the most parte in the contres of Braband. flandres holand and zeland" (*Recuyell*, in *Caxton*, 4). In Caxton's story of the London sailor caught in Kent stand the inscriptions of the printer's self in the reflections on linguistic change. In a story of a mercer blown from "zelande" back to Kent lies the negative example of the mercer Caxton having left his home for Holland. As he had put it in the *Recuyell* prologue:

> And afterward whan I remembryd my self of my symplenes and vnperfightnes that I had in bothe langages / that is to wete in frenshe 7 in englissh for in france was I neuer / and was born 7 lerned myn englissh in kente in the weeld where I doubte not is spoken as brode and rude englissh as is in ony place of englond.
>
> (*Caxton*, 4)

Nearly two decades later, the mercer of the *Eneydos* prologue finds himself in a wilderness of language: in a world where "egges" are "eyren," and where London English is mistaken for French. Blown back from his Burgundian journey, he finds himself in the rude world of Caxton's childhood, as this strange encounter writes out a new and personal account of the *errores* that blow Aeneas from his Rome to Carthage. Indeed, the *Eneydos* prologue is in itself a story of such romance-like *errores*: wanderings from place to place, but also possibilities of errors in translation and transmission, misprints that must be corrected by a knowing readership.

As Caxton's mercer had been linguistically rescued by a friend—translating so that the good Kentish woman "vnderstod hym wel" (*Caxton*, 108)—so Caxton will be saved from his errors by John Skelton. He appears only after we have run through the whole range of humankind: clerks and gentles, abbots and mercers, London men and Kentish women, the rude and the noble. Skelton *is* a discovery here, and Caxton crowns him laureate anew.

> But I praye mayster Iohn Skelton late created poete laureate in the vnyuersite of oxenforde to ouersee and correcte this sayd booke. And taddresse and expowne where as shalle be founde faulte to theym that shall requyre it. For hym I knowe for suffycyent to expowne and englysshe euery dyffyculte that is therin / For he hath late translated the epystlys of Tulle / and the boke of dyodorus syculus. and diuerse other werkes oute of latyn in to englysshe not in rude and olde langage. but in polysshed and ornate termes craftely. as he that hath redde vyrgyle / ouyde. tullye. and all the other noble poetes and oratours / to me vnknowen: And also he hath redde the ix. muses and vnderstande theyr musicalle scyences. and to whom of theym eche scyence is appropred. I suppose he hath dronken of Elycons well.
>
> *(Caxton,* 109)

Skelton's bold appearance here refers as much to the progress of Caxton's own work as it does to the externals of a Tudor literary patronage or the attempts of an English university to impersonate a European practice.[52] Caxton presents a narrative thematically concerned with naming and review. Its retrospections over his career create what might be called a discourse of self-referentiality: a discourse consciously concerned with rereading and rewriting the products of the press. Skelton's appearance toward the close of the *Eneydos* prologue reviews the traditions of a laureate authority invoked in the *Boece* and the second edition of the *Canterbury Tales*. The importations of a European *laureatus* and the vague imaginations of a Chaucer who "may wel" possess the title fade before an English "late created poete laureate in the vnyuersite of oxenforde." Armed with that education, Skelton controls the range of literary writing, a canon of classical *auctores* that includes both named and unnamed writers. Skelton reaches beyond the boundaries of Caxton's learning, but he also reaches outside the narrations of the *Eneydos* prologue. For in a narrative concerned with naming, where even an isolated mercer can be dubbed "sheffelde," Skelton's command of works "vnknowen" to Caxton takes him outside both the retrospections and the forecasts of his fame.

Chaucer is gone. Of course, he will appear throughout accounts of English literary history at the turn of the century. Grouped with Gower and Lydgate, maintained as the first in a line of writers that includes George Ashby, Stephen Hawes, and John Skelton, Chaucer does stand in the line of poetic inheritance.[53] But Caxton takes the business of writing literary history out of the realm of genealogy. He makes it bibliographical rather than personal, makes it a function of texts read rather than lives lived. Skelton is not to be compared with Chaucer or the other vernacular writers—as he would be, say, in the panegyrics of the 1510s.[54] Rather, he is to be assessed within the canon of *auctores*. As in Surigonus's epitaph on Chaucer, and as in the humanistic Latin poems on Skelton by Erasmus (1499) and Robert Whittinton (1519)—the latter, by the way, made poet laureate in 1513—the English poet is the heir to the classical tradition, not the heir to other English poets.[55] Skelton inaugurates a poetry in English, much as Chaucer had; but in the process, he effaces Chaucer. His "polisshed and ornate terms," though praised in the language of Chaucerian encomium, come not from the English poet but directly from the Latins.

The genealogical impulse at the close of the *Eneydos* prologue is political, not literary. Caxton rhetorically gives birth to Skelton much as Henry VII gave birth to Prince Arthur, and it is this latter "hye born" son who is the dedicatee of the volume. But certainly this is not a book for a four-year old child. There is no sense here that the *Eneydos* is "children's literature" in the manner of such other products of the press as the *Book of Curtesye* or *Aesop's Fables*. Nor is the printer's presentation as the prince's "moste humble subget 7 seruaunt" (*Caxton*, 110) an equivalent to Lydgate's subjugations before the infant Henry VI. What distinguishes this presentation of the child is the powerful presence of the father. Henry VII is as much the object of the dedication as the prince; he is as much the focus of his praise as Arthur. The status of this Prince of Wales as heir, as son, as focus of appeals for patronage, lies in the living presence of his father, and this fact of literary politics would have been familiar to Caxton and his readers from the laureate commissionings on Arthur's birth and Henry's right to rule.

Prince Arthur's birth in 1486 had focused energies both diplomatic and poetic operating to confirm the legitimacy of Henry's kingship since his assumption of the throne a year before.[56] For a king who had attained his power more by force of battle than by obvious birthright, the siring of a male heir (together with his linkages to other English and Continental royal families) became a public means of assuring the dynasty he sought to found. That birth was obviously a source of much public celebration and display, and Henry VII commissioned from his resident laureates commendations of his personal and dynastic paternity. Bernard André, Giovanni Gigli, and Pietro Carmeliano wrote poems on the prince's birth filled with the topoi of late-fifteenth-century humanist panegyric. That poetry is largely classicizing, and their versions of a new, dynastic security are drawn from Roman poetry on imperial conquest, from Virgilian prophecy, and from ancient mythography. In a certain sense, Arthur's birth restores an older, "Arthurian" glory that had also motivated Henry VII's claims for Tudor ancestry. But, as David Carlson has recently illustrated in a sensitive reading of these Latin poems, the controlled application of "antique myths to [this] historical present" outweighed whatever allusions these poets made to an earlier Arthur.[57] Carlson summarizes their achievement in terms that may explain Caxton's as well:

> By substituting fictions of Roman imperial glory, Virgilian messianism, and epic war for the Arthur myth, and so dissociating the birth of Prince Arthur from its medieval literary antecedants, the poets envisaged, if only by analogy, a solution to the so-called Tudor problem: freeing the Tudor dynasty from the threat of independent exercise of power by a feudal, medieval aristocracy. That threat had made the fifteenth-century dynastic struggles possible, but was now countered by the advent of the Tudors. The accession of Henry VII and then the birth of an heir to him were the political version of the solution to the problem of the immediate medieval past that Henry's court poets anticipated for him in making classical images, discontinuous with medieval traditions, for the birth of Prince Arthur.[58]

Primary among those classical images was that of the golden age. Arthur's birth restores a *seculum aureatum*, not of the Celtic Arthurian world but of the paradisical fantasies of Roman poets. *Aurea iam redeunt cum principe saecula tanto*, "Golden ages return now with such a prince," as Gigli put it, and his phrasing may recall the pleas of Lydgate in his Lancastrian mode for a return to the "world tho dayes callid aureat."[59] To a certain extent, the recollection is a valid one, for both the English propagandist and the Italian laureate draw on the same font of mythology for their vision. Yet, where Gigli's poem differs from Lydgate's, and in turn where the context of early Tudor panegryic differs from Lancastrian, is (to appropriate Carlson's terms) in its deliberately cultivated discontinuities between the recent medieval traditions and a deep classical past. The birth of Arthur, in the hands of Henry VII's humanists, looks back to the origins of both the social moment of imperial control and the poetic formulations of a golden age that had defined it.

Such retrospections frame the place of Skelton and the lacuna of Chaucer at the close of the *Eneydos* prologue. Caxton presents a Skelton in effect dissociated from his medieval literary antecedents. Not part of any genealogy of English writers, Skelton stands without named, English forebears. Much as the young prince's own "noble progenytours" are nameless here, buried in the dynastic conflicts of a century now past, so too are Skelton's. What are the books "vnknowen" to Caxton he has read? Who are these "other noble poetes and oratours"? They are, I would suggest, the unnamed English, the medieval antecedents Skelton's writing has replaced. The lists of English kings and English authors familiar from Lydgate are elided here, as Caxton skips past both the native and the recent to go back to that deep classical past. Its myths are those of the muses and of "Elycons well," not those of Arthur and Excalibur. Its authors are

Virgil, Ovid, and Tully, not Chaucer, Gower, and Lydgate. If Skelton is a
kind of a literary son or newborn star, like Arthur Tudor, he is one without the need to name the heritage of an immediate, medieval past.

To rephrase Carlson's argument, Caxton offers the *literary* version of
the solution to the problem of that past. What Henry's court poets antici-
pated for *him* was that strategy of discontinuity, a strategy that might be
labeled laureate hermeneutics. Reading like a laureate now means not just
reading for the past but writing for the present. It implies a political impulse for the translation of classical culture to current readers, an impulse
that goes beyond the panegyric and emendatory projects for which Caxton
had relied on them. Skelton may offer advice on the linguistic translation
of the *Eneydos*; but, in the end, Caxton invokes his authority as "poete
laureate" to address prince and king.

> I praye hym 7 suche other to correcte adde or mynysshe where as
> he or they shall fynde faulte / . . . And yf ony worde be sayd therin
> well / I am glad. and yf otherwyse I submytte my sayd boke to theyr
> correctyon / Whiche boke I presente vnto the hye born. my tocom-
> ynge naturell 7 souerayn lord Arthur . . .
>
> (*Caxton*, 110)

Read in this sequence, Skelton forms the bridge from the submissions of
the translator to the subjections of the "seruaunt." The unspecified "suche
other" are those who, like Skelton, have laureate authority: men like
André, Gigli, and Carmeliano, who put their knowledge of the classics to
the praise of newborn princes. Their present yet unnamed authority en-
ables Caxton to "submytte" his own book for the patronage of a royal father and son.

Laureation and paternity thus come together at the close of Caxton's
prologue to frame anew the production and reception of vernacular literature in the institutions that control it. As English laureate, Skelton replaces the imaginations of a Chaucerian laureation and the importations
of a European scholarship to provide the critical interpretation of past
texts for local readers. As royal father, Henry VII replaces the conjurings
of Chaucer's fatherhood and the paternity of bibliographic bequests to
provide a patronage for the work of the laureates. The process of textual
recovery—described in Caxton's previous prologues and epilogues as the
individuated hunts for books and tombs or as the chance encounters of
the bibliophile—now has the sanction of the university and court. The
"poet laureate" that Skelton will become is now akin more to the celebra-
tors of the birth of Arthur than to the elegist at Chaucer's tomb. His place
in the narrative of the *Eneydos* prologue links the personal with the political, the reflections on reading with the demands of patronage. Although

his crowning is from Oxford, his service lies with the King, and the father of this text is now the father of the nation.

In the end, what does it mean to read Chaucer "like a laureate"? In one sense, it means not to read him at all—or at least, not to read him as the source for literary imitation or domestic pleasure. Chaucer's *poetry* plays virtually no role in Caxton's construction of his authority as literary writer or in the deployments of his name. Instead, what he constructs is an idea of Chaucer's presence and his absence, a sense of how the name of Chaucer may be used in the articulations of a humanist recovery of texts or a commercial ploy for selling books. I do not claim that Caxton did not value Chaucer as poet, nor that his readers and clients paid little attention to his writings. Instead, what I have sought to show is how the praise of Chaucer finds a new place in the literary system of the sanctioned laureate. That he is absent from the last of Caxton's critical essays and absent from the literary birth of Skelton shows that Caxton and his readers now need neither invoke the name of Chaucer nor write genealogies of literary history out of his alignment with Gower, Lydgate, and others. Chaucer's tomb has been found, his texts clearly established, and his audience secured within the court and university.

But for this audience, Chaucer's paternity and laureateship are no longer (to borrow the words of A. C. Spearing) the "constitutive idea of the English poetic tradition."[60] To be a writer after Chaucer is no longer to be a rewriter of the poet. It may be to invoke him and his status in a pantheon of English and antique *auctores*, as Hawes does; it may be, too, to seek his imagined approval, as Skelton does. But it is not, primarily, to mime his forms. What I have sought to illustrate in this chapter, and seek to argue in the next, is how the fragmentation of Chaucerian authority splits the old, critical associations between rhetorical prowess, political approval, and patronized success. The concerns introduced here—of the relations of the book and tomb, of Continental humanist interpretation and vernacular poetic practice, of a coterie for manuscripts and a public for print—align themselves anew in Hawes and Skelton, as the celebration of the vernacular writer goes on not beside tombs of the poetic dead but at the courts and universities that sire laureates empowered to unclose and understand the volumes of the past.

CHAPTER SIX

Impressions of Identity: Print, Poetry, and Fame in Hawes and Skelton

AT THE conclusion to the "Prohemye" of his last published poem, *The Conforte of Louers* (printed in 1515), Stephen Hawes affirms his own ineptitude at literary composition. Drawing on what was by then a century-long tradition of self-deprecation and appeals to audience correction, Hawes submits himself so effusively that it has been hard for any modern reader to take seriously these lines as anything less than unthinking imitation.

> I lytell or nought / experte in this scyence
> Compyle suche bokes / to deuoyde ydlenes
> Besechynge the reders / with al my delygence
> Where as I offende / for to correct doubtles
> Submyttynge me to theyr grete gentylnes
> As none hystoryagraffe / nor poete laureate
> But gladly wolde folowe / the makynge of Lydgate
>
> Fyrst noble Gower / moralytees dyde endyte
> And after hym Cauncers / grete bokes delectable
> Lyke a good phylosophre / meruaylously dyde wryte
> After them Lydgate / the monke commendable
> Made many wonderfull bokes moche profytable
> But syth they are deed / & theyr bodyes layde in chest
> I pray to god to gyue theyr soules good rest.[1]

(15–28)

All the commonplaces of humility are here. There are the claims for lack of skill, the pleas for correction, the appeals to a laureate tradition, the construction of a canon of vernacular versemakers, and the lament for their deaths. But much has happened between Lydgate and Hawes, and these familiar effusions have been colored by the changes in the literary culture initiated by the early Tudor court. Hawes conjures up a vision of the poet laureate far different from Lydgate's imaginations; indeed, that poet laureate is set in opposition to Lydgate the maker. Hawes now contrasts the English inheritance against a literary system shaped by the university educated, politically sanctioned laureates. By 1510 or 1511, when the *Conforte of Louers* was composed, Henry VII's laureates and historiographers had come and gone, Skelton had made and lost a reputation (though he was soon to regain it), and a newly crowned Henry VIII had begun to populate his court with scholars of the likes of Thomas More.[2]

In this environment, the professed claims for an affiliation with Lydgate may seem deliberately if not perversely retrograde. They have been read as part of Hawes's own nostalgia for a literary past, or more sympathetically as a reflection of what may have been the popular literary culture of the age, one in which Lydgate was widely read and printed, and in which Chaucer and Gower had already received several editions from the press.[3] Hawes's affiliations, too, have been seen as part of his rivalry with Skelton.[4] Together with the poem's later possible allusions to Skelton's ascendancy at Henry VII's court—and, perhaps, its rejoinders to Skelton's digs at Hawes and Lydgate in his *Phyllyp Sparowe*—these lines may define what might be thought of as an anti-laureate poetics: an attempt not simply at preserving the old strategies of Lydgatean aureation, but of reconceiving the vernacular heritage of "making" in the age of print.

Hawes and Skelton have long been seen as two opposing poles of early Tudor culture: the one retrograde, the other innovative; the one abject, the other bold; the one rejected by the court, the other restored to political favor.[5] They are an effective pairing, representing two approaches to the various decisions faced by players in the literary politics of late-fifteenth- and early-sixteenth-century England. Much as Chaucer and Gower have been paired by modern scholars, Skelton and Hawes conveniently dichotomize the two paths to be taken at a cusp in literary history.[6] These poets come at the close of my book, too, but for a set of reasons different from the ones inherited from modern criticism. My concern is not so much with how they imitate or rewrite Chaucer's poetry, but rather how they use his name. Both poets confront the historicity of Chaucer in order to define themselves as vernacular authors. Although they appropriate his various personae and occasionally lift wholesale phrases from his work, they use him in a manner different from that of the imitators of the Lydgatean stripe. Their writings do not parasitically depend on their Chaucerian pretexts for their narrative sense or generic alignments. Skelton and Hawes use Chaucer for his citability, where the invocation of his name and writings fosters the occasion for reflecting on the nature of a literary culture and the social function of the English writer.

One of the themes of this book has been how the material culture of late-medieval literacy presented English poetry as a beheld thing. In discerning the narrative coherence of a manuscript assembly or in tracing the travels of a reading hero in a visionary romance, I have been concerned with how the fifteenth century *saw* poetry, and furthermore with how the various conventions and technologies of book production could be thematized within the critical response or poetic narration. My previous chapter had sought the intimations of those changes in the monumentalizing of the poet and the attitudes toward textual correction in Caxton. That chapter focused on reception and transmission: on the presentations of those figures who disseminated Chaucer to a public. Here, I turn to authorship itself. Skelton and Hawes are, to a certain extent, both products of the press: Skelton, given literary birth in Caxton's *Eneydos* prologue; Hawes, whose exclusive publishing arrangement with Caxton's successor Wynkyn de Worde formed a relationship of poet to printer not seen again in England for over a century.[7]

Yet, for all their apparent coexistence as writers in early print culture and for all their shared participation in the literary politics of early Tudor courts, Hawes and Skelton differ markedly in their uses of print technology, and as a consequence in their appropriations and appeals to Chaucer, their conceptions of a literary fame, and their articulations of authorial control. Though he had been occasionally printed in his lifetime, Skelton seems to have had little interest in the new technology.[8] For all his formal innovation and his topical concerns, he sustains the practice of manuscript coterie circulation in a fashion Hawes decisively abandons. The older poets speak in Skelton's writings in a manner far from Hawes's practice, and the implications of this difference define the two courses of English writing after Caxton. Hawes makes the technology of print a theme for his poetic narratives. He sustains the idea of a monumentalized Chaucer represented in the *Boece* epilogue, and this monumentalizing confirms the poet's historical distance from the present. His status as a buried *auctor* rather than a remembered maker affirms itself throughout Hawes's work, as he separates the "ancient" Chaucer from Lydgate.

Hawes reads the poet in what he identifies as "prynted bookes," and part of my argument will be that Hawes conceives of Chaucer's literary authority through Caxton's publications and his criticism. The idea of shaping an authorial presence through the technologies of print will thus inform Hawes's own project. De Worde's publishing blitz of 1509, in which all four of Hawes's then existing poems appeared from the press, together with their close attentions to the visual organization of the words on the page and the pictorial accompaniments to the poetry, reveal a careful coordination between poet and printer.[9] These attentions, I argue in what follows, complement the critical metaphors Hawes develops to express poetic understanding: images of seeing, impressing, engraving, and imprinting. Hawes's concerted appearance in print is an event in the "construction" of an author, and I use this word, familiar from a more contemporary critical vocabulary, in the historical sense that Hawes deploys it: as the work "harde in construccyon," a poetry made, fixed, and graven in the monuments of literary fame.

Skelton, by contrast, represents himself as a poet of the scripted page rather than the printed book, a poet of the oratorical performance rather than disseminated documents of booksellers. Though both Skelton and Hawes share in the literary milieu of an early Tudor, Burgundy-inspired humanism, it is Skelton who pursues the oratorical, performative roles shaped by both its practice and its ideologies. Gordon Kipling has persuasively argued for the influence of the Burgundian *rhetoriqueurs* on Skelton, and in *Phyllyp Sparowe* and the *Garlande of Laurell* the ideals of a performative poetics govern their thematic concerns and formal organization.[10] Both poems are, in some sense, works in progress, for their texts had been built up by accretion over several decades. Both poems, too, present the practice of Skeltonian revision as one of their themes, and I argue at this chapter's close that they constitute—in their reflections on the poet's craft and in their presentations of the English writers of the past—a sustained critical response to Hawes's monumentalizing of the aureate tradition. While Hawes reads Chaucer in the printed book, Skelton has the poet and his compeers speak in visionary colloquies.

For all this interest in the techno-culture of authority, however, Skelton and Hawes both confront what may be the most well known fact of Tudor literary history: the laureation. Skelton rests his fame on its attainment, and his presentation as a writer, right down to the attributions of his works, carries the laureate epithet inseparably from his name. In this, we might say he completes the process of rehistoricizing the laureation initiated in the last third of the fifteenth century—completes it not just in presenting himself as titled, sanctioned laureate, but, through the very writing of his name, in reenacting the originary Petrarchan gesture of the name and title linked together. If Petrarch was the eponymous poet laureate for the fourteenth century, Skelton becomes the eponymous laureate for the early sixteenth, and in this context no one—not even Hawes—may aspire to the degree of sanction or authority he has.

To these ends, Hawes constructs what I have called an anti-laureate poetics: one pendant not just on the humility topoi of a Lydgate (though those are there) but on the conception of literary fame bound to the new technology of print. Hawes offers up the idea of a literature in print to define the reception both of Chaucer and himself. Denied the offices of laureate, historiographer, or *orator regius* in the courts of Henry VII and VIII, denied the fame of poet while alive, Hawes seeks the monumental literary status of the Chaucer of the *Boece* epilogue. His fascination with his afterlife thus complements his interest in the inscribed. Hawes's poems, in effect, become his epitaphs, and this concretization of the written word contrasts distinctively with Skelton's parody of epitaphic praise in *Phyllyp Sparowe* and the wild excesses of his bibliography in the *Garlande of Laurell*.

Both Hawes and Skelton thus preoccupy themselves with the reception of their works and names, and in doing so they complete my own narration of the making of poetic identity after Chaucer. Authorship comes to be associated with the name, the externalization of a style, an origin, a status onto a persona with a history. In the anonymities of earlier manuscript compilations, as I illustrated in Chapters 2 and 3, the author's name is often absent, unnecessary to a literature pressed into service of a specific social function, be it education, entertainment, or group identification. The making of the Chaucer canon, as I sought to illustrate in Chapter 4, involved the scribal and the scholarly projection of a sense of Chaucer's work onto the named identity of the poet. The principle of appellation becomes the principle of authorship itself. It confers a human identity, rather than a social or a cultural function, on a given text. What happens at the close of the fifteenth century is the reestablishment of authorial identity around the name. Caxton's volumes are in some sense about naming, and in Chapter 5 I sought to illustrate how Caxton's sporting with names and titles in his prologues and epilogues suggests an idea of authorial control in tandem with the powers of the laureate editor or the commissioned printer.

In the work of Hawes and Skelton, then, it is the appeal to the named authority of writers that constructs the literary history in which the author names himself within his text. Skelton's near obsession with his name and title—with articulating a persona that has not just a historical or biographical identity ("John Skelton") but an institutional one as well ("poet laureate")—becomes a way of redefining the writer's relationship to the past. In Hawes's case, it is not so much the construction of a named authorial person as it is the invocation of the names of past English writers: an invocation that presents the name as living in perpetuity. Hawes writes of poets, heroes, and scholars as if only their names lived on, and his exploitation of the rhyme pair *name / fame* nicely encapsulates his fascinations. Hawes seeks to have his name survive not by inscribing it within the poem or by offering the power of its titles, as Skelton does, but by presenting it in printer's colophons. Hawes lives on in his printed books mechanically reproduced along with those of antique authors and their heroes.

I

The stanzas from the *Conforte of Louers* that begin this chapter come at the end of a literary career marked both by royal patronage and courtly rejection. As a groom of the chamber to Henry VII, Hawes would have served in a variety of functions as court tutor, rhetorician, and panegyrist for the king's projects.[11] In these roles, his work would have been akin to that of Bernard André, whose triumphal poems of the 1490s celebrated Henry's conquests; to William Cornish, responsible during that decade for what were labeled as "disguisings" keyed to diplomatic and political occasions; and to John English, who in the first decade of the new century had served as Master of the King's Players. Hawes himself had been paid ten shillings in 1506 "for a ballet that he gave to the kings grace in rewarde."[12] But just three years later, with the deaths of Henry VII and his mother, Margaret Beaufort (long thought of as a patroness of Hawes and his printer de Worde), Hawes's fortunes seem to have shifted. Although he composed *A Ioyful Medytacyon* for the coronation of Henry VIII (printed by de Worde soon after the king's ascension on June 24, 1509), it seems clear that the new king had little place for Hawes at his court. It may be, as Gordon Kipling has suggested, that Hawes had been too closely associated with the Burgundy-inspired humanists who lost out to the more Italianate, "classical" humanists favored by Henry VIII;[13] or it may be, as Alastair Fox has claimed, that Hawes had committed some transgression of amatory propriety and had allegorized it in his accounts of the visionary lovers in his poetry, such that he had been ostracized from public service.[14] For whatever reasons, it is clear that soon after Henry VIII became king, Hawes lost his position. In the title page to the *Conforte of Louers*, he is described as "sometyme grome of the honourable chambre of our late souerayne lorde kynge Henry ye seuenth," implying that he had no place in the new Henry's court, and throughout the *Conforte*, Hawes presents cryptically allusive comments on the critical responses to his earlier poetry and the fortunes of the more successful poet laureate, John Skelton.[15]

Though we may thus find much of Hawes's success in courtly records and in printer's colophons, what we find in the *Conforte of Louers*—and for that matter, in virtually all his surviving verse—is a chronicle of exclusions. Hawes never held, as far as we can tell, the title "poet laureate" as Skelton and André had; nor, in contrast to André, did he hold the position of "hystoryagraffe" to the king. The *Confort* details the rejection of his poetry, and in its dialogues between the lover/author and his allegorical La Belle Pucelle, Hawes writes a fable of his own reception: of the courtly reading and rejection of a work that was not simply out of fashion but out of form. Hawes represents his project as a synthesis of culture and technology. He seeks, in the traditions of Burgundian courtly humanism, in the ideologies of early Renaissance scholarship, and in the possibilities of print a conception of literary fame that can survive outside the confines of the court. Hawes imagines the idea of an absent author and his distant readers; he presents literature as a seen thing rather than as a performed piece; and he intimates, in his appeals to Gower, Chaucer, and Lydgate, a new alignment of the inheritance of English poetry in the world of the printed book.

To understand these various directions operating in his poetry, I first wish to review some of the cultural connections made and broken in the early Tudor period. Much recent work on the Anglo-Burgundian milieu of Hawes has stressed the public and performative features of its courtly discourse. Its literary figures, patronized by Henry VII, conceived of themselves more as "orators" than "poets," as rhetoricians whose command of panegyric would be pressed into the service of royal propaganda or display.[16] Such figures stood in the direct line of the Burgundian schools of rhetoric; and the professed blend of learning and chivalry articulated in the French, English, and Latin writings of the Valois and Henrician court— and translated into the self-presentations of such Englishmen as the Earl Rivers, Robert Tiptoft, and Lord Berners in the last quarter of the fifteenth century—painted a vision of the courtly life as one lived out before an audience.

It is the tournamentary and the chivalric that may be found in the poetry of the period, and Gordon Kipling calls attention to the popular allegories of chivalric education in Hawes's *Pastime of Pleasure* and John Skelton's idiosyncratic recreations of the metrical virtuosity and self-conscious wordplay of the Burgundian rhetoricians. In the *Pastime*, Hawes's treatments of *pronunciatio* and the arts of memory (the first of such treatments in the English language and distinguished for their detail and their length within the poem) testify to that concern with the orated, the said, and the performed that Kipling sees at the heart of the Anglo-Burgundian aesthetic alliance.[17] Graunde Amoure's education in that poem is an education in the arts of discourse, and the progress of his learning has long been appreciated as depicting, in the fashion of a mirror for courtiers, the specifics of a verbal tutelage at the early Tudor court.[18]

But there is, both for Hawes and for his cultural moment, a concern with the seen as much as with the heard, with the read as much as with the spoken. The texts of Cicero and the traditions of the *ars memorativa* had formed the spine of an approach to learning that inured the student to the visualization of the word.[19] The Italian humanist preoccupations with the monumentality of the literary artifice, together with the new technology of print that reinforced, to some degree, that interest, led to what has been discerned as a new spatialization of the ways of thinking.[20] And in the traditions of Burgundian intellectual life itself, a new interest in the visual appeal of the book had developed. Part of this new attitude toward books was no doubt due to the sophistication of the Flemish manuscript illuminators, and in turn to the creation of deluxe manuscripts valued for their visual appeal as much as for their content. It found its expression in Henry VII's patronage of European printers, men like the French Antoine Verard, who, unlike Caxton and de Worde, produced for the king's library sumptuous, hand-illuminated volumes in both French and Latin.[21]

But part of these changing attitudes toward books and bookmaking also developed from the changing habits of reading the text itself. The rise of silent reading as a social practice in the fifteenth century, together with the interest in the value of private study, had fostered what Paul Saenger considers as a shift in Northern European ideas of the book.[22] In tandem with the introduction of the printing press, a changing notion of the page itself shifted the governing metaphors for reading, prayer, and understanding.[23] Saenger describes the new distinctions working in the last third of the century as those between what one Burgundian treatise calls *oeuvre meritale* [*mentale*] (that is, the work of mental prayer) and *oeuvre vocale* (that is, the work of praying aloud).[24] The rise of silent prayer together with the cultivation of silent reading affected, as Saenger notes, the idioms of late-fifteenth-century theorizing on the act of reading. "References to the eyes and vision become more frequent in the rubrics of fifteenth-century prayers," Saenger notes, and there is a growing sense of visualization, rather than auralization, as the way of engaging with texts.[25]

In Guillaume Fillastre's *Toison D'Or*, the very manual of Burgundian courtly ideology and practice, Saenger finds a concise statement of this attitude toward texts and learning, and the terms of this account may stand as rubric for my own discussion of the idea of the book in Hawes's poetry. Fillastre had written:

> Furthermore, knowledge is not acquired by hearing alone, but also is acquired and increases by study, by reading and by subtly thinking and meditating on what one has read and studied, for as the sage says: Apply your mind to instruction and your ear to words of knowledge . . . because in this manner you will make my heart rejoice. Books are not given to men in vain or for amusement, but out of pure necessity, for they are made to supplement and come to the aid of the weakness of memory, which flows away and runs like water in the stream. By which it would profit little to hear or to ask questions to learn if memory does not retain it. Thus, for all its skill, as it is said, memory does not suffice for retention. This is why the study of books is necessary in order to retain what one has learned by inquiry and by hearing. In books there are also often found doctrines not heard by which man may learn and retain by reading and studying knowledge and wisdom without a teacher or instructor. For the sense of sight is much firmer than hearing and makes man much more certain, because the spoken word is transitory, but the written letter remains and impresses itself more on the understanding of the reader (*mais la lettre escript demeure et plus se imprime en l'endendement du lisant*).[26]

All the terms of Hawes's critical concerns are here: the visualization of the book, the need for books to supplement the memory, the possibilities of

learning without teachers or instructors, and the image of impression as
the form of readerly understanding. Hawes's poetics may be said to generate itself out of the collocations of these issues and their sources in the
classics, and in doing so it articulates not just an attitude to courtly life or
amatory culture but to the practice of reading itself.

In the most well known and most fully developed of his poems, the
Pastime of Pleasure, Hawes dovetails these developments in reading with
the rich inheritance of romance narrative to chart the hermeneutic journey of his chivalric reader.[27] The poem's hero, Graunde Amoure, works
through an education at the hands of a variety of allegorical tutors, each
representing one of the schoolroom *artes*, before battling a range of monstrous challengers drawn from more popular literatures. His journey and
Hawes's poem are often dismissed as derivations of received forms, coming together as a kind of *bricolage* of popular romance, commonplace instruction, and learned study. What I suggest, however, is that the *Pastime*
may be appreciated not just as a compilation of past literary techniques but
as a self-conscious retrospective of a century of literary practice. The
progress of Hawes's hero and his narrator defines a way of reading the
inheritance of Middle English literature in an age of printed bookmaking,
recasting the critical metaphors that control both the pedagogical and the
epistemological concerns of that literature. The story of Graunde Amoure
is, like the story of Hawes himself, the story of a reader: but it is a reader
seeking not the manuscript initials of the past but the printed letters of the
present.

Throughout the *Pastime*, Graunde Amoure confronts incised texts.
Everywhere he goes, he sees painted towers, gilded walls, inscribed objects. Like Lydgate's lover in the *Temple of Glas*—and like his many an-
cestors in Chaucer's dream verse, the *Knight's Tale*, such romances as *Flo-
ris and Blaunchefleur* and *Sir Orfeo*, and the *Romance of the Rose*—Graunde
Amoure finds the stories of the past told through pictorial displays. Even
before he sets out on his journey to recover the abducted heroine, La Belle
Pucelle, such architecture makes itself apparent to him. Seeking advice
from Lady Fame in the first of a series of instructions, he is told that
Pucelle dwells in a country

> . . . where the toure dothe stande
> Made all of golde / enameled aboute
> With noble storyes / whiche do appere without.
>
> (271–73)

In the course of his various instructions at the towers of the *artes*, he finds
stories pictured in the workings of a tapestry or the engravings of a stone.
Nearly three thousand lines after he has set out on his journey, he is still
encountering towers encrusted with "ymages" set into their walls, and
when he enters the Tower of Chivalry he sees "of golde so pure / Of wor-

thy Mars the meruaylous pycture" (3023–24).[28] These cases could be multi-plied almost—it seems in reading through the poem—indefinitely. Yet where they distinguish themselves from their origin in Lydgate and the earlier romance visions is in their repeatedly engraved, incised, golden, and monumental quality. Many of the pictures Graunde Amoure sees have captions, "scryptures" as Hawes calls them, "grauen" in the stone (see 4287–90). And Graunde Amoure's own reading of these texts and pictures is itself a kind of writing, now a printing in the thought, as if the mind and memory themselves were paper, plate, or wax on which the pen, engraver's tool, or student stylus could incise the truth. Graunde Amoure's journey is a romance of impressions, a progressive confrontation both with im-pressed signs and pictures and with the impressions formed within his own mind of their significance.

I had suggested that a source for Hawes's imagery may have been in the cultural directions of visualization and the ideas of impression shaped by a view of books exemplified in Guillaume Fillastre's treatise. There are, of course, further sources to this view as well, and Hawes draws on the tradi-tions of a classical vocabulary of impression to link his work both with the instructions of the schoolroom and the heritage of English verse.[29] The loci classici in English for Hawes's imagery are Chaucer's. In Book V, metrum 4, of his translation of Boethius's *Consolation of Philosophy*, Chau-cer presents Lady Philosophy's exposition of Stoic epistemology in terms that would shape the vocabulary of a century. In this translation, the Stoics believed

> that ymages and sensibilites ... weren enprientid into soules fro bodyes withoute-forth ... ryght as we ben wont somtyme by a swift poyntel to fycchen lettres empriented in the smothnesse or in the pleynesse of the table of wex. ...
>
> (Bk. V, metrum 4)[30]

This passage has a long literary afterlife, from Chaucer's own discussions of the amorous impressions of the January of the *Merchant's Tale* and the longer and more developed chronicle of *Troilus and Criseyde*'s "impres-siouns" of people, texts, and fantasies of love, to the advisory verses of the late fifteenth century.[31] The Envoy to the *Clerk's Tale* relies on the equa-tion of the memory with wax or parchment to enjoin the reader, "Em-prenteth wel this lessoun in youre mynde" (E 1193), and the *Book of Cur-tesye* develops this idiom to affirm the student's learning of its precepts.

> But as waxe resseyueth prynte or figure
> So children ben disposide of nature
>
> Vyce or vertue to folowe and enpresse
> In mynde. ...
>
> (6–9)

"Prynte ye trewly your memorie" (155), it will later command, and again, "Prynte in your mynde / clerly the sentence" (282). These acts of pedagogical impression are precisely what Graunde Amoure learns to do throughout his journeys. The memory—both literary and rhetorical—becomes a ground for writing, and in language strongly reminiscent of the *Book of Curtesye*, Hawes has his Lady Rhetoric describe the art of memory:

> So is enprynted / in his propre mynde
> Euery tale / with hole resemblaunce
> By this ymage / he dooth his mater fynde
> Eche after other / withouten varyaunce.
>
> (*Pastime* 1261–64)

But Graunde Amoure's texts are not the stark black-and-white documents of learning; nor is his story phrased in the self-deprecating monochromatics of Lydgate's apologies. Everything Graunde Amoure sees is golden or enameled. His is a journey through the *flores* and *colores rhetorici* given height and heft by some alchemist of the imagination. It is a journey through a beautifully embellished world—in a word, a journey through the aureate.

Hawes's representation of this fantasy aureate world, together with his own defense and practice of aureation, constitute the primary evidence in recovering his theory of literary fame and his thematizings of his professional relations with his printer.[32] Lydgate's uses of an aureate vocabulary and his promulgation of a cultural mythology of aureation were attempts to recreate a literary past in current practice. His fascinations with the golden world of antiquity were strategies for locating an originary moment in the history of English poetry in the rhetorical finesse and political sanction of a Chaucer "aureate" and "laureate." Hawes, by contrast, sees in aureation not the golden age of literary antiquity but the metallic uncorruptability of literature for the future. His development of an aureate diction and his presentations of the gilded texts of Graunde Amoure's encounters are designed to stress the immutability of work made in this metal. The quality of gold that captivates Hawes is not its color or its surface brilliance but its hardness and resistance to corrosion. The skills of elocution work to refine language into purified ingots of utterance.

> In fewe wordes / swete and sentencyous
> Depaynted with golde / harde in construccyon
> To the artyke eres / swete and dylycyous
> The golden rethoryke / is good refeccyon
> And to the reder / ryght consolacyon
> As we do golde / frome coper puryfy. . . .
>
> (911–16)

For Hawes, what makes aureate diction a suitable vehicle for poetry is both its luster and its physical hardness. Golden words do not, as Lydgate would have had it, look back to a golden past; they look forward to a distant future. They preserve the writings of the poet, much as the wondrously wrought towers of Graunde Amoure's journey preserve in both pictorial and scripted form the legends of the classical *auctores*. Both book and tower, poem and painting, function as monuments to past heroic narrative. They are "harde in construccyon," and that hardness is what ensures both the memory of fictive or historic heroes and the fame of poets. His statement that poetic diction works by analogy, "As we do golde frome coper puryfy," makes literary composition almost a form of smelting.

Hawes's conception of a golden, hardened literary diction may have several sources in the classical traditions of art criticism and rhetorical theory circulating at the close of the fifteenth century. Cicero's conception of training the young orator through actions akin to working clay, casting bronze, die stamping, or wax shaping (defined, respectively, in the Latin terms *limare, adfingere, exprimere*, and *effingere*) signaled a critical association between education in the verbal arts and crafting in the plastic.[33] The exemplary figures drawn from myth or literature become, in what is originally a forensic environment, models of social behavior generally, and Renaissance readers drew upon this notion of the pedagogically exemplary to recast theories of education and political behavior in these classicizing terms. Such readers would have been attuned to the vocabulary of the *Pro Archia*, for example, in which Cicero exclaims: "How many pictures of high endeavor the great authors of Greece and Rome have drawn for our use, and bequeathed to us not only for our contemplation but for our emulation."[34] They would have found, too, the reflections of this attitude in Pier Paolo Vergerio's treatise *De ingenuis moribus*, where the possibilities of literature to maintain both its writer's and its subject's fame derive from its very solidity: "With a picture, an inscription, a coin, books share a kind of immortality. In all these, memory is, as it were, made permanent."[35]

Hawes's *Pastime of Pleasure* is concerned with making memory permanent and with establishing itself as something "harde in construccioun" made from the impressions of the printer's type. Graunde Amoure's various imprintings on his mind are literalized at the *Pastime*'s conclusion. Echoing the Envoy from Chaucer's *Troilus*, Hawes fears not the misapprehensions of scribes but for the first time in English the typographical errors of printers.[36]

> Go lytell boke I pray god the saue
> Frome mysse metrynge / by wronge Impressyon.
>   (5803–4)

The fears of scribal culture, as articulated in the various personae cultivated by Chaucer, Lydgate, and Shirley, are the fears of individual corruption. They are the fears of variation by individual scribes, resulting in variation among different manuscripts of the same work. The hopes of scribal
culture, therefore, are responsive readers: figures like Strode or Gower, the
patrons of Lydgate's Envoys, or Shirley's London friends, who would correct the manuscripts and possibly return or recirculate them as authorized
copies. The fears of print culture, by contrast, are the fears of multiplicity;
corruption, when it does occur, is multiplied as often as the book itself is
reproduced. The hopes of print culture are thus the hopes of a discerning
reader—one who, like the son in Caxton's prologue to the 1483 *Canterbury
Tales*, will return the volume for reediting and reproduction. The new edition not only replaces but effaces the old. It functions not as a correction of
the earlier edition but as a wholly new text, and the responsibilities of
readers are thus not to "in ech" corrections of their own, in Chaucer's
phrasing, but to return it to the publisher or simply live with the printed
errors.

As a work of print technology, the *Pastime of Pleasure* needs no envoys
to correcting readers. Should there be error, Hawes states, the reader
should only "perceyue well thyn [i.e., the book's] entencyon" (5806). The
future of the *Pastime* thus lies not with readerly rescription but with public
memory, with the hope that the printed text will survive as one of the
"grete bokes to be in memory" (5815). The final several hundred lines of the
poem had presented, in sequence, a range of biblical, classical, and mythological heroes whose fame is preserved in books. Books save, Hawes states
repeatedly, "perpetually." At the poem's close, Lady Fame calls for Dame
Remembrance to inscribe for all time the details of Graunde Amoure's
journey (5594–99), and in this command for her "ryght truely for to wryte"
(5594), Hawes himself can remain "magnyfyed" (5600) in books of memory: "Thus after dethe I am all gloryfyed" (5602).

The perpetuity of books lies in their power to preserve the writer's name
and works after his death, and Hawes's fascination with the literary afterlife informs his attitudes toward earlier English poets. In the *Pastime*'s
extended treatment of the triumvirate poets Gower, Chaucer, and Lydgate, Hawes explores in a unique way the various reputations of the writers. This passage has long been discussed, and dismissed, as evidence of
Hawes's Lydgatean affiliations rather than his Chaucerian ones.[37] In terms
of sheer length, it takes two lines to define Gower, nineteen to list
Chaucer's achievements, and seventy to chronicle Lydgate's work and impact. Read quantitatively, it leaves us with the feeling of a poet imitative of
the imitator. But read qualitatively, it points to a distinction between
Chaucer and his heir that defines the role of printed books in making
literary reputations and helps explain the function of the literary inheritance throughout Hawes's poetry.

Hawes links Chaucer specifically and uniquely with survival in the printed book. The poet's works, his name, and his literary reputation all depend on print, and in this Chaucer differs markedly from both Gower and Lydgate. In the *Pastime* Hawes singles out Chaucer as the poet

> whose goodly name
> In prynted bokes / doth remayne in fame.
>
> (1336–37)

Read purely as a point of history, Hawes's notice is misleading. Chaucer, Gower, and Lydgate all had formed the core of vernacular productions in the early decades of English printing. Caxton had published works by all three by the early 1480s, and by 1509 when the *Pastime* appeared from de Worde's press, nearly all of the specific works Hawes mentions here had been printed: *The Canterbury Tales*, *The House of Fame*, and *Troilus and Criseyde* for Chaucer; *The Lyfe of Oure Lady*, *The Temple of Glas*, *The Fall of Princes*, and the *Churl and the Bird* for Lydgate.[38] Why, then, does Hawes single out Chaucer as his model for an English literature in print, and why does he maintain the old fictions of apprenticeship for Lydgate? Part of the answer may simply be chronological. Gower and Chaucer are the poets of the fourteenth century, poets not only in time but also in dynastic patronage distant from Lydgate and Hawes. In the *Conforte of Louers*, Gower and Chaucer are the "poetes rethorycall" who made their books "in antyquyte" (282–83). Yet, in the *Ioyfull Medytacyon*, it is Lydgate who receives the pride of place:

> The ryght eloquent poete and monke of bery
> Made many fayre bookes / as it is probable
> From ydle derkenes / to lyght our emyspery
> Whose vertuous pastyme / was moche commendable
> Presentynge his bookes / gretely prouffytable
> To your worthy predecessour the .v. kynge Henry
> Whiche regystred is in the courte of memory
>
> (8–14)

Here, Lydgate stands as the model for Hawes's public self, a poet who had written for a Henry, a poet too who had addressed in his own works the problematics of a patronage for kings. Invoked here in the *Ioyfull Medytacyon* as the antecedant of the current writer, Lydgate functions as he had functioned throughout Hawes's verse, as the instructor in a poetry of royal instruction. What makes his books "prouffytable" is their moral value, their engagement with the exemplary fables of past conduct, and their presentation of didactic entertainments. What Hawes learns from that poetry is how to write for kings.

Chaucer, by contrast, is the model for the afterlife of Hawes. He is the poet Hawes imagines himself to be after his death, a poet whose name resides in the books of Caxton and de Worde. Indeed, Hawes's conception of a printed Chaucer is so thoroughgoing that whenever he appropriates a Chaucerian phrase or idiom he filters it through the contexts of print culture and the terms of bibliographical physicality. The *Example of Virtu* begins with a cluster of allusions to Chaucer and Lydgate; its first stanzas bring together the ideas of remembrance culled from the Prologue to the *Legend of Good Women* with the idioms of dullness and ineptitude drawn from the spectrum of Lydgate's writings. The third of its four introductory stanzas concludes:

> I wyll now wryte for to fulfyll
> Saynt Powles wordes and true sentement
> All that is wryten is to oure document

(19–21)

The *OED* glosses Hawes's "document" as teaching in a general rather than a textual sense, and it is easy to imagine Hawes simply garbling the Nun's Priest's words that all is written "to our doctrine."[39] But Hawes clearly has documents on his mind—the books, quires, and "pamflets" that fill his various constructions of his work's textuality—and his creative misappropriation of Chaucer's vocabulary transforms the force of this injunction from the substance of what is taught to the means through which that teaching is preserved. Doctrine becomes document, teachings become texts. The *Example of Virtu* phrases epigrammatically what the *Pastime of Pleasure* had narrated dramatically: that the process of learning operates through the engagement with the book as object.

In an analogous manner, Hawes picks up on Chaucer's phrase "this litell treatise" used to describe the documentary status of several of his writings. Reserved by Chaucer for the characterization of prose discourse—the *Melibee*, the *Parson's Tale*, the *Astrolabe*, and the diplomatic correspondences in *Troilus and Criseyde*—the word *treatise* distinguishes formally a class of texts from the poetic narratives and largely fictive tales that constitute the bulk of his work.[40] *Treatise* signals not just prose itself but learned prose, that is, writings that convey a scholarly truth, a fact of moral life, or an instruction of a special kind.

Hawes uses the term to affirm his poetry's status as such kinds of documents. The *Conuercyon of Swerers* is explicitly a "treatyse" (54) designed to illuminate the readers' moral sense. The poem is, as well, a "lettre," offered for the reader to "prynte it in youre mynde" (61–62). What we see in the poem as de Worde printed it (see Figure 7) is a remarkable display of the coordinations of the letter and the print. Its presentation of Christ and the emblems of the passion—perhaps the first example of shaped poetry in English—arrests the reader's eye.[41] Not only does it unify the apprehension of the word and picture (indeed, it makes the word a picture) but it helps define the reader's response to the book itself. "See / me" (113–14),

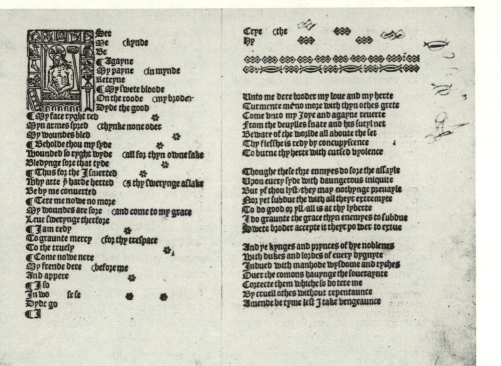

Figure 7. The poem as picture: Shaped poetry from Stephen Hawes,
The Conuercyon of Swerers, printed by Wynkyn de Worde (1509), Sigs.Aiiiv–Aiiir.

this bit of shaped verse begins, as it invites the reader both to meditate on Christ's signifying wounds and to marvel at the printer's craft. The book becomes a visually organized treatise, and at the poem's end Christ once again invites the audience to associate the body and the text, the incisions of his wounds with the impressions of both type and seal.

> With my blody woundes I dyde youre chartre seale
> Why do you tere it / why do ye breke it so
> Syth it to you is the eternall heale
> And the releace of euerlastynge wo
> Beholde this lettre with the prynte also
> Of myn owne seale by perfyte portrayture
> Prynte it in mynde and ye shall helthe recure.

(346–52)

Hawes textualizes, if not monumentalizes, the relationship of Christ to Christian, author to audience. Now the bond of religious fealty is a charter; the picture of Christ that accompanies the shaped poetry is a seal upon it. That seal may reaffirm the meaning of the charter, but it also serves as an impressed device, a figure in the wax that prints the meaning of Christ's passion so it can be printed in the mind of the beholder. The poem's imagery returns us at this moment to the locus classicus of the Chaucerian *Boece*, where knowledge is impressed like seals in wax and understanding is a form of printing. It returns us, too, to the use of the image in Guillaume Fillastre, where the visual experience of reading—the attentions of the eyes rather than the ears—becomes a way of impressing the text on the retentive mind. And it returns us to Chaucer, for in the envoy to the *Conuercyon of Swerers*, as well as the envoys to *A Ioyfull Medytacyon* and the *Confort of Louers*, Hawes recasts the familiar farewell of the *Troilus* into the specifics of the documentary. "Go little book" becomes, in these three envoys, "Go lytell treatyse," as if what Hawes sends off is a text both of the moral status and the documentary form of Chaucer's instructive prose writings. Hawes's envoys may be seen as transforming the Chaucerian and Lydgatean envoy into a description of the physicality of the book he sends off, and in this context we may now look back to the close of the *Pastime of Pleasure*. Hawes's fears of typographical error, of "wronge Impressyon," now fit into his sense of the reception of his own work on the Chaucerian model. If Chaucer is the pattern for a printed fame, then to articulate that fame means to recast the Chaucerian tag lines, idioms, and clichés in terms that reify the status of an author whose name and whose nature survives in "prynted bokes."

The question, though, remains, Why Chaucer? As I had illustrated in my previous chapter, Caxton's concern in his critical writings was to define the vernacular writer along the lines of laureation and paternity inherited, and newly redefined, from a near-century of Chaucer's reception. Caxton presents Chaucer in the *Boece*, the *House of Fame*, and the *Canterbury Tales* as the one English author worthy of a critical discussion in print. His publications of the works of Gower and Lydgate are not framed with reflections on their literary status, and this critical priority that Caxton gives to Chaucer, I believe, informs Hawes's impression of the English poet in the printed book. Though dead, Lydgate and Gower are not buried with the literary monumentalism or the complex cultural allusions that entomb Chaucer, and it is this burial of Chaucer that conditions Hawes's understanding of the fame of the dead writer. As he states in the *Pastime*, "Thus after dethe I am all gloryfyed" (5602), and that glorification lies in the "impressions" of printers and perhaps the elegists who cut the epitaph of Chaucer on his stone. The *name* of Chaucer, rhyming in the *Pastime* with his *fame* to seal the poem's stanzas on his work, stands as the incised name, the *Galfridus Chaucer* who at the close of Surigonus's epitaph is paired with his *fama* to seal the poet in his tomb.

Chaucer *is* a name for Hawes, different from Gower (who is just a

name) or Lydgate (who is both a name and literary legacy), but nevertheless, an author more appealed to than relied on. Nowhere does Hawes
recast the plots or engage with the themes of Chaucer's fictions. His borrowings from the poet are appropriations at the local level of the phrase or
idiom. Such phrases as the ones I have examined here had become, by
Hawes's day, part of the phraseology of English poetry. For Hawes, as
well as for much literate, late-medieval English culture, Chaucer supplied
the tag line, the familiar phrase, the cliché, much as, say, Shakespeare and
the King James Bible would for nineteenth-century educated discourse.
These phrases are the minutiae of Chaucer's legacy, but they define in
Hawes's writings in particular a way of understanding Chaucer's influence
more telling, though less critically noticed, than the large-scale imitation
of his work. Unlike Lydgate, who would insinuate his way into the poet's
fictions or impersonate his public voice, Hawes fills his poems with the
shards of Chaucer's verse. His use of Chaucer—what might well be called
his way of reading him—thus seems more passive than Lydgate's, less
overtly concerned with confronting the poetry by rewriting it. Chaucer's
text has become immutable, not because it has been made subject to the
canons of a more modern textual criticism, but rather because the poet's
words have been passed on in printed books—books that are as monumental as the incised texts and graven images that Graunde Amoure sees
on his journey, books that are seen as lasting as the ones Hawes hopes to
have composed.

   Hawes does not tell us what he thinks of Chaucer's work in any detail,
does not offer what we might consider "criticism" of the poet's writings.
What he does, both directly and allegorically, is envision a way of reading
poets in print, where appeals to their authority become citings of their
name rather than the creative—and creatively intrusive—quoting of their
verse. To say that Chaucer is a name for Hawes, as I have done, is thus to
say that reading has become citation. The snippets of the poet's verse and
the ensconcing of his name in printed books become, for Hawes and for
his fictive readers, the landmarks on a journey to self-presentation. The
goal of Stephen Hawes's poetry is, in a sense, to become "Stephen Hawes":
to become, if not as quotable as Lydgate, then as citable as Chaucer, one
whose name will reside in the closing colophons of printed books.

II

It is the fascination with the name, with the investment of authority in the
sign of the writer, that John Skelton raises almost to an obsession. Skelton's poetry is in large degree about self-naming and self-titling. It transforms strategies of citation into auto-citation, for instead of locating textual authority in outside canonical models or projecting it on dead and

buried antecedants, Skelton finds it in his living person. His poems depict a writing self whose identity is foremost, and the self-referentiality of so much of his work has challenged modern critics, who have variously attributed his stance to the exigencies of political preferment, aristocratic patronage, or simple egomania. What scholarship on Skelton largely bypasses, however, is the venue for his making: one distinguished by his maintenance of manuscript circulation and the attendant habits of reading as rewriting that formed the quality of literate engagement in the culture of script.

The differences between Skelton and Hawes that interest me lie in their attitudes toward books and consequently in how they read both the English literary past and their own works. For Hawes, books are monuments, static in the lithic immobility of "grauen" text or printed volume. The scenes of reading figured forth in Hawes's poems are scenes of passive response. Graunde Amoure's confrontations with incised texts are just that: confrontations, readings, and reactions, rather than dramatized attempts to recast the text or use writings as a goad for one's own writing of the self. The English authors in Hawes's narratives similarly stand as kinds of literary monoliths. Hawes does not claim to alter or recast their works, nor does he seek to rewrite his own texts. The reading of the *Pastime of Pleasure* described in the *Conforte of Louers* exemplifies this personal reception of an unalterable book. La Belle Pucelle's remark "Of late I sawe aboke of your makynge / Called the pastyme of pleasure / whiche is wondrous" (*Conforte* 785–86), is of a piece with Graunde Amoure's visions of graven scriptures. She sees the book as if it were a thing, and like the hero of the *Pastime* she conflates its physical journeys and its verbal pathways. "I redde there all your passage daungerous" (789), she notes, in an ambiguous allusion to the possibly censurable passages Hawes has written and/or to the dangerous passage of Hawes's fictional hero.[42] At such a moment, Hawes defines the reception of his book as a made object: one that may be explained, apologized for, or excused, but never altered after printing.

By contrast, Skelton is a poet of continuous rewriting. His many additions to his poems, the evidence that some of them were composed over many years, and his thematic concern with reading as a form of rewriting, all contribute to the sense of Skelton both enacting and inviting audience rescriptions of his text. His preoccupation with recasting his own works led Stanley Fish to dismiss many of the codas to the poems as a function of the poet's "disconcerting habit of attaching afterthoughts to his poems."[43] More sympathetically to Skelton, Susan Schibanoff has argued for a creative readerly response to the poet, one that requires Skelton's audience to perform what Skelton himself narrates in the text.[44] Schibanoff's reading of *Phyllyp Sparowe* identifies the locus of Skelton's reflective reading of his own work in the transitional passage of the poem, in lines 603–844 where

Jane Scrope searches in the literatures of England and Europe for appropriate models for her sparrow's epitaph. These lines, which form the core of Skelton's response to Chaucer, Gower, and Lydgate, also contain the sparrow's Latin epitaph, and I suggest that they recast—in witty, critical, and quite specific terms—the laureate panegyric and the monumentalism of the authorial text encoded in the epitaph on Chaucer printed at the close of Caxton's *Boece*. I find the laureate authority of Skelton in his various engagements with the textual authority of English literature: an authority centered in manuscript reading, rescription, and recirculation. *Phyllyp Sparowe*, it may be said, offers an anti-epigraphic notion of poetic fame. So, too, the *Garlande of Laurell* presents the heritage of English poetry not in the printed books or marble tombs of dead writers, but in the imagined voices of their dialogue. Chaucer, Lydgate, and Gower come alive in Skelton's dream world, as they crown him the living, writing heir to their productions.

Like Caxton's *Boece* epilogue, Skelton's *Phyllyp Sparowe* celebrates the dead; yet, as any reader of its opening lines will notice, it is not the great and literary dead that Skelton praises, nor is it even the poet's first-person voice that does the praising. *Phyllyp Sparowe* opens with the voice of the woman, Jane Scrope, lamenting the death of her pet sparrow at the paws of the house cat. Interspersed with passages from the Latin office for the dead, the poem's opening Skeltonics depict the woman grieving for the pet, remembering her joy at his responsiveness and seeking an appropriate venue for memorializing the bird. After six hundred lines of this reflection, Jane hits upon the idea of an epitaph for Phyllyp, though she seems at first daunted by the prospect of such writings.

> An epytaphe I wold have
> For Phyllyppes grave.
> But for I am a mayde,
> Tymerous, halfe afrayde,
> That never yet asayde
> Of Elyconys well,
> Where the muses dwell:
> Though I can rede and spell,
> Recounte, reporte, and tell
> Of the *Tales of Caunterbury*
> Some sad storyes, some mery . . .
>
> (605–15)

Jane Scrope is no John Skelton, for unlike the poet *she* has not drunk "Of Elyconys well," nor has she read in Ovid, Virgil, and Diodorus with the acumen described by Caxton in the *Eneydos* Prologue. As she says later, she "can but lytell skyll / Of Ovyd or Virgyll" (755–56); "These poetes of auncyente, / They ar to diffuse for me" (767–68). What she has read, however, is Chaucer, and her announcement at the opening of this bibliographic account points to the primacy of Chaucer's work, and of Chaucerian authority, in the construction of her literate persona. Chaucer's *Canterbury Tales* is the first text that comes to her mind, and her subsequent account of its contents—heavily weighted, as Schibanoff rightly notices, toward the Wife of Bath and a potentially gendered reading of the poem—dovetails with her interests in vernacular romance, fables, and historical tales.[45]

The list of books Jane reads (and does not read) makes up a virtual encyclopaedia of literature. Despite her professed tastes and her selective memory for the contents and emphases of these various works, the list she offers contains practically every writer who has ever written. Every name in classical, medieval, English, and European literatures is here; every major story in the literary tradition is announced and, at times, retold in abbreviated form. In this catenulate impulse, Jane's reading list resembles those ecphrastic catalogues of literary texts and characters descended from Chaucerian visions, through Lydgate's *Temple of Glas*, to Hawes's *Pastime of Pleasure*. They are anthologies of literature, reflections on reading that make the progress of these poems' heroes a progress through texts as much as contexts.

But, of course, the difference between *Phyllyp Sparowe* and the *Temple of Glas* is that Jane's texts are not graven in a wall; and of course Jane Scrope is different both in gender and in taste from Lydgate's hero or the other male reader/aristocrats who populate this kind of poetry throughout the fifteenth century. Skelton offers in the catalogue a critical response to this anthologistic tendency. It is a library more of the unread than the read, a list of great works and themes that, although apparently voicing the humility of the reader, only aggrandizes the power of the writer.

Now, at the close of this anthology, we get Jane's reflections on the triumvirate of English poets, one noteworthy for reflections not just on their matter but also on their style. Gower, Chaucer, and Lydgate—offered in what by now has become the sanctioned order—are assessed in terms of the relationship of manner and matter: Gower's worthless English contrasts with the moral value of his stories (784–87), Chaucer's translucent verse augments the "commendable" qualities of his subjects (788–803), while neither Lydgate's versifying nor his content comes in for much praise (804–12). This extended passage has been read as Skelton's criticism of the traditions of fifteenth-century writing. By going to the source in Chaucer, it is usually assumed, Skelton bypasses the excesses of Lydgatean imitation and makes possible the creation of his own literary authority. The passage has been read, too, as a dig at Hawes, whose praises of Lydgate had been effusive and whose characteristic phrases come in for witty impersonation here.[46] Skelton may well be working in this way, and there is evidence in Hawes's poetry, as well as in that of his contemporary Alexander Barclay, that Skelton and Hawes engaged in a literary flyting in the first decade of the sixteenth century.[47] But what makes this passage in *Phyllyp Sparowe* more than personal attack or topical allusion is the over-arching structure of the bibliographic interlude. Lines 605–844 mark a progress through the traditions of literature, carefully using the conventions of fifteenth-century poetry against themselves. The catalogue of authors, the recitation of received texts, the selective emphases of the viewer, the celebration of the English poets, are all progressively subverted by the gender of Skelton's speaker, the nature of her selections, and the cutting criticism of Lydgate himself.

Ultimately, after this range of critical responses, we get to the final undermining of the great fifteenth-century tradition itself: the Latin epitaph. In these lines, so many of whose phrases resonate with Surigonus's tomb poem on Chaucer and the tropes of humanist encomium it had employed, Skelton dazzlingly deflates the panegyrics of the older poets. He makes the business of celebrating literary fame the business of the living rather than of the dead. He transforms elegy into self-presentation, and he does so not by having himself speak but by having his female persona present a text he has authored. Jane Scrope stands in relation to Skelton as Caxton stands in relation to Surigonus, while the dead sparrow substitutes for Chaucer. In these lines, Skelton shifts the elements of encomiastic equation to critique not just the traditions of the genre but, I would venture, the whole project of Chaucerian reception I have chronicled throughout this book.[48]

> Flos volucrum formose, vale!
> Philippe, sub isto
> Marmore iam recubas,
> Qui mihi carus eras.
> Semper erunt nitido
> Radiantia sydera celo;
> Impressusque meo
> Pectore semper eris.
>   Per me laurigerum
> Britanum Skeltonida vatem
> Hec cecinisse licet
> Ficta sub imagine texta.
> Cuius eris volucris,
> Prestanti corpore virgo:
> Candida Nais erat,
> Formosior ista Joanna est:

Docta Corinna fuit,
Sed magis ista sapit.
                    Bien men souvient.

                                        (826–44)

[Best of birds, beautiful one, farewell. Phyllyp, beneath that marble
now you rest, who were dear to me. Always there will be shining stars
in the clear sky; and you will always be stamped in my heart.

Through me, Skelton the laureate poet of Britain, these compositions could be sung under a feigned likeness. She whose bird you were
is a maiden of surpassing physical beauty: the naiad was fair, but Jane
is more beautiful; Corinna was learned, but Jane knows more.

I recall it well.]

Now it is the bird instead of Chaucer who lies beneath the marble. Instead of the impressions of the typesetter or the incisions of the stonecut-
ter that memorialized Chaucer's poetry in book and tomb, what is "impressed" here is the personal remembrance of the bird in but a woman's
heart. The laureate authority that granted Surigonus the poetic right to
praise the deceased poet, and in turn that validated Caxton's own work,
now has changed; so too has the locus of both national and vatic literary
power. Here, Skelton is both laureate and *vates*, and Britannia is the na-
tionality of living poet rather than dead bard. The images of covering and
enclosure that in Surigonus's poem had defined the nature of the buried
author and the possibilites of opening his bound books work, in Skelton's
Latin, to define the literary process of cloaking the author's voice in a persona. These compositions are sung, he says, under feigned likeness, *Ficta
sub imagine texta*, and in defining the idea of narrative feigning in these
terms, Skelton can shift the focus of his praise. Now, the subject of encomium is neither bird nor poet but Jane Scrope herself; she is, as Schibanoff
observes, the feigned likeness.[49]

But we may also think of these words as referring, more directly, to
"imagined texts." The Latin epitaph becomes poem imagined as a text, the
verbal performance figured forth as incised object. The fiction of the poem
at this point is its own inscripted quality. In Caxton's *Boece* epilogue, incision and impression came together to associate the book and the tomb,
and in the process to equate the monumental epitaph with the handy volume that enclosed within its covers Chaucer's name and legacy. Here,
incisions and impressions contrast the all-pervading imagery of *Phyllyp
Sparowe*, an imagery of mouth and pen, of human speech and human
script. The epitaph is set up, not as in the *Boece*, to stand as a figure for the
book, but instead to stand in opposition to the poem. In the environment
of spoken liturgy, rewritten stories, and selectively read literature, the epitaph to Jane's dead bird stands as an anomalous monument—an epitaph

that celebrates the living rather than the dead; a text whose fiction is that it is a text.

What happens in the poem after the appearance of the epitaph confirms these tensions. When Skelton takes up his pen in his own persona in the poem's following "Commendacions" section (845–1267), he returns to the tropes of the fifteenth-century traditions to affirm his status as a poet of the manuscript rather than of the book. His first lines are a veritable parody of Lydgatean aureation. Their successive rhyme words—*imaginacion*, *medytacion*, *commendacyon*, *consyderacion*, *tolleracyon*—with their polysyllabic, Latinate ring take us back to the aureate chimings of earlier practice. Sustaining the Lydgatean mannerisms, Skelton then makes aureation the subject of his verse. His "pen hath enbybed / With the aureat droppes, /. . . Of Thagus, that golden flod" (872–75), and the repeated terms for flowing, golden inspiration, with the word *flod* repeated three times and with the references to the river's "golden sandes" and its "stremys" (877–82), form a catalogue of Lydgate's classic terms. We even get the touchstone reference to a "Brytons Albion" (887), familiar from Lydgate's political poems and Chaucerian kowtows.

Skelton invests heavily in these Lydgateanisms to maintain his persona as one who writes in a tradition of the scripted. His lines throughout the "Commendacions" section return again and again to acts of spoken praise and manual transcription. The structure of praise for Jane in this poem moves between these two poles, the spoken and the handwritten. *Labia mea laudabunt te* (901), "my lips shall praise thee," he quotes from the Psalms; yet the force of the line has less to do, I think, with scriptural allusion than with present literary practice. The "Commendacions" section figures forth the poet's voice, transcribed by the poet's own pen—"Now Phebus me ken / To sharpe my pen" (970–71)—as Skelton seeks to construct a poetics of presence in the poem. Skelton envisions a narrative self as one actively reading, speaking, writing, and rewriting. This is a world not of the fixity of Hawes's books and graven images but one of the fluidity of manuscript revision and public performance. Skelton, named and renamed throughout the poem, is the present speaker/writer; Skelton is the figure through whom the praise for bird, woman, and poet himself is filtered.

Through his appropriations of these Lydgatean strategies, Skelton also redefines the notion of emending that so frequently closed fifteenth-century poetry. The idea of the little book sent off for readerly correction—an idea, as I have stressed, central to fifteenth-century authorial constructions—is taken up by Skelton not to empower his reader as critic but instead to augment his own power as writer. Skelton emends his own work at the close of *Phyllyp Sparowe*, as the final movements of the "Commendacions" bring to the fore the impulse to rewrite received texts. Jane

herself appears as an emender ("And to amende her tale, / Whan she lyst
to avale," 1116–17) and when Skelton remarks, further on,

> And where my pen hath offendyd,
> I pray you it may be amendyd
> By discrete consyderacyon
> Of your wyse reformacyon,
>
> (1245–48)

his gesture seems curiously disingenuous. What he has "wrytten and sayd"
(1253), what he calls "This treatyse" (1252) is emendable only by the author, and at the poem's close we find the addition, apparently tacked on by
Skelton:

> Thus endeth the boke of Philip Sparow, and her foloweth an ad-
> dicyon made by Maister Skelton.

This "addicyon," it has long been assumed, is a late addendum to *Phyllyp
Sparowe* and appears, with minor variations, as lines 1261–1375 of the *Garlande of Laurell*.[50] Because the latter poem had been printed in 1523, it is
argued that the "addicyon" postdates the putative date for the earlier text
(generally assumed to be 1505) and represents a historical fact of Skelton's
returning to the poem for qualification and self-criticism.

What it represents, more generally, is the fluid nature of Skelton's texts:
the possibility of their emending, augmenting, and editing. Regardless of
whatever social circumstances we may reconstruct for *Phyllyp Sparowe*'s
earliest reception, and regardless of whatever criticisms we may think provoked this coda, the point remains that Skelton empowers himself, and
subjects his text, within the process of response and rewriting so characteristic of fifteenth-century poetry. What was a fiction for Chaucer and Lydgate is a fact for Skelton. There is no evidence that any readers of the
Troilus or of Lydgate's many poems acted on their Envoys for correction.
These earlier works, though they may circulate in manuscript, leave their
authors, apparently never to return. But Skelton seems to exercise a pro-
prietary authority over his poems. His revisions and recastings are of a
piece with his sense of the presence of himself within the text. Each poem
is an act, a performance—if not a verbal one, then an inscriptive one—and
as performance it is subject to review. Here and throughout his poetry,
Skelton enacts the central trope of fifteenth-century poetics: He performs,
himself, the acts of emendation or correction on his poems. Although
rhetorically he still appears to invite outside readers to emend, his intrusions into his own texts—combined with his own affirmations of his name
and title and the critical, as well as poetic, authority they grant him—vivify
what had, by this time, functioned as a trope of poetic humility.

The affirmations of Skeltonian authority thus operate at the levels of
both origination and reception. As laureate, he can present sanctioned lit-

erary documents and function as the sanctioned critic, mediating them to later readerships. He synthesizes the old Lydgatean imaginations of the poet laureate as textual originator with the newer Caxtonian sense of the poet laureate as editor, emender, and critic. In doing so, Skelton reserves for himself both the readerly and writerly authority of the performing poet. The reception of *Phyllyp Sparowe* itself forms a test case for this stance. Just at the moment in the *Garlande of Laurell* when he is about to introduce those lines that formed the "addycion" to *Phyllyp Sparowe*, Skelton challenges his critics:

> Of Phillip Sparow the lamentable fate,
> The dolefull desteny, and the carefull chaunce,
> Dyvysed by Skelton after the funerall rate;
> Yet sum there be therewith that take grevaunce
> And grudge therat with frownyng countenaunce;
> But what of that? Hard it is to please all men;
> Who list amende it, let hym set to his penne.
> *(Garlande* 1254–60)

Schibanoff notes that "Skelton's invitation at the end of the *Garlande of Laurell* is, in essence, a belated laureation of the reader, a recognition that the reader will always have the last word."[51] But I prefer to see these lines not as a capitulation but as a rhetorical challenge; this is the language of the dare. Just who could "amende" Skelton's lines? Whose pen is worthy to be set against the laureate's? No reader has the last word in this poem, for what follows is Skelton's own added text to *Phyllyp Sparowe*; and following that is the return to the narrations of the *Garlande*, with the poet entering into the triumphs of the Queen of Fame, and the succeeding string of envoys in English, Latin, French, and back again. No reader has the last word here, for the *Garlande of Laurell* is itself a poem that refuses to end: a poem that continues to emend itself in different languages, meters, and styles.

In *Speke Parrot*, Skelton distinguishes the role of author and reader along these lines, reserving for himself the power to emend and augment. The Latin lines that introduce the poem read:

> Lectoribus auctor recipit opusculy huius auxesim
>
> Crescet in immensum me vivo pagina presens;
> Hinc mea dicetur Skeltonidis aurea fama.

Through his readers, the author receives amplification of his little work.

Even while I live, the present page will grow to greatness; on the basis of it, the fame of Skelton will be proclaimed golden.[52]

It is a mistake, I believe, to read these lines as a claim to empower an emending reader. The idea here is that the little book (*opusculus*) does not grow in size through the readers but rather grows in reputation or status: From a little book it becomes a great work. The *lector* praises but the author augments, and I think that Skelton must have been alive to the received, medieval etymology of *auctor* as deriving from *augeo*, increase or make greater.[53] The fame of the poet, then, resides not in these pages themselves, not in what Hawes would call the "scryptures" or the "printed bokes," but in the speech of readers. Skelton's word is *dicetur*, "will be spoken," and at stake here is the idea of reputation, in the classical sense, as spoken fame. Again, Skelton relies on an adumbrated etymology, where *fama* comes from *fari*, "to be spoken about."[54] The gold of Skelton's fame thus lies not in the aureations of immutable diction or the hardness of the "construccioun" of his words, but rather in the glittering of public image.

What stands behind the idea of the laureation and of Skelton's pride in his new title, after 1513, of *orator regius*, is this glitter of the image.[55] These titles as he uses them attend to the education in the arts of rhetoric and the political approval of a poet who writes for a public occasion. Skelton performs both for and to his patrons, and nowhere is this stance clearer than in his last major statement of poetic purpose, the *Garlande of Laurell*. Eschewing now both the imaginations of an epitaph and the recognitions of the older poets' deaths, Skelton envisions a world of oratorical performances. For at its simplest level, the *Garlande* is a performance, something of a scripted play for the acknowledgment of present Howard family patronage. Its stretches of direct discourse, its rubrics that denote speakers and addressees, present the poem as a record of its acting.

I do not mean by these observations to claim that the *Garlande of Laurell* is in itself a play after the fashion of his earlier *Magnyfycence*. Nor do I mean to take as absolutely literal the claims made here for Howard patronage or royal sanction.[56] The evidence of early Tudor literary politics points strongly to conclusions that Skelton was far less successful in patronage than he might claim to be. His titles "laureate" and "orator regius," as Greg Walker recently has shown, did not confer the kind of royal approval granted by an earlier court to Bernard André, William Cornish, or John English.[57] And although Henry VIII may have harbored some sentiment for his old tutor, he most likely recalled Skelton from his rustication at Diss to serve as propagandist against the French. What I do wish to claim, however, is that Skelton presents the literary life as oratorical, laureate performance, and that such a performance has the sanctions of aristocratic patronage. He links the "poets and orators" so frequently in the *Garlande of Laurell* that we might think them one and the same. Demosthenes, "that oratour royall" (130), becomes a key projection of the poet's self-imaginings; and when the antique "poetis laureat" appear, they are distinguished by their qualities of declamation, eloquence, relation, and display (see 330–85). Moreover, though the poem opens under the aegis of Howard family patronage, its extant text remains a product of nearly three decades of revision, and it stands as one of the few poems printed during Skelton's lifetime (by Richard Fakes in an edition dated October 2, 1523). The *Garlande* may have started as a poem of occasion, originally written for the celebrations sponsored by the Duchess of Norfolk, Elizabeth Stafford Howard, in honor of Skelton's recent laureations by the universities.

But whatever the historical realities behind their origin and operation, Skelton's roles as orator and laureate function as literary fictions. They affirm his stance as patronized and public poet, one whose work is performed before a present audience and circulated among coterie readers. By appropriating this stance, Skelton returns to the kinds of visionary narratives of patronage I had discussed in Chapter 2: narratives brought together in the courtly house anthologies exemplified by the mid-century collections of the so-called Oxford Group of manuscripts. In seeking to maintain the fiction of performance and house circulation, therefore, Skelton's poem paradoxically denies the very form in which it is preserved for us. It is a printed book that tells a story of its manuscript rescription and its public presentation. It is a book that claims to be no book at all, a book that figures forth the poetic engagement with the English writers of the past not as an act of reading but as one of listening.

Gower, Chaucer, and Lydgate appear as early versions of the oratorical performing self that Skelton seeks to be. Not *auctores* of the book, not celebrated dead, the three poets appear in Skelton's poem as speaking personae. Each one speaks in his turn, and to each Skelton responds. Gower articulates the weighty moralisms of the *Confessio Amantis*, praising Skelton for deserving "meretoryously" entry into the "collage" of the famous poets (400–406). Chaucer's speech gives voice to what Skelton would call, in responding, that "pullisshyd eloquence" (421) that so characterizes his verse. His relatively straightforward syntax and facile blend of native English and imported words offer, in this stanza, a fine imitation of the Chaucer of the public mode. When Lydgate speaks, it is also in imitation of his public voice; but here the aureations of his rhyme words serve to parody rather than to praise:

> . . . welny nothynge there doth remayne
> Wherwith to geve you my regraciatory,
> But that I poynt you to be prothonatory
> Of Fames court.
>
> (430–33)

Such language provokes Skelton's double-edged thanks for Lydgate's "accustomable / Bownte" (436–37), and with these stanzas of praise and

thanks, the poet finds himself in Fame's abode. In Skelton's glib impersonations of their diction, Chaucer, Gower, and Lydgate become voiced
presences, markedly different in their literary fashionings from their appearance in Hawes. Hawes shows the poets as the authors of texts and the
makers of books—in Chaucer's case, of printed books. They cannot stand
with the imagined preceptors and guides of the *Pastime*. They are, instead,
their bibliographies, *auctores* dead and buried in their volumes.

Comparison with Hawes's *Pastime* may be tempting. Both poems offer
up encounters with the female tutors in the arts of discourse. Both poems,
too, imagine crafted, golden realms of literary fame, erections out of gems
and marble, peopled by the beautifully attired members of a literary court.
Yet Skelton outdoes Hawes, takes his aureations to such extremes that the
status of this crafted world, and of its crafted books, falls through the
weight of its encrustings. As if to beat Hawes at his own game, Skelton
places himself in the graven images of famous orators and heroes. Late in
the *Garlande*, having received the laurel from Occupacioun, he enters the
chamber of the Queen of Fame only to find himself.

> Castyng my syght the chambre aboute,
> To se how duly ich thyng in ordre was,
> Towarde the dore, as he were comynge oute,
> I sawe maister Newton sit with his compas,
> His plummet, his pensell, his spectacles of glas,
> Dyvysynge in pycture, by his industrious wit,
> Of my laurell the proces every whitte.
>
>   (1093–99)

Like many of the visionary, reading heroes of romance, Skelton sees "ich
thyng" set "in ordre." His visions of a crafted world by now familiarly introduce anthologies of heroism, love, and fame. Yet Skelton does not see
the pictures of the classic lovers or the medieval fighters blazoned on these
walls. He sees no history of literature but the history of himself. Master
Newton, armed with the various accoutrements of his divisings, represents
the possibilities of visual representation itself. He embodies all the Hawes-
like impulses to reify the literary imagination. The compass, plummet,
pencil, and his "spectacles of glas" are all the instruments of visualization.
But, of course, such instruments cannot encompass the entire range of
Skelton's work. For all the possibilities of portraiture, Skelton's poetry re-
sists the monumentalizing, if not the entombment, of the printed book or
painted portrait. For when the Queen of Fame asks Occupacioun to find
the volume of his works, what we soon realize is that no book can control
the poet's craft. Skelton ostentatiously displays the bound collection of his
texts only to move beyond it; he delights in the exquisite craft of book-
manship only to finish with a plea to public praise.

With that, of the boke losende were the claspis.
The margent was illumynid all with golden railles
And byse, enpicturid with gressoppes and waspis,
With butterfllyis and fresshe pecoke taylis,
Enflorid with flowris and slymy snaylis,
Envyvid pictures well towchid and quickly.
It wolde have made a man holde that he had ryght sekely,

To beholde how it was garnysshyd and bounde,
Encoverede over with golde of tissew fyne;
The claspis and bullyons were worth a thousande pounde;
With balassis and charbuncles the borders did shyne;
With *aurum musicum* every other lyne
Was wrytin; and so she did her spede,
Occupacyon, immediatly to rede.

(1156–69)

Gordon Kipling has relied on these lines to attest to Skelton's fascination with the products of Burgundian scriptoria.[58] But this is not so much of what Kipling calls a "loving" tribute to the masters among Flemish royal illuminators as it is a wild, excrescent fantasy upon them. This is the overstatement of the literary parodist, rather than the felt response of the courtier. It takes the aureate imaginings of Hawes—right down to his favorite vocabulary of illumination, garnishing, and gold—to their near-absurd ends, from the redundancies of "Enflorid with flowris" to the weird notice of the "slymy snaylis" and the hyperbole of claiming that a glance upon the volume could cure the sick. In these two stanzas, Skelton so elaborates the aureate traditions that his very lines appear written in *aurum musicum*, "mosaic gold" used for highlights in deluxe manuscript editions.[59] In this elaboration we may be reminded of the *aurum potabile* that Lydgate found in his letter to the Duke of Gloucester. There, Lydgate had presented a dull and dried-up world without the gold of inspiration or of coin. The only "aureate" thing in the poem, as I had suggested in Chapter 1, is the drinkable gold, the potion that might heal the sick. Now, in Skelton's *Garlande*, what is *aurum* in the book are the lines of its writing; they constitute the healing gold, a glitter that need not be ingested but simply beheld.

Skelton sets up this marvellously made book only to show how his works cannot be enclosed within it. Occupacioun, the following rubric notes, reads and expounds only "sum parte" of Skelton's works, "in as moche as it were to longe a proces to reherse all by name that he hath compylyd."[60] Just as the instruments of Maister Newton could not limn the range of Skelton's fame, so too the craftsmanship of bookmakers cannot enclose the poet, and at the end of over 400 lines of auto-bibliography, critical rejoinder, and self-praise, we leave the experience of reading for the unrestrained and public proclamation of his triumph. The reading of the poet's work is interrupted when Occupacioun comes to the account of Skelton's laureation.

> But when of the laurell she made rehersall,
> All orators and poetis, with other grete and smale,
>
> A thowsande, thowsande, I trow, to my dome,
> "*Triumpha, triumpha*!" they cryid all aboute.
> Of trumpettis and clariouns the noyse went to Rome;
> The starry hevyn, me thought, shoke with the showte;
> The grownde gronid and tremblid, the noyse was so stowte.
> The Quene of Fame commaundid shett fast the boke,
> And therwith, sodenly, out of my dreme I woke.
>
> (1503–11)

Not even the "sex volumis" (1502) of Skelton's Diodorus Siculus translation can compete with the thousands of voices that shout triumph. Texts are subsumed by noise, voice takes precedence over volume, and the very sound of shutting the book is enough to wake the poet from his dream. At the conclusion of the *Garlande of Laurell*, Skelton leaves the worlds of aureate bookmaking and physical inscription for the reputation of the poet in his world. Guarded by his patrons, sanctioned by the king, and inscribing their names in the text of his performance—from all the ladies of the Howard clan to *Henricum octavum* himself (1588)—Skelton can send off his book not for the corrections of his readers but for the praise of his public.

Skelton presents himself as a unique figure in the English literary landscape, and it is in this environment that we may reassess his notions of the influence of English poets and the responsibilites of current readers. In his earlier introduction of Gower, Chaucer, and Lydgate he had remarked, "Thei wantid nothynge but the laurell" (397). The line, of course, is ambiguous.[61] Does it mean that they lacked nothing but the formal laureation Skelton has received; or does it mean, by contrast, that they desired nothing save the kind of sanction Skelton had achieved? Coming after seventy-odd lines on "poetis laureat of many dyverse nacyons" (324)—stretching from Homer to Poggio, from ancient Greeks and Romans to fourteenth- and fifteenth-century Italians—Gower, Chaucer, and Lydgate seem distinguished in their lack of laureation. They are not part of the catalogue; the stanza in which they appear does not contain the refrain line of the previous eight, and it begins by rhetorically signaling a shift in Skelton's view: "And as I thus sadly amonge them avysid, / I saw Gower . . ." (386–87).

Skelton denies the laureation to the older English poets. He presents them last, outside the catalogue of laureates. They are invoked and vivified, now, to articulate the uniqueness of Skelton as the English poet laureate. No longer are we in the worlds of Lydgate, Shirley, and the posthumous imaginations of a laureate Chaucer; no longer can we even grant the double edge of Caxton's suppositions, that the English poet "may well" have the name of laureate poet. The poet laureate, for Skelton, is the unique bearer of the title, a title as personal, and as personalized, as the name of the writer himself. "John Skelton poet laureate" *becomes* the poet's name. In this imaginative realm, the English poets can only *want* the laurel, and I take the force of Skelton's verb in all the richness of its double meaning. They lacked the laurel, failed to garner from the universities or courts the public sanction of an educated and educating life. In what I have called the re-historicized conception of the laureation, these English poets cannot have what Skelton, in *A Replycacion*, would identify as "The fame matryculate / Of poetes laureate" (357–58). But these poets also desired the laurel, wanted it as Skelton wanted it, and in this Skelton projects back onto Gower, Chaucer, and Lydgate his own literary needs. He figures himself as poet in their tradition: a tradition of manuscript circulation and oratorical performance. But he figures himself as the culmination of that tradition, as the one English poet worthy of the titles that confirm it.

The "wanting" of the laurel is but one more of the many paradoxes I have charted through which Skelton affirms his identity. A writer of books posing as a performer; a maker of epitaphs who celebrates the living; a praiser of dead poets who revives them—in these, and many other ways, Skelton establishes uniquely his relations to the poets and traditions of the English language. Scattergood hints at this uniqueness in a suggestive account of the *Garlande*'s Chaucerianism when he notes that "fame and the laurel are his due, he feels, not necessarily because he is a better poet than his English predecessors, but because English poetry itself and its representatives, including Skelton, deserve more honour and in more formal terms than had been accorded them previously."[62] Although he may be modeling his laureation and his oratorship on classical or Burgundian example, Scattergood points out, "Skelton is the first English poet to feel able to do this."[63] The emphasis, I think should be on "first *English* poet," for it is not the case that Skelton necessarily believes that his poetic predecessors deserved laureation; as I have illustrated, he distinguishes them formally and narratively from the laureations of other nations in the poem. Rather, it is that *no* English poet until Skelton *could* be laureated— that he deserves, in the words of *A Replycacion*, "fame matryculate," fame garnered by receiving the degrees of British and Continental universities. Skelton's claim, in these terms, is for a title, and that title comes to blend with his own name to form an English eponym for laureate poetics.

A Replycacion is the last word in Skeltonian self-presentation, a work written in the heat of theological debate and quickly printed by Pynson soon after its composition in 1528. Its final movements, blending personal attack and biblical quotation, begin with the challenge,

> Why fall ye at debate
> With Skelton laureate

(300–301)

and the question is well taken. Who can debate with poets laureate, save those long dead who wore the crown? Who dares revise the poet's lines, save he who wrote them? Skelton, as I have suggested in this final chapter's closing pages, confronts the authority of Chaucer and his compeers not by seeking to rewrite their verses or aspiring to live within their fictions; he deals with their authority not by replacing but effacing it. In the *Garlande of Laurell*, Gower, Chaucer, and Lydgate have no bibliographies to affirm themselves as writers, as they do in Hawes, nor do they come as titled poets in their own right. They serve merely as the doorkeepers before the house of Fame, writers who may step aside to let the laureate go in. At the close of this poem, as at the close of so many of his works, Skelton denies the English poets the last word, refuses almost steadfastly to cling to the expected farewells of "Go little book" along the model of the *Troilus* Envoy. The *Garlande of Laurell* only seems to close with the words "Go, litill quaire, / Demene you faire" (1533–34).

Yet there are other envoys, Latin, French, and English, that remove us from the reminiscences of Chaucerian closure and bring us to the mention only of the poet's name and title: Mayster Skelton, Poete Laureate.[64] At the close of *A Replycacion*, Skelton quotes the Psalms and ends with Latin verses offering what he calls "Skeltonidis Laureati epitoma"—the epitome of Skelton laureate. Among the plethora of sophists, logicians, and theologians, poets, he avers, are few and rare: "sed sunt pauci rarique poetae." For this reason, the ancients always honored poets, and in final words that may imagine his own preoccupations with royal approval, Skelton remarks:

> Sic magnus Macedo, sic Caesar, maximus heros
> Romanus, celebres semper coluere poetas.

[Thus the great Macedonian (i.e., Alexander), thus Caesar, the greatest of Roman heroes, always honored famous poets.][65]

This is the epitome of Skelton: not just an account of literary learning or political approval, but an understanding of authorial identity. *Skeltonidis Laureati epitoma*. His epitome *is* the laureation, and the poem's final Latin word confirms on him the title and the vision of *poeta* that John Skelton and so many of his predecessors longed to be.

"All þis ys said vnder correctyon"

THIS HAS also been a book about endings. It has located the energies of fifteenth-century Chaucer reception and authorial self-definition in those moments of departure, dedication, or release that close the major fictions of the poet and that ground the literary identities of his inheritors. The Envoys to *Troilus and Criseyde* and the *Clerk's Tale*; the closing deferrals of the *Book of Cupid*; the broken endings to the *Thopas* and the *Squire's Tale*; the manuscript and printed book post-placement of the *Adam Scriveyn*; the epitaph that ends Caxton's *Boece* together with the retrospections of his *Eneydos*; and the farewells of Lydgate, Hawes, and Skelton—each, in its own way, seeks to establish the relations between an author's intention and a reader's response that can define the social function of the writer and the cultural and interpretive responsibilities of the audience. That function may have been didactic or celebratory; those responsibilities may have been directed toward the public arenas of ethical behavior or the private realms of fantasy. In any case, the readership of Chaucer's verse was challenged to become a writership as well. Accepting the invitations or the dares to "Doth therwithal right as youreselven leste," as he would put it in the *Troilus* (III.1330), Chaucer's readers complete or truncate, augment or diminish, complicate or simplify the narratives that would instruct them in the ways of making.

All this, of course, is said under correction. From the pleas to Strode and Gower at the close of *Troilus and Criseyde*, through the envoys of Hoccleve, Lydgate, and Hawes, to the conclusions of what may seem an innumerable group of undistinguished and anonymous late Middle English lyrics, Chaucer and his imitators appeal to their audiences not just to complete or alter texts, but to correct them. By presuming an empowered audience—one more knowing than the writer in the arts of love or the techniques of versemaking—Middle English writers seem to undermine both the authority of their work and the integrity of their texts. This ceding of control may, too, seem paradoxically to coexist with the insistences on correct copying by scribes and printers. Chaucer's fears of scribal miswriting become Hawes's anxieties about "wronge Impressyon." Shirley's preoccupations with coterie correction and response become Caxton's

concern with customer satisfaction. It is at times hard to distinguish between the rhetorical or fictional appeal for audience correction and the
facts of reader response. How much, we might ask, do medieval manuscripts embody this dynamic of correction; how much do they embody
actual responses to the work at hand or, by contrast, how much do they
maintain inherited interpretations? Is correction a social practice or a literary trope?

Such questions have been asked by literary theorists both medieval and
modern. From Geoffrey of Vinsauf's concern with structural integrity
based on rhetorical models, through Frank Kermode's and Barbara Herrnstein Smith's explorations of relationships between narrative form and cultural sensibility, to current deconstructive and feminist critiques of the
privileging of formal unity in literary studies, academic readers have
sought to describe our ease or our discomfort with the end.[1] One explanation for this fascination draws on shifts in the technologies of understanding. Orality and writing, script and print have long been the governing
dichotomies of histories of discourse. Is closure largely a concern of cultures in transition, a structural phenomenon identified in moments of self-
conscious technological or social change? Hans-Georg Gadamer has argued that communities of stable or traditional control are largely rhetorical
in orientation, concerned with the preservation and transmission of inherited discourse. By contrast, moments of transition provoke hermeneutical
communities, occupied with the recovery, interpretation, or critique of an
inheritance.[2] In what seems to me a similar gesture, David Hult tries to
locate "speculation on closure in literature" with shifts in the cultural
norm. "[I]t is a response to, and certainly a symptom of, a[n] . . . intellectual climate characterized by decenteredness, isolation and absence of
meaning (both in the world and in language)."[3]

Part of my purpose in this study has been to identify some of the changing contexts for the fifteenth-century literary system that provoke and sustain the critical fascination with the ending. Anxieties about dynastic succession, shifts in the system of patronage, patterns in book and manuscript
production, the rise of an advisory aesthetic, and the contact with humanist attitudes associated with the court and university—all may in varying
degrees have had an impact not just on the ways in which Chaucer was
read or poetry was written but on directing creative and interpretive energies largely to the ends of works. The implications of this study, therefore,
may be both critical and scholarly. For the former, I have been concerned
with tracing developments in certain genres, such as the envoy, as well as
certain canons, such as the construction of a moral, gallant, or epistolary
Chaucer. For the latter, I have been allied with an approach to editing that
seeks the interpretive integrity of manuscripts. Whenever possible, I have
tried to quote from early texts and to construct my arguments around the

structural norms or physical qualities of the material culture of late-medieval English literacy. For Chapter 3, in particular, I have sought to restore
certain ways of reading Chaucer by attending to texts long considered bad,
corrupt, or idiosyncratic. The Appendix at the end of my book is devoted
to presenting some of these particular documents; while they have been
edited before, my concern is not so much with correcting individual readings as with offering the possibilities of understanding the new poems that
the scribes have, in effect, created.

These various commitments may appear, in retrospect, to associate this
book with the interests of Paul Zumthor, Bernard Cerquiglini, and a
clutch of scholars who may loosely be associated under the rubric of a
"New Philology."[4] *Mouvance*, Zumthor's word for the variant condition of
the text, distills many of their concerns with relations between literate
transmission and popular performance in determining the origins of medieval literary works.[5] As both a product of retellings and a participant in its
potential understanding, the manuscript text is always *mouvante*, mobile,
uncertain in detail or design. As Zumthor puts it, in a recent and succinct
reformulation of his notion:

> [A]ny work, in its manuscript tradition, appears as a constellation of
> elements, each of which may be the object of variations in the course
> of time or across space. The notion of *mouvance* implies that the work
> has no authentic text properly speaking, but that it is constituted by
> an abstract scheme, materialized in an unstable way from manuscript
> to manuscript, from performance to performance.[6]

This notion of the instability of the literary text in manuscript culture
has, of late, been appropriated in discussions of the instability of the manuscript in *academic* culture. If the New Philology queries the stable or originary status of the work, it also queries the political and institutional environments that make it public for a scholarly readership. The motivations
of a modern philological discipline may be sought in national origins and
ideological consequences of professional literary study itself: in the tensions between French and German Romanists from the 1820s to World
War I; in the agendas of post–World War II American New Criticism
and its reception of such émigré philologists as Erich Auerbach and Leo
Spitzer; and, most recently, in the changing status of medieval studies in
the canons of graduate training.[7] Historicizing the profession of philology
has decentered the authority of its subjects. Manuscripts no longer remain
the locus of professionalization: No longer is the business of historical criticism grounded in the technical recovery of "readings" and their calibra-
tions in the reconstruction of an author's work or the originations of a
legend.

The philologist has become, in Bernard Cerquiglini's telling phrase,

"Monsieur Procuste," a creature caught between the two poles of nine-teenth-century academic culture: the romanticism of nationalist recovery and the positivism of linguistic taxonomy.[8] By historicizing manuscripts themselves—that is, by viewing them as documents of scribal practice or critical reception rather than as monuments of authorial identity—and by historicizing the practice of philology, the ministrations of the New Philology destabilize the subject and the practice of a medieval studies. As Cerquiglini puts it, in a formulation that has become something of a manifesto:

> Or l'écriture médiévale ne produit pas des variantes, elle est variance. La récriture incessante à laquelle est soumise la textualité médiévale, l'appropriation joyeuse dont elle est l'objet, nous invitent à faire une hypothèse forte: la variante n'est jamais ponctuelle.[9]

The *récriture incessante* of medieval textuality did not end with the advent of the printed book. As my last chapters had suggested, there is much about the uses of the early printed book in England to challenge the firm distinctions between script and print as cultural and technological distinctions. Hawes and Skelton exemplify two ways of coping with the challenges or the temptations of print and, in turn, with the idioms (if not the ideologies) of correction inherited from manuscript practice. Hawes seeks the library of bound and printed volumes; Skelton, the ever-present possibilities of rescription, revision, and increase. What is significant about the literary culture of their time, and what may be a point of departure for future work on the constructions of the Middle English literary canon, is the progressive interplay between the written and the printed. The text set in movable type is *mouvante*, too, as private readers copy out of printed books the poems, extracts, and exempla that reflect individual taste or political principles.

The printed book did not stanch the traditions of Chaucerian impersonation, either. Scribes and compilers throughout the century after Caxton maintained the habits of appropriating Chaucer and his imitators for particular personal and literary ends. Some of the fragmentary *Canterbury Tales* have sixteenth-century continuations, while private collectors supplemented old manuscripts with handwritten additions drawn from published volumes.[10] The search for closure—both for the traditions of Chauceriana and for my own book—may seem, therefore, a fruitless or an arbitrary enterprise, as strains of fifteenth-century literary practice continue well into the Tudor age.

The end of *Chaucer and His Readers* may be sought not in decisive shifts in technology or in radical departures in politics but, as I had sought its beginnings, in the impersonations of Chaucer's fictions. A controlling claim of this book has been that the poet's later readers, scribes, and imitators fashioned their personae against those of Chaucer's works, be they the Squire, Clerk, Adam Scriveyn, or Geffrey himself. One early Renaissance reader and recaster of Chaucer's verses took a somewhat different approach. Instead of modeling himself against the figures of subjection or childishness, he chose his template in the emblems of transgression. Pandarus and the narrator of *Troilus and Criseyde* constitute the compilatory persona of Humphrey Wellys, a Staffordshire lawyer and Tudor confidant who, in the 1520s and 1530s, put together a manuscript containing over sixty poems and prose pieces derived from Middle English examples.[11] Some of his work is highly conventional, some quite odd. Throughout, however, Wellys seems to take on the voyeuristic and transgressive ways of reading, writing, and interpreting that define the men of the *Troilus*.

Containing, in addition to its lyric poems, pieces of vulgar verse, satiric prose, and politically seditious prophecies, Wellys's manuscript represents the private compilations of a man close enough to the workings of political control to keep them secret. Though he had close professional relations to the Tudor court and personal connections to a rising regional gentry, Humphrey Wellys was nonetheless dangerously pro-papal and anti-Henrician in his sentiments. His manuscript contains an excerpt from among the most blunt of the anti-Wolsey propagandistic passages from Skelton's *Why Come Ye Nat to Courte?* It offers prophecies proclaiming that "The heed off the world is the pope," though on an earlier folio the word *pope* is heavily crossed out. Such writings, and the many others in the manuscript, would have been treasonous after the Act of Supremacy in 1534, and after 1542 it "shalbe deamed a Felonye . . . if any persone or persones prynte or write" anything challenging the king's temporal and religious authority.[12]

These political concerns dovetail with the larger literary project of the manuscript, a project governed by a fascination with the secrecy that attends transgressive correspondence, that hinges on the suppression of identity, and that generates the charge of surreptitiously observing and participating in potentially felonious activities. Women, throughout, are subject to derision as untrustworthy dissimulators, and the discourse of the woman is inherently transgressive. "Womans sayinges trust noot to trulye" (57.16); "doo nott euer beleve the womans compleynte . . . harlottes can collour bothe gloyse and paynt" (57.23, 25). Wantonness, harlotry, deception, elusiveness—all fit the women of these texts, as in the poem with the refrain line "She pat hathe a wantan eye" (21) or in the prose piece distinguishing between a "harlot, a hunter, and a whore" (29). Women are the object of erotic fantasy, as in the dream of poem 36, with its bereft lover, Troilus-like, clutching his empty pillow on awakening, or as in the glib autoeroticism of poem 46, in which the man awakens only to say "alas alas . . . / to wette myself Soo woo begone" (46.9–10).

Love is a secret, surreptitious, and suspicious thing, and what distinguishes a range of poems here—and what seems to have no real equivalent in late-medieval or early Tudor love poetry—is the emphasis on the namelessness of the love-letter writer. Poems 3, 5, 33, and 45 all end with the announcement that the letter comes from one that "hathe no name," and poem 13 concludes by enjoining secrecy through an appeal to the motto of, of all things, the Order of the Garter: "Si troue Si hony Soit qui mal y pense" ("If this poem is discovered, evil be to him who evil thinks").[13]

The women of this manuscript—whether they be the idealized ladies of the court or the friends who address each other as "amorous bune" and playfully curse, "I wolde yo were all beshetyn"—are women much like Criseyde herself.[14] They skirt the line between desire and duplicity, scared of public reputation, unsure of the effects of proclaiming their love. The men, too, of this manuscript are lovers lost among their fantasies, Troilan in their sickness and their fear of public humiliation. Both Troilus and Criseyde know of their reputations: as lovers, as letter writers, as betrayers and betrayed. As Criseyde puts it, in lines that would color centuries of critical reception:

> Allas, of me, unto the worldes ende,
> Shal neyther ben ywriten nor ysonge
> No good word, for this bokes wol me shende.[15]
>
> (V.1058–60)

And Troilus, too, for all his self-absorbtions, knows that his literary afterlife was guaranteed: "Men myght a book make of it, lik a storie" (V.585).

I would suggest that this is just what Humphrey Wellys has done. From lyrics possibly received or written for the occasion, he has constructed sequences of verse epistles that narrate a surreptitious love. Letters ostensibly by men and women alternate throughout the manuscript. Some focus on the anonymities attendant on their writing; some, on the problems of self-presentation in the letter; and some link themselves together in the imagery of printing and impression drawn from Chaucer, Lydgate, Hawes, and the traditions of didactic verse. Some of these poems are themselves cobbled together out of earlier verse. Four are made up of extracts from Hawes's *Pastime of Pleasure* and *Conforte of Louers*, and two draw on Lydgate for the idioms of envoy and submission.[16] Read as a group, they all explore in what by now are painfully familiar ways the "billes" and the complaints of love. Even the rough-hewn couplets of the letter between woman friends (item 7) or the missive to an apprentice (item 8) participate in the epistolary fiction of Wellys's work.[17]

And yet, perhaps the oddest of these seeming letters is the *cento* drawn from *Troilus and Criseyde* itself. A poem of nine stanzas culled apparently

at random from Chaucer's poem, item 38 in the collection seems at first
glance like the exercises in appropriation that fill fifteenth-century collections. Like Shirley's versions of the Chaucerian poems on Pity and the
scribal attempts to make generic and narrative sense out of the disparate
sections of *Anelida and Arcite* and the *Complaints* of *Mars* and *Venus*, this
poem tries to make a ballad and complaint out of the courtly fictions of the
poet. As such, it seems a pretty poor attempt: a garbled and miswritten
version of the *Troilus* stanzas that, in the words of Wellys's most recent
editors, is full of sudden shifts in tone and "strangely awkward" voicings.[18]
We are confused, the editors themselves complain, at the apparent anonymity of the messenger who opens the poem, and by the inconsistencies
in reference in what should be a complete love letter. But, I think, if we
return to Wellys's source, we see that there is little anonymity here. If
anything, the speakers of the stanzas are quite clear in Chaucer's poem,
and we need to hear their voices in Wellys's ear:

> Loo he that ys all holly yours Soo free
> hym recommendythe louly to your grace
> and hathe Send yow here a letter by me
> Aveyse yow on ytt whyle ye haue tyme and space
> And of Some goodly answere yow purchase
> or Soo helpe me god the truthe to sayne
> I thynke ye shall neuer See hym ageyne.
>
> (38.1–7)

These are the recognizable rehearsals of Pandarus, as he paraphrases
Troilus's first letter to Criseyde (II.1121–27). They form the introduction to
the poem in Wellys's manuscript, while in Chaucer's original they stand as
a complete account. What follows in the *Troilus* is Criseyde's blunt answer, "Scrit ne bille . . . that toucheth swich matere" (II.1130–31); yet that is
just what Wellys does, as his poem's following two stanzas offer something that looks much like a traditional lover's epistle. If we locate their
source in *Troilus and Criseyde*, however, we discern that they are not a
letter but a song, Antigone's song from earlier in Book II (corresponding
to 841–47 and 869–75, respectively). In Chaucer's poem, these are phrasings
of a spoken love, but in this manuscript, with its Hawes-like attentions to
the written and the seen, these lines take on a different focus. The exhortation "O my swete harte . . . of truthe the grounde myrrour of godlyhede"
(38.8–9) resonates with the imagery developed in the *Pastime of Pleasure*,
with its attentions to the grounds and mirrors on whose surfaces the lover
sees inscriptions of his love. Hawes's idioms have dominated in the manuscript, and Wellys's verse rewrites Chaucer's phrasings to bring the poem
into line with these preoccupations.[19] Instead of the original statement,

My deere herte and al myn owen knyght,
In which myn herte *growen* is so faste

(II.871–72)

Wellys's version reads:

o my dere harte and all my swete wyght
In whome my harte *grauyn* ys Soo faste.

(38.17–18, emphases added)

Stanza four of the poem, drawn from Troilus's lament in Book IV, seems to continue the direct address, but stanzas five and six are drawn from Criseyde's speeches and Wellys once again makes a telling alteration. Criseyde's address in Book V ends with a line in the narrator's voice: "An with that word she brast anon to wepe" (V.1078). In Wellys's poem, the last line of stanza five reads: "thys for to *wryte* my harte doeth brest to wepe" (38.35). Speech becomes text, "word" becomes "wryte," and what the lover writes, in stanza six, are lines from Criseyde's inner thoughts from Book II (778–84). The seventh stanza draws again on Pandarus, now in a maximal mood ("Men say to wretches ytt ys consolatyon," 38.43–46, corresponding to I.708–14) and ends with lines from Diomede's explanations to Criseyde (38.47–48, corresponding to V.139–40). Finally, in the last two stanzas of the poem, Troilus's voice appears again, as we hear the laments of Book IV but, of course, without the mention of Criseyde's name.[20]

I cannot claim to make precise sense out of Wellys's poem. Certainly, it has neither the generic control nor the dramatic unity of the many other experiments in compilation I have surveyed. But I think that I can propose a logic to its garblings, one that may define the essence of Wellys's project and may point to closure for the various traditions of reception he embodies. No single entry in a sequence of exchanges, poem 38 narrates a drama of its own. Announcement, bill, narrative comment, and return—the story of this poem is the story of the *Troilus* as a whole. Pandarus's voice introduces one lover's text, drawn from stanzas in a woman's voice; then we get the Troilan lament, the stanzas from Criseyde, the interruptions in the voices of Pandarus and Diomede, and Troilus's closing laments. This poem, I suggest, distills the scope of *Troilus and Criseyde* into a miniature version of the poem. Its stanzas are voiced texts, not discrete, disembodied fragments; its action transpires not just on the page but in the reader's mind, as the Pandaric narrator both brings together and comments upon two lovers' letters.

Pandarus is the go-between, the tutor in and reader of epistolary love. Throughout, he eavesdrops, transgresses, and edits. He had extracted Oenone's lament from Ovid's *Heroides*, pressing an existing text into the service of his arguments. He had, with Chaucer's narrator, looked in on

Criseyde in her "closet" as she wrote her first missive, looked upon the
lovers in Book III as if he read an "old romaunce," and stood as amatory
postman in Book V, transmitting the now wholly transcribed *litterae* of
Troilus and Criseyde.[21] He is the model for the reader and compiler
Humphrey Wellys, who writes out from the vast inheritance of late-medieval literature—Chaucer, Lydgate, Hawes, Skelton, and some oddly
Wyatt-like verse—only bits and pieces, glued together in a highly personal
collection.

In one sense Wellys has read the heritage of Chaucerian reception back-
ward, looking through both the lens of Stephen Hawes and the scrim of
contemporary politics to select and recast a poetry concerned with the imprintings of desire and the surreptitions of dissent. But in another sense,
he has read that tradition forward, taking up the Pandaric position of
transgressive reading to select those texts appealing to a taste for the erotic.
In this double vision, Wellys brings to a close the traditions of Chauceriana I have tried to trace. Like many of the compilers and scribes I have
analyzed, he brings a distinctively personal cast to the selection and organization of inherited material. His is, however, possibly the most extreme
of personalizations. Instead of paradigms of social conduct or public behavior, Wellys offers the temptations of transgression and of private fantasy. Rather than reading Chaucer and his heirs for their instruction in the
arts of decorum, he looks into their windows on the indecorous. Rather
than using *Troilus and Criseyde* to generate the delectations of a gentry
poetaster, he distills the poem to its central pattern of epistolary love and
spins out a personal anthology of surreptitious texts. A throwback to an
age of making in a time of laureate poetics, a curiosity of Lydgatean nostalgia in a climate of Skeltonic adventurism, a willful act of scribal labor in
a world of printed books—his manuscript closes the book on Chaucer and
his readers, not by affirming their teachings but by subverting their claims.

It may be little wonder, then, that Humphrey Wellys himself has only
recently been discovered as the compiler of this manuscript. Like his fictive correspondents, he took great pains to conceal his own name from the
text. In a bizarrely coded note, full of misspellings and corrections, on the
last leaf of his manuscript, he had written (in its deciphered form):

> homffrey Wellis est possessor huiu[s libri]
> pertinet liber iste ad me cognomine Wellis
> Si unqu[am] perdatur homfrido Restitu[m] sit.[22]

Edward Wilson, describing this inscription, calls attention to "its touching
faith in human nature that a finder would not only return the book but
would decipher the inscription in order to do so."[23] But there is little faith
in human nature, touching or otherwise, behind the coded privacies of this
volume. These are expressions of a fear and a concern that, should this

book be found, only those close to Humphrey Wellys and knowing of his habits would privately return it to him. The anxieties of being found out in this weird *ex libris* are less akin, say, to the versified requests of John Shirley than to the close of poem 13 in Wellys's manuscript, one of the poems cobbled out of Stephen Hawes yet ending with the personalized version of the motto of the Garter: If this be discovered, evil to him who evil thinks. Chaucerianism has become the voice and vehicle for fantasy. The privacy of making has become the making of privacy.

In this wholly internal world, the plea for correction can have no social meaning. One of Wellys's verse letters opened with the injunction to "prynte þis yn your mynde" and concluded with an envoy drawn from Lydgate's *Churl and the Bird*:

> goo lyttle queare and recommende me
> vnto my mastur with humble affectyon
> besechyng hym lowly of mercye and petye
> of my rude makyng to haue compassyon
>
> and as towchyng þis letter of translatyon
> owt of frenche how So euer þe englyshe be
> All þis ys said vnder correctyon
> with the supportatyon of youre benyngnyte.

(45.15–22)

There is no "queare" here, no "mastur" to correct the work; there is no evidence that, possibly like Lydgate's poem, the preceding verses were translated "owt of frenche"; and in a poem written by a woman (the "she" of its line 14), Lydgate's familiar tropes of male submission seem curiously out of place. Everything seems in error here, but in these errors lies the closure of Chaucerian remaking. True, the *récriture incessante* would go on for another century. But Humphrey Wellys has shown one way of shutting down the literary system. He has reduced the *Troilus* to a microcosm, stopped the invitations to his readers. The plea for correction that ends this little poem now launches itself not to the ears of kings or queens, famous friends or infamous patrons, but in all likelihood, to no one at all.

APPENDIX

THIS APPENDIX presents editions of material from Huntington Library MS HM 140 and from the Helmingham manuscript (Princeton University Library MS 100) discussed in Chapter 3. Abbreviations have been expanded and printed in brackets, but the texts have not been punctuated. All scribal corrections and deletions are transcribed as they appear in the manuscripts.

I. Conclusion of the *Clerk's Tale* with *Truth*, from HM 140 (Cf. *Riverside Chaucer: CT*, E 1142–1212; *Truth*, 1–21).

This story is seid not for that wyf[es] shulde   (fol.83r)
Ffolowe Gryseld as in humilite
Ffor it importable were though they wolde
But for ev[er]y wyght in his degree
Shulde be constannte in adv[er]site
As Griselde was so patrik writith
This story which with high stile endyng
Ffor sithen a woman was so pacient
Unto a mortall man well more us ought
Receyve all in gree that god us sent
Ffor grete skyll is he priuee that he wrought
But he temptith no man that he bought
As seith seint Jame yf ye his pistell rede
He prevyth folke all day yt nys no drede
And sufferith us for our ex[er]cise
With sharpe schoge of adv[er]site
Ssul often to be beten in sundry wyse
Not for to knowe for certis he
Or we were born knewe of our[e] freylete
And for our[e] best all is in his gou[er]n^ance
Lette us lyve then in vertuous suffraunce   amen
Griseld is dede and eke her paciens
And bothe at onys buried in Itali
Ffor which I cry in open audiens

No weddid man so hardy be to assey
His wyfis paciens in trust to fynde
Grisilde in certayn for he shall faile
O noble wyfe[s] full of high prudens
Let not humylite your tonge ayle
Ne let no clark haue cause or diligens
To wryte a story of you of such marvayle   (fol.83v)
As of worthy Grysylde[s] paciens
Lest chycheivache you swelowe in his entrayle
Ffoloweth Ecko that holdith no sylence
But ev[er] answerith at the countertayle
Beth not bedaffed for your innocens
But sharpely take upon you the gov[er]nayll
Empryntith in your mynde w^t true diligens
Ffor comyn p[ro]fit sen it may avayle
The archewyvis stondith at defence
Syn ye be stronge as is a grete camayll
Ne suffre not that men do you offence
And sklender wyvis feble in batayll
Bet egre as is a tygre yeend in ynde
Ay clappeth as a myll I you counseill
Ne dede hym not ne doo hym no rev[er]ens
For though thy husbond armyd be in mayle
The arowes of thy el crabbyd eloquens
In jelousy I rede thou hym bynde
If thou be faire there folke be in p[re]sens
Shewe thou thy visage and thyn apparaill
Shal p[er]issh his breste and eke his aventaill

And thou shalte make hym couche ^as doth̶ ̶l̶y̶k̶e̶ a quayle
If thou be foule be free of thy dispens
To gete the frende ay do thy travayll
Be ay of chere as light as lefe on lynde
And let hym care wepe wryng and wayle
Fflee from the prees and dwell w^t sothfastnesse
Suffise the thyne owne though it be small
Ffor horde hath hate and clymbyng tykylnesse
Press hath envye and wele blente ov[er] all
Ffavor nomore than thou behove shall
Rewle well thy self þ^t other forke canst rede
And treuth the shall deliv[er] it is no drede
Tempest the not al croke to redresse

In trust of her that turnyth as a ball
Muche wele stondith in litill besynes
Be ware therefore to spurne ayens an all   (fol.84r)
Stryv not as doth to crokke with the wall
Daunte thy self that dauntist an oþ[er]s dede
And treuth the shall delyv[er] it is no drede
That the is sente receyve in buxumnesse
The wrastlyng of the worlde asketh a fall
Here is noon home here nys but wyldernesse
Fforth pylgryme forth fforth best oute of þy stall
Knowe thy countrey loke up thanke god of all
Holde the high wey and let thy goste the lede
And treuth shall the delyv[er] it is no drede

II. The Pardoner on preaching, from the Helmingham manuscript
(Cf. *Riverside Chaucer*, *CT*, C 412–42).

Ffor when I dare nat othirwise debate   (fol.148v)
Than wol I styng him upon my tong smert
In preching so that he shal nat a stert
But shortly myn entent I wol devise
I prech no thing but of covetise
Therfor my entent no mon teme is yit & ev[er] was
Radix malorum est cupiditas
I wol nat lyve in povert wilfully
Nay nay I thought it nat trewly

III. The Pardoner on drunkenness, from the Helmingham manuscript
(Cf. *Riverside Chaucer*, *CT*, C 551–90).

O dronken man disfegured is thi fase   (fol.150r)
Ffoule is thy breth foul art þowe to enbrace
And thorowe thy dronkyn nose sownyth thy sown
As thogh thowe seydist Sampsoun Sampsoun
Nowe kepe yee ffro the white whyn of Lepe
That is to sel in Brigstrete or in Chepe
Of which ther risithe such fumosite
That er a man hath dronk draghtis thre
And wenyth that he is atte toun hede in Chepe
He is in Speyn ryght atte toun of Lepe
And now that I have spoke of glotonye
Nowe wol I defend yowe hazardry

IV. *Thopas/Melibee* Link, from the Helmingham manuscript
(Cf. *Riverside Chaucer, CT*, VII 919–66).

No more of this for Goddis dignite　　　　　　　　　(fol.161r)
Quod our hoost for thowe makist me
So wery of thy verry lewdnes
That also wis God my soule bles
Myn ere aken of thy drasty spech
Such anothir ryme the devil I betech
This may be a ryme dogerel quod he
Why so quod I wolt thow e let me
More of my tale than a nothir man
Syn it is the best ryme þat I can
Be God quod he ful pleynly at o word
Thy drasty rymyng is nat worth atord
Let se where thowe canst oght tel in gest
Or tel in prose some what atte lest
I wol ʒowe tel alitil thing in prose
That oght to like ʒowe as I suppose
Blamyth me nat for as in my centence
Shul yee no wher fynd dyference
Ffro the centence of this tretise lite
After the wich this mery tale I write
And therfor herkenyth what I shal sey
And let me tel my tale I ʒewe prey

NOTES

INTRODUCTION

1. For the appellation "Drab Age," see C. S. Lewis, *English Literature in the Sixteenth Century* (Oxford: Clarendon Press, 1954). Traditional assessments of the fifteenth century in English literature—with their sense of the decline in literary and metrical skill and the lack of continuity with either the fourteenth or the sixteenth century—include the following: George Saintsbury, *History of English Prosody* (London: Macmillan, 1906–1910), I:218–34; Eleanor Prescott Hammond, ed., *English Verse Between Chaucer and Surrey* (Durham: Duke University Press, 1927); H. S. Bennett, *Chaucer and the Fifteenth Century* (Oxford: Clarendon Press, 1947); and Alice S. Miskimin, *The Renaissance Chaucer* (New Haven: Yale University Press, 1975). For a valuable critique of the ideological motives behind this work, and a revisionary approach to the historiography of late-medieval literary study, see David A. Lawton, "Dullness and the Fifteenth Century," *ELH* 54 (1987): 761–99.

2. Studies that seek to revise preconceptions about fifteenth-century literary history, and the poetry of Lydgate, Hoccleve, and others, include Richard Firth Green, *Poets and Princepleasers: Literature and the English Court in the Late Middle Ages* (Toronto: University of Toronto Press, 1980); A. C. Spearing, *Medieval to Renaissance in English Poetry* (Cambridge: Cambridge University Press, 1985); Lois A. Ebin, *Illuminator, Makar, Vates: Visions of Poetry in the Fifteenth Century* (Lincoln: University of Nebraska Press, 1988); Paul Strohm, "Chaucer's Fifteenth-Century Audience and the Narrowing of the "'Chaucer Tradition,'" *Studies in the Age of Chaucer* 4 (1982): 3–32. See, too, the collected interpretive and bibliographical essays in Robert F. Yeager, ed., *Fifteenth-Century Studies: Recent Essays* (Hamden: Archon Books, 1984).

3. On Hoccleve, see the review of scholarship by Jerome Mitchell in Yeager, ed., *Fifteenth-Century Studies*, 49–63, and the recent reassessments by John A. Burrow, "Autobiographical Poetry in the Middle Ages: The Case of Thomas Hoccleve," *Proceedings of the British Academy* 68 (1982): 389–412; John M. Bowers, "Hoccleve's Huntington Holographs: The First 'Collected Poems' in English," *Fifteenth-Century Studies* 15 (1989): 27–51; Antony J. Hasler, "Hoccleve's Unregimented Body," *Paragraph* 13 (1990): 164–83. For Lydgate, the best single book-length treatment remains Derek Pearsall, *John Lydgate* (Charlottesville: University of Virginia Press, 1970). There is valuable commentary in Ebin, *Illuminator, Makar, Vates*, and in her *John Lydgate* (Boston: Twayne, 1985); and in P. M. Kean, *Chaucer and the Making of English Poetry* (London: Routledge and Kegan Paul, 1972), II: 210–39. For general, critical accounts of Hawes, see Florence Gluck and Alice Morgan, eds., *Stephen Hawes: The Minor Poems*, EETS OS 271 (London: Oxford University Press, 1974), xxxi–xlvii; Ebin, *Illuminator, Makar, Vates*, 133–62); A.S.G. Edwards, *Stephen Hawes* (Boston: Twayne, 1983); Alis-

tair Fox, *Politics and Literature in the Reigns of Henry VII and Henry VIII* (Oxford: Blackwell, 1989), 56–72.

4. For John Shirley and his projects, see the following: Aage Brusendorff, *The Chaucer Tradition* (London: Oxford University Press, 1925); A. I. Doyle, "More Light on John Shirley," *Medium Aevum* 30 (1961): 93–101; Richard F. Green, *Poets and Prince-pleasers*, especially 130–33; A. I. Doyle, "English Books in and out of Court from Edward III to Henry VII," in V. J. Scattergood and J. W. Sherborne, eds., *English Court Culture in the Later Middle Ages* (New York: St. Martin's, 1983), 163–81; A.S.G. Edwards, "Lydgate Manuscripts: Some Directions for Future Research," in Derek Pearsall, ed., *Manuscripts and Readers in Fifteenth-Century England* (Cambridge: D. S. Brewer, 1983), 15–26; Julia Boffey, *Manuscripts of English Courtly Love Lyrics in the Later Middle Ages* (Woodbridge: D. S. Brewer, 1985), especially 14–18, 65–66, 71–74. Jeremy Griffiths and Derek Pearsall, eds., *Book Production and Publishing in Britain 1375–1475* (Cambridge: Cambridge University Press, 1989) offers several detailed studies of manuscripts, scribes, and the social contexts for bookmaking in the period I discuss. Those which have had the greatest impact on my work, and on which I will draw in subsequent chapters, include the following: R. J. Lyall, "Materials: The Paper Revolution," 11–29; Kate Harris, "Patrons, Buyers, and Owners: The Evidence for Ownership, and the Role of Book Owners in Book Production and the Book Trade," 163–99; Carol Meale, "Patrons, Buyers and Owners: Book Production and Social Status," 201–38; A.S.G. Edwards and Derek Pearsall, "The Manuscripts of the Major English Poetic Texts," 257–78; Julia Boffey and John J. Thompson, "Anthologies and Miscellanies: Production and Choice of Texts," 279–315. The manuscripts of the Oxford Group (so named by Eleanor Hammond, *Chaucer: A Bibliographical Manual* [New York: Macmillan, 1908], 338–39) are now available in facsimile, and the introductions and notes to these publications contain valuable historical and interpretive information: Pamela R. Robinson, *Manuscript Tanner 346: A Facsimile* (Norman: Pilgrim Books, 1980); Pamela R. Robinson, *Manuscript Bodley 638: A Facsimile* (Norman: Pilgrim Books, 1982); John Norton-Smith, *Bodleian Library, MS Fairfax 16* (London: Scolar Press, 1979).

5. On the ideological motivations behind scholarship on fifteenth-century literature, and the "bourgeois individualism" of the generation of Eleanor Hammond in defining its place in English literary history, see Lawton, "Dullness and the Fifteenth Century."

6. Though sensitive to the various traditions of fifteenth-century writing, Spearing directs his energies primarily toward assessing in "detail the use made of Chaucer in specific works by his admiring successors" (*Medieval to Renaissance*, 65). For a similar account of Lydgate's "imitation . . . of particular passages in Chaucer" as central to the understanding of the later poet's meter, syntax, and style, see Derek Pearsall, "Chaucer and Lydgate," in Ruth Morse and Barry Windeatt, eds., *Chaucer Traditions: Studies in Honour of Derek Brewer*, 39–53. Although John Scattergood recognizes the limitations of studying Skelton's *Garlande of Laurell* by "citing parallel passages" for evidence of "dependence," he nonetheless seeks out the force of Skelton's poem in the ways in which "something of Chaucer's poem [i.e., the *House of Fame*] is recalled by Skelton." See "Skelton's *Garlande of Laurell* and the Chaucerian Tradition," in Morse and Windeatt, eds., *Chaucer Traditions*, 122–38, these quotations from 123–24.

7. Richard Helgerson, *Self-Crowned Laureates: Spenser, Jonson, Milton and the Literary System* (Berkeley and Los Angeles: University of California Press, 1983), 25–26.

8. My principles of exclusion are, I hope, not merely heuristic but grounded in certain historical and historiographical realities. Much recent work on late-medieval Scottish literature, for example, has exposed the unique qualities of its court culture, its intellectual inheritances, and its systems of patronage. Though a good deal of Scots poetry is clearly indebted to Chaucer's models, its differences in social and political climate from Chaucerian reception in London and the English provinces exclude an adequate discussion from my book. For a powerful reassessment of this literary system, see Louise Fradenburg, *City, Marriage, Tournament: Arts of Rule in Late Medieval Scotland* (Madison: University of Wisconsin Press, 1991). Similarly, the civic contexts for the cycle plays rely on structures of literary control and response different from the ones I find at work for Chaucer's English reception. For an articulation of those differences, especially between the northern towns and London, see Mervyn James, "Ritual, Drama, and Social Body in the Late Medieval English Town," *Past and Present* 98 (1983): 3–29, and Martin Stevens, *Four Middle English Mystery Cycles* (Princeton: Princeton University Press, 1987). Recent scholarship has also shown how the ideals of vernacular authorship and narrative authority articulate themselves in the traditions of late-medieval English history writing. These, too, are texts and contexts that might bear on the construction of a fifteenth-century literary system, yet, for purposes of my discussion, must be elided. I am, however, privileged to have seen the forthcoming study of Steven V. Justice, *Writing and Rebellion in England: The Literature of 1381*, a book that makes important connections between historiography, political polemic, and vernacular authorship in chronicles of the Rising of 1381 and in the work of Wyclif, Chaucer, Gower, Langland, and the cycle dramatists. Finally, though a discussion of Malory and the traditions of Arthuriana might bear on the constructions of fifteenth-century vernacular authorship and literary patronage (especially in the context of Caxton's publications and the polemics of early Tudor rule), a certain amount of recent criticism has pointed out the overemphasis of this tradition at the expense of other, competing humanist models of mythography and history (see, for example, David Carlson, "King Arthur and Court Poems for the Birth of Arthur Tudor in 1486," *Humanistica Louvaniensia* 36 [1987]: 147–83). These fifteenth-century writers and contexts, however, are not wholly absent from my study. On occasion, I seek to establish points of contact between Lydgatean public literature and dramatic spectacle, between the idea of the laureation and the kingly poetics of the Scottish James I's *Kingis Quair*, and between a taste for history writing and the making of personal anthologies.

9. Examples of this privileging of editorial technique, and the construction of a teleology to textual criticism, are the contributions collected in Paul G. Ruggiers, ed., *Editing Chaucer: The Great Tradition* (Norman: Pilgrim Books, 1984). For critiques of the editorial and critical traditions that have mediated Chaucer for twentieth-century audiences, and thus, for the creation of a qualified, academic community of interpreters, see Lee Patterson, *Negotiating the Past: The Historical Understanding of Medieval Literature* (Madison: University of Wisconsin Press, 1987), 3–39, 77–114; Carolyn Dinshaw, *Chaucer's Sexual Poetics* (Madison: University of Wisconsin Press, 1989), 28–64; and the following studies of Joseph A. Dane: "The Reception of Chaucer's Eighteenth-Century Editors," *Text* 4 (1988): 217–36; "Copy-Text and Its Variants in Some Recent Chaucer Editions," *Studies in Bibliography* 44 (1991): 164–83; and his review of Ruggiers, ed., *Editing Chaucer*, in *The Huntington Library Quarterly* 48 (1985): 172–79.

10. See Walter W. Skeat, *The Chaucer Canon* (Oxford: Clarendon Press, 1900), and

Brusendorff, *The Chaucer Tradition*, especially 43–52. Recent challenges to the authenticity of *Anelida and Arcite* and the *Canon's Yeoman's Tale* are, respectively, A.S.G. Edwards, "The Unity and Authenticity of *Anelida and Arcite*: The Evidence of the Manuscripts," *Studies in Bibliography* 41 (1988): 177–88; Norman F. Blake, "The Relationship Between the Hengwrt and the Ellesmere Manuscripts of the *Canterbury Tales*," *Essays and Studies*, new series 32 (1979): 1–18.

11. Stephen Orgel, "The Authentic Shakespeare," *Representations* 21 (1988): 1–25, responding to Gary Taylor's claims for the discovery of a new poem by Shakespeare ("Shall I die") and the media coverage of the event. These quotations from 2.

12. John Guillory, "Canonical and Non-Canonical: A Critique of the Current Debate," *ELH* 54 (1987): 483–527, this quotation from 494.

13. For fifteenth-century constructions of the Chaucer canon and the tales and poems most popular among different classes of readers, see Strohm, "Chaucer's Fifteenth-Century Audience"; Charles A. Owen, Jr., "The *Canterbury Tales*: Early Manuscripts and Relative Popularity," *JEGP* 54 (1955): 104–10; Daniel S. Silvia, "Some Fifteenth-Century Manuscripts of the *Canterbury Tales*," in Beryl Rowland, ed., *Chaucer and Middle English Studies in Honour of Rossell Hope Robbins* (London: George Allen and Unwin, 1974): 153–63.

14. On Hoccleve's autographs (now Huntington Library MSS HM 111 and HM 744, and Durham MS III.9), see the descriptions and bibliography in C. Deutschke et al., *A Guide to Medieval and Renaissance Manuscripts in the Huntington Library* (San Marino: Huntington Library, 1989), 146–47, 250–51; and Bowers, "Hoccleve's Huntington Holographs." For Hoccleve's work as a scribe in his own and his contemporaries' poetry, see A. I. Doyle and M. B. Parkes, "The Production of Copies of the *Canterbury Tales* and the *Confessio Amantis* in the Early Fifteenth Century," in M. B. Parkes and Andrew G. Watson, eds., *Medieval Scribes, Manuscripts and Libraries: Essays Presented to N. R. Ker* (London: Scolar Press, 1978), 163–210. The one surviving text, possibly in Chaucer's hand, is the *Equatorie of the Planets* (Cambridge University, Peterhouse College MS 75.1), edited by Derek J. Price and R. M. Wilson (Cambridge: Cambridge University Press, 1955), who suggest Chaucerian authorship based on the marginal notation in f.5v of the manuscript, "defferentia Christi et Radix Chaucer." The attribution to Chaucer is accepted by John Hurt Fisher, who prints the *Equatorie* in his edition, *The Complete Poetry and Prose of Geffrey Chaucer* (New York: Holt, Rinehart and Winston, 1977), and maintains its authenticity as a holograph in "Animadversions on the Text of Chaucer, 1988," *Speculum* 63 (1988): 779–93, especially 784.

15. For Gower's possible role in the production of his manuscripts, see Doyle and Parkes, "Production of Copies," and John Hurt Fisher, *John Gower: Moral Philosopher and Friend of Chaucer* (New York: New York University Press, 1964), 116. For suggestions about Lydgate's influence on the production and dissemination of his works, see Kathleen L. Scott, "Lydgate's *Lives of Saints Edmund and Fremund*: A Newly-Located Manuscript in Arundel Castle," *Viator* 13 (1982): 355–66, and A.S.G. Edwards, "Lydgate Manuscripts: Some Directions for Future Research."

16. For the claim that Gower and Langland revised their works in response to current political and social changes and perhaps even constructed their literary careers as trajectories of continuous revision, see Anne Middleton, "The Idea of Public Poetry in the Reign of Richard II," *Speculum* 53 (1978): 94–114.

17. Since the early 1980s, many critics have come to recognize the importance and

diversity of fifteenth-century manuscript transmissions of Chaucer's work. Much of this research has focused on the *Canterbury Tales*, and in particular on the relations between the Hengwrt and Ellesmere manuscripts in the establishment of an order, selection, and appearance of the *Tales* that reflects Chaucer's authorial control. The bibliography on these developments and others in the scholarly recovery of early fifteenth-century manuscript culture is vast and growing. Convenient summaries of evidence, argument, and polemic may be found in the following: A.S.G. Edwards and Derek Pearsall, "The Manuscripts of the Major English Poetic Texts"; John Hurt Fisher, "Animadversions on the Text of Chaucer, 1988"; Ralph Hanna III, "The Hengwrt Manuscript and the Canon of *The Canterbury Tales*," *English Manuscript Studies* 1 (1989): 64–84; Lee Patterson, *Chaucer and the Subject of History* (Madison: University of Wisconsin Press, 1991), 42–44.

18. This formulation comes from Victoria Kahn, "The Figure of the Reader in Petrarch's *Secretum*," *PMLA* 100 (1985): 154, though by using her phrases I do not mean to associate her with the New Historicist project implicit in my formulation. For an assessment of this project generally, and for a critique of the various historicisms at work in twentieth-century medieval studies, see Patterson, *Negotiating the Past*, 3–39. For a reconsideration of the New Historicism as a form of formalism, and in turn an assessment of the relations between formalism and historicism in professional literary study, see Alan Liu, "The Power of Formalism: The New Historicism," *ELH* 56 (1989): 721–71.

19. The phrase is from Herbert Lindenberger, "Toward a New History in Literary Study," *Profession 84* (1984): 16–23, quoted and discussed in Thomas G. Tanselle, "Historicism and Critical Editing," *Studies in Bibliography* 39 (1986): 2. Tanselle's entire review essay (2–46) provides me with many of the research guides and some of the critical idiom that I develop in the following paragraphs. Lindenberger's essay is now printed, with revisions, in his *The History in Literature* (New York: Columbia University Press, 1990).

20. Tanselle, "Historicism," 3–4.

21. Jerome J. McGann, *A Critique of Modern Textual Criticism* (Chicago: University of Chicago Press, 1983), 81. See also the collection of essays edited by him, *Textual Criticism and Literary Interpretation* (Chicago: University of Chicago Press, 1985). McGann's project is discussed, and in the end found wanting, in Tanselle, "Historicism," 19–27.

22. Among the many recent studies that illustrate how medieval scribes and readers understood and recast the texts they read and copied, see the following: B. A. Windeatt, "The Scribes as Chaucer's Early Critics," *SAC* 1 (1979): 119–41; Lee Patterson, "Ambiguity and Interpretation: A Fifteenth-Century Reading of *Troilus and Criseyde*," *Speculum* 54 (1979): 297–330, now reprinted with revisions in his *Negotiating the Past*, 115–56; John M. Bowers, "*The Tale of Beryn* and *The Siege of Thebes*: Alternate Ideas of *The Canterbury Tales*," *SAC* 7 (1985): 23–50; Derek Pearsall, "Editing Medieval Texts," in Jerome McGann, ed., *Textual Criticism and Literary Interpretation*, 92–106; Sylvia Huot, *From Song to Book: The Poetics of Writing in Old French Lyric and Lyrical Narrative Poetry* (Ithaca: Cornell University Press, 1987); David Hult, *Self-Fulfilling Prophecies: Readership and Authority in the First "Roman de la Rose"* (Cambridge: Cambridge University Press, 1987).

23. Although this is not the place to review exhaustively the historiography of sub-

jectivity in literary studies, it may be helpful to point to those works that have appropriated the idioms of Freudian and Lacanian analysis and applied it, specifically, to Chaucer. See Louise O. Fradenburg, "'Voice Memorial': Loss and Reparation in Chaucer's Poetry," *Exemplaria* 2 (1990): 169–202, and her earlier study, "The Wife of Bath's Passing Fancy," *Studies in the Age of Chaucer* 8 (1986): 31–58; Carolyn Dinshaw, *Chaucer's Sexual Poetics* (Madison: University of Wisconsin Press, 1989), especially 165–67; and H. Marshall Leicester, *The Disenchanted Self: Representing the Subject in the Canterbury Tales* (Berkeley and Los Angeles: University of California Press, 1990), especially 14–28, to which my following formulations are indebted. Works on the history and historiography of the "critique of the subject" in literary theory that have informed the idiom of my own approach include David Carroll, *The Subject in Question: The Languages of Theory and the Strategies of Fiction* (Chicago: University of Chicago Press, 1982) and Carolyn Dean, "Law and Sacrifice: Bataille, Lacan, and the Critique of the Subject," *Representations* 13 (1986): 42–62.

24. Originally published as "Qu'est-ce qu'un auteur?" *Bulletin de la Société Française de Philosophie*, 22 fevrier 1969, 73–95; English quotations from the translation of Donald F. Bouchard and Sherry Simon in Michel Foucault, *Language, Counter-Memory, Practice* (Ithaca: Cornell University Press, 1977), 113–38.

25. Among those critical projections, see in particular Hult, *Self-Fulfilling Prophecies*, 10–104. The recent studies of Joseph Loewenstein have sought to historicize the author function in Renaissance England through studies of copyright and textual production. For an approach that will bear directly on my work in the final chapters of this book, see his "*Idem*: Italics and the Genesis of Authorship," *JMRS* 20 (1990): 205–24.

26. "The Elizabethan Subject and the Spenserian Text," in Patricia Parker and David Quint, eds., *Literary Theory / Renaissance Texts* (Baltimore: Johns Hopkins University Press, 1986), 303–40, this quotation from 319. I have developed material from this quotation in another context in "*Transgressio Studii*: Writing and Sexuality in Guibert of Nogent," *Stanford French Review* 14 (1990): 243–66.

27. Foucault, "What is an Author?" in D. Bouchard and S. Simon, eds. and trans., *Language, Counter-Memory, Practice*, 131–32. These quotations are cited and discussed in Frank Lentricchia, *Ariel and the Police* (Madison: University of Wisconsin Press, 1988), 30–31.

28. An important early formulation of this set of distinctions is the widely quoted passage from Bonaventure:

> . . . quadruplex est modus faciendi librum. Aliquis enim scribit aliena, nihil addendo vel mutando; et iste mere dicitur scriptor. Aliquis scribit aliena addendo, sed non de suo; et iste compilator dicitur. Aliquis scribit et aliena et sua, sed aliena tamquam principalia, et sua tamquam annexa ad evidentiam; et iste dicitur commentator non auctor. Aliquis scribit et sua et aliena, sed sua tamquam principalia, aliena tamquam annexa ad confirmationem et debet dici auctor.

> The way of making a book is fourfold. For one man writes down others' works, adding or changing nothing, and he is simply to be called a scribe. Another writes others' works, adding material, but not of his own confection; and he is called a compiler. Another writes both the works of others and his own, but in such a way that the works of others are in principal place, and his own are added for the

purpose of clarification; and he is called a commentator, not an author. Another writes both his own works and those of others, but in such a way that his own are in principal place and the others are added for the sake of confirmation; and such a man should be called an author.

From Bonaventure, *Commentarius in primum librum sententiarum Petri Lombardi*, in his *Opera Omnia* (Quarracchi: Ex Typographia Collegi S. Bonaventurae), I:14–15, quoted and translated in David Hult, *Self-Fulfilling Prophecies*, 61n.99.

29. On the terms *auctor, auctores,* and *auctoritas,* see A. J. Minnis, *Medieval Theory of Authorship* (London: Scolar Press, 1984), 10–15, and the earlier discussion of M.-D. Chenu, "Auctor, actor, autor," *Bulletin du Cange - Archivum Latinitatis Medii Aevi* 3 (1927): 81–86. On *auctoritates* as "texts rather than persons," see M. B. Parkes, "The Influence of the Concepts of *Ordinatio* and *Compilatio* on the Development of the Book," in J.J.G. Alexander and M. T. Gibson, eds., *Medieval Learning and Literature: Essays Presented to Richard William Hunt* (Oxford: Clarendon Press, 1976), 115–41, this remark from 116n.1.

30. See Patterson, *Negotiating the Past,* 149–53.

31. Hult, *Self-Fulfilling Prophecies,* 34–51.

32. Ibid., 63–64.

33. Gerald L. Bruns, "The Originality of Texts in Manuscript Culture," *Comparative Literature* 32 (1980): 113–29, this quotation from 125. For a critique of Bruns's distinctions between open and closed texts as, potentially, devaluing "both the concept of authorship and the idea of a stable or closed text in a way not unlike that of deconstruction," see Lee Patterson, "The Logic of Textual Criticism and the Way of Genius: The Kane-Donaldson *Piers Plowman* in Historical Perspective," in Jerome McGann, ed., *Textual Criticism and Literary Interpretation,* 218n.56. Patterson appeals to Elizabeth Eisenstein's *The Printing Press as an Agent of Change* (Cambridge: Cambridge University Press, 1979) to show that "no unqualified distinctions of a theoretically powerful kind can be drawn between a print and scribal culture." (This discussion is eliminated from Patterson's reprinting of this essay in *Negotiating the Past.*) As I hope to illustrate throughout this book, however, members of manuscript and print societies can construct scribal or print *cultures* as self-conscious acts of theorizing their own historical condition, and furthermore, those historical constructions may or may not correspond to modern, scholarly distinctions.

34. For the importance of Bonaventure's distinctions in the scholarly recovery of medieval literary theory, see M. B. Parkes, "Influence of the Concepts of *Ordinatio* and *Compilatio*," especially 127–28, and Minnis, *Medieval Theory of Authorship.* The relations between vernacular practice and scholastic theory have been addressed in a variety of recent studies seeking to recover medieval notions of literary understanding. See, in particular, R. Howard Bloch, *Etymologies and Genealogies* (Chicago: University of Chicago Press, 1983), who is primarily concerned with finding a poetics of the origin in Old French narratives; Jesse Gellrich, *The Idea of the Book in the Middle Ages* (Ithaca: Cornell University Press, 1985), who argues for a mythology of writing in the self-presentation of medieval culture; Rita Copeland, *Rhetoric, Hermeneutics, and Translation in the Middle Ages* (Cambridge: Cambridge University Press, 1991), who notes in particular Chaucer's control over the vernacular tradition, "a control that allows the free play of a self-reflexive comedy" (186); and Anne Middleton, "William Langland's 'Kynde

Name': Authorial Signature and Social Identity in Late Fourteenth-Century England," in Lee Patterson, ed., *Literary Practice and Social Change, 1380–1530*, 15–82, who argues, "For the fourteenth century, the authorship question posed by Langland's work opens to view not only the ambiguous status of vernacular literary authority in this period, but the moral and political claims of vernacular cultural productivity in general to embody 'truth'" (18).

35. *Negotiating the Past*, 116.

36. General studies of fifteenth-century politics and society that influence the following account include J. R. Lander, *Government and Community, England, 1450–1509* (Cambridge: Harvard University Press, 1980); K. B. McFarlane, *Lancastrian Kings and Lollard Knights* (Oxford: Clarendon Press, 1972); G. L. Harriss, *Henry V: The Practice of Kingship* (Oxford: Oxford University Press, 1985), especially the survey of events on 1–51.

37. Lawton, "Dullness and the Fifteenth Century," 771.

38. Ibid., 773.

39. See Ralph A. Griffiths, *The Reign of King Henry VI: The Exercise of Royal Authority, 1422–1461* (London: Ernest Benn, 1981), 241. On the relevance of the quotation from Ecclesiastes to the reign of Richard II, and the topicality of Chaucer's excisions of the references to the "boy king" from his version of the *Melibee*, see the *Riverside Chaucer*, note to line 1199 (p.925).

40. On the problems of paternity in Henrician kingship, see McFarlane's chapter "Father and Son" in *Lancastrian Kings*, 102–113. For the larger social context that defines the changing status of paternity as a cultural category, and for the specifics of father-son relations in English political life, see Joel T. Rosenthal, *Patriarchy and Families of Privilege in Fifteenth-Century England* (Philadelphia: University of Pennsylvania Press, 1991), 23–101.

41. See McFarlane, *Lancastrian Kings*, 104–5. For contemporary responses, see the Latin poem on the reinterment of Richard's bones printed in Charles Augustus Cole, ed., *Memorials of Henry the Fifth, King of England* [*Rerum Britannicarum Medii Aevi Scriptores*, vol. 11] (London: Longman, Brown, Green, Longmans, and Roberts, 1858), 72; and Hoccleve's poem on the same occasion, printed in F. J. Furnivall, ed., *Hoccleve's Works, I. The Minor Poems*, EETS ES 61 (London: Kegan Paul, 1982), 47–49.

42. On the minority of Henry VI, see the impressionistic account in Lander, *Government and Community*, 175–79, and the full discussion in Griffiths, *The Reign of King Henry VI*, 11–230. For a vivid rendering of politics and personalities during the period, see G. L. Harriss, *Cardinal Beaufort* (Oxford: Oxford University Press, 1988), 114–90.

43. "Ballade to King Henry VI upon His Coronation," in Henry N. MacCracken, ed., *The Minor Poems of John Lydgate, Part II*, EETS OS 192 (London: Oxford University Press, 1934), 628, line 94. For Lydgate as Lancastrian propagandist during this period, see R. F. Green, *Poets and Princepleasers*, 187–90.

44. The quotations are from, respectively, a French observer of the King at Rouen in 1430 and the French envoy in 1433, quoted and discussed in Griffiths, *Reign of Henry VI*, 240–41. For more on Henry VI as a "child king," see the discussion of the iconography of the pageant on his entry into London in 1432 in Richard Osberg, "The Jesse Tree in the 1432 London Entry of Henry VI: Messianic Kingship and the Rule of Justice," *JMRS* 16 (1986): 213–32, especially 219.

45. From an anonymous chronicler, writing in the mid-1460s about the state of

England in 1459, two years before his deposition by Richard of York. See J. S. Davies, ed., *An English Chronicle of the Reigns of Richard II, Henry IV, Henry V, and Henry VI*, Camden Society, Old Series, 64 (1856), 79, quoted and discussed in Griffiths, *Reign*, 2.

46. For John Hardyng's remarks, see Griffiths, *Reign*, 242, and Lander, *Government and Community*, 179.

47. For Whethamstede's remarks, see Griffiths, *Reign*, 242.

48. For narratives of Henry VI's last years and his brief reattainment of the throne in 1470–71, see Lander, *Government and Community*, 270–71, noting, "As the London chronicler sarcastically said, it was 'more like a play than the showing of a prince to win men's hearts.'"

49. For modern, scholarly reconstructions of the literary culture at the court of Richard II, see John A. Burrow, *Ricardian Poetry* (New Haven: Yale University Press, 1971); Anne Middleton, "The Idea of Public Poetry in the Reign of Richard II," *Speculum* 53 (1978): 94–114; and the essays collected in V. J. Scattergood and J. W. Sherborne, eds., *English Court Culture in the Later Middle Ages* (New York: St. Martin's, 1983). For a critique of the historiography on Ricardian culture, especially of the construction of the court as the locus for literary patronage, see Ralph Hanna III, "Sir Thomas Berkeley and His Patronage," *Speculum* 64 (1989): 878–916, especially 912–16.

50. Arguments and evidence for the political topicality of *Lak of Stedfastnesse* are assembled in George Pace and Alfred David, eds., *The Minor Poems, Part I, Variorum Chaucer*, Vol. 5, Part 1 (Norman: University of Oklahoma Press, 1982), 77–79. See, too, the discussion in Paul Strohm, *Social Chaucer* (Cambridge: Harvard University Press, 1989), 50–51 and 204n.14. Claims that the poem is addressed to Richard II are due to the Shirlean headnote to the text in BL MS Harley 7333, fol.147v: "This balade made Geffrey Chaunciers the Laureall Poete of Albion and sent it to his souerain lorde Kynge Richarde the secounde þane being / in his Castell of / Windesore /." For discussion of the reliability of such headnotes and the critical presuppositions behind their fifteenth-century transmission and twentieth-century acceptance, see Chapter 4.

51. For the modern scholarship that construes the *Complaint to His Purse* as addressed to Henry IV and "written out of genuine financial need," see Pace and David, *Minor Poems*, 121–22. The Shirlean headnote from Harley 7333, fol. 178r, however, calls it "A supplicacioun to Kyng Richard by Chaucier."

52. See the poems titled, in MacCracken's edition, "The Title and Pedigree of Henry VI," "Roundel for the Coronation of Henry VI," "Soteltes at the Coronation Banquet of Henry VI," "Ballade to King Henry VI upon his Coronation," "King Henry VI's Triumphal Entry into London, 21 Feb. 1432," and "Ballade on a New Year's Gift of an Eagle, Presented to King Henry VI." For the political contexts and literary antecedents to this kind of poetry, and for Lydgate as a propagandist to the Lancastrians, see Richard H. Osberg, "The Jesse Tree in the 1432 London Entry of Henry VI."

53. Among the many studies that have shaped my understanding of the changing nature of literary patronage during the fifteenth century are the following: R. F. Green, *Poets and Princepleasers*, 135–67; Peter J. Lucas, "The Growth and Development of English Literary Patronage in the Late Middle Ages and Early Renaissance," *The Library*, sixth series, 4 (1982): 219–48; Ralph Hanna III, "Sir Thomas Berkeley and His Patronage."

54. On Duke Humphrey, see the early studies of Kenneth H. Vickers, *Humphrey Duke of Gloucester* (London: Constable, 1907), and more specifically, Eleanor P. Ham-

mond, "Poet and Patron in the *Fall of Princes*: Lydgate and Humphrey of Gloucester," *Anglia* 38 (1914): 121–36. For Humphrey's role in disseminating "humanist" texts and ideas in fifteenth-century England, see Roberto Weiss, *Humanism in England During the Fifteenth Century*, 3d ed. (Oxford: Blackwell, 1957). For the outlines of a revisionary account of Humphrey as "an erratic, unprincipled and attractively unsuccessful politician who dabbled in letters partly because he saw in them a way to prestige and profit," see Derek Pearsall, *John Lydgate* (Charlottesville: University of Virginia Press, 1970), 223–30 (this quotation from 224).

55. Representative is the view of Carol M. Meale, "Patrons, Buyers, and Owners," especially 215 on the question of a "national identity" consolidated through patronage commissions.

56. See R. F. Green, *Poets and Princepleasers*, who notes that certain of Chaucer's poems "acquired their authoritative status in the 'game of love,' owing their popularity at least in part to the opportunities they offered for both social and literary plunder (Chaucer's *Troilus* seems to have achieved this position in England by the end of the Middle Ages)" (129); and the remarks of John Stevens in *Music and Poetry in the Early Tudor Court* (London: Methuen, 1961), 213, forming the basis of Patterson's construction of a late-medieval courtly literature parasitic on the example of the *Troilus* (see his *Chaucer and the Subject of History*, 58).

57. See his formulations in *John Lydgate*, 68–70.

58. The phrasing is from Gail M. Gibson, *The Theater of Devotion* (Chicago: University of Chicago Press, 1989), 105.

59. For arguments and bibliography on late-medieval children's literature, and Chaucer's possible place in it, see Chapter 3 of this book.

CHAPTER ONE

1. For various approaches to the *Troilus* frontispiece and to the Corpus Christi manuscript in general, see the following studies: Derek Pearsall, "The *Troilus* Frontispiece and Chaucer's Audience," *Yearbook of English Studies* 7 (1977): 68–74, and Elizabeth Salter, "The 'Troilus Frontispiece,'" in M. B. Parkes and Elizabeth Salter, eds., *Troilus and Criseyde: A Facsimile of Corpus Christi College Cambridge MS 61* (Cambridge: D. S. Brewer, 1978), 15–23 (both of whom associate the picture of Chaucer with the iconography of preaching and with what Salter calls "the development of a lively 'recital' scene, with poet-monk addressing an appropriately mixed audience from his pulpit" [19]). For arguments that the frontispiece represents the acting out of scenes from the *Troilus* itself and that its iconography is therefore grounded in the visualizations of the Medieval *puy*, see Laura Kendrick, *Chaucerian Play* (Berkeley and Los Angeles: University of California Press, 1988), 163–74. On the manuscript, see the account of its making and provenance by M. B. Parkes in *Troilus and Criseyde: A Facsimile*, 1–13.

2. Among the many medieval images of authors and bookmakers proffering their works to patrons, some of the most well known and most widely reproduced include the frontispiece to the Bible of Charles V, with its presentation of the book by Jean de Vaudetar (Rijksmuseum Meermanno, Westreenianum, The Hague, MS 10323, dated 1372); the frontispiece to Jacques de Guise, Chroniques de Hainault, showing Philip the Good receiving the manuscript from the publisher Simon Nockart (Bibliothèque

Royale, Brussels MS 9242, dated 1448); folio 3r of the manuscript of Christine de Pisan's works, showing Christine presenting her book to Isobel of Bavaria (London, BL MS Harley 4431, dated early fifteenth century). For color reproductions of these pictures, see Joan Evans, ed., *The Flowering of the Middle Ages* (New York: McGraw-Hill, 1966), 286, 149, respectively. For Lydgate in this role, see the frontispiece to *The Pilgrimage of the Life of Man*, where the author and a palmer present the book to Thomas Montacute, Earl of Salisbury (BL MS Harley 4826), reproduced in Pearsall, *John Lydgate* (Charlottesville: University of Virginia Press, 1970), following 166, and as the frontispiece to John Norton-Smith, ed., *John Lydgate: Poems* (Oxford: Clarendon Press, 1966). Kathleen L. Scott defines the conventions of authorial representation as follows: "Fifteenth-century English illustrations with patrons or contemporary authors are of two sorts: presentation scenes . . . , and a second type in which a patron or . . . an author is an intrusion on established pictorial matter" ("Lydgate's *Lives of Saints Edmund and Fremund*," *Viator* 13 [1982]: 347n.50). Several late-medieval manuscripts survive that appear to have been presentation copies. For brief discussion of the phenomenon, see John Hurt Fisher, "Animadversions on the Text of Chaucer, 1988," *Speculum* 63 (1988): 781. For discussion of examples from the work of Lydgate and Hoccleve, see Pearsall, "The *Troilus* Frontispiece," 72. For pictures of Gower, see J. J. Griffiths, "The *Confessio Amantis*: The Poem and Its Pictures," in A. J. Minnis, ed., *Gower's Confessio Amantis: Responses and Reassessments* (Cambridge: D. S. Brewer, 1983), 163–77.

3. For the author as university clerk, see the study (with many illustrations) of Julie Smith, "The Poet Laureate as University Master: John Skelton's Woodcut Portrait," in Maryanne Cline Horowitz et al., eds., *Renaissance Rereadings: Intertext and Context* (Urbana: University of Illinois Press, 1988), 159–83.

4. John Norton-Smith discusses the conventions of armigerous display in fifteenth-century vernacular manuscripts in his introduction to *Bodleian Library, MS Fairfax 16*, (London: Scolar Press, 1979), xii–xvi. A more comprehensive survey is Kate Harris, "Patrons, Buyers, and Owners," in Griffiths and Pearsall, eds., *Book Production and Publishing*, 166–69. She remarks at 188n.34, "The absence of such [armigerous] evidence" from Corpus Christi College MS 61 "has proved tantalizing" and compares the similar, puzzling "absence of contemporary coats of arms and notes of ownership in lavishly produced copies of Lydgate's [*Troy Book*]."

5. Pearsall, "The *Troilus* Frontispiece," 70.

6. On Hoccleve's relationship to "father Chaucer" in these terms, see the discussions of A. C. Spearing, *Medieval to Renaissance* (Cambridge: Cambridge University Press, 1985), 90–92; Antony Hasler, "Hoccleve's Unregimented Body," *Paragraph* 13 (1990): 164–83; and those that begin Chapter 2 of this book.

7. Hoccleve's role in the dissemination of vernacular literature is discussed by Doyle and Parkes, "The Production of Copies of the *Canterbury Tales*," in Parkes and Watson, eds., *Medieval Scribes, Manuscripts*, especially 198–99, and reviewed by A.S.G. Edwards and Derek Pearsall, "The Manuscripts of the Major English Poetic Texts," in Griffiths and Pearsall, eds., *Book Production and Publishing*, 259. Manly-Rickert (I:168) linked Hoccleve's energies to the production of one manuscript of the *Canterbury Tales* in particular (Fitzwilliam McClean 181). For arguments that Hoccleve had a role in organizing the order of the *Tales* and that he may have written some of the links of the *Tales*, see David Lawton, *Chaucer's Narrators* (Woodbridge: D. S. Brewer, 1985), 127–29.

8. For an account of Chaucer portraiture and the assumptions of a late-medieval

and Renaissance biographical criticism, see R. F. Yeager, "British Library Additional MS 5141: An Unnoticed Chaucer *Vita*," *JMRS* 14 (1984): 261–81; and David R. Carlson, "Thomas Hoccleve and the Chaucer Portrait," *Huntington Library Quarterly* 54 (1991): 283–300, both of whom offer full bibliographies of earlier scholarship on the iconography of Chaucer.

9. One way of measuring the popularity of Chaucer's *Tales* in the fifteenth century is by their appearance as separate items in manuscript anthologies. The *Clerk's Tale* appears more frequently (six times) than does any other: Longleat, Marquess of Bath 257; Naples, Biblioteca Nazionale XIII.B.29; Huntington Library MS HM 140; Oxford, Bodleian Library Rawlinson C.86; BL MS Harley 1239; and a single leaf bound in a later collection in BL MS Harley 5908. Arguments for the relative popularity of individual *Tales* based on the frequency of their appearance in collections have been put forward by Charles A. Owen, Jr., "The Canterbury Tales: Early Manuscripts and Relative Popularity," *JEGP* 54 (1955): 104–10; Daniel S. Silvia, "Some Fifteenth-Century Manuscripts of the *Canterbury Tales*," in B. Rowland, ed., *Chaucer and Middle English Studies*, 153–63; and Paul Strohm, "Chaucer's Fifteenth-Century Audience and the Narrowing of the 'Chaucer Tradition,'" *SAC* 4 (1982): 3–32, especially 24–28. For fifteenth-century manuscript revisions of the *Clerk's Tale* as forms of critical interpretation, see my discussion in Chapter 3.

10. Montrose, "The Elizabethan Subject and the Spenserian Text," in P. Parker and D. Quint, eds., *Literary Theory*, 319, quoted and discussed in my Introduction, above.

11. E. H. Wilkins, "The Coronation of Petrarch," in *The Making of the "Canzoniere" and Other Petrarchan Studies* (Rome: Edizioni di Storia e Letteratura, 1951), 9–69. For the impact of Petrarch's laureation on later literary history and authorial self-representation, see the studies of J. B. Trapp, "The Owl's Ivy and the Poet's Bays," *JWCI* 21 (1958): 227–55, and "The Poet Laureate: Rome, *Renovatio*, and *Translatio Imperii*," in P. A. Ramsey, ed., *Rome in the Renaissance: The City and the Myth* (Binghamton: Center for Early Medieval and Renaissance Studies, 1982), 93–130. Other discussions relevant to late-medieval English literature include those of Pamela Gradon, *Form and Style in Early English Literature* (London: Methuen, 1971), 332–33; and R. F. Green, *Poets and Princepleasers* (Toronto: University of Toronto Press, 1980), 209–10. For the construction of a "Petrarchan Academy" in Italy designed to foster the dissemination of the poet's work and reputation, and the impact of that activity on the possible reception of his work by Chaucer, see David Wallace, "'Whan She Translated Was': A Chaucerian Critique of the Petrarchan Academy," in Lee Patterson, ed., *Literary Practice and Social Change*, 156–215.

12. Wilkins, "Coronation," and his translation and commentary on the Coronation Oration, published as an appendix to his *Studies in the Life and Works of Petrarch* (Cambridge: Mediaeval Academy of America, 1955).

13. For Petrarch as the eponymous poet laureate, see Trapp, "Owl's Ivy." For the appellation *poeta laureato* (and other variations) in manuscripts of the story of Griselda (headed *Boccaccii Griseldis historia*), see Nicholas Mann, *Petrarch Manuscripts in the British Isles* (Padua: Antenore, 1975), originally published in *Italia Medioevale e Umanistica* 18 (1975): 139–527. A representative selection includes Corpus Christi College Cambridge MS 275, before 1439 (" . . . Ffrancisci Petrarche lauriati poete . . ."); British Library MS Add.10094, fifteenth century (" . . . Francisco Petrarcha florentino poeta laureato . . ."); and British Library MS Harley 2492, second half of the fifteenth century (which calls Petrarch "poeta laureatissimo").

14. All quotations from Boccaccio will be from Giovanni Boccaccio, *Genealogie Deorum Gentilium Libri*, ed. Vincenzo Romano (Bari: Giuseppe Laterza et Figli, 1951), with references cited by book and chapter number in my text; all translations will be from Charles G. Osgood, trans., *Boccaccio on Poetry* (New York: Liberal Arts Press, 1956).

15. Osgood, trans., *Boccaccio on Poetry*, 91.

16. Ibid.

17. Ibid., 92 (*Genealogie Deorum* xiv.19).

18. From *Francisci Petrarcae epistolae de rebus familiaribus*, ed. I. Fracassetti (Florence, 1859–63), III:258; translation: M. E. Cosenza, *Petrarch's Letters to Classical Authors* (Chicago: University of Chicago Press, 1910), quoted in A. J. Minnis, *Medieval Theory of Authorship* (London: Scolar Press, 1984), 211.

19. Osgood, *Boccaccio on Poetry*, 115–16 (*Genealogie Deorum* xv.6).

20. For an interpretation of this moment in the Clerk's Prologue, see Warren Ginsburg, "'And Speketh so Pleyn': The *Clerk's Tale* and Its Teller," *Criticism* 20 (1978): 307–23, especially 311–12.

21. Middleton, "Chaucer's 'New Men' and the Good of Literature," in Edward Said, ed., *Literature and Society*, Papers from the English Institute, 1978 (Baltimore: Johns Hopkins University Press, 1980), 45.

22. On Lynyan and his place in this comparison, see notes to the *Riverside Chaucer*, 879–80 and the studies cited therein.

23. I paraphrase Anne Middleton, "Chaucer's 'New Men,'" 37. The distinctions between "making" and "poetry" summarized in my discussion have been codified into a critical orthodoxy in Chaucer studies, beginning with the essays of Glending Olson, "Deschamps' *Art de Dictier* and Chaucer's Literary Environment," *Speculum* 48 (1973): 714–23, and "Making and Poetry in the Age of Chaucer," *Comparative Literature* 31 (1979): 272–90, and sustained and refined in Middleton, "Chaucer's 'New Men'"; Winthrop Wetherbee, *Chaucer and the Poets: An Essay on Troilus and Criseyde* (Ithaca: Cornell University Press, 1984), 17–29; Lee Patterson, "'What Man Artow?': Authorial Self-Definition in the *Tale of Sir Thopas* and the *Tale of Melibee*," *SAC* 11 (1989): 117–75, especially 118–20; and Patterson, *Chaucer and the Subject of History* (Madison: University of Wisconsin Press, 1991), 59–60.

24. My capsule interpretation of the Clerk's performance in what follows is indebted to the following critical studies of the *Tale*: Middleton, "The Clerk and His Tale: Some Literary Contexts," *SAC* 2 (1980): 121–50, and her "Chaucer's 'New Men'," 45–48; Judith Ferster, *Chaucer on Interpretation* (Cambridge: Cambridge University Press: 1985), 94–121; Carolyn Dinshaw, *Chaucer's Sexual Poetics* (Madison: University of Wisconsin Press, 1989), 132–55; John M. Ganim, *Chaucerian Theatricality* (Princeton: Princeton University Press, 1990), 79–91.

25. Louise O. Fradenburg, "The Manciple's Servant Tongue: Politics and Poetry in the *Canterbury Tales*," *ELH* 82 (1985): 85–118, this quotation from 89.

26. For arguments that the Clerk is presented as a feminized tale-teller before the Host's authority, and that his relationship to that male authority mirrors that of his fictive Griselda, see Dinshaw, *Chaucer's Sexual Poetics*, 136–37.

27. Daniel Poirion, *Le Poète et le prince: L'évolution du lyrisme courtois de Guillaume de Machaut à Charles d'Orleans* (Paris: Presses Universitaires de France, 1965), 372–74.

28. For some aspects of that challenge, see Ganim, *Chaucerian Theatricality*, 79–91, especially 81–82.

29. It has been widely recognized that Chaucer's usage of the term "heigh style" derives from a misreading of Petrarch's own words in his Latin letter to Boccaccio— where he remarks how he had translated his friend's Italian into "stylo . . . alio," a different style or language as "stylo . . . alto." See the discussion of J. Burke Severs in W. F. Bryan and Germaine Dempster, eds., *Sources and Analogues of Chaucer's Canterbury Tales* (Chicago: University of Chicago Press, 1941), 330. The Latin gloss to the stanza beginning at line 1142, preserved in several manuscripts of the *Tales*, notes, "This story it seemed good to weave anew in a high style (*stilo alto*) . . ." (quoted and translated in *Riverside Chaucer*, 883).

30. Wallace, "'Whan She Translated Was,'" 191.

31. Lydgate coins the terms *aureate* and *aureation*, and much critical discussion of these words centers on the polysyllabic, Latinate vocabulary he developed and, in turn, on the rhetorical brilliance, immutability of diction, and nobility of sentiment praised in Chaucer as an "aureate" poet. For Lydgate's aureate vocabulary, see John Norton-Smith, *John Lydgate: Poems*, 192–95. For the sense of Chaucer as an "aureate" and hence a "noble" poet, see P. M. Kean, *Chaucer and the Making of English Poetry* (London: Routledge and Kegan Paul, 1972), II: 210–39. For a conception of the term *aureate* as suggesting "the special nature of the poet's medium, the heightened poetic quality that sets it off from ordinary speech and writing," see Ebin, *Illuminator, Makar, Vates* (Lincoln: University of Nebraska Press, 1988), 25.

32. Lydgate's *Mumming for Mercers*, and John Shirley's annotations as preserved in his manuscript, now Bodleian Library MS Ashmole 59, are quoted from the edition of McCracken, *Minor Poems II*, 696.

33. On the autobiographical content of these passages in the *Fall of Princes*, see Pearsall, *John Lydgate*, 223–54, and the earlier study of Eleanor Hammond, "Poet and Patron in the *Fall of Princes*," *Anglia* 38 (1914): 12–36.

34. Early critics considered the *Letter to Gloucester* as having been written between Lydgate's completion of Book II of the *Fall of Princes* and his start on Book III. Norton-Smith makes the case that the poem was written after the completion of the entire work, finding verbal parallels between the complaints of the *Letter* and the envoy in Book XI of the *Fall* (*John Lydgate: Poems*, 114–16). Here, I rely on Norton-Smith's edition of the poem.

35. "Nat sugre-plate maad by th'appotecarye" (41); Norton-Smith glosses "sugre-plate" as "*sucra crustalis*, a sweet lozenge for medicinal use" (*John Lydgate: Poems*, 118).

36. See Norton-Smith's note to the line, ibid.

37. For the comparison between Lydgate's *Fall* and his source in Laurent de Premierfrait's French translation of Boccaccio's *De Casibus* collection, see part 4 of Bergen's edition (EETS ES 124), 137–397. For specific comparisons with the Prologue to Book VIII of the *Fall*, see 291–96, with Bergen's summary statement, "Thus the chapter as it stands in the *Fall of Princes* is for the most part Lydgate's own" (296).

38. See my discussion in Chapter 4 on the impact of the *Troilus* Envoy on the forms of late Middle English poetry and the generic expectations of Chaucerian verse. For a consideration of the envoy in the patronage relationships of late-fifteenth-century English literature, see Russell Rutter, "William Caxton and Literary Patronage," *SP* 84 (1987): 440–70, especially 449–53 on the "epistolary tone" generated by the uses of the envoy.

39. See the description of this manuscript in C. Deutschke, *Guide to Medieval and Renaissance Manuscripts in the Huntington Library* (San Marino: Huntington Library,

1989), 230–32. The manuscript has been dated between the years 1445 and 1450, and A.S.G. Edwards considers it "almost certainly a presentation copy of this popular fifteenth-century poem" ("The Huntington *Fall of Princes* and Sloane 2452," *Manuscripta* 16 [1972]: 37–40, this quotation from 40).

40. See A.S.G. Edwards, "Lydgate Manuscripts: Some Directions for Future Research," in Pearsall, ed., *Manuscripts and Readers*, 15–26, and "The Huntington *Fall*'"; Kathleen L. Scott, "Lydgate's *Lives of Saints Edmund and Fremund*."

41. Bergen, ed., *Lydgate's Fall of Princes*, Part IV, EETS ES Vol. 124, 101, "Lydgate presenting his book to Duke Humphrey"; C. Deutschke, *Guide to Medieval and Renaissance Manuscripts*, 231, which describes the picture as "a monk (?) presenting a book to a man seated in a chair"; M. C. Seymour, "Manuscript Pictures of Duke Humphrey," *Bodleian Library Record* 12 (1986): 95–105.

42. On the visual representation of the poet/author as a schoolmaster, and the details of the kinds of chairs presented in late-medieval manuscript illumination and early printed books, see Julie Smith, "The Poet Laureate as University Master," in M. C. Horowitz et al., eds., *Renaissance Rereadings*, especially 161–63.

43. On the *pileum*, see Hastings Rashdall, *The Universities of Europe in the Middle Ages*, ed. F. M. Powicke and A. B. Emden, Volume 3 (London: Oxford University Press, 1936), 390n.2: "Gascoigne, in his Theological Dictionary . . . tells us that at Oxford the round cap was worn by doctors in all the superior faculties: he declares that this ornament was bestowed by God himself on the doctors of Mosaic law."

44. On the gowns of Oxford and Paris, see Rashdall, *Universities*, 389n.3: "At Paris as at Oxford the doctors of all superior faculties wore red; . . . the rector wore purple with a cap, and apparently stockings of the same color . . . *Habits rouges* (*rubeae*) are often mentioned as characteristic of doctors of canon law. . . . In England . . . scarlet was certainly worn by D.D.S." In HM 268, fol.18r (see Figure 1), the figure I am taking to be Bochas wears a blue robe with a red cape or hood. On fol.79v (see Figure 2), the Bochas at his desk wears a pink robe with blue stockings on his feet. For illustrations of Boethius in late-medieval manuscripts, see the pictures reproduced in Pierre Courcelle, *La Consolation de la Philosophie et la tradition littéraire* (Paris: Etudes Augustiniennes, 1967), especially those of plates 37.1, 40, 44, 46.2, 46.3, 47. Comparisons between the picture on 153r (see Figure 3) and the Boethius pictures are particularly striking, where the model for the HM 268 manuscript seems to be the visionary appearance of Lady Philosophy before a bed-ridden Boethius; in the English manuscript, Bochas and Petrarch appear modeled, respectively, on Boethius and Philosophy.

45. On Lydgate's sonic effects, see Pearsall, *John Lydgate* (Charlottesville: University of Virginia Press, 1970), 7–11, 268–75. On the taste for pun and wordplay in late-medieval European poetry generally, see Paul Zumthor, "From Hi(story) to Poem, or the Paths of Pun: The Grands Rhétoriqueurs of Fifteenth-Century France," *New Literary History* 10 (1979): 231–63.

46. I quote from the edition of George F. Reinecke, *Saint Albon and Saint Amphibalus by John Lydgate* (New York: Garland, 1985). Another example of the association of the two terms appears in Book IX of the *Fall of Princes*, where Patience is personified as a "Laureate queen" (2380) sitting on an "aureat Throne" (2391). For an example of Lydgate's reception couched in these terms, see Dunbar's phrasing in *The Goldyn Targe*: "O morall Gower, and Ludgate laureate, / Your sugurit lippis and tongis aureate, . . ." (quoted in Spurgeon, *Five-Hundred Years of Chaucer Criticism and Allusion* [London: Kegan Paul, Trench, Trübner, 1914–25], 66).

47. See, in particular, Kean, *Chaucer and the Making of English Poetry*, II: 232–33.

48. Shirley's headnotes are printed (with some variation from his own spelling) in Spurgeon, *Five-Hundred Years of Chaucer Criticism and Allusion*; these are from page 47. For a bibliography on Shirley and a more detailed account of both the biographical and critical function of these headnotes, see Chapter 4.

49. I quote from the manuscript here.

50. For discussion of this annotation, see my account of Shirley's MS, BL Harley 78, in Chapter 4.

51. Lydgate, or at the very least his scribes, consistently spell the word *envoy* as "lenvoy." See, for example, the headings to the final stanzas of *The Complaint of a Lover's Life* ("Lenvoye de quare"), *A Ballade, of Her that Hath All Virtues* ("Lenvoy"), *The Churl and the Bird* ("Lenvoie"), *Fabula Duorum Mercatorum* ("Lenvoye"), and many others (all texts printed in McCracken's editions). In the *Fall of Princes*, the envoys that conclude the individual legends are routinely headed *Lenvoy* (with some variation in spelling). In the text of the *Fall*, Lydgate spells the word *lenvoie* even with a previous indefinite article (see, for example, II.151, VII.775, and Bergen's note in his edition, part 3, 796); see, too, the heading to the final stanzas of the *Letter to Gloucester* in MSS Landsdowne 699 and Vossius 9 (MacCracken, ed., *Minor Poems II*, 667). More generally, entries from the *MED* point to a habit of fourteenth- and fifteenth-century scribes of spelling certain loan words from French with the proclitic *l-*. Thus, the word for *andiron* is occasionally spelled "laundiren" (s.v. *laundiren*, with examples from 1362 and 1459–60); the word for *amber* is spelled "laumbre" (s.v. *laumbre*, with a range of spellings cited from 1332 to 1500, including one from Caxton's *Book of Curtesye* of 1477). Further scribal confusions may derive from the various spellings of *aureole* (the crown of a halo and a saint) and *laurel* (the tree and the crown of leaves on the victor's head). The *MED* lists a variant spelling of the former as "aureall," in, for example, *St. Jerome* (dated 1500), 339/22: "That crowne . . . is the aureall of martirdom, by which y endid my bodely lyff." It also records a variant of the latter as "laureole," in particular in manuscripts of the *Nun's Priest's Tale* in the *Canterbury Tales* at line B 4153. Because both of these words share a similar semantic field ("crown" and "honor"), there may be possible confusions between them that contribute to the scribal confusions and sonic pairings of *laureate* and *aureate* in Lydgate's poetry and in Shirley's and the Shirley-derived headnotes. For another example of this possible confusion, see Lydgate's description of Bochas's fame in the *Fall*, "With laureat stremys shad foorth to peeplis all" (VI:440). In keeping with Lydgate's metaphorics of a golden, flowing diction and a sort of liquid poetics, this phrasing should, I think, more accurately refer to "aureat stremys." For reflections on this spelling problem in French writing from the period, see Peter Rickard, *A History of the French Language*, 2d ed. (London: Unwin Hyman, 1989), 68: "Hesitation and uncertainty in the use of the [definite] article led to its agglutination to the substantive in a few cases" (with examples cited). For reflections on the problems posed for textual critics in Anglo-Norman manuscripts that illustrate this usage, see Bernard Cerquiglini, *Éloge de la variante: Histoire critique de la philologie* (Paris: Seuil, 1989), 44–46 (with examples cited).

52. Henry N. MacCracken, ed., *Minor Poems I*, 41, edited from Shirley's MS TCC R.3.20.

53. Walter F. Schirmer, *John Lydgate: A Study in the Culture of the XVth Century*, trans. Ann E. Keep (Berkeley and Los Angeles: University of California Press, 1961),

31. There is no manuscript authority for this poem, however; it first appears in Thynne's Chaucer edition of 1532 and was later attributed to Lydgate by John Stowe. For a review of this history and for the argument that the poem "is Lydgate's by supposition only," see Pearsall, *John Lydgate*, 97. I quote from the edition in MacCracken, *Minor Poems I* (410–18), who prints Thynne's edition without apparent emendation.

54. I quote these lines from the selection printed in Spurgeon, *Five-Hundred Years*, 19. The one modern critical edition of this poem—of J. Lauritis, R. Kleinfelter, and V. Gallagher, *Duquesne Studies, Philological Series* 2 (Pittsburgh, 1961)—was unavailable to me. For citation of this edition and of other works on the poem, together with a characteristically sensitive reading, see Pearsall, *John Lydgate*, 285–90 and nn.48–49. Pearsall reviews the difficulties of dating the poem, usually associated with the patronage of Henry V, and though he records scholarly opinions ranging from 1409 to 1434, he seems to favor the dating of the "modern edition" of 1421–22 (286). Norton-Smith, however, dates the poem "?1434+" in his chronology of Lydgate's works (*John Lydgate: Poems*, xiv) without explanation, though Pearsall's remark ("all the internal chronology and arrangements of the poem suggest that it was written for reading aloud to members of a monastic community," 286) may identify those features that led Norton-Smith to date it after Lydgate's return to Bury St. Edmunds sometime after 1434.

55. On the propagandistic motives behind much of Henry V's literary patronage, see R. F. Green, *Poets and Princepleasers*, 183–87; and G. L. Harriss, *Henry V: The Practice of Kingship* (Oxford: Oxford University Press, 1985), 1–30.

56. See Jeanne E. Krochalis, "The Books and Reading of Henry V and His Circle," *Chaucer Review* 23 (1988): 50–77.

57. Henry V's role in the restoration of English as the language of court and commerce has been the subject of a number of studies by John Hurt Fisher. See his "Chancery and the Emergence of Standard Written English in the Fifteenth Century," *Speculum* 52 (1977): 870–99; the remarks throughout his "Animadversions on the Text of Chaucer, 1988," *Speculum* 63 (1988): 779–93; and *The Importance of Chaucer* (Carbondale: Southern Illinois University Press, 1992). Fisher's interests inform Malcolm Richardson's dissertation, "The Influence of Henry V on the Development of Chancery English" (University of Tennessee, 1978), and the article deriving from it, "Henry V, the English Chancery, and Chancery English," *Speculum* 55 (1980): 726–50. The associations between Henry V's "conversion" to English and the rise in Chaucer's reputation stand behind some of Fisher's formulations and inform Richardson's averral: "Henry's shift to English in 1417 marks a firm commitment to the vernacular—equivalent in the public world to Chaucer's commitment to English in the literary world, and of equal importance" ("Henry V," 727). In the year of Henry V's death, 1422, the Brewer's Guild of London adopted English as the "mother tongue" and associated its official sanction with Henry V (ibid., 739–40), and "by the end of the 1420s . . . Chancery English was well on its way toward standardization" (ibid., 741). For an account of this standardization in philological, historical, and orthographical detail, together with a collection of representative texts, see John H. Fisher, Malcolm Richardson, and Jane L. Fisher, *An Anthology of Chancery English* (Knoxville: University of Tennessee Press, 1984).

58. Lydgate's practice has been seen by R. F. Green as characteristic of (*Poets and Princepleasers*, 207–8)

a general campaign of self-justification undertaken by authors in the later Middle Ages. We can sense an attempt to promote his own cause even in so simple a matter as the poet's eagerness to allude to his illustrious predecessors as his "mas-ters." . . . Indeed, the lavish praise which fifteenth-century writers heaped on Chaucer, Gower, and, later, Lydgate was rarely completely disinterested; living poets were manifestly raising their own stock by venerating their predecessors.

59. See Peter J. Lucas, "The Growth and Development of English Literary Patron-age in the Later Middle Ages and Early Renaissance" (*The Library*, sixth series, 4 [1982]: 231–36, 241–42) and the narrative account in Pearsall, *John Lydgate*, 160–91.

60. Pearsall, *John Lydgate*, 223–30.

61. See Richard H. Osberg, "The Jesse Tree in the 1432 London Entry of Henry VI: Messianic Kingship and the Rule of Justice," *JMRS* 16 (1986): 213–32.

62. I quote from the edition of Carleton F. Brown, "Lydgate's Verses on Queen Margaret's Entry into London," *Modern Language Review* 7 (1912): 225–34. Lydgate's authorship of the text of this pageant has recently been challenged by Gordon Kipling, "The London Pageants for Margaret of Anjou: A Medieval Script Restored," *Medieval English Theatre* 4 (1982): 5–27. Kipling notes that Lydgatean authorship rests on the attributions of John Stowe in his *Annales of England* (1592) and argues:

> The script we have, in fact, contrasts sharply with Lydgate's stylistic habits as a writer, stands at variance with his status as a commemorative describer rather than a deviser of civic triumphs, and contradicts what we know of the poet's final years. . . . Once removed from the canon of Lydgate's poems, these verses find their proper context in the history of the medieval English theater. We can now see them as a successful experimental script rather than as a failed commemorative poem, as the journeyman work of one or more civic pageant devisers rather than as the garbled effusion of an enfeebled poet.
>
> (13)

In addition to accepting Kipling's rejection of Lydgate's authorship for the 1445 pag-eant, Martin Stevens also reports that "John Lydgate's role in the 1432 triumph has long been questioned," though he does not cite those who have questioned it. Relying on reports of Kipling's unpublished work in progress, Stevens further discounts any role for Lydgate in the production or organization of early fifteenth-century drama. See *Four Middle English Mystery Cycles* (Princeton: Princeton University Press, 1987), 53 and n.44. By contrast, Lydgate's authorship for the pageants is accepted by Osberg ("The Jesse Tree") and by P. H. Parry, "On the Continuity of English Civic Pageantry: A Study of John Lydgate and the Tudor Pageant," *Forum for Modern Language Studies* 15 (1979): 222–36. Although my argument does not necessarily stand or fall on the facts of Lydgatean authorship, it does rely on the maintenance of certain idioms and narra-tive stances by the pageant texts. To that end, the pervasive imagery of an idealized Edenic or aureate world and the notion of a laureate ruler articulated in these texts is Lydgatean: not narrowly as proof of authorship, but rather as witness to the pervasive influence of Lydgate's diction on the public poetry of Henry VI's early reign.

63. Carleton Brown notes that *crist* "has been interlined by a different hand of about the same date" (230). The manuscript of the pageant text, BL MS Harley 3869, fols.2r–4v, is considered written in a mid fifteenth-century hand by Kipling ("The London Pageants," 9). Although Kipling's edition of the text does not distinguish the word *crist* as interlineated, his textual notes do call attention to many other interlineations in the manuscript.

64. For the dating, authorship, circumstances of composition, and transmission of the poem, see John Norton-Smith, ed., *James I of Scotland, The Kingis Quair* (Oxford: Clarendon Press, 1971), xi–xxv. At issue in the poem's dating are the astrological observations at its opening and its numerological account of the author's captivity in stanza 25. For the former, Norton-Smith identifies the poem's opening as set "during the period 10–18 February 1424" (52); for the latter, he establishes the author's age as "28/9, and the year of composition 1424" (61). Norton-Smith reconstructs a date for James's return to England as after his marriage to Joan Beaufort during the beginning of February 1424 (xxiv). For an opposing view of the poem's composition, see John Mac-Queen, "The Literature of Fifteenth-Century Scotland," in Jennifer M. Brown, ed., *Scottish Society in the Fifteenth Century* (New York: St. Martin's, 1977), 184–208 (claiming that the *Kingis Quair* was "written probably at some time between his return to Scotland in 1424 and his death in 1437" [187]). The *Kingis Quair* is preserved in only one manuscript copy, Oxford Bodleian Library MS. Arch. Selden B.24, most likely written in 1488 on a commission from the Sinclair family (see MacQueen, *Literature*, 201; Norton-Smith, *James I of Scotland*, xxxi–xxxv; and Louise O. Fradenburg, *City, Marriage, Tournament* [Madison: University of Wisconsin Press, 1991], 123–34).

65. On the Pageant of 1392, see Glynne Wickham, *Early English Stages 1300–1600*, vol. 1: *1300 to 1576* (London: Routledge and Kegan Paul, 1959), 64–71. On the return of Richard II's bones to Westminster, see the bibliography cited in my Introduction, n.41.

66. Maydiston's poem is printed and translated in Wickham, *Early English Stages*, 1:64–71, from which I take my references. Citing unpublished work by Gordon Kipling, Martin Stevens considers the pageants in the 1392 entry as "an allegorical scenario" on a par with "the Entry into Jerusalem pageant in the York cycle." According to Stevens, Kipling "shows that 'long before European cities began decorating their streets with pageantry, they imagined themselves transformed into another Zion, a celestial Jerusalem, whenever a king made his ceremonial entry'" (*Four Middle English Mystery Cycles*, 53n.43).

67. On the origins of the *orator regius*, see R. F. Green, *Poets and Princepleasers*, 174–76.

> One of the earliest clear-cut uses of the title is in the *Defence of the Proscription of the Yorkists of 1459* (possibly written by Sir John Fortescue), in which an "orator regius" debates the question of royal clemency. . . . All other unequivocal uses of the term (with the exception of Frulovisi's title as Duke Humphrey's 'poet and orator') appear to belong, like this one, to the second half of the century.
>
> (175)

68. On Shirley's ownership of the manuscript, see M. B. Parkes's introduction to *Troilus and Criseyde: A Facsimile*, 11.

CHAPTER TWO

1. The Man of Law had condemned the "wike ensample of Canacee" (*CT*, B 78) and the story of her incestuous relationship with her brother. For arguments that this reference in the Prologue to the *Man of Law's Tale* is a satiric jab at Gower (who tells the story in the *Confessio Amantis*, III.143–336), see the bibliography cited in *Riverside Chaucer*, 890–91. For the suggestion that the Franklin cuts off the *Squire's Tale* before this indelicate story can be told, see Haldeen Braddy, "The Genre of Chaucer's *Squire's*

Tale," *JEGP* 41 (1942): 279–90. Throughout this chapter, my account of the *Squire's Tale,* its thematic and rhetorical emphases, and aspects of its reception, is guided by Anne Middleton, "Chaucer's 'New Men' and the Good of Literature in the *Canterbury Tales,*" in E. Said, ed., *Literature and Society,* 15–56, and by David Lawton, *Chaucer's Narrators* (Woodbridge: D. S. Brewer, 1985), 106–29.

2. This remark, in the hand of the scribe John Duxworth, appears in Bibliothèque Nationale MS Anglais 39 (c. 1422–39), after breaking off the *Squire's Tale* at line 28. For discussion of the manuscript and this remark in particular, see Paul Strohm, "Jean of Angoulême: A Fifteenth-Century Reader of Chaucer," *Neuphilologische Mitteilungen* 72 (1971): 69–76. David Lawton considers the judgment "singular" (*Chaucer's Narrators,* 107).

3. Strohm, "Chaucer's Fifteenth-Century Audience and the Narrowing of the 'Chaucer Tradition,'" *SAC* 4 (1982): 26.

4. Lydgate singles out the story of the *Squire's Tale* for mention in the *Temple of Glas* (see my discussion below) and in *Horse, Goose, and Sheep* ("Chaunser remembrith the swerd, the ryng, the glas, / Presented wern vpon a stede of bras," 76–77). For the possible influence of the *Squire's Tale* on Hoccleve, see the speculations in Lawton, *Chaucer's Narrators,* 128–29, who also suggests that Hoccleve may have had a hand in writing the eight-line introduction to the *Tale.*

5. See the chronicle of responses and rewritings in Lawton, *Chaucer's Narrators,* 106–23.

6. On the history of the idea of a "father Chaucer," see A. C. Spearing, *Medieval to Renaissance in English Poetry* (Cambridge: Cambridge University Press, 1985), 88–110, this quotation from 92. Spearing develops the idea of Chaucerian "paternity," however, through the fictional representations of fathers and children, and of a God the father, in the stories Chaucer tells, rather than through the relationship between the Knight, Squire, and Franklin (for a brief mention of this triangle, see 95). See, too, the discussion in Patterson, *Chaucer and the Subject of History* (Madison: University of Wisconsin Press, 1991), 13–22.

7. Antony J. Hasler, "Hoccleve's Unregimented Body," *Paragraph* 13 (1990): 164–83, this quotation from 174.

8. Middleton, "Chaucer's 'New Men'," 16.

9. Ibid., 30.

10. Ibid., 29.

11. The phrasing originates in Anglo-American criticism with the publication of Wolfgang Iser, *The Implied Reader: Patterns of Communication in Prose Fiction from Bunyan to Beckett* (Baltimore: Johns Hopkins University Press, 1974), though the origins may be traced back to notions of implied authorship in Wayne Booth, *The Rhetoric of Fiction* (Chicago: University of Chicago Press, 1961) and through the traditions of what may be called a "rhetorical" school of criticism in Stanley Fish, *Surprised by Sin: The Reader in Paradise Lost* (Berkeley and Los Angeles: University of California Press, 1966); Walter J. Ong, S. J., "The Writer's Audience Is Always a Fiction," *PMLA* 90 (1975): 9–21; and for medieval studies in particular, Franz Bäuml, "Varieties and Consequences of Medieval Literacy and Illiteracy," *Speculum* 55 (1980): 237–65, especially his statement:

> For just as the author is absent from the public, which must "constitute" a narrator on the basis of the text, and an "author" implied by the text, the public is absent

from the author, who must "constitute" the public whom he addresses in his text. And just as the function of the narrator in the text, that of the fictional public may be explicit or implicit, and it serves to provide the "real" public with a mask . . . by means of which its relationship to the text may be manipulated.

(253)

Paul Strohm has distinguished between the "implied" and "real" or social audiences for Chaucer along these lines in "Chaucer's Audience(s): Fictional, Implied, Intended, Actual," *Chaucer Review* 18 (1983): 137–45.

12. For a full description of the Tanner manuscript, see the introduction to the facsimile edition by Pamela R. Robinson, *Manuscript Tanner 346: A Facsimile* (Norman: Pilgrim Books, 1982). Tanner 346 is traditionally associated with two other Bodleian library manuscripts, Bodley 638 and Fairfax 16, in what Eleanor Hammond called the Oxford Group of manuscripts collecting Chaucer's minor verse (see *Chaucer: A Bibliographical Manual* [New York: Macmillan, 1908], 338–39). They share many of the same texts in similar order, though Tanner is the shortest of the three. Full descriptions of these manuscripts may be found in their facsimile editions: Pamela R. Robinson, *Manuscript Bodley 638: A Facsimile*; and John Norton-Smith, *Bodleian Library, MS Fairfax 16* (London: Scolar Press, 1979). The *Book of Cupid* appears in all three of these manuscripts, as well as in the Scottish Sinclair Manuscript of the late 1480s (Bodleian Library MS Arch. Selden B.24) and the Findern Anthology of the late fifteenth century (Cambridge University Library MS Ff.1.6), where it receives its sole attribution, "Explicit Clanvowe." For discussion of the textual relationships among these five manuscripts of the *Book of Cupid*, and the problems of dating and authorship they raise, see V. J. Scattergood, *The Works of Sir John Clanvowe* (Cambridge: D. S. Brewer, 1975), 14–18, from whose edition I also quote the poem (abbreviated as *BC*).

13. Robinson dates Tanner 346 on paleographic grounds, reporting information received from Malcolm Parkes (*Tanner 346*, xxiv). Norton-Smith dates Fairfax 16 to the 1450s (*Fairfax 16*, xi–xii), while Bodley 638 is generally believed to date from the later half of the century (see Robinson, *Bodley 638*, xxii–xxiii). The chronological order of the Oxford Group texts is thus Tanner, Fairfax, Bodley.

14. Robinson traces the scribal stints as follows: Scribe A wrote folios 1–33 and 120–131, Scribe B wrote folios 34–75 and 110–119, and Scribe C wrote folios 76–109. Thus, Scribe A began the *Legend of Good Women* in the first booklet; Scribe B completed the booklet; Scribe C wrote the entire second booklet and began the third; Scribe B completed the third booklet; and Scribe A wrote the entire fourth booklet (*Tanner 346*, xvii–xviii, xxii, xxv). Robinson's findings lead her to suppose a "lack of coordination among the scribes," where "each was working independently of the others" (xxv). Julia Boffey and John J. Thompson, however, reviewing the same evidence, conclude that the manuscript was copied from "collaborating scribes" who shared exemplars. The manuscript's separate sections, they conclude, "were probably copied from the outset for some single, defined purpose, and furthermore . . . they were copied simultaneously." See their study, "Anthologies and Miscellanies: Production and Choice of Texts," in Griffiths and Pearsall, eds., *Book Production and Publishing in Britain, 1375–1475*, 279–315, these quotations from 281.

15. Robinson calls attention to the signature "JGraystok" [*sic*] and the name "John graystok" [*sic*] on the closing folios of the manuscript, names she identifies as Sir John Greystoke (d. 1501), second son and later heir of Ralph, Baron Greystoke (d. 1487)

(*Tanner 346*, xxvi). On the family and the public service of Ralph and John, see A. H. Doubleday, et al., *The Complete Peerage* (London: St. Catherine Press, 1926), VI:199–201. It is, Robinson admits, only speculation as to whether the manuscript was commissioned by a member of the Greystoke family or whether it was purchased by John Greystoke several decades after its original making. The physical features of the manuscript, however, such as its modest but carefully planned decorations, its clear organization of stichic and stanzaic poetry, and the fact that it is wholly on parchment, all suggest that Tanner is closer to the ambience of Fairfax 16 (a presentation text commissioned by a member of the armigerous gentry) than it is to Bodley 638 (perhaps representative of "amateur productions, copied by individuals for their own use," Boffey and Thompson, "Anthologies and Miscellanies," 282). Although Tanner 346 has not received the detailed study that such manuscripts as the Findern Anthology and the Sinclair manuscript have as a product of gentry or aristocratic patronage, some of the defining features of this kind of patronage may be applied to such a study, and in my analysis I draw on materials and interpretations collected in the following: Peter J. Lucas, "The Growth and Development of English Literary Patronage in the Late Middle Ages and Early Renaissance," *The Library*, sixth series, 4 (1982): 219–48; Ralph Hanna III, "Sir Thomas Berkeley and His Patronage," *Speculum* 64 (1989): 878–916; Joel T. Rosenthal, "Aristocratic Cultural Patronage and Book Bequests, 1350–1500," *Bulletin of the John Rylands Library* 64 (1982): 522–48; Derek Pearsall, *John Lydgate* (Charlottesville: University of Virginia Press, 1970); and Carol Meale, "Patrons, Buyers and Owners: Book Production and Social Status," in Griffiths and Pearsall, eds., *Book Production and Publishing in Britain*, 201–38. Among recent specialized studies of individual manuscripts and patrons, I have found the following particularly helpful: George R. Keiser, "Lincoln Cathedral Library MS. 91: Life and Milieu of the Scribe," *Studies in Bibliography* 32 (1979): 158–79; Kate Harris, "The Origins and Make-Up of Cambridge University Library MS Ff.1.6," *Transactions of the Cambridge Bibliographical Society* 8 (1983): 299–333; and Ralph Hanna III, "The Production of Cambridge University Library MS. Ff.1.6," *Studies in Bibliography* 41 (1988): 62–70.

16. Quoted from Meale, "Patrons, Buyers," 216.

17. See Malcolm Parkes, "The Literacy of the Laity," in David Daiches and Anthony Thorlby, eds., *The Mediaeval World* (London: Aldus Books, 1973), 555–77. On the relationship between schooling and changing literary taste, see the suggestive remarks in JoAnn Hoeppner Moran, *The Growth of English Schooling 1340–1548* (Princeton: Princeton University Press, 1985), 185–220. For an influential, general assessment of the relationship between education, class, and taste in the fifteenth century, see F.R.H. Du Boulay, *An Age of Ambition: English Society in the Late Middle Ages* (London: Nelson, 1970), 61–79.

18. On court patronage generally, and more specifically for an argument that fifteenth-century literary culture was shaped by the rise of a self-conscious "court" readership, see R. F. Green, *Poets and Princepleasers* (Totonto: University of Toronto Press, 1980). For the idea of a "Ricardian" poetic sponsored by the patronage of the royal court, see John Burrow, *Ricardian Poetry* (New Haven: Yale University Press, 1971) and the arguments developed by Anne Middleton, "The Idea of Public Poetry in the Reign of Richard II," *Speculum* 53 (1978): 94–114. Hanna offers a useful caveat on the "difficulties of discussing as any unity court culture, especially under Richard II and Henry IV" ("Sir Thomas Berkeley," 913n.83). The relationship between such courtly patronage

and that of what Hanna calls "magnate culture" of the fifteenth century is subject to a variety of interpretations. Hanna's argument is that "the creation of magnate culture" may have preceded "a formed national literary culture" (912), and that "court culture moved *through* London ... rather than radiating *from* it. . . . London encouraged a disparate national court culture by allowing decentralization, by facilitating a kind of exportable use which joined together quite diverse rural environments" (913, emphases his). For the notion that the aristocracy, and then the gentry and the middle classes, imitated their superiors in the commissioning of books, see the formulations of Lucas, "English Literary Patronage" ("The gentry imitated the magnates in wanting to possess books and in turn wealthy merchants imitated the gentry," 241), and Pearsall, *John Lydgate* ("To buy books, to own them, perhaps even to commission one or two, will set the seal on status," 72).

19. Pearsall, *John Lydgate*, 69.

20. John Stanley of Hooton commissioned the Fairfax 16 manuscript, with its opening illustration of the allegory of Mars and Venus and the Stanley coat of arms emblazoned on it. For a discussion of this commission and its implications for the study of magnate patronage in the fifteenth century, see Norton-Smith, *Fairfax 16*, xxi and Boffey and Thompson, "Anthologies and Miscellanies," 282. On Robert Thornton and his manuscripts, see Keiser, "Lincoln Cathedral Library MS. 91" who notes, in passing, on "the availability and importance of books in late medieval Yorkshire" (158) and finds among the prospective readership of such books "various Yorkshiremen associated with manors, some of whom held prestigious rank and some of whom must have been fairly well educated" (161), among whom he lists Ralph, Baron of Greystoke, the possible first owner of Tanner 346.

21. Sylvia Huot, *From Song to Book* (Ithica: Cornell University Press, 1987) esp. 11–45.

22. Ibid., 15.

23. Ibid., 20.

24. John Norton-Smith, *Fairfax 16*, vii.

25. A. J. Minnis, *Medieval Theory of Authorship* (London: Scolar Press, 1984), 201.

26. Implicit in my argument here is the claim that the *idea* of a Chaucerian anthology originates with Chaucer himself and that the fifteenth-century readers and writers who produce Chaucerian collections are responding to dramatic and interpretive problems in the poetry itself, rather than inventing the idea wholly in response to specific economic, aesthetic, or social pressures. It is generally assumed by modern scholars that the idea of the Chaucerian anthology is an invention of the fifteenth century. See, for example, Boffey and Thompson, "Anthologies and Miscellanies": "A growing taste for such anthologies made itself felt in the second half of the fifteenth century, seemingly generated by a small number of exemplars" (280). Robinson similarly voices the received interpretation: "The notion of such a collection probably did not arise until the mid-fifteenth century when John Shirley began publishing his verse anthologies and two of the manuscripts of the so-called Oxford group [i.e., Tanner 346 and Fairfax 16] were compiled" (*Tanner 346*, xxiv). Malcolm Parkes and Richard Beadle come closer to the mark in their assessment of the origins of Cambridge University Library MS Gg.4.27, the earliest surviving manuscript anthology of Chaucer's works, which they date to the second half of the first quarter of the fifteenth century (*Geoffrey Chaucer: Poetical Works: A Facsimile of Cambridge University Library Gg.4.27* [Cambridge: Cam-

bridge University Press, 1980], 7). They suggest that "interest in Chaucer's writings was encouraged by responses to the poetic persona which emerges in his works," and that "enthusiasm for the poetry of a particular literary persona" influenced the rise of the Chaucerian collection (64).

27. Hanna, "The Production of Cambridge University Library MS Ff.1.6," 68. For the principles of fascicular, or booklet, construction in medieval manuscripts, and for the implications of its study for an understanding of fourteenth- and fifteenth-century literary culture generally, see Pamela R. Robinson, "The 'Booklet': A Self-Contained Unit in Composite Manuscripts," *Codicologica* 3 (1980): 46–69, and Ralph Hanna, "Booklets in Medieval Manuscripts: Further Considerations," *Studies in Bibliography* 39 (1986): 100–111. For a skeptical response to the booklet theory of production, especially as it applies to Tanner 346, see N. F. Blake's review of Robinson, *Tanner 346*, in *English Studies* 63 (1982): 71–73.

28. Hanna, "Production of Cambridge University Library MS Ff.1.6," 68n.14.

29. Middleton, "Chaucer's 'New Men'," 28.

30. Ibid.

31. Ibid.

32. For Lydgate's appellations, see *Fall of Princes* I.1783, where the poet directs his audience, "Redith the legende of martirs off Cupide" for more on the story of Erysichthon; and *Fall of Princes* VI.3624, where he defers to Chaucer for the story of Antony and Cleopatra "In his book, the Legende of Cupide." In the *Letter of Cupid*, Hoccleve has the god of love refer to Chaucer's poem as "my legende of martres" (316). Furnivall's collations of different manuscripts of the poem, however, show the following variations in this line: The Ashburnham MS reads "our" for "my," and Shirley's copy of the poem in Trinity College Cambridge MS R.3.20 reads "þe" for "my." See F. J. Furnivall, ed., *Hoccleve's Works, I. The Minor Poems*, EETS ES 61 (London: Kegan Paul, 1892), 252. Interestingly, the editors of the *Riverside Chaucer* adopt the Man of Law's characterization of the *Legend* as a subtitle to their edition of the poem (588, and see the notes on 1179).

33. On the textual tradition of the *Temple of Glas*, and the three versions of the poem, possibly representing different stages of its composition as they survive in seven manuscripts, see the account in John Norton-Smith, *John Lydgate: Poems* (Oxford: Clarendon Press, 1966), 176–79 (from whose edition I quote from the *Temple of Glas*). Norton-Smith bases his edition on the text in Tanner 346, whose copy of the poem he calls "the most perfect example" of "the completed draft of the poem" (176). In Tanner 346 the *Temple of Glas* begins the second booklet, folio 76 of a total of 132 folios in the volume. It is rubricated "The tempil of Glas" by the scribe who wrote the text (Scribe C), and it and the A Scribe's rubricated heading for the fourth booklet ("The parlement of Briddis") form the only titled poems in English in the manuscript. The title for Hoccleve's *Letter of Cupid* is in Latin ("Litera Cupidinis dei Amoris directa subditis suis amatoribus") and unrubricated, written in the same ink as the text by the B Scribe.

34. The English phrase "set in order" is most likely a translation of the Latin *ordinare*, the specific term for the organization of a manuscript book or collection. Together with the term *compilatio*, *ordinatio* defines the processes by which disparate materials were organized into volumes and through which narrative and encyclopaedic works were given shape. For the origin, development, and critical implications of these terms, see Malcolm Parkes, "The Influence of the Concepts of *Ordinatio* and *Compila-*

tio on the Development of the Book," in Alexander and Gibson, eds., *Medieval Learning and Literature*, 115–41; and for the development of this approach, see A. J. Minnis, *Medieval Theory of Authorship*. Lydgate clearly thinks of the *Legend of Good Women* in these terms, when he states in the *Fall of Princes*: "Redith the legende of martirs off Cupyde / Which that Chaucer, *in ordre* as thei stood, / *Compiled* off women that wer callid good" (I.1782–84, emphases added). In the Kalendar of John Shirley (probably dating from the late 1420s and surviving in the copy made by John Stowe in his manuscript, BL MS Add. 29729), he remarks that he has brought together the contents of his manuscript anthology: "thus haue I them in ordre sete" (line 15, quoted from Brusendorff, *The Chaucer Tradition* [London: Oxford University Press, 1925], 457). The fifteenth-century English translator of Higden's *Polychronicon* writes of "the ordre of the processe" governing the collection and incorporation of materials into the narrative (quoted in Minnis, *Theory of Authorship*, 200).

35. For the sources of Lydgate's lines in Chaucer's works, see Norton-Smith's notes to the poem in *John Lydgate: Poems*, 181–82 (though he misses the allusion to the *Squire's Tale*).

36. Lydgate's list of specifically named lovers runs from lines 55 to 142; Chaucer's name appears at line 110. In the Tanner manuscript a late-fifteenth-century hand has written "Nota" beside line 110 (fol. 77v; see Robinson, *Tanner 346*, xxiii).

37. The *Book of Cupid* follows the *Temple of Glas* in Tanner 346. It is also associated with Lydgate's poem in Bodley 638 (where it precedes the *Temple*), and it appears with the *Temple* in Fairfax 16.

38. Clanvowe's poem has received a variety of sensitive assessments since the publication of Scattergood's edition. See in particular A. C. Spearing, *Medieval Dream-Poetry* (Cambridge: Cambridge University Press, 1976), 176–81; Charles S. Rutherford, "The *Boke of Cupide* Reopened," *Neuphilologische Mitteilungen* 78 (1977), 350–58; Paul Strohm, "Fourteenth- and Fifteenth-Century Writers as Readers of Chaucer," in Piero Boitani and Anna Torti, eds., *Genres, Themes, and Images in English Literature* (Tübingen: Gunter Narr, 1988), 90–104, and his *Social Chaucer* (Cambridge: Harvard University Press, 1989), 78–82. Based on its appellation in the Findern Anthology (the "Explicit Clanvowe"), the poem is now generally assumed to be the work of John Clanvowe (d. 1391), one of the so-called Lollard Knights affiliated with Chaucer in the 1380s. For remarks on his personal relationship to Chaucer (for example, he was one of the witnesses to the legal documents of the Cecily Champagne incident) and for his place in Richard II's court, see Richard F. Green, *Poets and Princepleasers*, 65, 130, and 196. For assessments of the *Book of Cupid* in the tradition of Valentine's Day poetry, perhaps first brought to England or even invented by Chaucer, see Jack B. Oruch, "St. Valentine, Chaucer, and Spring in February," *Speculum* 56 (1981): 534–65; and Henry A. Kelly, *Chaucer and the Cult of St. Valentine* (Leiden: E. J. Brill, 1986), esp. 128–30, who challenges, however, John Clanvowe's authorship of the poem and its dating as a fourteenth-century work.

39. The lines quote from the *Knight's Tale* A 1785–86. Several of the earliest manuscripts of the *Canterbury Tales* call attention to this speech of Theseus: Hengwrt signals the opening of the speech with a "Nota" and Hengwrt, Ellesmere, and Corpus Christi College Cambridge MS 198 begin the couplet with a paragraph marker or large capital.

40. Spearing, *Medieval Dream-Poetry*, 176; but see Thomas Hill, "'Half-Waking,

Half-Sleeping': A Tropological Motif in a Middle English Lyric and Its European Context," *Review of English Studies*, new series 29 (1978): 50–56.

41. For a survey of Chaucer's uses of the rhyming pair, and for an overview of the philosophical underpinnings of his notion of intention, see P. B. Taylor, "Chaucer's *Cosyn to the Dede*," *Speculum* 57 (1982): 315–27. For a reading of one of the *Canterbury Tales* as thematically concerned with the issue, see Richard H. Passon, "'Entente' in Chaucer's *Friar's Tale*," *Chaucer Review* 2 (1968): 166–71; and Robert B. Burlin, *Chaucerian Fiction* (Princeton: Princeton University Press, 1977), 162–64. For the role of *intentio* in the medieval study of law, see Hermann Kantorowicz, *Studies in the Glossators of Roman Law* (Cambridge: Cambridge University Press, 1938), 51. For the place of the study of intention in the history of medieval theories of signification (especially as derived from the work of Priscian and Abelard), see the account in Brian Stock, *The Implications of Literacy* (Princeton: Princeton University Press, 1983), 376–77; and see, too, the suggestive article of Russell A. Peck, "Chaucer and the Nominalist Questions," *Speculum* 53 (1978): 745–60.

42. For a review of the literary history behind the pun, see Scattergood's note to these lines in *The Works of Sir John Clanvowe*, 84.

43. Scattergood prints line 282, "The morowe of Seynt Valentynes day," but the Tanner manuscript, along with the Findern Anthology and Thynne's edition in the 1532 *Chaucer's Works* all offer "The morowe after Seynt Valentynes day." It is possible that these alternative readings are designed to bring out the meaning of "morowe" already present in Clanvowe's Middle English, that is, they may function as translations of an idiom that had passed out of use by the mid-fifteenth century. "Morwe" frequently could mean the day after as well as the morning of, and it appears recorded and cited in the *MED*, s.v. *morwe*, 3. Metrical arguments for the line are equivocal: With the probable syncopation of "morowe" by the mid-fifteenth century, and with the elision of the final *-e*, the line with *after* scans. For another example of scribal revision of Clanvowe's lines to suit revised interpretations or changes in usage, see line 80. The birds will choose their mates, in Scattergood's edition, "In Marche, vponn Seynt Valentynes day." Tanner and Thynne, however, have "In feviȝere vponn Seynt Valentynes day." Kelly suggests that this revision represents a fifteenth-century change in the assignation of Valentine's Day (*Chaucer and the Cult of St. Valentine*), and that the Tanner scribe has sacrificed meter for calendrical accuracy.

44. "Chaucer's 'New Men,'" 42.

45. "Though Chaucer implies he is working from a source . . . none has been discovered nor is likely to be" (*Riverside Chaucer*, 890).

46. "Chaucer's 'New Men,'" 30.

47. Louise Fradenburg, "The Scottish Chaucer," in R. J. Lyall and Felicity Riddy, eds., *Proceedings of the Third International Conference on Scottish Language and Literature (Medieval and Renaissance)* (Sterling and Glasgow: William Culross and Son, Ltd., 1981), 185.

48. The *Book of Cupid* ends at the top of Tanner 346, fol.101r and is followed by an "Explicit." What follows are three rhyme-royal stanzas, stretching to fol.101v, and then "The lenvoye," the six-line anagrammatic stanza whose first letters spell out the name Alison. Beneath this stanza a seventeenth-century hand has written "Explicit Cuck. & Nighting." These four stanzas have been considered a separate poem since Skeat

printed them as *The Envoy to Alison* in 1900 (*Oxford Chaucer* [Oxford: Oxford University Press, 1894–97] VII:359–60). The poem also appears in MS Fairfax 16 (fols.147v–148r), between the *Book of the Duchess* and the *Chance of the Dice*. Commenting on the poem, Norton-Smith notes, "This could be described as a 'false item'; these four stanzas are not an independent poem," and he holds with the critical opinion that they form an envoy to the *Book of Cupid*. (*Fairfax 16*, xxv).

49. For Hoccleve's envoy to the *Regiment*, see Furnivall, ed., *Hoccleve's Works I. The Minor Poems*, 61. These three stanzas were separated out of the *Regiment* by Hoccleve himself and included in his holograph manuscript (now Huntington Library MS HM III) under the title "Ceste balade ensuyante feust mise en le fin du liure del Regiment des Princes." Compare, for example, the opening lines of both poems:

> O lewde book, with thy foole rudenesse,
> Sith thou hast neither beautee n'eloquence,
> Who hath thee caused, or yeve thee hardiness
> For to appere in my ladyes presence?
>
> > (*Alison*, 1–4, ed. Skeat)

> O litil book / who yaf thee hardynesse
> Thy wordes to pronounce in the presence
> Of kynges ympe and Princes worthynesse,
> Syn thow al nakid art of eloquence?
>
> > (*Balade*, 1–4, ed. Furnivall)

Compare, also, the paired uses of *sentence / reverence* in the second stanzas of both poems, and the imperative for the book to beseech the reader-patron as the opening word of the third stanzas.

50. Anne Middleton, "William Langland's 'Kynde Name': Authorial Signature and Social Identity in Late Fourteenth-Century England," in Patterson, ed., *Literary Practice and Social Change*, 15–82, these quotations from 34–35.

51. I borrow the phrasing of Chris Given-Wilson, *The English Nobility in the Late Middle Ages* (London: Routledge and Kegan Paul, 1987), 57, as quoted in Lee Patterson, "'What Man Artow?'" (*SAC* 11 [1989]:119).

CHAPTER THREE

1. I quote from the edition of Caxton's 1477 print as published in F. J. Furnivall, ed., *Caxton's Book of Curtesye*, EETS ES 3 (London: Trübner, 1868). Two other versions of this work survive and are printed in parallel edition by Furnivall: one from Oriel College Oxford, MS 79; the other from a copy in Richard Hill's commonplace book, Balliol College Oxford, MS 354. The relationship between these three texts is still debated. Curt Bühler considered the Oriel manuscript a copy of Caxton's print, a relation rejected by N. F. Blake, "Manuscript to Print," in Griffiths and Pearsall, eds., *Book Production and Publishing in Britain 1375–1475*, 425 (citing Bühler, "*The Fasciculus Temporum*," *Speculum* 27 [1952]: 183). Blake identifies Hill's manuscript as an early-sixteenth-century compilation, and notes, "The text of the *Book of Courtesy* in Balliol 354 is similar to that in Caxton's print, but it has not been identified as a copy of it" (425).

Although the *Book of Curtesye* may thus have circulated in various forms in the late fifteenth century, I rely on Caxton's print as the earliest extant copy.

2. On the manuscript traditions of the *Treatise on the Astrolabe*, see the notes in the *Riverside Chaucer*, 1193–95. The manuscripts that title it "Brede and milke for children" are identified as Bodleian Library MSS Bodley 68 and 619 and E. Museo 54, and Aberdeen University Library MS 123. For an account of the *Astrolabe*'s teaching in relation to the various traditions of astronomy in medieval Europe, together with assumptions that it is a children's book, see J. D. North, *Chaucer's Universe* (Oxford: Oxford University Press, 1988), 38–86. Although there is some discussion of Chaucer's poetry as a form of children's literature, there seems little current, critical awareness of the place of the paternal voice of the *Astrolabe* in that discussion. One treatment is that of Thomas J. Jambeck and Karen K. Jambeck, "Chaucer's *Treatise on the Astrolabe*: A Handbook for the Medieval Child," *Children's Literature* 3 (1974): 177–22. Some broader gestures in this direction are made by Lee Patterson, "'What Man Artow?'" (*SAC* 11 [1989]: 117–75), who notes in the contexts of a discussion on the traditions of advisory literature, "Is it too much to suggest, then, that *Melibee*, no less than *Astrolabe*, is a piece of children's literature?" (149).

3. Though Patterson, "'What Man Artow?'" says much about the thematics of childhood in Chaucer's poetry—and although portions of this chapter are concerned with qualifying or responding to the challenge of his arguments—he does not explore the possibilities of Chaucer's work as actually read by children in late-medieval England. For suggestions on the place of Chaucer in a children's literature of the time, and for the idea of a category of children's literature before the publication in the eighteenth century of volumes explicitly for children, see the collection of articles published as "A Symposium on Children and Literature in the Middle Ages," in *Children's Literature* 4 (1975): 36–63, especially the study of Bennett A. Brockman, "Children and Literature in Late Medieval England," 58–63, and his later study, "Robin Hood and the Invention of Children's Literature," *Children's Literature* 10 (1982): 1–17.

4. The Helmingham Manuscript is now Princeton University Library, MS Princeton 100. For published descriptions, see Manly-Rickert, I:256–65, and my catalogue entry to David Anderson, ed., *Sixty Bookes Olde and Newe* (Knoxville: New Chaucer Society, 1986), 7–9.

5. The manuscript is described as Phillipps 8299 in Manly-Rickert I:433–38, and more fully in Deutschke et al., *A Guide to Medieval and Renaissance Manuscripts in the Huntington Library* (San Marino: Huntington Library, 1989), 185–90.

6. I paraphrase from Lawton, "Dullness in the Fifteenth Century," *ELH* 54 (1987): 761.

7. Manly-Rickert's response to Helmingham is representative: "A careless copy of a very bad and much edited ancestor, [Helmingham] is worth little in the making of the text" (I:258). Kate Harris, "John Gower's 'Confessio Amantis': The Virtues of Bad Texts," in Derek Pearsall, ed., *Manuscripts and Readers in Fifteenth-Century England*, 26–40, defines "bad" texts as "those in which the intrusions of a medieval manuscript compiler or editor (or both) are most obvious . . . appearing in the form of extracts . . . [or] containing an abridged text" (27–28). For an exhortation to the study of such documents as evidence of medieval critical responses to literature, see Derek Pearsall, "Editing Medieval Texts," in McGann, ed., *Textual Criticism and Literary Interpretation*, 92–106.

8. The controlling didacticism of late-medieval literature has long been recognized in the rise of courtesy books and a pictorial and narrative fascination with domestic behavior. An early collection of texts may be found in F. J. Furnivall, ed., *The Babees Book*, EETS OS 32 (London: Trübner, 1868). A survey of key issues is in Pearsall, *John Lydgate* (Charlottesville: University of Virginia Press, 1970), 68–70, and, with reference to specific commissions, Carol Meale, "Patrons, Buyers, and Owners," in Griffiths and Pearsall, eds., *Book Production and Publishing*, 201–38. Paul Zumthor has located the late-medieval concern with an education in manners not so much in the rise of an ambitious commercial class (the way that Pearsall and Meale do) as in a shift in attitudes toward the body and its social representations: a concern with the symbolic, and a cultivation of the cultivated in courtly discourse ("From Hi(story) to Poem or the Paths of Pun," *New Literary History* 10 [1979]: 231–63). Louise Fradenburg develops Zumthor's suggestions to define the latter Middle Ages as "a time when the refusal of the real by the symbolic is intensely elaborated. One index of its elaboration is a new interest in manners" ("The Manciple's Servant Tongue," *ELH* 82 [1985]: 89–90.).

9. For an exemplary account of the impact of these various traditions on vernacular poetics, see Theodore Silverstein, "Sir Gawain in a Dilemma, or Keeping Faith with Marcus Tullius Cicero," *Modern Philology* 75 (1976): 1–17. A survey of courtesy books and chivalric manuals, with an eye to their place in the study of English literature, is found in Diane Bornstein, *Mirrors of Courtesy* (Hamden: Archon Books, 1975).

10. See Carol Meale, "Patrons, Buyers, and Owners." For a survey of the impact of paper on the making of late-medieval books, see R. J. Lyall, "Materials: The Paper Revolution," in Griffiths and Pearsall, eds., *Book Production and Publishing*, 11–29. A.S.G. Edwards and Derek Pearsall note that it is only in the last third of the fifteenth century that vernacular literary works come to be written on paper with any degree of regularity ("Manuscripts of the Major English Poetic Texts," in Griffiths and Pearsall, eds., *Book Production and Publishing*, 260).

11. Patterson, "'What Man Artow?'" 172. See, too, the bibliography assembled in notes 161 and 162 on that page.

12. For the ironies of the Prioress's table manners, see John V. Fleming, "Daun Piers and Dom Pier: Waterless Fish and Unholy Hunters," *Chaucer Review* 15 (1981): 287, who notes, characteristically, "That the Prioress learned her table manners from the most notorious old whore in Europe can be regarded as a simple fact of 'source study' or an exciting critical challenge." For critiques of the critical tradition of reading Chaucer and his sources ironically in these ways, see the account of Leonard Koff, *Chaucer and the Art of Storytelling* (Berkeley and Los Angeles: University of California Press, 1988), 7–36, and Joseph A. Dane, *The Critical Mythology of Irony* (Athens: University of Georgia Press, 1991), 135–45.

13. See, for example, the injunctions to good table manners in the two manuscript versions of Lydgate's *Stans Puer ad Mensam*, printed by Furnivall, *Babees Book*, 28–31; the descriptions of eating properly in the anonymous *Urbanitatis* (*Babees Book*, 13–15); and the similar descriptions in *The Young Children's Book* (*Babees Book*, 17–20); and the *Babees Book* itself, 6–7.

14. See, for example, *Stans Puer ad Mensam* in Furnivall's *Babees Book* edition from BL MS Harley 2251, p.30 line 61 ("Be quyke and redy, meke and seruisable"), and the overall description of serviceable qualities in *The Schoole of Vertue* (published in 1557 and printed in Furnivall, *Babees Book*, especially 341–43).

15. On the Squire's carving, see the discussion in the *Riverside Chaucer*, 802. Furnivall prints de Worde's *Boke of Keruynge* (1513) in *Babees Book*, 264–86, and the *Boke of Nurture* by John Russell (described as "sum tyme seruande with Duke Vmfrey of Glowcetur . . . ") on 117–99.

16. Manly-Rickert, I:261–64. The names written in the childish scribbles of the manuscript have been identified as the playmates of Lionel Tollemache III (1536–75). By positing a period of friendship from Lionel's age 9 to 14, Manly and Rickert date the bulk of the scribbles to the period 1545–50.

17. Manly and Rickert date the handwriting on the vellum folios to ca. 1420–30, on the paper ca. 1450–60. By my examination of the manuscript, the earlier hand has a more squarish look and a more careful duct than does that of the paper section. The latter also has more apparent secretary features to the overall Anglicana bookhand (in particular, formations of the letters *g* and *w*) and has the look of a more current, hurried execution.

18. Manly and Rickert mention this flyleaf (I:259), but it has never been fully described. It is a single sheet of paper bearing a stag's head watermark very close, but not identical, to section II number 209 (Cologne 1478) in G. Piccard, *Wasserzeichen Hirsch* (Stuttgart: Verlag W. Kohlhammer, 1987). The handwriting of the table of sunrises and sunsets bears strong similarities to the "set hands" dated to the period of the reign of Henry VII by Hilary Jenkinson, *The Later Court Hands in England from the Fifteenth to the Seventeenth Century, Illustrated from the Common Paper of the Scriveners' Company of London, the English Writing Masters, and the Public Records* (Cambridge: Cambridge University Press, 1927). No other paper in the manuscript is of this stock, and it appears to have been added to the Helmingham manuscript after the paper quires had been made and just before its original binding. Though the opening of the *Canterbury Tales* is lost from the manuscript as it stands now (the opening of what is now fol.1r begins at the *Knight's Tale*, A 1975), the flyleaf's annotations that repeat the opening line of the *General Prologue* indicate that it must have been bound into the text before the opening leaves had been lost. What I would posit is that the Helmingham manuscript, like many vernacular books in private hands, existed for a time in unbound quires, and that sometime at the end of the fifteenth or beginning of the sixteenth century it was bound together with the paper flyleaf. For examples of such volumes kept in unbound quires, see the discussion of the books bequeathed by Richard Fox in his will of 1454 in Kate Harris, "Patrons, Buyers, and Owners," in Griffiths and Pearsall, eds., *Book Production and Publishing 1375–1475*, 184n.5.

19. Rossell Hope Robbins, "English Almanacks of the Fifteenth Century," *Philological Quarterly* 18 (1934): 321–31, calls attention to the many kinds of astronomical and calendrical annotations to late-medieval commonplace books, which he calls "the obvious repository for household hints as well as entertaining songs and stories" (322). Robbins also notes the preponderance of prose and verse materials in flyleaves bound into fifteenth-century manuscripts (see 324n.20, and 330). Robbins discerns that many of these calendrical pieces (in both verse and prose) center on determining the dates and the weather of holidays. The table in the Helmingham manuscript similarly begins with a grounding in the liturgical feast day, as the first entry for January reads: "ffyrst on Newe yeers day called þᵉ cyrcu[m]sysyon of o[ure] lorde þᵉ sonne ryseth att q[uar]ter of an our after viii. of clokke yn þᵉ morwe / and goth down a q[uar]ter of an

hour befor iii of þᵉ clokke at afternoon." For more recent work on lay interests in astronomy and observation, see the remarks of Linda E. Voigts, "Scientific and Medical Books," in Griffiths and Pearsall, eds., *Book Production and Publishing in Britain 1375–1475*, 345–402, especially 365 and the reproduction of plates of astronomical tables on 362–63. Of 178 manuscripts containing some scientific material examined by Voigts, she reports 52 containing "astronomical and mathematical relationships set forth in tables and charts" (365). J. D. North's chapter "On Diverse Tables" (*Chaucer's Universe*, 86–133) details the kinds of astronomical and calendrical accounts kept in late-medieval compilations; such tables included records of the length of day and night throughout the year (101–3). North's information is pressed into the service of reading Chaucer's poetry as, in effect, astrological and computistical allegories, and at the close of his chapter he illustrates how late-medieval concerns with the times of sunrise and sunset inform Chaucer's astrological introduction in the *General Prologue* and the astronomical allusions in the Prologue to the *Pardoner's Tale*. One might speculate, therefore, that the Helmingham manuscript prefaces the *Canterbury Tales* with a table designed to figure out the dating and the length of the Canterbury pilgrimage and furthermore to illustrate the possibilities of the kind of astronomical interpretation North posits in his juxtaposition of Chaucer's *Astrolabe* and *Canterbury Tales*.

20. Rough squares appear at the top of fol.161r. Next to Chaucer's line in the *Thopas / Melibee* Link, "After the wich this mery tale I write," a different, late-fifteenth-century hand has written a capital *Q* followed by an *r* and a brief flourish, which I read as the abbreviation for the Latin "Quaeritur" (see A. Cappelli, *Lexicon abbreviaturarum: Dizionario di abbreviature latine et italiane usate nelle carte e codici specialmente del medio evo*, 3d. ed. [Milan: V. Hoepli, 1929]). At the bottom of the page, a child's version of a late-sixteenth-century secretarial hand has written, "The man that sitteth fel."

21. The following studies may exemplify the range of responses to the *Tale of Sir Thopas* and the *Tale of Melibee* in recent Chaucer criticism: Alan T. Gaylord, "Sentence and Solaas in Fragment VII of the *Canterbury Tales*: Harry Bailly as Horseback Editor," *PMLA* 82 (1967): 226–35, and his later studies "Chaucer's Dainty 'Dogerel': The 'Elvyssh' Prosody of *Sir Thopas*," *SAC* 1 (1979): 84–104, and "The Moment of *Sir Thopas*: Towards a New Look at Chaucer's Language," *Chaucer Review* 16 (1982): 311–29; Donald R. Howard, *The Idea of the Canterbury Tales* (Berkeley and Los Angeles: University of California Press, 1976), 309–16; Glending Olson, "A Reading of the Thopas-Melibee Link," *Chaucer Review* 10 (1975): 147–53; C. David Benson, "Their Telling Difference: Chaucer the Pilgrim and His Two Contrasting Tales," *Chaucer Review* 18 (1983): 60–76; John Burrow, "Four Notes on Chaucer's *Sir Thopas*," in his *Essays on Medieval Literature* (Oxford: Clarendon Press, 1984), 60–78; Lee Patterson, "'What Man Artow?'"

22. A history of the late-medieval reception of the *Melibee* remains to be written. For some remarks on the fifteenth-century appearance of the *Tale*, abstracted from the *Canterbury Tales* and included in anthologies, see Daniel Silvia, "Some Fifteenth-Century Manuscripts," in B. Rowland, ed., *Chaucer and Middle English Studies*, 153–63. One such manuscript, Huntington Library MS HM 144, titles it simply *Prouerbis* and pares down the allegorical narrative of the tale to highlight the assemblage of Prudence's *sententiae*. On this manuscript, Silvia simply notes that "The heading 'Prouerbis' for the *Melibeus* can hardly be the product of literary awareness" (159–60). By contrast,

A. J. Minnis, in his dissertation "Medieval Discussions of the Role of the Author" (Queen's University, Belfast, 1976), suggests that, along with the tales of the Monk and the Parson, "*The Tale of Melibee* can be regarded as a *compilatio*" (206), in whose manuscripts the margins "are filled with the names of the *auctores* cited. This practice may be understood to imply a literary judgment: these tales are being presented as repositories of *auctoritates*; Chaucer's text is being edited as a *compilatio*" (218). This material has not been included in the book developed from Minnis's dissertation, *Medieval Theory of Authorship* (London: Scolar Press, 1984).

23. The phrase "unimpersonated artistry" originates with Donald R. Howard, *The Idea of the Canterbury Tales*, 230–31, and is developed by H. Marshall Leicester, Jr., "The Art of Impersonation: A General Prologue to the *Canterbury Tales*," *PMLA* 95 (1980): 213–24, and incorporated in *The Disenchanted Self* (Berkeley and Los Angeles: University of California Press, 1990), especially 1–13.

24. John Burrow, "*Sir Thopas* in the Sixteenth Century," in Douglas Gray and E. G. Stanley, eds., *Middle English Studies Presented to Norman Davis in Honour of his Seventieth Birthday* (Oxford: Clarendon Press, 1983), 69–91.

25. On the background to these associations, see Bennett A. Brockman, "Robin Hood and the Invention of Children's Literature."

26. For the possibilities of family audiences for the Middle English romance, see Bennett A. Brockman, "Children and Literature in Late Medieval England."

27. This remark comes from Edward Dering, *The Bryfe and Necessary Catechisme* (London, 1572), writing on Guy of Warwick and quoted in Brockman, "Robin Hood," 4–5 and 16n.16. For a review of responses (from Erasmus, Vives, and Tyndale to Dering) to "children's attachment to romance and to the corruption its foolishness engenders in them," see 4 and nn.13–15.

28. For the complete text of the Helmingham version of the *Thopas / Melibee* Link, see the Appendix, 222.

29. See Patterson's remark in "'What Man Artow?'": "As the primacy of the theme in *The Prioress's Tale* suggests, the tales of fragment VII (B²) are particularly focused upon the question of childhood" (162).

30. Ibid., 164.

31. See, for example, R. A. Shoaf, "Notes Towards Chaucer's Poetics of Translation," *SAC* 1 (1979): 64–66.

32. As opposed to what Patterson identifies as the original version of the Link's "exaggerated, slow-motion version of a narrowly conservative defense of writing that was widespread throughout the Middle Ages" ("'What Man Artow?'" 153).

33. Barry Windeatt, "The Scribes as Chaucer's Early Critics," *SAC* 1 (1979): 119–41, this quotation from 132.

34. See *OED*, s.v. *dangerous*, defs. I.a, b; *MED*, s.v. *daungerous*, def. 2.b. Elsewhere in Chaucer, *daungerous* carries almost a moral force, as when the narrator describes the Parson:

> He was to synful men nat despitous,
> Ne of his speche daungerous ne digne.

> (A 516–17)

35. See, for example, the "scribal bowdlerization" noted by the *Riverside Chaucer* (1131) from Corpus Christi College Oxford MS 198:

"By God," quod he, "pleynly I þe say
Þou shalt no lenger rymen heere today."

36. Manly and Rickert call attention to this summary, I:259–60.

37. The relevant lines from the Pardoner's Prologue omitted by Helmingham correspond to *Riverside Chaucer*, C 361–64, 391–94, and C 415–22, 427–40, respectively. For the texts of these portions of the *Pardoner's Prologue and Tale* revised in Helmingham, see the Appendix, 221.

38. The manuscript omits the following lines from the *Tale* itself: C 547–50, 555–62, 565–66, 571–88, 599–602, 617–20, 622, 627–28, 643–48.

39. Missing is the section including the line "Of this mateere it oghte ynogh suffise" (C 434) and the long list of examples of the evils of drunkenness, concluding, "Namoore of this, for it may wel suffise" (C 588). For these episodes, see the Appendix to this book. On the uses of *occupatio* relevant to this context, see H. A. Kelly, "*Occupatio* as Negative Narration: A Mistake for *Occultatio / Praeteritio*," *Modern Philology* 74 (1976–77): 311–15.

40. George Lyman Kittredge, *Chaucer and His Poetry* (Cambridge: Harvard University Press, 1915), 211–18; Donald R. Howard, *The Idea of the Canterbury Tales*, 339–57; H. Marshall Leicester, Jr., *The Disenchanted Self*, 161–220. For a sensitive account of the traditions of reading the Pardoner as performer and character, see Leonard Koff, *Chaucer and the Art of Storytelling*, 158–73.

41. Significantly, almost all the passages from the *Pardoner's Prologue and Tale* that Howard quotes and discusses as being representative of the pilgrim and of Chaucer's conception of his *Tale* are omitted by the Helmingham manuscript (*Idea of the Canterbury Tales*, 347–51).

42. The manuscript divides into two parts as follows: quires 1–9, fols. 1–123; quire 10, fols. 124–170. Folios 92–123 are blank, save for sixteenth-century scribblings, and it is clear that they constitute the final leaves of an incomplete but unitary manuscript. As many as six separate hands have been identified in the first section of the manuscript, but I do not think this vitiates the likelihood of an overriding thematic interest governing the commission of the text and as expressed in the poems' juxtapositions within the compilation. The order of the contents of the first section of HM 140 is as follows (cited by folio numbers, author and modern title, and current edition, from which, unless otherwise noted, I quote the poems here).

Fols. 1–67v, Lydgate, *Saint Albon and Saint Amphibalus*; ed. George F. Reinecke (New York: Garland, 1985).

Fols. 68–84v, Chaucer, *Clerk's Tale* and *Truth*; ed. *Riverside Chaucer*.

Fols. 84v–85, Lydgate, "Vppone a crosse nayled I am for the"; ed. H. N. MacCracken, *Minor Poems I*, EETS ES 107, 252–54.

Fols. 85v–87, Chaucer, Anelida's Complaint from *Anelida and Arcite*; ed. *Riverside Chaucer*.

Fols. 87v–89, Lydgate, "As a Midsummer Rose"; ed. MacCracken, *Minor Poems II*, EETS OS 192, 780–85.

Fols. 90v–91, Lydgate, "Song of Vertue"; ed. MacCracken, *Minor Poems II*, EETS OS 192, 835–38.

Fols. 91–92v, Lydgate, "Testament" (first fourteen stanzas only); ed. MacCracken, *Minor Poems I* EETS ES 107, 329–33.

Fols. 93–96v, Anonymous, Middle English Life of Job, eds. G. N. Garmonsway and R. R. Raymo, "A Middle English Metrical Life of Job," in Arthur Brown and Peter Foote, eds., *Early English and Norse Studies Presented to Hugh Smith* (London: Methuen, 1963), 77–98.

43. Manly-Rickert, I:438 and 609–10. On Chaworth's will and what it may suggest about reading tastes among the gentry in the mid-fifteenth century, see R. M. Wilson, *The Lost Literature of Medieval England*, 2d ed. (London: Methuen, 1970), 149–51. Kate Harris questions the reliability of the will in representing the range of Chaworth's reading tastes. She calls attention to the fact that the will "notices none of the extant manuscripts he is known to have commissioned," that is, manuscripts of Trevisa's translation of the *De Proprietatis Rerum*, Lydgate's *Troy Book*, and an Antiphonal. For details see "Patrons, Buyers, and Owners," 164 and 184n.5.

44. For a definition of the Middle English *Lyf* as a literary genre, see Paul Strohm, "Middle English Narrative Genres," 380.

45. The Huntington Library *Guide* (ed. Deutschke) identifies the watermarks as follows: "*Main* somewhat similar to Briquet 11322, Naples 1478 for the first 6 quires; *Tête de boeuf* similar to Briquet 14261, Trier 1473 for quires 7–9; *Ciseaux* similar to Briquet 3754, Palermo 1456 for the last quire, except for its outer bifolium, with the *Tête de boeuf* as above" (189). Of the writing, the *Guide* notes, "Written in England during the third and fourth quarters of the fifteenth century." Manly and Rickert date the handwriting to 1450–80 (I:434).

46. See the Huntington Library *Guide*, 189–90. On the features associated with "commonplace books" or "household miscellanies," see Boffey and Thompson, "Anthologies and Miscellanies," in Griffiths and Pearsall, eds., *Book Production and Publishing*," 292–94. If the first portion of HM 140 is indeed the book mentioned in Chaworth's will, then one possible explanation for its binding together with a London manuscript might be that it went to London with Chaworth's heirs. Ralph Hanna reports on another of Chaworth's books: "The Plimpton manuscript [of Trevisa's *Properties*] was commissioned by a noted bibliophile of the mid-fifteenth century, Sir Thomas Chaworth of Wiverton (Notts.). And it was again available in London, although the property of Chaworth's heirs, the Willoughbys, when in 1495 the merchant Roger Thorney lent it to de Worde to provide copy for his editio princeps" ("Sir Thomas Berkeley and His Patronage," *Speculum* 64 [1989]: 912).

47. This headnote appears in TCC MS R.3.20, p.106; I quote from the edition in Brusendorff, *Chaucer Tradition* (London: Oxford University Press, 1925), 219.

48. As, for example, Henry Scogan's remark, "That in his langage he was so curious," in his *Moral Balade* (edited by Skeat, *The Oxford Chaucer* 7: 239).

49. This and the following quotations from *Truth* are from the version in the Helmingham manuscript, which together with BL MS Add.10340 constitutes the *alpha* group of manuscript versions of the poem and which differs in occasional wording and spelling from the standard, edited text as presented in the *Riverside Chaucer* (653). For textual variants and manuscript affiliations, see the *Riverside Chaucer*, 1189 and the discussion in Ralph Hanna III, "Authorial Versions, Rolling Revision, Scribal Error? Or, the Truth about *Truth*," *SAC* 10 (1988): 23–40. For the complete text of the conclusion of the *Clerk's Tale* in HM 140, see my edition in the Appendix, 219–21.

50. Strohm considers Chaucer's fifteenth-century audience more generally drawn to "familiar materials treated within stable generic frames and to thematic reaffirmations

of divine, social, and inner hierarchies" ("Chaucer's Fifteenth-Century Audience," *SAC* 4 [1982]: 27).

51. Silvia, "Some Fifteenth-Century Manuscripts," 163n.15.

52. See A. S. G. Edwards, "Lydgate Manuscripts: Some Directions for Future Research," in Pearsall, ed., *Manuscripts and Readers*, 22–23, who also notes that the manuscript evidence suggests "that Lydgate and Chaucer were viewed as hagiographers of equal merit."

53. Edwards, "Lydgate Manuscripts," 23, who, however, does not mention that it is the concluding Envoy to *Doublenesse* which ends the Naples manuscript of the *Clerk's Tale*. For descriptions of this manuscript and its contents, see Manly-Rickert I:378, and William McCormick, *The Manuscripts of Chaucer's Canterbury Tales* (Oxford: Clarendon Press, 1933), 549.

54. Of the manuscripts that anthologize the *Clerk's Tale* apart from the Canterbury collection, Naples, Rawlinson C 86, and Longleat omit the Wife of Bath stanza. Of the manuscripts of the complete *Canterbury Tales* listed by McCormick, sixteen omit the stanza.

55. The editors of the *Riverside Chaucer* note concerning the spelling of Petrarch's name at E 31 in the Prologue to the *Clerk's Tale*: "Both here and in MkT VII.2325, the best MSS support the spelling *Petrak* rather than *Petrark*. There are parallels for it in French, Latin, and Italian documents" (879). For a summary of the different spellings of Petrarch's name at E 1147 where HM 140 has "patrik," see Manly-Rickert VI:377, recording variants as follows: Patrak, Petrayke, Patrik, Petrark.

56. I quote from the edition of the headnote printed in the Huntington Library *Guide* (ed. Deutschke), 185–86.

57. The poem's fourth stanza begins: "Thinke ageyn pride on myn humylyte; / Kom to scole, recorde weell this lessoun" (25–26), and it enjoins further on, "Afforn thyn herte hang this lytel table" (30), as if the poem itself had become something like a maximal school text or writing slate for the student's meditation. I quote from Mac-Cracken's edition in *Minor Poems I*, 253.

58. The manuscript inserts an additional stanza between those numbered 4 and 5 in MacCracken's edition. MacCracken edits the stanza from HM 140 and prints it in a note on 253.

59. The poem's refrain line reads at lines 8, 16, 40, 48, 56, 64, 72, 80, 88, and 96: "Al stant on chaung like a mydsomyr roose" (with some variations in spelling).

60. The refrain line in this form appears at lines 16, 24, 40, 48, 56.

61. *Guide* (ed. Deutschke), 187.

62. For a description of the quiring and history of binding of the manuscript, see the *Guide* (ed. Deutschke), 189–90.

63. One of the earliest to read the poem in this literal way was Furnivall, who introduces it in his discussion of the habits of courtesy literature in his edition of *The Babees Book*, xliii–xliv. For other, biographical uses of the *Testament*, see Pearsall, *John Lydgate*, 294–96.

64. The "Poem to Apprentices" appears as an untitled entry on fols.167v–168r of the second section of HM 140. To my knowledge, it has only been edited once, in Thomas Wright and James Orchard Halliwell, *Reliquiae Antiquae* (London: William Pickering, 1843), II:223–24. My quotations are from the manuscript, with abbreviations expanded and printed in square brackets. Another example of a poem to apprentices in a late

Middle English compilation is the text headed "A Letter Send by R. W. to A. C." and beginning, "Right welbeloued prentise / I commende me to your gentilnesse" in Bodleian Library MS Rawlinson C.813, datable to the second quarter of the sixteenth century and in the hand of the Staffordshire lawyer and Tudor confidant Humphrey Wellys. For the text of this poem, see the edition in Sharon L. Jansen and Kathleen H. Jordan, eds., *The Welles Anthology: MS. Rawlinson C. 813* (Binghamton: Medieval and Renaissance Texts and Studies, 1991), item 8, 103–5. For discussion of its social context and literary analogues, see Edward Wilson, "Local Habitations and Names in MS Rawlinson C 813 in the Bodleian Library, Oxford," *Review of English Studies* new series 41 (1990): 12–44. Wilson offers an edition of his own of this poem on 15–16 and identifies the figures named in the text and reviews the social and literary notions of apprenticeship on 16–22. For a discussion of the literature addressed to apprentices in later Tudor England, see Mark Thornton Burnett, "Apprentice Literature and the 'Crisis' of the 1590s," *Yearbook of English Studies* 21 (1991): 27–38.

65. In this comparison, I do not mean to overlook the banal conventionalities of both Lydgate's *Testament* and the "Poem to Apprentices." For an example of the commonplace quality of the advice in both, see text Furnivall calls "Maxims in -ly," from BL MS Landsowne 762, fol.16v, which, though written out in prose, is printed as verse (*Babees Book*, 359). See the following selection:

> Aryse erly,
> serue God devowtely
> and the worlde besely,
> doo thy werk wisely
> yeue thyne almes secretely,
> goo by the waye sadly,
> answer the people demuerly,
> goo to thy mete apetitely
> etc.

This "-ly" pattern, together with certain specifics of phrasing, similarly controls the pattern of the "Poem to Apprentices." N. F. Blake notes that the items on fols.16r–v of Landsdowne 762 "may have been copied from the *Boke of St Albans*" ("Manuscript to Print," in *Book Production and Publishing*, 427). The *Boke of St. Albans* (STC 3308) has been dated at 1486, making the Landsdowne entries, and perhaps those of HM 140, later than that.

66. *OED*, s.v. *commodity*, defs. 5, 6. See, too, *MED*, s.v. *commodite*, citing this line from Lydgate's *Song of Virtue* under the meaning "Benefit, profit, welfare." But the *MED* cites a range of fifteenth-century usages in which it is hard to distinguish between moral benefit and commercial profit. See, for example, their citation from Lydgate's *Siege of Thebes* 3126, "For high profit and gret comodite."

67. Mervyn James, "Ritual, Drama, and Social Body in the Late Medieval English Town," *Past and Present* 98 (1983): 22n.9.

68. See Sylvia Thrupp, *The Merchant Class of Medieval London 1300–1500* (Chicago: University of Chicago Press, 1948), 162–63.

69. F. Harth, "Carpaccio's Meditation on the Passion," *Art Bulletin* 22 (1940): 25–35, this quotation from 28. Michaela Paasche Grudin notes the changing popularity of the Job story in post-plague Europe. See "Chaucer's *Clerk's Tale* as Political Paradox," *SAC* 11 (1989): 63–92, especially 87 and n.50, citing Millard Meiss's observation that the

story's "popularity after the plague" lay in the perceived "similarity between Job's suffer-ing and the experience of contemporary Italy" (from *Painting in Florence and Siena After the Black Death* [New York: Harper and Row, 1964], 68). For a survey of the medieval fortunes of the Job story, see Lawrence L. Besserman, *The Legend of Job in the Middle Ages* (Cambridge: Harvard University Press 1979), who briefly discusses the Middle English Job from HM 140 on 90–91. General remarks on Job and the tradi-tions of patience in late-medieval Europe can be found in Gerald Schiffhorst, ed., *The Triumph of Patience: Medieval and Renaissance Studies* (Orlando: University Presses of Florida, 1978), especially the contributions of Schiffhorst, "Some Prolegomena for the Study of Patience, 1480–1680," 1–64, and Ralph Hanna, "Some Commonplaces of Late Medieval Patience Discussions: An Introduction," 65–87.

70. Patterson, "'What Man Artow?'" writes, "In the *Clerk's Tale* it [i.e., childhood] appears primarily as pathos, for both the threatened children and—not often noticed—for the youthful Griselda herself" (161). See the suggestive development of this notion on 161–62.

71. On the importance of the vocabulary of *sadness* in the *Clerk's Tale*, in its moral, philosophical, and social contexts, see Grudin, "Chaucer's *Clerk's Tale* as Political Para-dox," 63–92, especially the pointed discussion and full, bibliographical apparatus at 88–91.

72. On the thematics of *array* in the *Clerk's Tale*, see Kristine Gilmartin Wallace, "Array as Motif in the *Clerk's Tale*," *Rice University Studies* 62 (1976): 99–100, and the development of this discussion in Carolyn Dinshaw, *Chaucer's Sexual Poetics* (Madison: University of Wisconsin Press, 1989), 144–48, and 253n.38.

73. Though they are, of course, related issues, I wish to distinguish here between the narrative stance of an apprenticeship to Chaucer on the one hand, and, on the other, the practice of a literature for apprentices, together with a growing sense that amateur writers could consider their productions as acts of literary apprenticeship. Thus, a distinction needs to be made between the latter phenomenon as I describe it here, and the former as exemplified in George Ashby's appeals to "Maisters Gower, Chauucer & Lydgate" and his claim to write "Not as a master but as a prentise." See the prologue to his *Active Policy of a Prince* as printed in Spurgeon, *Five-Hundred Years of Chaucer Criticism and Allusion* (London: Kegan Paul, Trench, Trübner, 1914–25), 54–55, and the brief discussion of Ashby's literary apprenticeship in the context of a "master Chaucer" by Patterson, *Chaucer and the Subject of History* (Madison: University of Wisconsin Press, 1991), 17.

CHAPTER FOUR

1. Scogan's poem appears only in John Shirley's manuscript, now BL MS Ashmole 59, and is published by Skeat, who calls it a *Moral Balade*, in *The Oxford Chaucer*, 7:237–44. For discussion of the manuscript transmission of the *Balade* and its impor-tance in chronicling the early reception of Chaucer's lyrics, see Brusendorff, *Chaucer Tradition* (London: Oxford University Press, 1925), 254–56. For a reading of the *Balade* in the contexts of Chaucerian paternity and the cultivation of a "master" Chaucer in the early fifteenth century, see Patterson, *Chaucer and the Subject of History* (Madison: University of Wisconsin Press, 1991), 16–22.

2. For general accounts of such manuscript collections, see Julia Boffey, *Manuscripts of English Courtly Love Lyrics in the Later Middle Ages* (Woodbridge: D. S. Brewer,

1985) and with John J. Thompson, "Anthologies and Miscellanies: Production and Choice of Texts," in Griffiths and Pearsall, eds., *Book Production and Publishing*, 279–315. Earlier scholarship on these productions is summarized in R. H. Robbins, "The Chaucerian Apocrypha," in Severs and Hartung, eds., *Manual*, IV: 1061–86.

3. For a treatment of early printers' attitudes toward Chaucer's shorter poems, see R. F. Yeager, "Literary Theory at the Close of the Middle Ages: William Caxton and William Thynne," *SAC* 6 (1984): 135–64, especially 141–47. See, too, the essays on individual editors, beginning with Caxton, in Paul Ruggiers, ed., *Editing Chaucer: The Great Tradition* (Norman: Pilgrim Books, 1984).

4. William Thynne, *The Workes of Geffray Chaucer newly printed, with dyverse workes which were neuer in print before . . .* (London: Thomas Godfray, 1532); I use the facsimile edition of Derek Brewer, *Geoffrey Chaucer, The Works, 1532, With Supplementary Material from the Editions of 1542, 1561, 1598, and 1602* (Menston: Scholar Press, 1969). For discussion of Thynne's preface, see Yeager, "Literary Theory," and James E. Blodgett, "William Thynne," in P. G. Ruggiers, ed., *Editing Chaucer*, 32–52.

5. For the prehistory of these developments, see Anthony Grafton, *Defenders of the Text: The Traditions of Scholarship in an Age of Science, 1450–1800* (Cambridge: Harvard University Press, 1991). For the origins of stemmatics, see Giorgio Pasquali, *Storia della tradizione e critica del testo*, 2d ed. (Firenze: Le Monnier, 1962), and Sebastiano Timpanaro, *La genesi del metodo del Lachmann*, 2d ed. (Padua: Antenore, 1985). For a review of nineteenth-century stemmatic criticism pressed into the service of a critique of Middle English editorial practice, see Lee Patterson, "The Logic of Textual Criticism and the Way of Genius," in *Negotiating the Past* (Madison: University of Wisconsin Press, 1991), 77–114. For the relations among nineteenth-century lexicography and philology, see Hans Aarsleff, *The Study of Language in England, 1780–1860* (Princeton: Princeton University Press, 1967). For the ideological component, see Jerome J. McGann, *A Critique of Modern Textual Criticism* (Chicago: University of Chicago Press, 1983). A prospectus for a history of Middle English editing is A.S.G. Edwards, "Observations on the History of Middle English Editing," in Derek Pearsall, ed., *Manuscripts and Texts: Editorial Problems in Later Middle English Literature* (Cambridge: D. S. Brewer, 1987), 34–48.

6. See Patterson, *Negotiating the Past*, 9–18.

7. W. W. Skeat, *The Chaucer Canon* (Oxford: Clarendon Press, 1900):

> The object of this treatise is to explain clearly the chief peculiarities of Chaucer's grammar and versification. If these are once exactly and accurately comprehended, it becomes easy, even for a reader who has had not previous training, to distinguish his genuine poems from those that have been attributed to him, at various times, by the carelessness or wantonness of editors and critics. (1)

See the discussions in Brusendorff, *Chaucer Tradition*, 43–53, who while attending to grammar and versification as the primary criteria, notes that the "unsettled state of the Canon is really due to the comparative neglect of our most important body of evidence, the ascriptions of the scribes" (49). In discussing the inclusion of certain minor poems labeled by Robinson as "doubtful," Larry D. Benson in the *Riverside Chaucer* notes that "we believe" certain of those poems to be by Chaucer, though his account does not articulate the bases of that belief (see *Riverside Chaucer*, xxvi–xxviii).

8. For an account of the major lines of criticism on the short poems, see George Pace and Alfred David, eds., *The Minor Poems, Part 1*, in *A Variorum Edition of the*

Works of Geoffrey Chaucer, Volume 5, Part 1 (Norman: University of Oklahoma Press, 1982). For the tensions between "making" and "poetry" as centering in particular on Chaucer's shorter courtly poems, see Patterson, *Chaucer and the Subject of History*, 47–61.

9. For Shirley generally, see Brusendorff, *Chaucer Tradition*; A. I. Doyle, "More Light on John Shirley," *Medium Aevum* 30 (1961): 93–101; Cheryl Greenberg, "John Shirley and the English Book Trade," *The Library*, sixth series, 4 (1982): 369–80. On the various contexts—courtly, commercial, personal—for Shirley's compilations, see A. I. Doyle, "English Books in and out of Court from Edward III to Henry VII," in V. J. Scattergood and J. W. Sherborne, eds., *English Court Culture in the Later Middle Ages*, 163–81; A.S.G. Edwards, "Lydgate Manuscripts: Some Directions for Future Research," in Derek Pearsall, ed., *Manuscripts and Readers in Fifteenth-Century England*, 15–26; Julia Boffey, *Manuscripts of English Courtly Love Lyrics*, 14–18, 65–66, 71–74; Boffey and Thompson, "Anthologies and Miscellanies," 284–87; R. J. Lyall, "The Paper Revolution," in Griffiths and Pearsall, eds., *Book Production and Publishing*, 11–29.

10. Shirley attributes the following to Chaucer: *Anelida and Arcite*, *The Complaint of Mars*, *The Complaint of Venus*, *The Complaint to a Lady*, *Lak of Stedfastnesse* (which Shirley calls "Envoy to King Richard"), *Adam Scrivyen*, and *Womanly Noblesse* (called by Shirley "Envoy to a Lady"). The poem labeled by Brusendorff "Balade of a Reeve" (*Chaucer Tradition*, 278–84) and assumed by him to bear Shirley's attribution to Chaucer is rejected in Robinson's *Works of Geoffrey Chaucer*, 2d ed. (Boston: Houghton Mifflin, 1957) and remains unprinted in the *Riverside Chaucer*.

11. Strohm, *Social Chaucer* (Cambridge: Harvard University Press, 1989), though Strohm's study is not in any sense limited to the coterie productions of the poet. See his description of the project, "I view Chaucer not only as producing but as responding to the social implications of his material" (xii). For his discussion of the contexts that generated and the individuals who may have received Chaucer's shorter poetry, see 24–46, 75–83. For a survey of critical responses to the idea of Chaucer as a coterie poet, see 204–5n.14. In his reconstruction of what he calls "the social meaning of Chaucer's poetry," Patterson broadens Strohm's categories to include "the institutional context from which it derived, the audience to which it was addressed, [and] above all the class values it expressed" (*Chaucer and the Subject of History*, 47).

12. A history of the literature of the scribe remains to be written. For surveys of the material, see Wilhelm Wattenbach, *Das Schriftwesen im Mittelalter*, 3d ed. (Leipzig: S. Hirzel, 1896), 416–534; E. R. Curtius, *European Literature and the Latin Middle Ages*, trans. W. R. Trask (Princeton: Princeton University Press, 1953), 308–15; Rosamond McKitterick, *The Carolingians and the Written Word* (Cambridge: Cambridge University Press, 1989), 115–34. For a delightful collection of poems to and on the scribe in the twelfth century, see the poetry of Baudri of Bourgeuil, ed. Karlheinz Hilbert, *Baldricus Burgulianus Carmina* (Heidelberg: Carl Winter, 1979), poems numbered 9, 10, 84, 85, 92, 105, 108, 144, 148, 196. For Petrarch's letter on his scribes, see *Petrarch: Four Dialogues for Scholars*, ed. and trans. C. H. Rawski (Cleveland: Western Reserve University Press, 1967), 34–37. Jan Gerson's *De laude scriptorum* dates from 1423 and is printed in his *Oeuvres complètes*, ed. P. Glorieux (Paris: Desclée, 1973), IX:423–34. Perhaps the last articulation of the ideals of a scribal culture, in the face of print technology, is that of Johannes Trithemius, *In Praise of Scribes: De laude scriptorum*, ed. Klaus Arnold, trans. R. Behrendt (Lawrence: Coronado Press, 1974), dated 1492.

13. Biographically oriented approaches are summarized in Pace and David, *Minor*

Poems, 133–34. Allegorical or figural readings are attempted by Russell A. Peck, "Public Dreams and Private Myths: Perspective in Middle English Literature," *PMLA* 90 (1975): 461–68, and Robert E. Kaske, "*Clericus Adam* and Chaucer's *Adam Scriveyn*," in Edward Vasta and Zacharias P. Thundy, eds., *Chaucerian Problems and Perspectives: Essays Presented to Paul E. Beichner C.S.C.* (Notre Dame: Notre Dame University Press, 1979), 114–18.

14. Shirley's copy of the *Boece* opens his anthology, now BL MS Add.16165. Although *Troilus and Criseyde* does not seem to have formed one of his major scribal projects, he did at one time own the manuscript that is now Corpus Christi College Cambridge MS 61.

15. Brusendorff, *Chaucer Tradition*, 460–67; Greenberg, "John Shirley and the English Book Trade," 377, 380.

16. Boffey, *Manuscripts of English Courtly Love Lyrics*, 65.

17. Ibid., 66.

18. In quoting from Shirley's Kalendars, I use the edition printed in Brusendorff, *Chaucer Tradition*, 453–60, and cite by original manuscript and line number in my text.

19. This Kalendar survives in the copy made by John Stowe in the mid-sixteenth century. On the possible original manuscript it prefaced, and on Stowe's transcription, see Kathryn Walls, "Did Lydgate Translate the 'Pèlerinage de Vie Humaine'?" *Notes and Queries* 24 (1977): 103–5.

20. For the details of the appellative and textual history of *Lak of Stedfastnesse*, see Pace and David, *Minor Poems*, 77–89.

21. On the popularity and textual transmission of *Truth*, see Ralph Hanna III, "Authorial Versions, Rolling Revision, Scribal Error? Or, the Truth about *Truth*," *SAC* 10 (1988): 23–40, and Pace and David, *Minor Poems*, 49–65.

22. The variations between Shirley's copy of the poem in TCC R.3.20 and the "received" text published by modern editors (and based on the text in BL Cotton Cleopatra D.VII) may be attributed to Shirley's lapses of memory or to his responses to the sounds of the verse, rather than to details of a separate textual tradition. Pace and David, *Minor Poems*, report that two lines from the poem are quoted in a longer work in MS, Ipswich County Hall Deposit, Hillwood (80n.1). TCC MS R.3.21 presents the Envoy to the poem written twice (fols. 245v, 319r). For the pervasiveness of *Troilus and Criseyde* in fifteenth- and early-sixteenth-century amateur poetry and private compilations, see the brief discussion in Patterson, *Chaucer and the Subject of History*, 58. An excellent example of this phenomenon is the work of Humphrey Wellys, whose personal mansucript (Bodleian Library MS Rawlinson C.813) offers, among other things, a long poem constructed out of individual stanzas of the *Troilus*, rearranged to form a lover's complaint narrative. See *The Welles Anthology*, item 38, 195–98 (with detailed correspondences listed on 303), and my discussion in the Envoy to this book.

23. In addition to my own investigation of the manuscripts, my discussion relies on the following accounts. For Harley 7333, Manly-Rickert, I:207–18, and Boffey, *Manuscripts*, 17, 19, 108–11. For TCC R.3.20, M. R. James, *The Western Manuscripts in the Library of Trinity College, Cambridge* (Cambridge: Cambridge University Press, 1900–1904), II:75–82; N. R. Ker, *Medieval Manuscripts in British Libraries* (Oxford: Clarendon Press, 1969), I:290–91; R. J. Lyall, "The Paper Revolution," 19–21; Boffey, *Manuscripts*, 16, 36, 65, 67, 72, 76–77; and the collection of notes and bibliography in Boffey and Thompson, "Anthologies and Miscellanies," 305–7. For the Cotton Otho A.XVIII

text, see the description in Pace and David, *Minor Poems*, 80, and the title printed on 85. In quoting from and citing manuscripts, I use folio numberings, with the exception of TCC R.3.20, whose leaves are paginated and for which it is traditional to refer to page numbers.

24. For such a recovery, see Strohm, *Social Chaucer*, 50–51, 204–5.

25. See Manly-Rickert, I:214–17; Edwards and Pearsall, "Manuscripts of the Major English Poetic Texts," in Griffiths and Pearsall, eds., *Book Production and Publishing*, 268; Boffey, *Manuscripts*, 128.

26. For discussion of the relevance of these and other headnotes to the manuscript compilation, and their influence on later editors, see Boffey, *Manuscripts*, 17, 65–66.

27. The headnote appears on fol.37r, column 1, where it is headed, "Prologue to the Knights Tale." It has been printed by Caroline Spurgeon, *Five-Hundred Years of Chaucer Criticism and Allusion* (London: Kegan Paul, Trench, Trübner, 1914–25), 53–54, and by Manly-Rickert, I:213. My quotations are from the manuscript, checked against Manly-Rickert's readings.

28. Harley 7333, fol.132r. It also appears, with some slight variations, at the close of the text of the *Parlement of Foules* in TCC MS R.3.19, a compilation usually dated to the last decade of the fifteenth century. The text is printed in Spurgeon, *Five-Hundred Years*, 53.

29. Manly-Rickert, I:211–12.

30. For an account of the manuscript's contents, see M. R. James, *The Western Manuscripts*, II:75–82.

31. TCC R.3.20, page 53; see MacCracken, *Minor Poems of John Lydgate I*, 288, and Boffey, *Manuscripts*, 65.

32. TCC R.3.20, 35; see Boffey, *Manuscripts*, 65.

33. Boffey, *Manuscripts*, 65.

34. The headnotes are printed in Brusendorff, *Chaucer Tradition*, 263–64.

35. The title is in Shirley's hand on page 144. Shirley wrote out the poem again on page 357 with the title "Balade by Chaucier" and a later hand (perhaps Stowe's) wrote afterward "on his dethe bede."

36. From BL MS Add.5467, fol.72v, quoted from Brusendorff, *Chaucer Tradition*, 214.

37. Patricia Parker, *Inescapable Romance* (Princeton: Princeton University Press, 1979), especially 67–69, 99, 127. The quotation is from her use of Frederick Jameson, "Magical Narratives: Romance as Genre," *New Literary History* 6 (1974): 161.

38. David Hult, *Self-Fulfilling Prophecies* (Cambridge: Cambridge University Press, 1987), 34–60.

39. From Gui de Mori's supplemental lines to the *Roman de la Rose*, quoted and translated by Hult, 35.

40. Hult, *Self-Fulfilling Prophecies*, 52.

41. It has long been assumed that Shirley's scribal work occasionally drifts from the sustained transcription of complete texts to the erratic jottings of remembered fragments. There is much evidence that Shirley transcribed some of his texts from memory; especially in shorter works or those datable to his last years, variations in phraseology and diction indicate the workings of the oddities of memory, rather than the diversities of manuscript exemplars. Behind my argument is the assumption that such reveries govern the associations on the final leaves of TCC R.3.20. Boffey and Thomp-

son assemble the complete evidence for and review the scholarship on Shirley's habits of transcription and the workings of his memory in the series of notes 26–43 of "Anthologies and Miscellanies," 305–6.

42. The stanza is printed in its entirety by James, *The Western Manuscripts*, II:81. Shirley included this stanza, with minor variations in spelling, in another of his manuscripts, Bodleian Library Oxford MS Ashmole 59, fol.59v, where it is followed by the words, "Lenvoy . by . Lydgate." This version is printed in Brusendorff, *Chaucer Tradition*, 460, who implies that the stanza is in fact by Lydgate: "The Monk repaid Shirley for his good wishes by composing what is really a kind of poetic equivalent to the notices to subscribers, found in modern circulating library copies."

43. The poem is printed as one of the poems on the virtues of the mass by Mac-Cracken, *Minor Poems I*, 116–17.

44. Printed from this manuscript by MacCracken, *Minor Poems II*, 608–13, from whose edition I quote. The only other copy, though incomplete, is in Shirley's Ashmole 59 manuscript, fols.57–58v.

45. I quote from the edition of Shirley's copy by Pace and David, *Minor Poems*, 136–37.

46. For details, see Boffey and Thompson, "Anthologies and Miscellanies," 306n.43, who conclude, "In both manuscripts Shirley produced a peculiarly random assortment of fragments which might have emerged in roughly associated fashion from the recesses of his memory."

47. Brusendorff prints and makes much of Shirley's marginal addresses to Lydgate (*Chaucer Tradition*, 461–66).

48. For the figurations of the medieval writer as a scribe, see the suggestive remarks of Gabriel Josipovici, *The World and the Book* (London: Paladin, 1971), Chapters 1 and 2. For the epistolary flavor of late Middle English complaint poetry, see the account in John Norton-Smith, *Geoffrey Chaucer* (London: Routledge and Kegan Paul, 1974), 16–34; W. A. Davenport, *Chaucer: Complaint and Narrative* (Woodbridge: D. S. Brewer, 1988); and Martin Camargo, *The Middle-English Verse Love Epistle* (Tübingen: Niemeyer, 1991). For the influence of patronage relationships on the epistolary rhetoric of fifteenth-century writing, traced from Hoccleve, through Osborn Bokenham, to Caxton, see Russell Rutter, "William Caxton and Literary Patronage," *SP* 84 (1987): 440–70.

49. The two poems are printed in the *Riverside Chaucer*, 640–41 and 642–43, respectively. Frederick Furnivall published Shirley's versions of the poems separately as follows: For the *Complaint Unto Pity*, see *A Parallel-Text Edition of Chaucer's Minor Poems*, Chaucer Society Publications, Series 1, Volume 21, Part 1 (London: Trübner, 1881), 41, 43, 45, 47, 49; for the *Complaint to a Lady*, titled by Furnivall as *The Balade of Pitee*, see *Odd Texts of Chaucer's Minor Poems*, Chaucer Society Publications, Series 1, volume 23, part 1, *Appendix of Poems Attributed to Chaucer* (London: Trübner, 1871), ii–v.

50. The only complete description of the contents of this manuscript remains the original one by Humphrey Wanley, in R. Nares, *A Catalogue of the Harleian Manuscripts in the British Museum* (London: G. Eyre and A. Strahan, 1808–12), Volume I, no. 78. For Stowe's role in assembling the manuscript and some aspects of its contents, see A. I. Doyle, "An Unrecognized Piece of *Piers the Ploughman's Creed* and Other Works by Its Scribe," *Speculum* 34 (1959): 428–36.

51. For the relationships among these manuscripts, and various suggestions as to

their original construction and later dismemberment, see N. R. Ker, *Medieval Manuscripts in British Libraries*, I:291; Kathryn Walls, "Did Lydgate Translate the 'Pèlerinage de Vie Humaine'?" 103; R. J. Lyall, "The Paper Revolution," 19–21.

52. See Eleanor Hammond, "Two British Museum Manuscripts. (Harley 2251 and Add.34360). A Contribution to the Bibliography of John Lydgate," *Anglia* 28 (1905): 1–28. One of the scribes who contributed to Add.34360 was the London stationer John Multon, who also wrote the piece of *Piers the Ploughman's Creed* in Harley 78, though he does not appear to be the scribe of the double *Complaint Unto Pity / Complaint of a Lady* poem copied from Shirley. On Multon, see A. I. Doyle, "An Unrecognized Piece of *Piers the Ploughman's Creed*," *Speculum* 34 (1959): 428–36, and C. Paul Christianson, "Evidence for the Study of London's Late Medieval Manuscript-Book Trade," in Griffiths and Pearsall, eds., *Book Production and Publishing*, 107n.43.

53. F. N. Robinson, *Works of Geoffrey Chaucer*, noted that Add.34360 "contains an additional stanza at the end" (916). The *Riverside Chaucer* states that the manuscript "adds a unique stanza at the end," implying that Add.34360 put something in the text of the poem not in its exemplar (1186; the notes are attributed to R. T. Lenaghan).

54. See my "British Library MS Harley 78 and the Manuscripts of John Shirley," *Notes and Queries* 37 (1990): 402.

55. Derek Pearsall, *John Lydgate* (Charlottesville: University of Virginia Press, 1970), 92–93.

56. I rely here on the exposition and argument of A.S.G. Edwards, "The Unity and Authenticity of *Anelida and Arcite*: The Evidence of the Manuscripts," *Studies in Bibliography* 41 (1988): 177–88. Patterson's interpretation of this poem, though acknowledging the vicissitudes of its manuscript transmission, nonetheless assumes its published version as largely authorial. See *Chaucer and the Subject of History*, 47–83, and the revealing aside that "the present discussion means to demonstrate the unity of the poem (less the final stanza), its poetic sophistication, and above all *its profoundly Chaucerian character* (62n.55, emphasis added).

57. Boffey, *Manuscripts*, 36. For the textual history of the two poems, see the notes in the *Riverside Chaucer*, 1186–87. For arguments that the two poems may have originally been one, see Rodney Merrill, "Chaucer's *Broche of Thebes*: The Unity of 'The Complaint of Mars' and 'The Complaint of Venus,'" *Literary Monographs* 5 (1973): 1–61. Patterson seems to accept this argument, considering the putative original "Broche of Thebes" as the "closest analogue in the Chaucerian canon" to *Anelida and Arcite* and characterizing it as "a diminutive poem with similarly divided loyalties that literally fell apart in the fifteenth century, becoming the poems we now know as the 'Complaint of Mars' and the 'Complaint of Venus'" (*Chaucer and the Subject of History*, 62–63). By bringing the two Pity poems of Harley 78 into the critical ambiance of the *Complaints* and *Anelida and Arcite*, I do not mean to argue definitively either for Chaucer's original writing of one long poem on Pity or for Chaucer's original composition of two distinct poems. Instead, my discussion hopes to focus on the fifteenth-century critical and scribal climate in which such double poems could circulate in various and—from a modern perspective—potentially contradictory forms, each reflecting the taste of the compiler or the reader. These are, I believe, texts in flux rather than poems in decay.

58. Boffey, *Manuscripts*, 36.

59. Boffey, *Manuscripts*, 36, citing Robinson, *Works of Geoffrey Chaucer*, 586–87.

60. Paul M. Clogan, "The Textual Reliability of Chaucer's Lyrics: *A Complaint to His Lady*," *Medievalia et Humanistica*, new series 5 (1974): 183–89, this quotation from 188.

61. John Norton-Smith, *Geoffrey Chaucer*, 20n.2.

62. *Riverside Chaucer*, 1077.

63. See, for example, Wolfgang Clemen, *Chaucer's Early Poetry*, trans. C.A.M. Sym (London: Methuen, 1963).

64. G. C. Macaulay, ed., *The English Works of John Gower*, vol. 2, EETS ES 89 (London: Oxford University Press, 1901), 466. These lines, indicated by the asterisk in Macaulay's edition, appear only in the first recension of the *Confessio Amantis*; they are eliminated from the revised version of the poem's epilogue, traditionally ascribed to the years 1392–93.

65. My phrasing is from John Guillory, "Canonical and Non-Canonical: A Critique of the Current Debate," *ELH* 54 (1987): 483–527, passim.

66. Stanley Fish, *Is There a Text in This Class?* (Cambridge: Harvard University Press, 1980), 10–11.

67. *The Former Age* survives in two manuscript copies, the earliest of which inscribes it into the prose translation of the *Boece* and places it after Book 2, metrum 5 (Cambridge University Library MS Ii.3.21), where it is titled "Chawcer vp on this fyfte metur of the second book" (see Pace and David, *Minor Poems*, 91, 93, 97). The *ABC* appears in sixteen manuscript copies, six of which (including Shirley's copy now in Sion College, London, MS Arc. L.10.2/E.44) include it in the prose translation of Deguilleville's *Pilgrimage of the Life of Man* (see *Riverside Chaucer*, 1185).

68. On Stowe's collecting habits and his recovery, annotation, and subsequent reliance on Shirley's manuscripts, see the discussion throughout Anne Hudson, "John Stowe," in Ruggiers, ed., *Editing Chaucer*, 53–70 and the notes on 259–65.

69. On the differences between "laureate" and "amateur" in Tudor literary self-presentation, see Richard Helgerson, *Self-Crowned Laureates* (Berkeley and Los Angeles: University of California Press, 1983), 25–34. The relationships between manuscript circulation and print publication in the sixteenth and seventeenth centuries have been the ongoing concern of Arthur F. Marotti. See, in particular, his *John Donne, Coterie Poet* (Madison: University of Wisconsin Press, 1986), and his recent essay, "Patronage, Poetry, and Print," *Yearbook of English Studies* 21 (1991): 1–20.

CHAPTER FIVE

1. All quotations from Caxton's prologues and epilogues will be from W.J.B. Crotch, ed., *The Prologues and Epilogues of William Caxton*, EETS OS 176 (London: Oxford University Press, 1928), cited simply as *Caxton*, by page number in my text. I have silently retained Crotch's editorial expansions.

2. With the exception of those volumes Caxton dates himself, it is notoriously difficult to assign a particular occasion for his printings. In dating Caxton's publications, I rely on evidence and arguments in George Painter, *William Caxton, A Quincentenary Biography of England's First Printer* (London: Chatto and Windus, 1976), especially his "Chronological List of Caxton's Editions," 211–15. A somewhat different chronology is offered in Paul Needham, *The Printer and the Pardoner* (Washington, D. C.: Library of Congress, 1986), Appendix D, 83–91. *The Book of Curtesye* is dated by Needham and

Crotch as 1477, though Painter puts it anywhere from 1477–78; *The Canterbury Tales* and *House of Fame* are assigned to 1483 by Painter, largely on the internal evidence of the Prologue to the *Canterbury Tales* edition in which Caxton states that the first edition had appeared "vi. yeeres" before and on the basis of the details of the selection of typefaces (see 134–35).

3. The following discussion draws on a range of recent reconsiderations of the origin of European humanism in the projects of philology, textual criticism, and pedagogy developed out of Petrarch's initiatory gestures and sustained in fifteenth-century scholarship. For much of my vocabulary, I draw on Thomas Greene, *The Light in Troy: Imitation and Discovery in Renaissance Poetry* (New Haven: Yale University Press, 1982). For a probing account of exemplarity in Renaissance hermeneutics and historiography rephrasing many of Greene's formulations, see Timothy Hampton, *Writing from History: The Rhetoric of Exemplarity in Renaissance Literature* (Ithaca: Cornell University Press, 1990), especially 1–80. For the origins of humanist textual criticism, see Anthony Grafton, *Defenders of the Text* (Cambridge: Harvard University Press, 1991), especially 1–75.

4. Greene, *Light in Troy*, 81–88.

5. Ibid., 82, working from Gerald L. Bruns, "The Originality of Texts in Manuscript Culture," *Comparative Literature* 32 (1980): 125–26.

6. These motives have been exposed by the many studies of Norman F. Blake. The arguments are summarized in his *Caxton and His World* (London: Andre Deutsch, 1969) and developed, with special reference to the prologues and epilogues, in two articles: "Continuity and Change in Caxton's Prologues and Epilogues: The Bruges Period," *Gutenberg Jahrbuch* (1979): 72–77, and "Continuity and Change in Caxton's Prologues and Epilogues: Westminster," *Gutenberg Jahrbuch* (1980): 38–43. For a challenge to these views and a reassessment of Caxton's relations to his patrons and his readers, see Russell Rutter, "William Caxton and Literary Patronage," *SP* 84 (1987): 440–70.

7. See R. F. Yeager, "Literary Theory at the Close of the Middle Ages: William Caxton and William Thynne," *SAC* 6 (1984): 135–64.

8. See Beverly Boyd, "William Caxton," in Paul G. Ruggiers, ed., *Editing Chaucer: The Great Tradition*, 13–34. For emerging textual criticism in Europe in the last decades of the fifteenth century, see Grafton, "The Scholarship of Poliziano in Its Context," in *Defenders of the Text*, 47–75.

9. See Hampton, *Writing from History*, 12–14.

10. Discussions of Caxton as a literary critic tend to devolve to arguments about his relative autonomy from patronage. For Blake (see n.6), Caxton's publications and his prefatory writings are so keyed to the demands of patronage or the requirements of commercial sale that they cannot constitute independent critical activities. For Rutter (see n.6), Caxton's work was, for the most part, independent of specific patronage commissions or political demands, and the obeisances to apparent patronizing figures in his writings are largely rhetorical. For Yeager (see n.7), Caxton's "literary theory" is to be sought in the selection of his publications rather than in anything he wrote himself. One attempt to define Caxton as a literary critic, in an evaluative sense, is Donald B. Sands, "Caxton as a Literary Critic," *Papers of the Bibliographical Society of America* 51 (1957): 312–18.

11. For the elegiac impulse as the motivating force in literary history, see Peter M.

Sacks, *The English Elegy: Studies in the Genre from Spenser to Yeats* (Baltimore: Johns Hopkins University Press, 1985). For the specifics of the humanist elegy—both in social performance and in the announcements of the literary career—see George W. Pigman III, *Grief and English Renaissance Elegy* (Cambridge: Cambridge University Press, 1985); John M. McManamon, S. J., *Funeral Oratory and the Cultural Ideals of Italian Humanism* (Chapel Hill: University of North Carolina Press, 1989).

12. This sense of post-Chaucerian writing as elegiac is embedded in the arguments of Louise O. Fradenburg that *all* of Chaucer's writing is elegiac and by consequence, also that of his imitators. See her "'Voice Memorial': Loss and Reparation in Chaucer's Poetry," *Exemplaria* 2 (1990): 168–202, especially 178–80.

13. For much of what follows, I am indebted to J. B. Trapp, "Ovid's Tomb: The Growth of a Legend from Eusebius to Laurence Sterne, Chauteaubriand and George Richmond," *JWCI* 34 (1973): 35–76, and the more specialized study of B. L. Ullman, "The Post-Mortem Adventures of Livy," in his *Studies in the Italian Renaissance* (Rome: Edizioni di Storia e Letteratura, 1955), 55–80.

14. See the two studies of Iiro Kajanto, *Classical and Christian: Studies in the Latin Epitaphs of Medieval and Renaissance Rome* (Helsinki: Suomalainen Tiedeakatemia, 1980), 11–16, and *Papal Epigraphy in Renaissance Rome* (Helsinki: Suomalainen Tiedeakatemia, 1982), 11–19. Christopher De Hamel reports that Poggio Bracciolini took Cosimo de Medici the Elder "exploring in Grottaferrata, Ostia, and the Alban Hills to look for Roman inscriptions" (*A History of Illuminated Manuscripts* [Boston: Godine, 1986], 224). For the sustained humanist fascination with Roman epigraphy in the second half of the fifteenth century, see the evocative discussion in James Wardrop, *The Script of Humanism: Some Aspects of Humanistic Script 1460–1560* (Oxford: Clarendon Press, 1963), 13–18. Noteworthy is the tradition of the *sillogi*, collections of transcriptions made by the humanists from Roman monuments and tombs. For examples of individual *sillogi* and their influence on humanist letter forms, see the reproductions of the work of Bartolomeo Sanvito in Wardrop, plates 22 and 23 and the discussion on pp.27–28. These manuscript recreations of monumental tomb inscriptions are dated by Wardrop as c.1478 and from "the last decade of the fifteenth, and the first of the sixteenth, centuries" respectively (p.28). For the possible relevance of this tradition to Caxton's printing of Surigonus's epitaph on Chaucer, see my suggestions in n.31.

15. See McManamon, *Funeral Oratory*, 29–30.

16. Ibid., 153, and see the discussion on 153–61.

17. On these journeys, see Phyllis W. G. Gordan, trans., *Two Renaissance Book Hunters: The Letters of Poggius Bracciolini to Nicolaus de Niccolis* (New York: Columbia University Press, 1974), and Roberto Weiss, *Humanism in England During the Fifteenth Century*, 3d ed. (Oxford: Blackwell, 1957), 11–24. Caxton appeals to the authority of Poggio in the prologue to his *Caton* (1483) as follows:

> There was a noble clerke named pogius of Florence / And was secretary to pope Eugenye / 7 also to pope Nycholas whiche had in the cyte of Florence a noble 7 well stuffed lybrarye / whiche alle noble straungyers comynge to Florence desyred to see / And therin they fonde many noble and rare bookes And whanne they had axyd of hym whiche was the best boke of them alle / and that he reputed for best / He sayd / that he helde Cathon glosed for the best book of his lyberarye.
>
> (*Caxton*, 78)

18. Trapp, "Ovid's Tomb," 45–46.

19. Quoted and translated in Trapp, "Ovid's Tomb," 41–42. For the Latin, see Paul Klopsch, *Pseudo-Ovidius De Vetula: Untersuchungen und Text* (Leiden: E. J. Brill, 1967), 193. On the textual and cultural traditions of *De Vetula*, see Klopsch's study and Wolfgang Speyer, *Bücherfunde in der Glaubenswerbung der Antike. Mit einem Ausblick auf Mittelalter und Neuzeit* (Göttingen: Vandenhoeck und Ruprecht, 1970), 102–3.

20. Trapp, "Ovid's Tomb," 42.

21. See O. B. Hardison, Jr., *The Enduring Monument: A Study of the Idea of Praise in Renaissance Literary Theory and Practice* (Chapel Hill: University of North Carolina Press, 1962), 123–62.

22. For a reading of the poem complementing my own, see Hardison, *Enduring Monument*, 131–37. For Politian's elegy, I use the text and translation in Fred J. Nichols, *An Anthology of Neo-Latin Poetry* (New Haven: Yale University Press, 1979), 254–69.

23. *Ioannis Iovani Pontani, Carmina*, ed. Johannes Oeschger (Bari: Giuseppi Laterza et Figli, 1948), 189–258. Poems that bear directly on my discussion of Surigonus's elegy include Pontanus's poems on buried orators and poets, numbered XIV to XX, in ibid., 198–201. Note, in particular, the similar references to the tears of the Pierian Muses (ibid., 198, line 102; 200, lines 11–12; 201, lines 13–14), and to the arbitrary cuttings of the Parcae (ibid., 198, line 15).

24. George Puttenham, *The Arte of English Poesie* (1589), from Book I, chapter 28, quoted and discussed in Hardison, *Enduring Monument*, 111; for traditions in antiquity and developments in the Renaissance, see Pigman, *Grief and English Renaissance Elegy*, 40–51.

25. Text (reprinted from Caxton's *Boece*) and translation from Derek Brewer, ed., *Chaucer: The Critical Heritage, Volume I 1385–1837* (New York: Barnes and Noble, 1974) 78–79, where the translation is attributed to R.G.G. Coleman (material in square brackets is from Coleman's translation). The elegy and its later reception are discussed in N. F. Blake, "Caxton and Chaucer," *Leeds Studies in English*, new series 1 (1967): 19–36, especially 27–30. For a dazzling reading of another similar representation of a tomb inscription in the contexts of an early humanist hermeneutic, see Timothy Hampton on Guillaume Budé's story of Alexander's visit to the tomb of Achilles in his *Livre de l'institution du prince* (1517). Hampton's remarks are worth quoting at length, because they bear on my own understanding of the "bookishness" of Caxton's printing of Surigonus's tomb poem:

> It is important that this scene of the tomb appears in conjunction with a praise of writing. For just as the courage of Achilles is represented by the stony icon of the sepulcher, so too the great deeds of the hero have sense for future generations only when hardened into textual form. . . . Writing is a kind of funereal inscription. The histories are seen as a series of stones wherein the hero is preserved for eternity, with the hope that his virtue will be reanimated by a future animator. . . . The tomb, of course, signifies by a single sign the "pourtraicture" of Achilles, whereas the narratives of the historians and poets work through the syntagmatic interplay of an entire series of signs. The compact form of the image is pedagogically useful, since the reduction of the hero's life to a single sign imposes coherence on it, making it easy to define or interpret.
>
> (*Writing from History*, 38–39)

26. Coleman's interpretive note reads: "Taking *dixeris* as addressed to the reader. *Hunc latuisse virum nil* is difficult. I have rendered it as if it were classical, viz. 'this man lay hidden in nothing'; but the unclassical meaning 'nothing was hidden from this man' might be better in the context" (Pearsall, ed., *Critical Heritage*, 80).

27. Taking *latuisse* as transitive, rather than intransitive as Coleman does, and *nil* as adverbial (for advice on this translation, I am indebted to George W. Pigman III). There is, I believe, a similar use of this idiom in John Rastell's 1517 printing of Thomas Linacre's *Progymnasmata*. The Latin poem that prefaces Linacre's text begins: "Pagina que falso *latuit* sub nomine nuper / Que fuit et multo co[m]maculata luto / Nunc tandem authoris p[er]scribens nomina veri / Linacri dulces pura recepit aquas" ("The Page which not long since *lay hidden* beneath a false name, caked thick with muck, now printing out the true author's name—Linacre, is cleansed, washed in fresh water," emphases mine). What the poems in Caxton and Rastell share is the sense of printing as an act of revealing that which has lain hidden: in both cases, the name of an author and the reputation of his work. For the text and translation of this poem, see Joseph Loewenstein, "*Idem*: Italics and the Genetics of Authorship," *JMRS* 20 (1990): 221–22.

28. See Blake, "Caxton and Chaucer," summarizing nineteenth- and twentieth-century interpretations and concluding, "I do not think that Caxton's Latin lines were engraved on the tablet [i.e., of the tomb]. They were written for the edition" (28).

29. On Caxton's typefaces, cut by Johannes Veldener, see Blake, *Caxton and His World*, 50, 56, and Painter, *William Caxton*, 61–62.

30. See Painter, *William Caxton*, 98 and plate IIb.

31. Painter confirms that Caxton's types 1 and 2 were modeled on a Burgundian bookhand derived from the batard, whereas type 3 is modeled on a Latin Gothic textura, display hand. Painter notes, "The gothic type 3 is here used for the first time (in the *Boece*) with its intended function as a heading and a Latin type" (*William Caxton*, 92). My claims here for the "monumental" look of Caxton's display type in the *Boece* should not be construed as challenging the specifics of European type-history. The Roman monumental capital had, for fifteenth-century scribes and printers, formed the model for an inscriptional hand or typeface, and there are many examples of attempts to reproduce on the page the look of epigraphic incision (see De Hamel, *History of Illuminated Manuscripts*, 242–44; Wardrop, *The Script of Humanism*, 13–18). But, within systems of typography, different faces could be used to evoke different styles of written communication. Thus, as Joseph Loewenstein has argued, Aldus Manutius's development of italic type was designed to evoke handwriting, in contrast to the Roman typfaces that had imitated "antique, monumental, incised letterforms." When these typefaces were imported into England in the early sixteenth century, Roman came to replace black-letter and the former "soon lost its emphatic quality" (quotations from "*Idem*: Italics and the Genetics of Authorship," 222, 224). My argument, therefore is that the *Boece* represents a very early case of using contrasting typfaces—one restricted to vernacular text, the other to Latin display headings—to evoke the visual impression of distinctions in the function of the type. What I would further suggest is that Caxton's printing of Surigonus's tomb-poem, together with the epilogue's English directions for finding it, represent a version of the *sylloge*, that is, an attempt to capture on the page the look of a discovered inscription.

32. For the history of post-Petrarchan laureation ceremonies in Europe, see J. B. Trapp, "The Owl's Ivy and the Poet's Bays," *JWCI* 21 (1958): 227–55.

33. Henry de Vocht, *History of the Foundation and the Rise of the Collegium Trilingue Lovaniense 1517–1550* (Louvain: University of Louvain, 1951–55), I:159.

34. On Surigonus, see Roberto Weiss, *Humanism in England During the Fifteenth Century*, 138–40, 153–55; Richard Walsh, "The Coming of Humanism to the Low Countries," *Humanistica Louvaniensia* 25 (1975): 162–63; de Vocht, *History of the Foundation*, 159 and n.8 (from which I quote the matriculation records of the University of Louvain); Jozef Ijsewijn, "The Coming of Humanism to the Low Countries," in Heiko Oberman and Thomas A. Brady, Jr., eds., *Itinerarium Italicum: The Profile of the Italian Renaissance in the Mirror of Its European Transformations* (Leiden: Brill, 1975), especially 234–35. Surigonus's collection of Latin poetry (mostly epigrams and panegyrics) is preserved in British Library, MS Arundel 249, fols.94–117, which is titled "Versus laureati poete Stephani Surigoni ad varios transmissi." This collection may have circulated in England during Surigonus's residency there. For this suggestion, see David R. Carlson, "Reputation and Duplicity: The Texts and Contexts of Thomas More's Epigram on Bernard André," *ELH* 58 (1991): 277n.23. Although there is no modern published edition of these poems, a description of their contents and a selection of texts appears in H. Keussen, "Der Humanist Stephan Surigonus und sein Kölner Aufenthalt," *Westdeutscher Zeitschrift für Geschichte und Kunst* 18 (1899): 352–69. Jozef Ijsewijn prints one of the poems ("Coming of Humanism," 234), stating that it was written in Louvain in 1472 (and thus could not have circulated in England, as Carlson supposes). Painter writes of Surigonus's writing of the epitaph: "Surigonus was used to such work for printers, having written a Latin verse advertisement for the first edition of Virgil printed by Johann Mentelin at Strassburg about 1469" (*William Caxton*, 92, and see n.4).

35. See Gordon Kipling, *The Triumph of Honour: The Burgundian Origins of the Elizabethan Renaissance* (The Hague: University of Leiden Press, for The Sir Thomas Browne Institute, 1977), and "Henry VII and the Origins of Tudor Patronage," in Guy Fitch Lytle and Stephen Orgel, eds., *Patronage in the Renaissance* (Princeton: Princeton University Press, 1981), 117–64.

36. Summarized in Blake, "Caxton and Chaucer."

37. Recounted in Blake, "Continuity and Change . . . The Bruges Period."

38. See Kipling, "Henry VII," 118–19.

39. The following information is drawn from William Nelson, *John Skelton, Laureate* (New York: Columbia University Press, 1939), whose opening chapters still remain the best overall account of early Tudor "laureates." For the scholars mentioned here, see in particular 15, 42, 63. John Kay appears to be the first English-born writer to call himself a "poet laureate" in his dedication to Edward IV in his translation of Guillaume Caoursin's *Siege of Rhodes* (1482).

40. On Kay, see the facsimile edition of the *Siege of Rhodes*, ed. Douglas A. Gray (Delmar: Scholars' Facsimiles and Reprints, 1975); on André, see Nelson, *John Skelton, Laureate*, 15; on Skelton's laureations, see ibid., 61–63, and Greg Walker, *John Skelton and the Politics of the 1520s* (Cambridge: Cambridge University Press, 1988), 35–40.

41. See Blake, *Caxton and His World*, 196; Painter, *William Caxton*, 135.

42. Painter, *William Caxton*, 136.

43. For a survey of Caxton as editor, and the features of his two editions of the *Canterbury Tales*, see Beverly Boyd, "William Caxton." For a description of his edition of c.1478, see Manly-Rickert I:79–81.

44. For the details of the second edition, see Boyd, "William Caxton." Manly and Rickert dismiss this edition as having "no textual authority" (I:81).

45. For Dryden's phrasing, see his "Preface to Fables Ancient and Modern," in George Watson, ed., *Of Dramatic Poesy and Other Critical Essays* (London: Dent, 1962), 2:280.

46. According to the *OED*, Caxton is the first to use the word in his translation of the *Game and Play of Chess* (first edition, c.1475; s.v. *historiographer*). Bernard André was appointed royal historiographer to Henry VII in c.1490. For André's title as "Poete laureati ac Regii hystorici," see the printing of the catalogue of André's works from MS Arsenal 418 (dated 1500) in Nelson, *John Skelton, Laureate*, 239. For André's other titles in royal and literary documents, see Walker, *John Skelton and the Politics of the 1520s*, (Cambridge: Cambridge University Press, 1988), 36.

47. Anthony Grafton, *Defenders of the Text*, 47–75.

48. The story appears in Poliziano's *Miscellanea* (I.25), published in 1489. I quote from the translation in Grafton, *Defenders*, 60 (for the Latin, see 265n.52). For discussion of Poliziano's attentions to naming of both authors and authoritative owners, and his development of a "genealogical method of source criticism" designed to prove "that one extant manuscript was the parent of all the others," see Grafton's discussion at 51–65.

49. See Blake, "Continuity and Change . . . Westminster."

50. For a challenge to the patron-oriented scholarship on Caxton, and arguments that Caxton develops strategies of presentation designed to shift the reading audience from the commissioning patron to the purchasing reader, see Russell Rutter, "Caxton and Literary Patronage." Though Rutter does not discuss the prologues and epilogues I analyze here, his remarks bear directly on my account. He summarizes:

> [The] focus on multiple audiences, even in patronized books, together with Caxton's obvious efforts to address nonreaders and to identify special book-buying groups, shows that he aggressively sought markets for his books. Compelling evidence for all this can be seen in Caxton's prologues and epilogues as long as inquiry is not closed off by the hasty assumption that patrons paid all the expenses, took the books off Caxton's hands, and obviated the need for him to develop on his own a dependable clientele.
>
> (464)

See, too, Rutter's earlier arguments for Caxton's advertising and the profit motive in his printing programs (458–59).

51. See, for example, the discussion in W. F. Bolton, *A Living Language: The History and Structure of English* (New York: Random House, 1982), 172–76. For linguistic developments leading up to Caxton's usages and his remarks in the *Eneydos* prologue, see John Hurt Fisher, "Chancery and the Emergence of Standard Written English in the Fifteenth Century," *Speculum* 52 (1977): 870–99.

52. For interpretations of Skelton's place in the *Eneydos* prologue, see A.S.G. Edwards, *Skelton: The Critical Heritage* (London: Routledge and Kegan Paul, 1981), 2, who refers to it as a kind of "publisher's blurb," and Greg Walker, *John Skelton and the Politics of the 1520s*, 38–40. The passage has also been read as testimony to Skelton's growing reputation at court, inaugurated in his first datable poem on the death of the Earl of Northumberland (*Upon the Dolorus Dethe and Muche Lamentable Chaunce of the*

Mooste Honorable Erle of Northumberlande, written in 1489 at the behest of Henry VII). Caxton's reference to Skelton having drunk from "elycons well" may be a conscious allusion to Skelton's appeal at the beginning of that poem for the Muses "Myne homely rudnes and drighnes to expelle / With the freshe waters of Elycons welle" (lines 13–14). See the text and discussion in John Scattergood, ed., *John Skelton: The Complete English Poems* (New Haven: Yale University Press, 1983), 29, 389.

53. This range of texts is conveniently available in Spurgeon, *Five-Hundred Years of Chaucer Criticism and Allusion* (London: Kegan Paul, Trench, Trübner, 1914–25), I.54, 66, 69. The first to appeal to the triumvirate of Gower, Chaucer, and Lydgate may have been Osbern Bokenham in his *The Leuys of Seyntys* (c. 1443–47): "For I dwellyd neuere / wt the fresh rethoryens / Gower / Chauncers / ner with lytgate" (Spurgeon, *Five-Hundred Years*, I:46).

54. See the texts printed in Edwards, *Skelton: The Critical Heritage*, 46–48.

55. Edwards, *Skelton: The Critical Heritage*, considers Erasmus's "fulsome" praise of Skelton in 1499 not so much the critical account of a then young poet but "the effusion of a courteous visitor to the court of Henry VII, disinclined to afford any possibility of offence to his powerful hosts" (3). On Whittington, see ibid., 6–7. For a reading of the praise of Skelton as a mark of the "conditions of the market of humanism" rather than as records of the poet's contemporary reputation as such, see David R. Carlson, "Reputation and Duplicity," 280n.44.

56. For much of what follows, I draw on David R. Carlson, "King Arthur and Court Poems for the Birth of Arthur Tudor in 1486," *Humanistica Louvaniensia* 36 (1987): 147–83. See, too, Sydney Anglo, *Spectacle, Pageantry, and Early Tudor Policy* (Oxford: Clarendon Press, 1969), 19–20, 46–51.

57. Carlson, "Court Poems," 161.

58. Ibid., 169.

59. From Giovanni Gigli, *Genethliacon in principem Arturum*, edited and printed in Carlson, "Court Poems," 171–83; I quote from line 273.

60. Spearing, *Medieval to Renaissance in English Poetry* (Cambridge: Cambridge University Press, 1985), 92.

CHAPTER SIX

1. All quotations from *The Conforte of Louers*, as well as from *The Example of Vertu*, *A Ioyfull Medytacyon*, and *The Conuercyon of Swerers* will be from Florence W. Gluck and Alice B. Morgan, eds., *Stephen Hawes: The Minor Poems*, EETS ES 271 (London: Oxford University Press, 1974) and will be cited by line numbers in my text. I have silently retained their editorial expansions.

2. The title page of the *Confort* notes that the book was compiled "in the seconde yere of the reygne of our most naturall sourayne lorde ky[n]ge Henry the eyght," thus dating it between April 1510 and April 1511. De Worde's printing is usually dated to 1515 (see Gluck and Morgan, *Stephen Hawes*, xix–xx). On the shifts in humanist patronage from the courts of Henry VII to Henry VIII, see Gordon Kipling, "Henry VII and the Origins of Tudor Patronage," in Lytle and Orgel, eds., *Patronage in the Renaissance*, 1179–64; David R. Carlson, "Reputation and Duplicity," *ELH* 58 (1991): 261–81; and Alistair Fox, *Politics and Literature in the Reigns of Henry VII and Henry VIII* (Oxford: Blackwell, 1989).

3. Accounts that chronicle the critical reputation of Hawes, especially with reference to his adoration of Lydgate and his practice of aureation, may be found in Elizabeth J. Sweeting, *Early Tudor Criticism, Linguistic and Literary* (Oxford: Blackwell, 1940), 1–22; in the remarks made throughout in Stanley E. Fish, *John Skelton's Poetry* (New Haven: Yale University Press, 1965); and in Alice Miskimin, *The Renaissance Chaucer* (New Haven: Yale University Press, 1975), 166 (who calls Hawes's *Pastime of Pleasure* "one of the most crippled and myopic of early sixteenth-century allegorical poems"). For more sympathetic views, see the appreciation in Gluck and Morgan, *Stephen Hawes*, xxi–xlvii; A.S.G. Edwards, *Stephen Hawes* (Boston: Twayne, 1983); and Ebin, *Illuminator, Makar, Vates* (Lincoln: University of Nebraska Press, 1988), 133–62.

4. On the rivalry with Skelton, see the review of evidence in Gluck and Morgan, *Stephen Hawes*, 160–62; on its historical background, see Edwards, *Stephen Hawes*, 5–8. David Carlson ("Reputation and Duplicity," 271) writes about the competition between the Latin poetry of Thomas More and Bernard André in terms that may bear on the rivalry of Hawes and Skelton as vernacular poets:

> That the early Tudor humanists should have attacked one another from time to time is to be expected, in light of the ongoing struggle to win reputation enjoined by the dominant system of literary exchange, of literary labor for patronage. Ridiculing others, as objectionable as it was pretended to be, was a tactic acknowledged in practice to be an effective means of self-promotion.

5. See the account in A. C. Spearing, *Medieval to Renaissance in English Poetry* (Cambridge: Cambridge University Press, 1985), 224–34.

6. For the pairing of Gower and Chaucer as a trope in recent medieval criticism, see Carolyn Dinshaw, "Rivalry, Rape and Manhood: Gower and Chaucer," in R. F. Yeager, ed., *Chaucer and Gower: Mutability, Difference, Exchange*, ELS Monograph Series, No.51 (Victoria: English Literary Studies, 1991), 130–52.

7. For a precise account of that relationship, see A.S.G. Edwards, "Poet and Printer in Sixteenth Century England: Stephen Hawes and Wynkyn de Worde," *Gutenberg Jahrbuch* (1980): 82–88. In a personal communication I received after this book had gone to press, David Carlson informs me that I may exaggerate the unusualness of Hawes's relationship to de Worde. He has called my attention to the contemporary relationship of Alexander Barclay to Robert Pynson, the details of which have yet to be spelled out in a full scholarly article of the sort that Edwards wrote about Hawes and de Worde. For now, however, Carlson recommends Julie Smith, "Woodcut Presentation Scenes in Books Printed by Caxton, de Worde, Pynson," *Gutenberg Jahrbuch* (1986): 338, and (on Robert Whittinton and de Worde) N. F. Blake, "Wynkyn de Worde: The Later Years," *Gutenberg Jahrbuch* (1972): 135–36. The norm, however, for the early sixteenth century seems to have been that English humanists tended to rely on Continental printers such as Manutius, Bade, and Froben, who had early on established publishing relationships with a variety of European writers. For an account of this apparent gap between English writers and English printers, see Carlson, "Reputation and Duplicity," 263 and n.10. For accounts of the relationship between writers and printers as contributing to Renaissance conceptions of authorship and to the idea of intellectual property, see Joseph Loewenstein, "For a History of Literary Property: John Wolfe's Reformation," *English Literary Renaissance* 18 (1988): 389–412, and "*Idem*: Italics and the Genesis of Authorship," *JMRS* 20 (1990): 205–24.

8. Based on information in Scattergood, *John Skelton: The Complete English Poems* (New Haven: Yale University Press, 1983), the only publications of Skelton's work datable before his death in 1529 are the following: *The Bowge of Court* (de Worde, 1499 and 1510); *A Ballade of the Scottysshe Kynge* (Fakes, 1513); *Elynour Rummynge* (de Worde or Henry Pepwell, c.1521); *The Garlande of Laurell* (Fakes, October 3 1523); *Agaynste a Comely Coystrowne* (Rastell, c.1527); *Dyvers Ballettys and Dyties Solacyous* (Rastell, c.1527); and *A Replycacion Agaynst Certayne Yong Scolers Abjured of Late* (Pynson, c.1528). On the impulse to print courtly lyrics in the 1520s and the place of Skelton's printed editions in this context, see Julia Boffey, *Manuscripts of English Courtly Love Lyrics* (Woodbridge: D. S. Brewer, 1985), 29–33.

9. De Worde printed the following, in separate editions, in 1509: *The Pastime of Pleasure*, *The Conuercyon of Swerers*, *The Example of Virtu*, and *A Ioyfull Medytacyon*. On the visual coordination between the layout of poetic passage and the selection of illustrative woodcuts in these editions, see Edwards, "Poet and Printer in Sixteenth Century England."

10. Kipling, "Henry VII," 132–33, and *Triumph of Honour* (The Hague: University of Leiden Press, 1977), 22–30.

11. See Edwards, *Stephen Hawes*, 2, and more generally, R. F. Green, *Poets and Princepleasers* (Toronto: University of Toronto Press, 1980), 38–70.

12. Quoted and discussed in Edwards, *Stephen Hawes*, 2.

13. Kipling, "Henry VII," 124–25.

14. Fox, *Politics and Literature*, 56–72, and his earlier formulation, "Stephen Hawes and the Political Allegory of *The Comfort of Lovers*," *English Literary Renaissance* 17 (1987): 3–21.

15. The centerpiece of the possible rivalry with Skelton in the *Confort* appears at lines 890–96; for discussion, see the notes in Gluck and Morgan, *Stephen Hawes*, 160–62.

16. For much of what follows, I am indebted to Kipling, "Henry VII," and *Triumph of Honour*.

17. Hawes's treatment of *pronunciatio* (*Pastime of Pleasure*, 1184–1239) has received much attention from scholars of the history of rhetoric. See, in particular, W. S. Howell, *Logic and Rhetoric in England 1500–1700* (Princeton: Princeton University Press, 1956), 46–49, 81–88, and the remarks in Michael Murrin, *The Veil of Allegory* (Chicago: University of Chicago Press, 1969), 3, 68, 178.

18. On the *Pastime* as an allegory of education, see Gluck and Morgan, *Stephen Hawes*, xlii–xliii.

19. For these traditions, see Frances Yates, *The Art of Memory* (Chicago: University of Chicago Press, 1966), and the more recent and compelling study of Mary Carruthers, *The Book of Memory: A Study of Memory in Medieval Culture* (Cambridge: Cambridge University Press, 1990), especially on Hawes at 41–42.

20. See Walter Ong, S. J., *Ramus: Method and the Decay of Dialogue* (Cambridge: Harvard University Press, 1958), especially 83–119; Elizabeth Eisenstein, *The Printing Press as an Agent of Change* (Cambridge: Cambridge University Press, 1979), especially 43–159, 163–225. In appealing to these authorities, however, I do not mean to elide recent criticism of the teleologies behind their notions of cultural change and technological innovation. Among the many studies that stress the continuities between manuscript and print "cultures," two pointedly technical accounts are Linda Ehrsam

Voigts, "Scientific and Medical Books," in Griffiths and Pearsall, eds., *Book Production and Publishing*, 345–402, and N. F. Blake, "Manuscript to Print," in ibid., 403–32. For a vigorous criticism of the "techno-determinism" identified with the work of Ong, Eisenstein, and Marshall McLuhan, see Michael Warner, *The Letters of the Republic: Publication and the Public Sphere in Eighteenth-Century America* (Cambridge: Harvard University Press, 1990). The studies of Roger Chartier have sought to redefine the qualities of print culture less in the terms of technological determinism and more in the contexts of the social changes operating simultaneously with and complementing the development of movable type. For a useful summary of his ideas, see his "General Introduction: Print Culture," in Roger Chartier, ed., *The Culture of Print: Power and the Uses of Print in Early Modern Europe*, trans. Lydia G. Cochrane (Princeton: Princeton University Press, 1989), 1–10.

21. See Kipling, "Henry VII," 125.

22. Paul Saenger, "Silent Reading: Its Impact on Late Medieval Script and Society," *Viator* 13 (1982): 367–414.

23. Paul Saenger, "Books of Hours and the Reading Habits of the Later Middle Ages," in Chartier, ed., *The Culture of Print*, 141–73.

24. Ibid., 144.

25. Ibid., 147.

26. Quoted and translated in ibid., 167–68 n.76. For discussion of the *Toison D'Or* as the model for English courtly practice, in particular its impact on the making of the *Liber Niger* (1478) of Edward IV, see Kipling, "Henry VII," 118–19.

27. W. E. Mead, ed., *The Pastime of Pleasure by Stephen Hawes*, EETS OS 173 (London: Oxford University Press, 1928). All subsequent references will be cited by line number in my text.

28. For a detailed report of these encounters, see my article "The Rhetoric of Fame: Stephen Hawes's Aureate Diction," *Spenser Studies* 5 (1984): 169–84.

29. For the inheritance in Latin rhetorical traditions, see, for example, Cicero's discussion of the impressions on the mind of patterns of understanding at *Topica* 27 (ed. and trans. H. M. Hubbell, Loeb Library Classics [Cambridge: Harvard University Press, 1927]); and John of Salisbury's discussion of sensations impressed on the imagination and his awareness of the Aristotelian theory behind Cicero's idiom in the *Topica*, at *Metalogicon* IV.11 (ed. C.C.I. Webb [Oxford: Clarendon Press, 1929], 177).

30. From the edition in the *Riverside Chaucer*, 464.

31. For the many uses of "impressioun" in Chaucer's writings, see the listing in J.S.P. Tatlock, ed., *A Concordance to the Complete Works of Geoffrey Chaucer* (Washington, D.C.: The Carnegie Institution of Washington, 1927). For the Middle English idiom "to print or imprint in the mind," possibly deriving from these Chaucerian sources, see *MED*, s.v. *prente* (verb), defs. 3 c and d. In fifteenth-century lyrics, preserved in the early-sixteenth-century anthology of Bodleian Library, Oxford, MS Rawlinson C.813, the idiom appears in several poems pendant on (and at times incorporating) the poetry of Lydgate and Hawes (see my discussion in the Envoy to this book). One of the poems of this manuscript (item 3) incorporates lines from a late Middle English song, "So ys emprentid in my remembraunce," preserved in the Mellon Chansonnier (Yale University, Beinecke Library MS 91). On this appropriation, see Boffey, *Manuscripts of English Courtly Love Lyrics*, 91, and Jansen and Jordan, eds., *The Welles Anthology* (Binghamton: Medieval and Renaissance Texts and Studies, 1991), 88–89.

32. For Hawes's and Lydgate's *practice* of aureation, as opposed to the mythologies of the aureate I have explored here, see the discussions throughout Ebin, *Illuminator, Makar, Vates*, which incorporates (without acknowledgment) material from her earlier essay, "Lydgate's Views on Poetry," *Annuale Mediaevale* 18 (1977): 76–105.

33. The following discussion is adapted, with some changes of emphasis, from my "Rhetoric of Fame," where I had suggested that the recovery of complete Ciceronian texts in the fifteenth century stimulated the development of a vocabulary of impression in humanist discourse. For development of a Ciceronian vocabulary through which terms for artistic representation describe literary processes, see Elaine Fantham, "Imitation and Evolution: The Discussion of Rhetorical Imitation in Cicero *De Oratore* 2.87–97 and Some Related Problems of Ciceronian Theory," *Classical Philology* 73 (1978): 1–16; A. E. Douglas, "The Intellectual Background of Cicero's Rhetorica," in H. Temporini, ed., *Aufstieg und Niedergang der Römischen Welt*, I, no.4 (Berlin: De Gruyter, 1973), especially 108–15; and Wesley Trimpi, "The Quality of Fiction: The Rhetorical Transmission of Literary Theory," *Traditio* 30 (1974): 1–118, especially 31–40.

34. *Pro Archia* 21, ed. and trans. N. H. Watts, *The Speeches of Cicero*, Loeb Classical Library (Cambridge: Harvard University Press, 1965). Such sentiments inform, too, the defense of exemplary fable and the presentation of judicial verity in *De Officiis*, III.ix.39 and III.xvii.69 (on these texts, see Trimpi, "Quality of Fiction," 34–35).

35. Quoted in William H. Woodward, *Vittorino da Feltre and Other Humanist Educators* (Cambridge: Harvard University Press, 1897), 105. For discussion of Vergerio in the context of emerging Humanist ideas of exemplarity, see Timothy Hampton, *Writing from History*, 10, 15. Cicero, too, had used the language of art to distinguish true glory from popular fame at *Tusculan Disputations*, III.ii.3.

36. Although the *OED* cites a 1508 quotation as the first English usage of the word *impress* to mean "to print," the Latin word *impressor* was early on used to characterize printers. Fifteenth-century colophons and grants of privilege record *impressit* as the word for "printed" and *impressor* as "printer." See Eisenstein, *The Printing Press as an Agent of Change*, 57n.52; Cora E. Lutz, "Manuscripts Copied from Printed Books," in her *Essays on Manuscripts and Rare Books* (Hamden: Archon Books, 1975), 129–38, especially 134; Joesph Loewenstein, "*Idem*: Italics and the Genesis of Authorship," 210–11.

37. *Pastime of Pleasure*, 1317–1407. For a summary of Hawes's debts to Lydgate, see Edwards, *Stephen Hawes*, 10–12, who reports Antony á Wood's comment from the seventeenth century that Hawes "could repeat by heart most of our English poets; especially Jo. Lydgate, a monk of Bury, whom he made equal, in some respects with Geff. Chaucer" (12).

38. The printing history of these texts up to 1509 follows. Information on dates and printers is drawn from A. W. Pollard and G. R. Redgrave, eds., *A Short-Title Catalogue of Books Printed in England, Scotland, and Ireland and of English Books Printed Abroad 1475–1640*, 2d ed., revised and enlarged by W. A. Jacobs, F. S. Furguson, and Katherine F. Panzer (London: The Bibliographical Society), Volume 1 (1986), Volume 2 (1976) [*sic*], and hereafter referred to as *STC*. Numbers in square brackets refer to *STC* numbers.

> *The Canterbury Tales* (Caxton, 1478 [5082], 1483 [5083]; Pynson, 1492 [5084]; de Worde, 1498 [5085])
> *The House of Fame* (Caxton, 1483 [5087])
> *Troilus and Criseyde* (Caxton, 1483 [5094])

The Temple of Glas (Caxton, 1477 [17032]; de Worde, 1495 [17032a], 1500 [17033],
   and 1506? [17033.7]; Pynson, 1503 [17033.3])
The Fall of Princes (Pynson, 1494 [3175])
The Churl and the Bird (Caxton, 1477 [17008], 1478 [17009]; Pynson, 1493 [17010];
   de Worde, 1497 or 1500 [17011])
The Court of Sapience (Caxton, 1480 [17015])

Hawes also refers to Lydgate's authorship "Of our blyssed lady / the conuersacyon"
(*Pastime*, 1343), which Mead considers an error for "The Balade in Commendation of
our Lady" (note to 1343, p.231). Such a poem by Lydgate survives in two fifteenth-
century manuscripts and in Thynne's 1532 Chaucer edition (MacCracken prefers the
title "Ballade at the Reverence of Our Lady Qwene of Mercy," *Minor Poems I*, xii).
MacCracken, however, considers Hawes's "conuersacyon" as referring to "conduct"
and takes this as a reference to Lydgate's *The Life of Our Lady* (Caxton, 1484 [17024]).
Spurgeon notes that in Caxton's printing of this poem the passage in praise of Chaucer
is entitled "A commendacion of chauceres" (as it is in BL MS Harley 629; see *Five-
Hundred Years of Chaucer Criticism* [London: Kegan Paul, Trench, Trübner, 1914–25],
19). It is possible, then, that Hawes conflated his memory of two texts, and I believe his
reference is to *The Life of Our Lady*. MacCracken considers Hawes's lines about a book
"bytwene vertue and the lyfe vycyous / Of goddes and goddes" (*Pastime*, 1362–63) as
referring either to the *Assembly of Gods* or to *Reason and Sensuality* (the former published by de Worde in his Chaucer edition of 1498, the latter not printed until the
nineteenth century). Of the two other works by Lydgate mentioned by Hawes, *The
Troy Book* was printed by Pynson in 1513 [5579], and the *Life of St. Edmund*, though
extant in nine manuscripts, was not printed until the nineteenth century. For Mac-
Cracken's discussion of Hawes's Lydgate references, see *Minor Poems I*, xxxiv–xxxvi.
Of Chaucer's works mentioned in the *Pastime*, the only unprinted poem would have
been the *Legend of Good Women* (Thynne's 1532 edition is the first). Among what
Hawes calls the "many other bokes" (*Pastime*, 1335) among Chaucer's "prynted bokes"
(*Pastime*, 1337), the following would have appeared by 1509: *Mars and Venus* (Julian
Notary, 1500? [5089]); *Anelida and Arcite* (Caxton, 1477? [5090]); *The Parlement of
Foules* (called *The Temple of Brass*, Caxton, 1477? [5091]). For additional information
on the printing history of Chaucer's and Lydgate's works, some of which differs in
dating and attribution from the *STC*, see the following: H. S. Bennett, *English Books
and Readers 1475–1557* (Cambridge: Cambridge University Press, 1952), 259 (on de
Worde's printings of Lydgate); the chronologies of Painter, *William Caxton* (London:
Chatto and Windus, 1976), and Needham, *Printer and Pardoner* (Washington, D.C.:
Library of Congress, 1986), on Caxton's printings; and H. Bergen, ed., *Lydgate's Fall of
Princes*, Part 4, 109–15.

   39. OED, s.v. *document*. But see *MED*, s.v. *document*, where fifteenth-century usages point toward a growing awareness of the physical, visible, "documentary" (in the
modern sense of the word) nature of such teaching. See, for example, the citations
from Pecock, *Rule* 212 (c.1443), "In which *text* may be *seen* . . . þat þo wroȝtist myraclis
and þat þou tauȝtist . . . documents"; and another citation from the same, "If he *marke*
alle þe moral documents *conteyned* in hem [þe gospels], in how many *placis* þei sownen
from or aȝens þe verry moral trouþe of resoun" (all emphases mine).

   40. On Chaucer's uses of the word *treatise*, see the discussion in Donald R. Howard, *The Idea of the Canterbury Tales* (Berkeley and Los Angeles: University of California Press, 1976), 59.

41. On this section of the *Conuersion* (lines 113–58) as an early form of "shaped" poetry, see the discussion in Gluck and Morgan, *Stephen Hawes*, 147.

42. Alistair Fox reads the *Confort of Lovers* as a thinly veiled account of Hawes's love of none other than Mary Tudor, Henry VII's daughter, who figures as the Pucelle of his poems. For a development of this notion, together with a survey of the various anti-Tudor plots at work in the last decade of the fifteenth and the first decade of the sixteenth century, see his *Politics and Literature*, 56–72.

43. Fish, *John Skelton's Poetry*, 98. See, too, the remarks of John Scattergood, "Skelton's *Garlande of Laurell* and the Chaucerian Tradition," in Morse and Windeatt, eds., *Chaucer Traditions*, 122–38, especially 122, "Skelton's poems frequently grow by addition and augmentation."

44. Susan Schibanoff, "Taking Jane's Cue: *Phyllyp Sparowe* as a Primer for Women Readers," *PMLA* 101 (1986): 832–47.

45. Schibanoff, "Taking Jane's Cue," 839.

46. See Spearing, *Medieval to Renaissance*, 234–40; Gluck and Morgan, *Stephen Hawes*, 160–61.

47. For the rivalry with Alexander Barclay, see the texts and discussion in Gluck and Morgan, *Stephen Hawes*, 160–61.

48. The translation of the following text is from Scattergood's edition, 413.

49. Schibanoff, "Taking Jane's Cue," 838–39.

50. See Scattergood's edition (*Skelton: The Complete English Poems*), 406, for discussion and summary of critical responses.

51. Schibanoff, "Taking Jane's Cue," 843.

52. The Latin is from Scattergood's edition, *Skelton: The Complete English Poems*, 230. I am grateful to David Carlson for providing the translation here, which differs somewhat from Scattergood's (454).

53. For the medieval etymology of *auctor* out of *augere*, "to grow," see Minnis, *Medieval Theory of Authorship* (London: Scolar Press, 1984), 10, 219–20, who calls attention to late-medieval dictionary entries. Hugotio of Pisa begins the defintion of *augeo* in his *Magnae derivationes* "by glossing *augere* as *amplificare*, 'to increase,' 'to grow': hence *auctor*, written with a 'u' and a 'c,' means *augmentator*" (219–20). Other dictionaries with similar definitions cited by Minnis are *Papias: De linguae latinae vocabulis* (published in 1476) and *Joannes de Janua: Catholicon* (published in Venice in 1495). The etymology goes back at least as far as Isidore of Seville's *Etymologies*: "Auctor ab augendo dictus" (*Etymologiarum siue originum libri XX*, ed. W. M. Lindsay [Oxford: Clarendon Press, 1911], X.2).

54. For the Isidorian etymology, see *Etymologiarum*, V.xxvii.26: "Fama autem dicta quia fando, id est loquendo, . . ."

55. On the circumstances of Skelton's attainment of the title *orator regius*, see Greg Walker, *John Skelton and the Politics of the 1520s* (Cambridge: Cambridge University Press, 1988), 35–52.

56. On the possible contexts in commission and patronage that generated the *Garlande of Laurell*, see Walker, *John Skelton*, 5–34.

57. Ibid., 36–37, 40–43.

58. Kipling, "Origins," 128–30, recasting material from *The Triumph of Honour*, 47–48.

59. See Scattergood's gloss on this line in his edition, *Skelton: The Complete English Poems*, 507.

60. Ibid., 345.

61. For various interpretations, see Scattergood, "Skelton's *Garlande of Laurell* and the Chaucerian Tradition," and Ebin, *Illuminator, Makar, Vates*, 182–87.

62. Scattergood, "Skelton's *Garlande of Laurell*," 126.

63. Ibid.

64. Scattergood, *Skelton: The Complete English Poems*, 358.

65. Translation from ibid., 520.

ENVOY

1. See Geoffrey of Vinsauf's remarks:

> Let the beginning of your poem, as if it were a courteous servant, welcome in the subject matter. Let the middle, as if it were a conscientious host, graciously provide it hospitality. Let the ending, as if it were a herald announcing the conclusion of a race, dismiss it with due respect. In each section, let everything in its own way do honor to the poem; neither let anything in any section sink or in any way suffer eclipse.

These words come from *The New Poetics*, trans. Jane Baltzell Kopp, in J. J. Murphy, ed., *Three Medieval Rhetorical Arts* (Berkeley and Los Angeles: University of California Press, 1971), 35. For Kermode's now famous phrase, see *The Sense of an Ending: Studies in the Theory of Fiction* (New York: Oxford University Press, 1967); for Barbara Herrnstein Smith's meditations on closure, see *Poetic Closure: A Study of How Poems End* (Chicago: University of Chicago Press, 1968). For a review of the critical problems attendant on Chaucer's enigmatic endings, see Michaela Paasche Grudin, "Discourse and the Problem of Closure in the *Canterbury Tales*," *PMLA* 107 (1992): 1157–67.

2. See the two essays "On the Scope and Function of Hermeneutical Reflection" and "On the Problem of Self-Understanding" in Hans-Georg Gadamer, *Philosophical Hermeneutics*, ed. and trans. David E. Linge (Berkeley and Los Angeles: University of California Press, 1976), 18–43 and 44–58.

3. David Hult, "Editor's Preface," *Concepts of Closure*, Yale French Studies 67 (1984): iv. Hult's provocative remarks throughout his preface (iii–vi) bear on the relationship between the problematics of closure and the invitation to completion, interpretation, and scribal intrusion.

4. The idea of a "New Philology" is both propagated and critiqued in the January 1990 special issue of *Speculum*, edited by Stephen G. Nichols. See, in particular, the following contributions for the positions I abstract in my discussion: Stephen G. Nichols, "Introduction: Philology in a Manuscript Culture" (1–10); Suzanne Fleischman, "Philology, Linguistics, and the Discourse of the Medieval Text" (19–37); R. Howard Bloch, "New Philology and Old French" (38–58). Without necessarily implicating him in these critical developments, the work of Paul Zumthor, especially his brief, retrospective *Parler du Moyen Age* (*Speaking of the Middle Ages*, trans. Sarah White [Lincoln: University of Nebraska Press, 1986]), has informed many of the self-historicizing interests of the New Philology. So, too, has Bernard Cerquiglini, *Éloge de la variante: Histoire critique de la philologie* (Paris: Seuil, 1989). For a vigorous rebuttal to the terms and interests of the New Philology, especially in the contexts of profes-

sional textual criticism, see Mary B. Speer, "Editing Old French Texts in the Eighties: Theory and Practice," *Romance Philology* 45 (1991): 7–43.

5. Zumthor develops the idea of *mouvance* in *Essai de poétique médiévale* (Paris: Seuil, 1972) and hones it in the retrospections of *Speaking of the Middle Ages*, 59–62.

6. *Speaking of the Middle Ages*, 96 n.49.

7. For a survey of these traditions in Medieval Studies, see Hans-Ulrich Gumbrecht, "'Un Souffle d'Allemagne ayant passé': Friedrich Diez, Gaston Paris, and the Genesis of National Philologies," *Romance Philology* 40 (1986): 1–37, and Bloch, "New Philology and Old French."

8. Cerquiglini, *Éloge de la variante*, 33–54, and see the brief discussion in Fleischman, "Philology, Linguistics, and the Discourse of the Medieval Text," 19, 25.

9. *Éloge de la variante*, 111. "For medieval writing is not the product of variants, it is variance. The incessant rewriting to which medieval textuality is subject, the joyous appropriation which is its object, invite us to pose a strong hypothesis: the variant is never precise."

10. The late-fifteenth- and early-sixteenth-century practice of using printed books as copy-texts for personal manuscripts is surveyed by N. F. Blake, "Manuscript to Print." Noteworthy among such collections is Trinity College Cambridge MS R.3.19, which relies on Caxton's 1478 *Canterbury Tales*. Princeton University Library MS 128 (c.1600) contains a handwritten copy of Caxton's *Eneydos*. In Cambridge University Library MS Gg.4.27, 35 leaves were added after 1598, supplementing the manuscript's contents with material drawn from Speght's edition (see Manly-Rickert, I:182). Sixteenth- and seventeenth-century annotators corrected and added material derived from printed sources to what is now Bodleian Library MS Fairfax 16 (see Norton-Smith, *Bodleian Library MS Fairfax 16*, xvi–xvii for details). Book IV of Spenser's *Faerie Queene* may be the most well known continuation of a Chaucerian fragment, the *Squire's Tale*; one was also written by John Lane in the first decades of the seventeenth century (see *Riverside Chaucer*, 891). The phenomena to which I am alluding, however, differ from what J. W. Saunders and Arthur Marotti have called the "stigma of print" in the coterie poetics of sixteenth- and seventeenth-century gentleman amateurs. See Marotti, *John Donne, Coterie Poet* (Madison: University of Wisconsin Press, 1986), 3–5, especially these remarks: "For most sixteenth-century poetry, the book was an alien environment. Gentlemen-amateurs avoided what J. W. Saunders has called the 'stigma of print' by refusing to publish their verse, publishing it anonymously, or (accurately or inaccurately) disclaiming responsibility for its appearance in book form" (3, working from J. W. Saunders, "The Stigma of Print: A Note on the Social Bases of Tudor Poetry," *Essays in Criticism* 1 [1951]: 139–64).

11. All quotations from the poetry in this manuscript will be from the edition of Jansen and Jordan, *The Welles Anthology* (Binghamton: Medieval and Renaissance Texts and Studies, 1991). Following Edward Wilson, "Local Habitations and Names," (*Review of English Studies*, new series 41 [1990]: 12–44), however, I spell the anthologist's name "Wellys." Rossell Hope Robbins, *Secular Lyrics of the Fourteenth and Fifteenth Centuries* (Oxford: Clarendon Press, 1952), draws on Rawlinson C.813 for five poems (numbers 129, 130, 200, 204, and 207 in his edition) which "I have taken as being late fifteenth century, because of their content, form, language, as well as their general tone" (xliv). He also prints one in *Historical Poems of the Fourteenth and Fifteenth Centuries* (New York: Columbia University Press, 1959), number 74 in his edition.

12. I quote from the text printed by Wilson, "Local Habitations," 40–41, who also provides information on the larger political and social contexts for Wellys's political work.

13. On the erotic poems in the manuscript, see the early study of P. J. Frankis, "The Erotic Dream in Middle English Lyrics," *Neuphilologische Mitteilungen* 57 (1956): 228–37, and the review of texts and scholarship in Jansen and Jordan, *The Welles Anthology*, 22–29.

14. Editors from Robbins through Jansen and Jordan do not question the authenticity of the female-voiced lyrics in the manuscript as women's poetry. For some presuppositions governing such assumptions, in both textual and literary criticism and in the construction of a woman's literary history in the Middle Ages, see Sarah McNamer, "Female Authors, Provincial Settings: The Re-Visiting of Courtly Love in the Findern Manuscript," *Viator* 22 (1991): 279–310. For the influence of the epistolary exchanges of Troilus and Criseyde on later poetry, see Martin Camargo, *The Middle-English Verse Love Epistle* (Tübingen: Niemeyer, 1991). For the impact of Ovid's *Heroides* (with special reference to Spanish literature, but with discussion and bibliography relating to medieval European writing generally), see Marina Scordilis Brownlee, "Hermeneutic Transgressions in the *Heroides* and *Bursario*," *Stanford French Review* 14 (1990): 95–115, and *The Severed Word* (Princeton: Princeton University Press, 1990). Implicit in my argument is thus that the female-voiced lyrics in the poem are not necessarily by women, and in fact, that they may be examples of the kind of "literary transvestism" recently explored for medieval and more modern literatures. For recent theoretical approaches that may generate new readings of the poetry I am discussing here, see Nancy K. Miller, "'I's' in Drag: The Sex of Recollection," *The Eighteenth Century, Theory and Interpretation* 22 (1981): 47–57. Miller develops her argument in the context of eighteenth-century "women's" literature written by men, though her claims may be extended to the general phenomenon of literary transvestism. For claims that the cycle of male appropriations of a woman's voice must end in the reassertions of patriarchal authority, see Madeleine Kahn, *Narrative Transvestism: Rhetoric and Gender in the Eighteenth-Century English Novel* (Ithaca: Cornell University Press, 1991). The issue of Chaucer's own literary impersonation, ventriloquism, or transvestism has been a central theme of much recent criticism, one I have not explored fully in this study. Indeed, one implication of this criticism is that, through such impersonations, Chaucer himself stages a critique of patriarchal (and, for that matter, heterosexualist) authority in his fictions. For the core arguments, see Carolyn Dinshaw, *Chaucer's Sexual Poetics* (Madison: University of Wisconsin Press, 1989), and H. Marshall Leicester, *The Disenchanted Self* (Berkeley and Los Angeles: University of California Press, 1990). A challenging development of these arguments is Glenn Burger, "Kissing the Pardoner," *PMLA* 107 (1992): 1143–50. For an account of fifteenth-century responses to Chaucerian impersonation in the Wife of Bath, discerned in manuscript marginalia to the *Canterbury Tales*, see Susan Schibanoff, "The New Reader and Female Textuality in Two Early Commentaries on Chaucer," *SAC* 10 (1988): 71–108.

15. For a review of Criseyde's history and afterlife, see Gretchen Mieszkowski, "The Reputation of Criseyde, 1155–1500," *Transactions of the Connecticut Academy of Arts and Sciences* 43 (1971): 71–153. The poem titled in the manuscript "A lettre sende by on yonge woman to anoder, whiche aforetyme were ffelowes togeder" (item 7), is printed and discussed in Jansen and Jordan, *The Welles Anthology*, 100–103, and by Wilson,

"Local Habitations," on 23–25. Wilson refers to its "fireside vulgarity" and "its analogues in the genre of Good Gossips and Ale-wife poems" (23).

16. For the details of these borrowings, see Jansen and Jordan, *Welles Anthology*, 18–29, 300–304, and the bibliography cited therein. A point not noticed is that Wellys borrows from among the most popular of Middle English poems by Hawes, Lydgate, and Chaucer available in print. Publications before 1540 (the latest probable date of compilation of Wellys's anthology) are as follows (numbers in square brackets refer to *STC* numbers): Hawes, *Pastime of Pleasure,* de Worde 1509 [12948], de Worde 1517 [12949]; *Conforte of Louers*, de Worde 1515 [12942.5]; Chaucer, *Troilus and Criseyde*, Caxton 1483 [5094], de Worde 1517 [5095], Pynson 1526 [5096]. In addition to the early printings of Lydgate recorded in my discussion of Hawes (Chapter 6, n.38), printings before 1540 are as follows: *Temple of Glas*, Berthelet 1529 [17034]; *Churl and the Bird*, de Worde 1510 [17012].

17. For item 7, see n.15. Item 8 is titled, "A Letter Send by R. W. to A. C.," printed in Jansen and Jordan, *The Welles Anthology*, 103–5, and by Wilson ("Local Habitations") on 15–17.

18. Jansen and Jordan, *Welles Anthology*, 195. I quote from their edition of the poem on 195–97. They identify the borrowings from *Troilus and Criseyde* on 303, though they do not comment on the possible significance of the selections.

19. Wellys's anthology begins, for example, with a stanza drawn from one of Grande Amoure's complaints in the *Pastime of Pleasure*. Item 13 is drawn almost entirely from stanzas of the *Pastime* and the *Conforte of Louers*. "Regarde and See" are the exordial injunctions (13.1), while toward its conclusion the narrator announces that his lady's "goodly countenance and fygure" had been "engrauyd" in his mind (13.128, 127). For the complete list of borrowings from Hawes, see Jansen and Jordan, *Welles Anthology*, 300–303.

20. The last two stanzas are drawn from IV.266–73.

21. For a review of Pandarus's textual transgressions from a critical perspective somewhat different from my own, see John V. Fleming, *Classical Imitation and Interpretation in Chaucer's Troilus* (Lincoln: University of Nebraska Press, 1990), 155–252.

22. "Humphrey Wellys is the owner of this book. That book belongs to me with the last name Wellys. If it is ever lost, may it be returned to Humphrey." For reproduction of the flyleaf with the original encoded inscription, and remarks on its writing, see Jansen and Jordan, *The Welles Anthology*, 1–3. Wilson, "Local Habitations," offers a slightly different transcription and discussion on 14–15.

23. Wilson, "Local Habitations," 15.

WORKS CITED

Aarsleff, Hans. *The Study of Language in England, 1780–1860*. Princeton: Princeton
   University Press, 1967.
Anderson, David, ed. *Sixty Bookes Olde and Newe*. Knoxville: New Chaucer Society,
   1986.
Anglo, Sydney. *Spectacle, Pageantry, and Early Tudor Policy*. Oxford: Clarendon Press,
   1969.
Bäuml, Franz H. "Varieties and Consequences of Medieval Literacy and Illiteracy."
   Speculum 55 (1980): 237–65.
Bennett, H. S. *Chaucer and the Fifteenth Century*. Oxford: Clarendon Press, 1947.
———. *English Books and Readers 1475–1557*. Cambridge: Cambridge University Press,
   1952.
Benson, C. David. "Their Telling Difference: Chaucer the Pilgrim and His Two Con-
   trasting Tales." *Chaucer Review* 18 (1983): 60–76.
Benson, Larry D., et al., eds. *The Riverside Chaucer*, 3d edition. Boston: Houghton
   Mifflin, 1987.
Bergen, Henry, ed. *Lydgate's Fall of Princes*. Parts 1–4. EETS ES 121–24. London: Ox-
   ford University Press, 1924.
Besserman, Lawrence L. *The Legend of Job in the Middle Ages*. Cambridge: Harvard
   University Press, 1979.
Blake, Norman F. "Caxton and Chaucer." *Leeds Studies in English*, new series 1 (1967):
   19–36.
———. *Caxton and His World*. London: Andre Deutsch, 1969.
———. "Wynkyn de Worde: The Later Years." *Gutenberg Jahrbuch* (1972): 128–38.
———. "Continuity and Change in Caxton's Prologues and Epilogues: The Bruges
   Period." *Gutenberg Jahrbuch* (1979): 72–77.
———. "The Relationship Between the Hengwrt and the Ellesmere Manuscripts of
   the *Canterbury Tales*." *Essays and Studies*, new series 32 (1979): 1–18.
———. "Continuity and Change in Caxton's Prologues and Epilogues: Westminster."
   Gutenberg Jahrbuch (1980): 38–43.
———. Review of Pamela R. Robinson, ed. *Manuscript Tanner 346: A Facsimile*. *En-
   glish Studies* 63 (1982): 71–73.
———. "Manuscript to Print." In Griffiths and Pearsall, eds. *Book Production and Pub-
   lishing in Britain 1375–1475*. 403–32.
Bloch, R. Howard. *Etymologies and Genealogies: A Literary Anthropology of the French
   Middle Ages*. Chicago: University of Chicago Press, 1983.
———. "New Philology and Old French." *Speculum* 65 (1990): 38–58.
Blodgett, James E. "William Thynne." In Ruggiers, ed. *Editing Chaucer: The Great
   Tradition*. 32–52.

Boccaccio, Giovanni. *Genealogie Deorum Gentilium Libri*. Ed. Vincenzo Romano. Bari: Giuseppe Laterza et Figli, 1951.

Boffey, Julia. *Manuscripts of English Courtly Love Lyrics in the Later Middle Ages*. Woodbridge, Suffolk, England: D. S. Brewer, 1985.

Boffey, Julia, and John J. Thompson. "Anthologies and Miscellanies: Production and Choice of Texts." In Griffiths and Pearsall, eds. *Book Production and Publishing in Britain 1375–1475*. 279–315.

Bolton, W. F. *A Living Language: The History and Structure of English*. New York: Random House, 1982.

Bonaventure, St. *S. Bonaventurae Opera Omnia*. Quaracchi: Ex Typographia Collegi S. Bonaventurae. 10 vols. 1892–1903.

Booth, Wayne. *The Rhetoric of Fiction*. Chicago: University of Chicago Press, 1961.

Bornstein, Diane. *Mirrors of Courtesy*. Hamden: Archon Books, 1975.

Bowers, John M. "*The Tale of Beryn* and *The Siege of Thebes*: Alternate Ideas of *The Canterbury Tales*." *SAC* 7 (1985): 23–50.

———. "Hoccleve's Huntington Holographs: The First 'Collected Poems' in English." *Fifteenth-Century Studies* 15 (1989): 27–51.

Boyd, Beverly. "William Caxton." In Ruggiers, ed. *Editing Chaucer: The Great Tradition*. 13–34.

Braddy, Haldeen. "The Genre of Chaucer's *Squire's Tale*." *JEGP* 41 (1942): 279–90.

Brewer, Derek, ed. *Geoffrey Chaucer, the Works, 1532, With Supplementary Material from the Editions of 1542, 1561, 1598, and 1602*. Menston: Scholar Press, 1969.

———. ed. *Chaucer: The Critical Heritage*. 2 volumes. New York: Barnes and Noble, 1974.

Brockman, Bennett A. "Children and Literature in Late Medieval England." *Children's Literature* 4 (1975): 58–63.

———. "Robin Hood and the Invention of Children's Literature." *Children's Literature* 10 (1982): 1–17.

Brown, Carleton. "Lydgate's Verses on Queen Margaret's Entry into London." *Modern Language Review* 7 (1912): 225–34.

Brownlee, Marina Scordilis. "Hermeneutic Transgressions in the *Heroides* and *Bursario*." *Stanford French Review* 14 (1990): 95–115.

———. *The Severed Word*. Princeton: Princeton University Press, 1990.

Bruns, Gerald L. "The Originality of Texts in Manuscript Culture." *Comparative Literature* 32 (1980): 113–29.

Brusendorff, Aage. *The Chaucer Tradition*. London: Oxford University Press, 1925.

Bryan, W. F., and Germaine Dempster, eds. *Sources and Analogues of Chaucer's Canterbury Tales*. Chicago: University of Chicago Press, 1941.

Bühler, Curt F. "The *Fasciculus Temporum* and Morgan Manuscript 801." *Speculum* 72 (1952): 178–83.

Burger, Glenn. "Kissing the Pardoner." *PMLA* 107 (1992): 1143–56.

Burlin, Robert B. *Chaucerian Fiction*. Princeton: Princeton University Press, 1977.

Burnett, Mark Thornton. "Apprentice Literature and the 'Crisis' of the 1590s." *Yearbook of English Studies* 21 (1991): 27–38.

Burrow, John A. *Ricardian Poetry*. New Haven: Yale University Press, 1971.

———. "Autobiographical Poetry in the Middle Ages: The Case of Thomas Hoccleve." *Proceedings of the British Academy* 68 (1982): 389–412.

_____. "*Sir Thopas* in the Sixteenth Century," in Douglas Gray and E. G. Stanley, eds. *Middle English Studies Presented to Norman Davis in Honour of his Seventieth Birthday*. Oxford: Clarendon Press, 1983. 69–91.

_____. "Four Notes on Chaucer's *Sir Thopas*." In Burrow, *Essays on Medieval Literature*. Oxford: Clarendon Press, 1984. 60–78.

Camargo, Martin. *The Middle-English Verse Love Epistle*. Tübingen: Niemeyer, 1991.

Cappelli, A. *Lexicon abbreviaturarum: Dizionario di abbreviature latine et italiane usate nelle carte e codici specialmente del medio evo*. 3d edition. Milan: V. Hoepli, 1929.

Carlson, David R. "King Arthur and Court Poems for the Birth of Arthur Tudor in 1486." *Humanistica Louvaniensia* 36 (1987): 147–83.

_____. "Reputation and Duplicity: The Texts and Contexts of Thomas More's Epigram on Bernard André." *ELH* 58 (1991): 261–81.

_____. "Thomas Hoccleve and the Chaucer Portrait." *Huntington Library Quarterly* 54 (1991): 283–300.

Carroll, David. *The Subject in Question: The Languages of Theory and the Strategies of Fiction*. Chicago: University of Chicago Press, 1982.

Carruthers, Mary. *The Book of Memory: A Study of Memory in Medieval Culture*. Cambridge: Cambridge University Press, 1990.

Cerquiglini, Bernard. *Éloge de la variante: Histoire critique de la philologie*. Paris: Seuil, 1989.

Chartier, Roger, ed. *The Culture of Print: Power and the Uses of Print in Early Modern Europe*. Trans. Lydia G. Cochrane. Princeton: Princeton University Press, 1989.

Chenu, M.-D. "Auctor, actor, autor." *Bulletin du Cange - Archivum Latinitatis Medii Aevi* 3 (1927): 81–86.

Christianson, C. Paul. "Evidence for the Study of London's Late Medieval Manuscript-Book Trade." In Griffiths and Pearsall, eds. *Book Production and Publishing in Britain 1375–1475*. 87–108.

Cicero. *Topica*. Ed. and trans. H. M. Hubbell. Loeb Classical Library. Cambridge: Harvard University Press, 1927.

_____. *Pro Archia Poeta*. In N. H. Watts, ed. and trans. *The Speeches of Cicero*. Loeb Classical Library. Cambridge: Harvard University Press, 1961.

Clemen, Wolfgang. *Chaucer's Early Poetry*. Trans. C. A. M. Sym. London: Methuen, 1963.

Clogan, Paul M. "The Textual Reliability of Chaucer's Lyrics: *A Complaint to His Lady*." *Medievalia et Humanistica*, new series 5 (1974): 183–89.

Cole, Charles Augustus, ed. *Memorials of Henry the Fifth, King of England. Rerum Britannicarum Medii Aevi Scriptores*, vol. 11. London: Longman, Brown, Green, Longmans, and Roberts, 1858.

Copeland, Rita. *Rhetoric, Hermeneutics, and Translation in the Middle Ages*. Cambridge: Cambridge University Press, 1991.

Cosenza, M. E., trans. *Petrarch's Letters to Classical Authors*. Chicago: University of Chicago Press, 1910.

Courcelle, Pierre. *La Consolation de la Philosophie dans la tradition littéraire*. Paris: Etudes Augustiniennes, 1967.

Crotch, W.J.B., ed. *The Prologues and Epilogues of William Caxton*. EETS OS 176. London: Oxford University Press, 1928.

Curtius, Ernst Robert. *European Literature and the Latin Middle Ages.* Trans. W. R. Trask. Princeton: Princeton University Press, 1953.

Dane, Joseph A. Review of Paul Ruggiers, ed. *Editing Chaucer: The Great Tradition.* *Huntington Library Quarterly* 48 (1985): 172–79.

———. "The Reception of Chaucer's Eighteenth-Century Editors." *Text* 4 (1988): 217–36.

———. "Copy-Text and Its Variants in Some Recent Chaucer Editions." *Studies in Bibliography* 44 (1991): 164–83.

———. *The Critical Mythology of Irony.* Athens: University of Georgia Press, 1991.

Davenport, W. A. *Chaucer: Complaint and Narrative.* Woodbridge: D. S. Brewer, 1988.

Davies, J. S., ed. *An English Chronicle of the Reigns of Richard II, Henry IV, Henry V, and Henry VI.* Camden Society, old series, 64 (1856).

Dean, Carolyn. "Law and Sacrifice: Bataille, Lacan, and the Critique of the Subject." *Representations* 13 (1986): 42–62.

De Hamel, Christopher. *A History of Illuminated Manuscripts.* Boston: Godine, 1986.

Deutschke, Consuela, et al. *A Guide to Medieval and Renaissance Manuscripts in the Huntington Library.* San Marino: Huntington Library, 1989.

de Vocht, Henry. *History of the Foundation and the Rise of the Collegium Trilingue Lovaniense 1517–1550.* 4 volumes. Louvain: University of Louvain, 1951–55.

Dinshaw, Carolyn. *Chaucer's Sexual Poetics.* Madison: University of Wisconsin Press, 1989.

———. "Rivalry, Rape and Manhood: Gower and Chaucer." In R. F. Yeager, ed. *Chaucer and Gower: Mutability, Difference, Exchange.* ELS Monograph Series No. 51. Victoria: English Literary Studies, 1991. 130–52.

Doubleday, A. H., et al. *The Complete Peerage.* London: St. Catherine Press, 1926.

Douglas, A. E. "The Intellectual Background of Cicero's Rhetorica." In H. Temporini, ed. *Aufstieg und Niedergang der Römischen Welt.* I, no.4. Berlin: De Gruyter, 1973.

Doyle, A. I. "An Unrecognized Piece of *Piers the Ploughman's Creed* and Other Works by Its Scribe." *Speculum* 34 (1959): 428–36.

———. "More Light on John Shirley." *Medium Aevum* 30 (1961): 93–101.

———. "English Books in and out of Court from Edward III to Henry VII." In Scattergood and Sherborne, eds. *English Court Culture in the Later Middle Ages.* 163–81.

Doyle, A. I., and M. B. Parkes. "The Production of Copies of the *Canterbury Tales* and the *Confessio Amantis* in the Early Fifteenth Century." In M. B. Parkes and A. G. Watson, eds., *Medieval Scribes, Manuscripts and Libraries: Essays Presented to N. R. Ker.* London: Scolar Press, 1978. 163–210.

Dryden, John. *Of Dramatic Poesy and Other Critical Essays.* 2 volumes. Ed. George Watson. London: J. M. Dent, 1962.

Du Boulay, F.R.H. *An Age of Ambition: English Society in the Late Middle Ages.* London: Nelson, 1970.

Duff, E. Gordon. *Fifteenth-Century English Books.* London: Oxford University Press for the Bibliographical Society, 1917.

Ebin, Lois. "Lydgate's Views on Poetry." *Annuale Mediaevale* 18 (1977): 76–105.

———. *John Lydgate.* Boston: Twayne, 1985.

————. *Illuminator, Makar, Vates: Visions of Poetry in the Fifteenth Century.* Lincoln: University of Nebraska Press, 1988.

Edwards, A.S.G. "The Huntington *Fall of Princes* and Sloane 2452." *Manuscripta* 16 (1972): 37–40.

————. "Poet and Printer in Sixteenth-Century England: Stephen Hawes and Wynkyn de Worde." *Gutenberg Jahrbuch* (1980): 82–88.

————. ed. *Skelton: The Critical Heritage.* London: Routledge and Kegan Paul, 1981.

————. "Lydgate Manuscripts: Some Directions for Future Research." In Pearsall, ed. *Manuscripts and Readers in Fifteenth-Century England.* 15–26.

————. *Stephen Hawes.* Boston: Twayne, 1983.

————. "Observations on the History of Middle English Editing." In Derek Pearsall, ed. *Manuscripts and Texts: Editorial Problems in Later Middle English Literature* Cambridge: D. S. Brewer, 1987. 34–48.

————. "The Unity and Authenticity of *Anelida and Arcite*: The Evidence of the Manuscripts." *Studies in Bibliography* 41 (1988): 177–88.

Edwards, A.S.G., and Derek Pearsall. "The Manuscripts of the Major English Poetic Texts." In Griffiths and Pearsall, eds. *Book Production and Publishing in Britain 1375–1475.* 257–78.

Eisenstein, Elizabeth. *The Printing Press as an Agent of Change.* Cambridge: Cambridge University Press, 1979.

Evans, Joan, ed. *The Flowering of the Middle Ages.* New York: McGraw-Hill, 1966.

Fantham, Elaine. "Imitation and Evolution: The Discussion of Rhetorical Imitation in Cicero *De Oratore* 2.87–97 and Some Related Problems of Ciceronian Theory." *Classical Philology* 73 (1978): 1–16.

Ferster, Judith. *Chaucer on Interpretation.* Cambridge: Cambridge University Press, 1985.

Fish, Stanley E. *John Skelton's Poetry.* New Haven: Yale University Press, 1965.

————. *Surprised by Sin: The Reader in Paradise Lost.* Berkeley and Los Angeles: University of California Press, 1966.

————. *Is There a Text in This Class? The Authority of Interpretive Communities.* Cambridge: Harvard University Press, 1980.

Fisher, John Hurt. *John Gower: Moral Philosopher and Friend of Chaucer.* New York: New York University Press, 1964.

————. "Chancery and the Emergence of Standard Written English in the Fifteenth Century." *Speculum* 52 (1977): 870–99.

————. ed. *The Complete Poetry and Prose of Geoffrey Chaucer.* New York: Holt, Rinehart and Winston, 1977.

Fisher, John Hurt, Malcolm Richardson, and Jane L. Fisher. *An Anthology of Chancery English.* Knoxville: University of Tennessee Press, 1984.

————. "Animadversions on the Text of Chaucer, 1988." *Speculum* 63 (1988): 779–93.

————. *The Importance of Chaucer.* Carbondale: Southern Illinois University Press, 1992.

Fleischman, Suzanne. "Philology, Linguistics, and the Discourse of the Medieval Text." *Speculum* 65 (1990): 19–37.

Fleming, John V. "Daun Piers and Dom Pier: Waterless Fish and Unholy Hunters." *Chaucer Review* 15 (1981): 287–94.

Fleming, John V. *Classical Imitation and Interpretation in Chaucer's Troilus*. Lincoln: University of Nebraska Press, 1990.

Foucault, Michel. "Qu'est-ce qu'un auteur?" *Bulletin de la Société Francaise de Philosophie* (22 February 1969): 73–95.

———. "What is an Author?" [translations of the above] In Donald F. Bouchard and Sherry Simon, eds. and trans., *Michel Foucault: Language, Counter-Memory, Practice*. Ithaca: Cornell University Press, 1977. 113–38.

Fox, Alistair. "Stephen Hawes and the Political Allegory of The *Comfort of Lovers*." *English Literary Renaissance* 17 (1987): 3–21.

———. *Politics and Literature in the Reigns of Henry VII and Henry VIII*. Oxford: Blackwell, 1989.

Fradenburg, Louise. "The Scottish Chaucer." In R. J. Lyall and Felicity Riddy, eds. *Proceedings of the Third International Conference on Scottish Language and Literature (Medieval and Renaissance)*. Glasgow: William Culross and Sons, Ltd., 1981. 177–90.

———. "The Manciple's Servant Tongue: Politics and Poetry in the *Canterbury Tales*." *ELH* 82 (1985): 85–118.

———. "The Wife of Bath's Passing Fancy." *SAC* 8 (1986): 31–58.

———. "'Voice Memorial': Loss and Reparation in Chaucer's Poetry." *Exemplaria* 2 (1990): 169–202.

———. *City, Marriage, Tournament: Arts of Rule in Late Medieval Scotland*. Madison: University of Wisconsin Press, 1991.

Frankis, P. J. "The Erotic Dream in Middle English Lyrics." *Neuphilologische Mitteilungen* 57 (1956): 228–37.

Furnivall, F. J., ed. *The Babees Book*. EETS OS 32. London: Trübner, 1868.

———. ed. *Caxton's Book of Curtesye*. EETS ES 3. London: Trübner, 1868.

———. ed. *Odd Texts of Chaucer's Minor Poems*. Chaucer Society Publications, Series 1, Volume 23, Part 1, *Appendix of Poems Attributed to Chaucer*. London: Trübner, 1871.

———. ed. *A Parallel-Text Edition of Chaucer's Minor Poems*. Chaucer Society Publications, Series 1, Volume 21, Part 1. London: Trübner, 1881.

———. ed. *Hoccleve's Works, I. The Minor Poems*. EETS ES 61. London: Kegan Paul, 1892.

Gadamer, Hans-Georg. *Philosophical Hermeneutics*. Ed. and trans. David E. Linge. Berkeley and Los Angeles: University of California Press, 1976.

Ganim, John M. *Chaucerian Theatricality*. Princeton: Princeton University Press, 1990.

Garmonsway, G. N., and R. R. Raymo. "A Middle English Metrical Life of Job." In Arthur Brown and Peter Foote, eds. *Early English and Norse Studies Presented to Hugh Smith*. London: Methuen, 1963. 77–98.

Gaylord, Alan T. "Sentence and Solaas in Fragment VII of the *Canterbury Tales*: Harry Bailly as Horseback Editor." *PMLA* 82 (1967): 226–35.

———. "Chaucer's Dainty 'Dogerel': The 'Elvyssh' Prosody of *Sir Thopas*." *SAC* 1 (1979): 84–104.

———. "The Moment of *Sir Thopas*: Towards a New Look at Chaucer's Language." *Chaucer Review* 16 (1982): 311–29.

Gellrich, Jesse. *The Idea of the Book in the Middle Ages*. Ithaca: Cornell University Press, 1985.

Gerson, Jean. *De laude scriptorum.* In *Oeuvres complètes*, ed. P. Glorieux. Paris: Desclée 1973. IX: 423–34.

Gibson, Gail M. *The Theater of Devotion: East Anglian Drama and Society in the Late Middle Ages.* Chicago: University of Chicago Press, 1989.

Ginsburg, Warren. "'And Speketh so Pleyn': *The Clerk's Tale* and Its Teller." *Criticism* 20 (1978): 307–23.

Given-Wilson, Chris. *The English Nobility in the Late Middle Ages.* London: Routledge and Kegan Paul, 1987.

Gluck, Florence, and Alice Morgan, eds. *Stephen Hawes: The Minor Poems.* EETS OS 271. London: Oxford University Press, 1974.

Gordan, Phyllis W. G., trans. *Two Renaissance Book Hunters: The Letters of Poggius Bracciolini to Nicolaus de Niccolis.* New York: Columbia University Press, 1974.

Gower, John. *Confessio Amantis.* In G. C. Macaulay, ed. *The English Works of John Gower.* 2 vols. EETS ES 81, 82. London: Oxford University Press, 1900, 1901.

Gradon, Pamela. *Form and Style in Early English Literature.* London: Methuen, 1971.

Grafton, Anthony. *Defenders of the Text: The Traditions of Scholarship in an Age of Science, 1450–1800.* Cambridge: Harvard University Press, 1991.

Green, Richard Firth. *Poets and Princepleasers: Literature and the English Court in the Late Middle Ages.* Toronto: University of Toronto Press, 1980.

Greenberg, Cheryl. "John Shirley and the English Book Trade." *The Library*, sixth series, 4 (1982): 369–80.

Greene, Thomas M. *The Light in Troy: Imitation and Discovery in Renaissance Poetry.* New Haven: Yale University Press, 1982.

Griffiths, Jeremy J. "*Confessio Amantis*: The Poem and Its Pictures." In A. J. Minnis, ed. *Gower's Confessio Amantis: Responses and Reassessments.* Cambridge: D. S. Brewer, 1983. 163–78.

Griffiths, Jeremy J., and Derek Pearsall, eds. *Book Production and Publishing in Britain 1375–1475.* Cambridge: Cambridge University Press, 1989.

Griffiths, Ralph A. *The Reign of King Henry VI: The Exercise of Royal Authority, 1422–1461.* London: Ernest Benn, 1981.

Grudin, Michaela Paasche. "Chaucer's *Clerk's Tale* as Political Paradox." *SAC* 11 (1989): 63–92.

———. "Discourse and the Problem of Closure in the *Canterbury Tales*." *PMLA* 107 (1992): 1157–67.

Guillory, John. "Canonical and Non-Canonical: A Critique of the Current Debate." *ELH* 54 (1987): 483–527.

Gumbrecht, Hans-Ulrich. "'Un Souffle d'Allemagne ayant passé': Friedrich Diez, Gaston Paris, and the Genesis of National Philologies." *Romance Philology* 40 (1986): 1–37.

Hammond, Eleanor Prescott. "Two British Museum Manuscripts. (Harley 2251 and Add.34360). A Contribution to the Bibliography of John Lydgate." *Anglia* 28 (1905): 1–28.

———. *Chaucer: A Bibliographical Manual.* New York: Macmillan, 1908.

———. "Poet and Patron in the *Fall of Princes*: Lydgate and Humphrey of Gloucester." *Anglia* 38 (1914): 121–36.

———. ed. *English Verse Between Chaucer and Surrey.* Durham: Duke University Press, 1927.

Hampton, Timothy. *Writing from History: The Rhetoric of Exemplarity in Renaissance Literature*. Ithaca: Cornell University Press, 1990.

Hanna, Ralph III. "Some Commonplaces of Late Medieval Patience Discussions: An Introduction." In Schiffhorst, ed. *The Triumph of Patience, Medieval and Renaissance Studies*. 65–87.

———. "Booklets in Medieval Manuscripts: Further Considerations." *Studies in Bibliography* 39 (1986): 100–111.

———. "Authorial Versions, Rolling Revision, Scribal Error? Or, the Truth about *Truth*." *SAC* 10 (1988): 23–40.

———. "The Production of Cambridge University Library MS. Ff.i.6." *Studies in Bibliography* 41 (1988): 62–70.

———. "Sir Thomas Berkeley and His Patronage." *Speculum* 64 (1989): 878–916.

———. "The Hengwrt Manuscript and the Canon of the *Canterbury Tales*." *English Manuscript Studies* 1 (1989): 64–84.

Hardison, O. B., Jr. *The Enduring Monument: A Study of the Idea of Praise in Renaissance Literary Theory and Practice*. Chapel Hill: University of North Carolina Press, 1962.

Harris, Kate. "John Gower's 'Confessio Amantis': The Virtues of Bad Texts." In Derek Pearsall, ed. *Manuscripts and Readers in Fifteenth-Century England*. 26–40.

———. "The Origins and Make-Up of Cambridge University Library MS Ff.i.6." *Transactions of the Cambridge Bibliographical Society* 8 (1983): 299–333.

———. "Patrons, Buyers, and Owners: The Evidence for Ownership and the Role of Book Owners in Book Production and the Book Trade." In Griffiths and Pearsall, eds. *Book Production and Publishing in Britain 1375–1475*. 163–99.

Harriss, G. L. *Henry V: The Practice of Kingship*. Oxford: Oxford University Press, 1985.

———. *Cardinal Beaufort: A Study of Lancastrian Ascendancy and Decline*. Oxford: Oxford University Press, 1988.

Harth, F. "Carpaccio's Meditation on the Passion." *Art Bulletin* 22 (1940): 25–35.

Hasler, Antony J. "Hoccleve's Unregimented Body." *Paragraph* 13 (1990): 164–83.

Helgerson, Richard. *Self-Crowned Laureates: Spenser, Jonson, Milton and the Literary System*. Berkeley and Los Angeles: University of California Press, 1983.

Hilbert, Karlheinz, ed. *Baldricus Burgulianus Carmina*. Heidelberg: Carl Winter, 1979.

Hill, Thomas D. "'Half-Waking, Half-Sleeping': A Tropological Motif in a Middle English Lyric and Its European Context." *Review of English Studies*, new series 29 (1978): 50–56.

Howard, Donald R. *The Idea of the Canterbury Tales*. Berkeley and Los Angeles: University of California Press, 1976.

Howell, W. S. *Logic and Rhetoric in England 1500–1700*. Princeton: Princeton University Press, 1956.

Hult, David. "Editor's Preface" to *Concepts of Closure*. *Yale French Studies* 67 (1984): iii–vi.

———. *Self-Fulfilling Prophecies: Readership and Authority in the First "Roman de la Rose."* Cambridge: Cambridge University Press, 1987.

Huot, Sylvia. *From Song to Book: The Poetics of Writing in Old French Lyric and Lyrical Narrative Poetry*. Ithaca: Cornell University Press, 1987.

Ijsewijn, Jozef. "The Coming of Humanism to the Low Countries." In Heiko Oberman and Thomas A. Brady, Jr., eds. *Itinerarium Italicum: The Profile of the Italian Renaissance in the Mirror of Its European Transformations.* Leiden: Brill, 1975. 193–301.

Iser, Wolfgang. *The Implied Reader: Patterns of Communication in Prose Fiction from Bunyan to Beckett.* Baltimore: Johns Hopkins University Press, 1974.

Jambeck, Thomas J., and Karen K. Jambeck. "Chaucer's *Treatise on the Astrolabe*: A Handbook for the Medieval Child." *Children's Literature* 3 (1974): 117–22.

James, M. R. *The Western Manuscripts in the Library of Trinity College, Cambridge. A Descriptive Catalogue.* 4 volumes. Cambridge: Cambridge University Press, 1900–1904.

James, Mervyn. "Ritual, Drama, and Social Body in the Late Medieval English Town." *Past and Present* 98 (1983): 3–29.

Jansen, Sharon L., and Kathleen H. Jordan, eds. *The Welles Anthology: MS Rawlinson C.813.* Binghamton: Medieval and Renaissance Texts and Studies, 1991.

Jenkinson, Hilary. *The Later Court Hands in English From the Fifteenth to the Seventeenth Century, Illustrated from the Common Paper of the Scrivener's Company of London, the English Writing Masters, and the Public Records.* Cambridge: Cambridge University Press, 1927.

Josipovici, Gabriel. *The World and the Book: A Study of Modern Fiction.* London: Paladin, 1971.

Justice, Steven V. *Writing and Rebellion in England: The Literature of 1381.* Forthcoming.

Kahn, Madeleine. *Narrative Transvestism: Rhetoric and Gender in the Eighteenth-Century English Novel.* Ithaca: Cornell University Press, 1991.

Kahn, Victoria. "The Figure of the Reader in Petrarch's *Secretum*." *PMLA* 100 (1985): 154–66.

Kajanto, Iiro. *Classical and Christian: Studies in the Latin Epitaphs of Medieval and Renaissance Rome.* Helsinki: Suomalainen Tiedeakatemia, 1980.

———. *Papal Epigraphy in Renaissance Rome.* Helsinki: Suomalainen Tiedeakatemia, 1982.

Kantorowicz, Hermann. *Studies in the Glossators of Roman Law.* Cambridge: Cambridge University Press, 1938.

Kaske, Robert E. "*Clericus Adam* and Chaucer's *Adam Scriveyn*." In Edward Vasta and Zacharias P. Thundy, eds. *Chaucerian Problems and Perspectives: Essays Presented to Paul E. Beichner C.S.C.* Notre Dame: Notre Dame University Press, 1979. 114–18.

Kay, John. *The Siege of Rhodes.* London, 1482. Reprinted in facsimile. Ed. Douglas A. Gray. Delmar: Scholars' Facsimiles and Reprints, 1975.

Kean, P. M. *Chaucer and the Making of English Poetry.* 2 volumes. London: Routledge and Kegan Paul, 1972.

Keiser, George R. "Lincoln Cathedral Library MS. 91: Life and Milieu of the Scribe." *Studies in Bibliography* 32 (1979): 158–79.

Kelly, Henry A. "*Occupatio* as Negative Narration: A Mistake for *Occultatio / Praeteritio*." *Modern Philology* 74 (1976–77): 311–15.

———. *Chaucer and the Cult of St. Valentine.* Leiden: E. J. Brill, 1986.

Kendrick, Laura. *Chaucerian Play: Comedy and Control in the Canterbury Tales.* Berkeley and Los Angeles: University of California Press, 1988.

Ker, N. R. *Medieval Manuscripts in British Libraries*. Oxford: 2 volumes. Clarendon Press, 1969.

Kermode, Frank. *The Sense of an Ending: Studies in the Theory of Fiction*. New York: Oxford University Press, 1967.

Keussen, H. "Der Humanist Stephan Surigonus und sein Kölner Aufenthalt." *Westdeutscher Zeitschrift für Geschichte und Kunst* 18 (1899): 352–69.

Kipling, Gordon. *The Triumph of Honour: The Burgundian Origins of the Elizabethan Renaissance*. The Hague: University of Leiden Press, for the Sir Thomas Browne Institute, 1977.

———. "Henry VII and the Origins of Tudor Patronage." In Guy Fitch Lytle and Stephen Orgel, eds. *Patronage in the Renaissance*. Princeton: Princeton University Press, 1981. 117–64.

———. "The London Pageants for Margaret of Anjou: A Medieval Script Restored." *Medieval English Theatre* 4 (1982): 5–27.

Kittredge, George Lyman. *Chaucer and His Poetry*. Cambridge: Harvard University Press, 1915.

Klopsch, Paul. *Pseudo-Ovidius De Vetula: Untersuchungen und Text*. Leiden: E. J. Brill, 1967.

Koff, Leonard M. *Chaucer and the Art of Storytelling*. Berkeley and Los Angeles: University of California Press, 1988.

Krochalis, Jeanne E. "The Books and Reading of Henry V and His Circle." *Chaucer Review* 23 (1988): 50–77.

Lander, J. R. *Government and Community, England, 1450–1509*. Cambridge: Harvard University Press, 1980.

Lawton, David A. *Chaucer's Narrators*. Woodbridge: D. S. Brewer, 1985.

———. "Dullness and the Fifteenth Century." *ELH* 54 (1987): 761–99.

Leicester, H. Marshall, Jr. "The Art of Impersonation: A General Prologue to the *Canterbury Tales*." *PMLA* 95 (1980): 213–24.

———. *The Disenchanted Self: Representing the Subject in the Canterbury Tales*. Berkeley and Los Angeles: University of California Press, 1990.

Lentricchia, Frank. *Ariel and the Police*. Madison: University of Wisconsin Press, 1988.

Lerer, Seth. "The Rhetoric of Fame: Stephen Hawes's Aureate Diction." *Spenser Studies* 5 (1984): 169–84.

———. "Rewriting Chaucer: Two Fifteenth-Century Readings of the Canterbury Tales." *Viator* 19 (1988): 311–26.

———. "British Library MS Harley 78 and the Manuscripts of John Shirley." *Notes and Queries* 37 (1990): 400–403.

———. "Textual Criticism and Literary Theory: Chaucer and His Readers." *Exemplaria* 2 (1990): 329–45.

———. "*Transgressio studii*: Writing and Sexuality in Guibert of Nogent." *Stanford French Review* 14 (1990): 243–66.

Lewis, C. S. *English Literature in the Sixteenth Century, Excluding Drama*. Oxford: Clarendon Press, 1954.

Lindenberger, Herbert. "Toward a New History in Literary Study." *Profession 84* (1984): 16–23.

———. *The History in Literature: On Value, Genre, Institutions*. New York: Columbia University Press, 1990.

Liu, Alan. "The Power of Formalism: The New Historicism." *ELH* 56 (1989): 721–71.

Loewenstein, Joseph. "For a History of Literary Property: John Wolfe's Reformation." *English Literary Renaissance* 18 (1988): 389–412.

——. "*Idem*: Italics and the Genesis of Authorship." *JMRS* 20 (1990): 205–24.

Lucas, Peter J. "The Growth and Development of English Literary Patronage in the Late Middle Ages and Early Renaissance." *The Library*, sixth series, 4 (1982): 219–48.

Lutz, Cora E. "Manuscripts Copied from Printed Books." In her *Essays on Manuscripts and Rare Books*. Hamden: Archon Books, 1975. 129–38.

Lyall, R. J. "Materials: The Paper Revolution." In Griffiths and Pearsall, eds. *Book Production and Publishing in Britain 1375–1475*. 11–29.

Macaulay, G. C., ed. *The English Works of John Gower*. EETS ES 88–89. London: Oxford University Press, 1900–1901.

McCormick, William. *The Manuscripts of Chaucer's Canterbury Tales*. Oxford: Clarendon Press, 1939.

MacCracken, Henry N., ed. *The Minor Poems of John Lydgate, Part I*. EETS ES 107. London: Kegan Paul, Trench, Trübner, 1911.

——. *The Minor Poems of John Lydgate, Part II*. EETS OS 192. London: Oxford University Press, 1934.

McFarlane, K. B. *Lancastrian Kings and Lollard Knights*. Oxford: Clarendon Press, 1972.

McGann, Jerome J. *A Critique of Modern Textual Criticism*. Chicago: University of Chicago Press, 1983.

——. ed. *Textual Criticism and Literary Interpretation*. Chicago: University of Chicago Press, 1985.

McKitterick, Rosamond. *The Carolingians and the Written Word*. Cambridge: Cambridge University Press, 1989.

McManamon, John M., S. J. *Funeral Oratory and the Cultural Ideals of Italian Humanism*. Chapel Hill: University of North Carolina Press, 1989.

McNamer, Sarah. "Female Authors, Provincial Settings: The Re-Visiting of Courtly Love in the Findern Manuscript." *Viator* 22 (1991): 279–310.

MacQueen, John. "The Literature of Fifteenth-Century Scotland." In Jennifer M. Brown, ed. *Scottish Society in the Fifteenth Century*. New York: St. Martin's, 1977. 184–208.

Mann, Nicholas. *Petrarch Manuscripts in the British Isles*. Padua: Antenore, 1975. Originally published in *Italia Medioevale e Umanistica* 18 (1975): 139–527.

Marotti, Arthur. *John Donne, Coterie Poet*. Madison: University of Wisconsin Press, 1986.

——. "Patronage, Poetry, and Print." *Yearbook of English Studies* 21 (1991): 1–26.

Mead, W. E., ed. *The Pastime of Pleasure by Stephen Hawes*. EETS OS 173. London: Oxford University Press, 1928.

Meale, Carol M. "Patrons, Buyers, and Owners: Book Production and Social Status." In Griffiths and Pearsall, eds. *Book Production and Publishing in Britain 1375–1475*. 201–38.

Meiss, Millard. *Painting in Florence and Siena After the Black Death*. New York: Harper and Row, 1964.

Merrill, Rodney, "Chaucer's *Broche of Thebes*: The Unity of 'The Complaint of Mars' and 'The Complaint of Venus.'" *Literary Monographs* 5 (1973): 1–61.

Middleton, Anne. "The Idea of Public Poetry in the Reign of Richard II." *Speculum* 53 (1978): 94–114.

———. "Chaucer's 'New Men' and the Good of Literature in the *Canterbury Tales*." In Edward Said, ed. *Literature and Society*. Papers from the English Institute, 1978. Baltimore: Johns Hopkins University Press, 1980. 15–56.

———. "The Clerk and His Tale: Some Literary Contexts." *SAC* 2 (1980): 121–50.

———. "William Langland's 'Kynde Name': Authorial Signature and Social Identity in Late Fourteenth-Century England." In Lee Patterson, ed. *Literary Practice and Social Change in Britain, 1380–1530*. 15–82.

Mieszkowski, Gretchen. "The Reputation of Criseyde, 1155–1500." *Transactions of the Connecticut Academy of Arts and Sciences* 43 (1971): 71–153.

Miller, Nancy K. "'I's' in Drag: The Sex of Recollection." *The Eighteenth Century, Theory and Interpretation* 22 (1981): 47–57.

Minnis, A. J. "Medieval Discussions of the Role of the Author." Ph. D. Dissertation, Queen's University, Belfast, 1976.

———. *Medieval Theory of Authorship*. London: Scolar Press, 1984.

Miskimin, Alice S. *The Renaissance Chaucer*. New Haven: Yale University Press, 1975.

Mitchell, Jerome. "Hoccleve Studies, 1965–1981." In Yeager, ed. *Fifteenth-Century Studies*. 49–63.

Montrose, Louise Adrian. "The Elizabethan Subject and the Spenserian Text." In Patricia Parker and David Quint, eds. *Literary Theory / Renaissance Texts*. Baltimore: Johns Hopkins University Press, 1986. 303–40.

Moran, JoAnn Hoeppner. *The Growth of English Schooling, 1340–1548*. Princeton: Princeton University Press, 1985.

Morse, Ruth, and Barry Windeatt, eds. *Chaucer Traditions: Studies in Honour of Derek Brewer*. Cambridge: Cambridge University Press, 1990.

Murphy, James J., ed. *Three Medieval Rhetorical Arts*. Berkeley and Los Angeles: University of California Press, 1971.

Murrin, Michael. *The Veil of Allegory*. Chicago: University of Chicago Press, 1969.

Nares, Robert. *A Catalogue of the Harleian Manuscripts in the British Museum*. London: G. Eyre and A. Strahan, 1808–12.

Needham, Paul. *The Printer and the Pardoner*. Washington, D.C.: Library of Congress, 1986.

Nelson, William. *John Skelton, Laureate*. New York: Columbia University Press, 1939.

Nichols, Fred J. *An Anthology of Neo-Latin Poetry*. New Haven: Yale University Press, 1979.

Nichols, Stephen G. "Introduction: Philology in a Manuscript Culture." *Speculum* 65 (1990): 1–10.

North, J. D. *Chaucer's Universe*. Oxford: Clarendon Press, 1988.

Norton-Smith, John. *Geoffrey Chaucer*. London: Routledge and Kegan Paul, 1974.

———. *Bodleian Library, MS Fairfax* 16. London: Scolar Press, 1979.

———. ed. *John Lydgate: Poems*. Oxford: Clarendon Press, 1966.

———. ed. *James I of Scotland, The Kingis Quair*. Oxford: Clarendon Press, 1971.

Oeschger, Johannes, ed. *Ioannis Iovanni Pontani, Carmina*. Bari: Guiseppi Laterza et Figli, 1948.

Olson, Glending. "Deschamps' *Art de Dictier* and Chaucer's Literary Environment." *Speculum* 48 (1973): 714–23.

———. "A Reading of the *Thopas-Melibee* Link." *Chaucer Review* 10 (1975): 147–53.

———. "Making and Poetry in the Age of Chaucer." *Comparative Literature* 31 (1979): 272–90.

Ong, Walter J., S. J. *Ramus: Method and the Decay of Dialogue*. Cambridge: Harvard University Press, 1958.

———. S. J. "The Writer's Audience Is Always a Fiction." *PMLA* 90 (1975): 9–21.

Orgel, Stephen. "The Authentic Shakespeare." *Representations* 21 (1988): 1–25.

Oruch, Jack B. "St. Valentine, Chaucer, and Spring in February." *Speculum* 56 (1981): 534–65.

Osberg, Richard. "The Jesse Tree in the 1432 London Entry of Henry VI: Messianic Kingship and the Rule of Justice." *JMRS* 16 (1986): 213–32.

Osgood, Charles G., trans. *Boccaccio on Poetry*. New York: Liberal Arts Press, 1956.

Owen, Charles A., Jr. "*The Canterbury Tales*: Early Manuscripts and Relative Popularity." *JEGP* 54 (1955): 104–10.

Pace, George B., and Alfred David, eds. *The Minor Poems, Part I. A Variorum Edition of the Works of Geoffrey Chaucer*. Vol. 5, Part 1. Norman: University of Oklahoma Press, 1982.

Painter, George D. *William Caxton, A Quincentenary Biography of England's First Printer*. London: Chatto and Windus, 1976.

Parker, Patricia. *Inescapable Romance: Studies in the Poetics of A Mode*. Princeton: Princeton University Press, 1979.

Parkes, M. B. "The Literacy of the Laity." In David Daiches and Anthony Thorlby, eds. *The Medieval World*. London: Aldus Books, 1973. 555–77.

———. "The Influence of the Concepts of *Ordinatio* and *Compilatio* on the Development of the Book." In J.J.G. Alexander and M. T. Gibson, eds. *Medieval Learning and Literature: Essays Presented to Richard William Hunt*. Oxford: Clarendon Press, 1976. 115–41.

Parkes, M. B., and Richard Beadle, eds. *Geoffrey Chaucer: Poetical Works: A Facsimile of Cambridge University Library Gg.4.27*. Cambridge: Cambridge University Press, 1980.

Parkes, M. B., and Elizabeth Salter, eds. *Troilus and Criseyde: A Facsimile of Corpus Christi College Cambridge MS 61*. Cambridge: D. S. Brewer, 1978.

Parry, P. H. "On the Continuity of English Civic Pageantry: A Study of John Lydgate and the Tudor Pageant." *Forum for Modern Language Studies* 15 (1979): 222–36.

Pasquali, Giorgio. *Storia della tradizione e critica del testo*. 2d edition. Firenze: Le Monnier, 1962.

Passon, Richard H. "'Entente' in Chaucer's *Friar's Tale*." *Chaucer Review* 2 (1968): 166–71.

Patterson, Lee. "Ambiguity and Interpretation: A Fifteenth-Century Reading of *Troilus and Criseyde*." *Speculum* 54 (1979): 297–330.

———. "The Logic of Textual Criticism and the Way of Genius: The Kane-Donaldson *Piers Plowman* in Historical Perspective." In Jerome McGann, ed. *Textual Criticism and Literary Interpretation*. 55–91, 212–19.

———. *Negotiating the Past: The Historical Understanding of Medieval Literature*. Madison: University of Wisconsin Press, 1987.

Patterson, Lee. "'What Man Artow?': Authorial Self-Definition in the *Tale of Sir Thopas* and the *Tale of Melibee*." *SAC* 11 (1989): 117–75.

———. ed. *Literary Practice and Social Change in Britain, 1380–1530*. Berkeley and Los Angeles: University of California Press, 1990.

———. *Chaucer and the Subject of History*. Madison: University of Wisconsin Press, 1991.

Pearsall, Derek. *John Lydgate*. Charlottesville: University of Virginia Press, 1970.

———. "The *Troilus* Frontispiece and Chaucer's Audience." *Yearbook of English Studies* 7 (1977): 68–74.

———. ed. *Manuscripts and Readers in Fifteenth-Century England*. Cambridge: D. S. Brewer, 1983.

———. "Editing Medieval Texts." In Jerome McGann, ed., *Textual Criticism and Literary Interpretation*. 92–106.

———. "Chaucer and Lydgate." In Morse and Windeatt, eds. *Chaucer Traditions*. 39–53.

Peck, Russell A. "Public Dreams and Private Myths: Perspective in Middle English Literature." *PMLA* 90 (1975): 461–68.

———. "Chaucer and the Nominalist Questions." *Speculum* 53 (1978): 745–60.

Piccard, Gerhard. *Wasserzeichen Hirsch*. Stuttgart: Verlag W. Kohlhammer, 1987.

Pigman, George W. III. *Grief and English Renaissance Elegy*. Cambridge: Cambridge University Press, 1985.

Poirion, Daniel. *Le Poète et le prince: L'Evolution du lyrisme courtois de Guillaume de Machaut à Charles d'Orleans* (Paris: Presses Universitaires de France, 1965).

Pollard, A. W., and G. R. Redgrave, eds. *A Short-Title Catalogue of Books Printed in England, Scotland, and Ireland and of English Books Printed Abroad, 1475–1640*. 2d ed., revised and enlarged by W. A. Jacobs, F. S. Ferguson, and Katherine F. Panzer. 2 vols. London: The Bibliographical Society, 1976 (vol. 2), 1986 (vol. 1).

Price, D. J., and R. M. Wilson, eds. *Chaucer's Equatorie of the Planets: Edited from Peterhouse MS 75.I*. Cambridge: Cambridge University Press, 1955.

Rashdall, Hastings. *The Universities of Europe in the Middle Ages*. Ed. F. M. Powicke and A. B. Emden. London: Oxford University Press, 1936.

Rawski, Conrad H., ed. and trans. *Petrarch: Four Dialogues for Scholars*. Cleveland: Western Reserve University Press, 1967.

Reinecke, George F., ed. *Saint Albon and Saint Amphibalus by John Lydgate*. New York: Garland, 1985.

Richardson, Malcolm. "The Influence of Henry V on the Development of Chancery English." Ph.D. dissertation, University of Tennessee, 1978.

———. "Henry V, the English Chancery, and Chancery English." *Speculum* 55 (1980): 726–50.

Rickard, Peter. *A History of the French Language*. 2d ed. London: Unwin Hyman, 1989.

Robbins, Rossell Hope. "English Almanacks of the Fifteenth Century." *Philological Quarterly* 18 (1934): 321–31.

———. *Secular Lyrics of the Fourteenth and Fifteenth Centuries*. Oxford: Clarendon Press, 1952.

———. *Historical Poems of the Fourteenth and Fifteenth Centuries*. New York: Columbia University Press, 1959.

——. "The Chaucerian Apocrypha." In J. Burke Severs and Albert E. Hartung, eds. *A Manual of Writings in Middle English, 1050–1500*. New Haven: Yale University Press, 1967. IV: 1061–86.

Robinson, F. N., ed. *The Works of Geoffrey Chaucer*. 2d ed. Boston: Houghton Mifflin, 1957.

Robinson, Pamela R. *Manuscript Tanner 346: A Facsimile*. Norman: Pilgrim Books, 1980.

——. "The 'Booklet': A Self-Contained Unit in Composite Manuscripts." *Codicologica* 3 (1980): 46–69.

——. *Manuscript Bodley 638: A Facsimile*. Norman: Pilgrim Books, 1982.

Rosenthal, Joel T. "Aristocratic Cultural Patronage and Book Bequests, 1350–1500." *Bulletin of the John Rylands Library* 64 (1982): 522–48.

——. *Patriarchy and Families of Privilege in Fifteenth-Century England*. Philadelphia: University of Pennsylvania Press, 1991.

Ruggiers, Paul G., ed. *Editing Chaucer: The Great Tradition*. Norman: Pilgrim Books, 1984.

Rutherford, Charles S. "The *Boke of Cupide* Reopened." *Neuphilologische Mitteilungen* 78 (1977): 350–58.

Rutter, Russell. "William Caxton and Literary Patronage." *SP* 84 (1987): 440–70.

Sacks, Peter. *The English Elegy: Studies in the Genre from Spenser to Yeats*. Baltimore: Johns Hopkins University Press, 1985.

Saenger, Paul. "Silent Reading: Its Impact on Late Medieval Script and Society." *Viator* 13 (1982): 367–414.

——. "Books of Hours and the Reading Habits of the Later Middle Ages," in Roger Chartier, ed., *The Culture of Print*, 141–73.

Saintsbury, George. *History of English Prosody From the Twelfth Century to the Present Day*. 4 volumes. London: Macmillan, 1906-10.

Salter, Elizabeth. "The 'Troilus Frontispiece.'" In Parkes and Salter, eds., *Troilus and Criseyde*. 15–23.

Sands, Donald B. "Caxton as a Literary Critic." *Papers of the Bibliographical Society of America* 51 (1957): 312–18.

Saunders, J. W. "The Stigma of Print: A Note on the Social Bases of Tudor Poetry." *Essays in Criticism* 1 (1951): 139–64.

Scattergood, V. J[ohn], ed. *The Works of Sir John Clanvowe*. Cambridge: D. S. Brewer, 1975.

——. ed. *John Skelton: The Complete English Poems*. New Haven: Yale University Press, 1983.

——. "Skelton's *Garlande of Laurell* and the Chaucerian Tradition." In Morse and Windeatt, eds. *Chaucer Traditions*. 122–38.

Scattergood, V. J[ohn], and J. W. Sherborne, eds. *English Court Culture in the Later Middle Ages*. New York: St. Martin's, 1983.

Schibanoff, Susan. "Taking Jane's Cue: *Phyllyp Sparowe* as a Primer for Women Readers." *PMLA* 101 (1986): 832–47.

——. "The New Reader and Female Textuality in Two Early Commentaries on Chaucer." *SAC* 10 (1988): 71–108.

Schiffhorst, Gerald, ed. *The Triumph of Patience: Medieval and Renaissance Studies*. Orlando: University Presses of Florida, 1978.

Schiffhorst, Gerald. "Some Prolegomena for the Study of Patience, 1480–1680." In Schiffhorst, ed. *The Triumph of Patience: Medieval and Renaissance Studies*. 1–64.

Schirmer, Walter F. *John Lydgate: A Study in the Culture of the XVth Century*. Trans. Ann E. Keep. Berkeley and Los Angeles: University of California Press, 1961.

Scott, Kathleen L. "Lydgate's *Lives of Saints Edmund and Fremund*: A Newly-Located Manuscript in Arundel Castle." *Viator* 13 (1982): 335–57.

Seymour, M. C. "Manuscript Pictures of Duke Humphrey." *Bodleian Library Record* 12 (1986): 95–105.

Shoaf, R. A. "Notes Toward Chaucer's Poetics of Translation." *SAC* 1 (1979): 55–66.

Silverstein, Theodore. "Sir Gawain in a Dilemma, or Keeping Faith with Marcus Tullius Cicero." *Modern Philology* 75 (1976): 1–17.

Silvia, Daniel S. "Some Fifteenth-Century Manuscripts of the *Canterbury Tales*." In Beryl Rowland, ed. *Chaucer and Middle English Studies in Honour of Rossell Hope Robbins*. London: George Allen and Unwin, 1974. 153–63.

Skeat, Walter W. *The Oxford Chaucer*. 7 volumes. Oxford: Oxford University Press, 1894–97.

———. *The Chaucer Canon*. Oxford: Clarendon Press, 1900.

Smith, Barbara Herrnstein. *Poetic Closure: A Study of How Poems End*. Chicago: University of Chicago Press, 1968.

Smith, Julie. "Woodcut Presentation Scenes in Books Printed by Caxton, de Worde, Pynson." *Gutenberg Jahrbuch* (1986): 322–43.

———. "The Poet Laureate as University Master: John Skelton's Woodcut Portrait." In Maryanne Cline Horowitz et al., eds. *Renaissance Rereadings: Intertext and Context*. Urbana: University of Illinois Press, 1988. 159–83.

Spearing, A. C. *Medieval Dream-Poetry*. Cambridge: Cambridge University Press, 1976.

———. *Medieval to Renaissance in English Poetry*. Cambridge: Cambridge University Press, 1985.

Speer, Mary B. "Editing Old French Texts in the Eighties: Theory and Practice." *Romance Philology* 45 (1991): 7–43.

Speyer, Wolfgang. *Bücherfunde in der Glaubenswerbung der Antike. Mit einem Ausblick auf Mittelalter und Neuzeit*. Göttingen: Vandenhoeck und Ruprecht, 1970.

Spurgeon, Caroline. *Five-Hundred Years of Chaucer Criticism and Allusion, 1357–1900*. 3 volumes. London: Kegan Paul, Trench, Trübner, 1914–25.

Stevens, John. *Music and Poetry in the Early Tudor Court*. London: Methuen, 1961.

Stevens, Martin. *Four Middle English Mystery Cycles*. Princeton: Princeton University Press, 1987.

Stock, Brian. *The Implications of Literacy*. Princeton: Princeton University Press, 1983.

Strohm, Paul. "Jean of Angoulême: A Fifteenth-Century Reader of Chaucer." *Neuphilologische Mitteilungen* 72 (1971): 69–76.

———. "Middle English Narrative Genres." *Genre* 13 (1980): 379–88.

———. "Chaucer's Fifteenth-Century Audience and the Narrowing of the 'Chaucer Tradition.'" *SAC* 4 (1982): 3–32.

———. "Chaucer's Audience(s): Fictional, Implied, Intended, Actual." *Chaucer Review* 18 (1983): 137–45.

———. "Fourteenth- and Fifteenth-Century Writers as Readers of Chaucer." In Piero

Boitani and Anna Torti, eds., *Genres, Themes, and Images in English Literature*. Tübingen: Günter Narr, 1988. 90–104.

———. *Social Chaucer*. Cambridge: Harvard University Press, 1989.

Sweeting, Elizabeth J. *Early Tudor Criticism: Linguistic and Literary*. Oxford: Blackwell, 1940.

Tanselle, Thomas G. "Historicism and Critical Editing." *Studies in Bibliography* 39 (1986): 2–46.

Tatlock, J.S.P., ed. *A Concordance to the Complete Works of Geoffrey Chaucer and to the Romaunt of the Rose*. Washington, D.C.: The Carnegie Institution of Washington, 1927.

Taylor, P. B. "Chaucer's 'Cosyn to the Dede.'" *Speculum* 57 (1982): 315–27.

Thrupp, Sylvia L. *The Merchant Class of Medieval London 1300–1500*. Chicago: University of Chicago Press, 1948.

Thynne, William. *The Workes of Geffray Chaucer newly printed, with dyuerse workes which were neuer in print before* . . . . London: Thomas Godfray, 1532.

Timpanaro, Sebastiano. *La genesi del metodo del Lachmann*. 2d edition. Padua: Antenore, 1985.

Trapp, J. B. "The Owl's Ivy and the Poet's Bays." *JWCI* 21 (1958): 227–55.

———. "Ovid's Tomb: The Growth of a Legend from Eusebius to Laurence Sterne, Chauteaubriand and George Richmond." *JWCI* 34 (1973): 35–76.

———. "The Poet Laureate: Rome, *Renovatio*, and *Translatio Imperii*." In P. A. Ramsey, ed., *Rome in the Renaissance: The City and the Myth*. Binghamton: Center for Early Medieval and Renaissance Studies, 1982. 93–130.

Trimpi, Wesley. "The Quality of Fiction: The Rhetorical Transmission of Literary Theory." *Traditio* 30 (1974): 1–118.

Trithemius, Johannes. *In Praise of Scribes: De laude scriptorum*. Ed. Klaus Arnold, trans. R. Behrendt. Lawrence: Coronado Press, 1974.

Ullman, B. L. "The Post-Mortem Adventures of Livy." In his *Studies in the Italian Renaissance*. Rome: Edizioni di Storia e Letteratura, 1955. 55–80.

Vickers, Kenneth H. *Humphrey Duke of Gloucester: A Biography*. London: Constable, 1907.

Voigts, Linda E. "Scientific and Medical Books." In Griffiths and Pearsall, eds. *Book Production and Publishing in Britain 1375–1475*. 345–402.

Walker, Greg. *John Skelton and the Politics of the 1520s*. Cambridge: Cambridge University Press, 1988.

Wallace, David. "'Whan She Translated Was': A Chaucerian Critique of the Petrarchan Academy." In Lee Patterson, ed., *Literary Practice and Social Change*. 156–215.

Wallace, Kristine Gilmartin. "Array as Motif in the *Clerk's Tale*." *Rice University Studies* 62 (1976): 99–110.

Walls, Kathryn. "Did Lydgate Translate the 'Pèlerinage de vie Humaine'?" *Notes and Queries* 24 (1977): 103–5.

Walsh, Richard. "The Coming of Humanism to the Low Countries." *Humanistica Louvaniensia* 25 (1975): 146–97.

Wardrop, James. *The Script of Humanism: Some Aspects of Humanistic Script, 1460–1560*. Oxford: Clarendon Press, 1963.

Warner, Michael. *The Letters of the Republic: Publication and the Public Sphere in Eighteenth-Century America.* Cambridge: Harvard University Press, 1990.

Wattenbach, Wilhelm. *Das Schriftwesen im Mittelalter.* 3d edition. Leipzig: S. Hirzel, 1896.

Webb, C.C.I., ed. *Johannes Saresberiensis . . . Metalogicon.* Oxford: Clarendon Press, 1929.

Weiss, Roberto. *Humanism in England During the Fifteenth Century.* 3d edition. Oxford: Blackwell, 1957.

Wetherbee, Winthrop. *Chaucer and the Poets: An Essay on Troilus and Criseyde.* Ithaca: Cornell University Press, 1984.

Wickham, Glynne. *Early English Stages 1300–1600.* 2 volumes. London: Routledge and Kegan Paul, 1959–81.

Wilkins, Ernest Hatch. *The Making of the "Canzoniere" and Other Petrarchan Studies.* Rome: Edizioni di Storia e Letteratura, 1951.

———. *Studies in the Life and Works of Petrarch.* Cambridge: Mediaeval Academy of America, 1955.

Wilson, Edward. "Local Habitations and Names in MS Rawlinson C.813 in the Bodleian Library, Oxford." *Review of English Studies,* new series 41 (1990): 12–44.

Wilson, R. M. *The Lost Literature of Medieval England.* 2d edition. London: Methuen, 1970.

Windeatt, B. A. "The Scribes as Chaucer's Early Critics." *SAC* 1 (1979): 119–41.

Woodward, William H. *Vittorino da Feltre and Other Humanist Educators.* Cambridge: Harvard University Press, 1897.

Wright, Thomas, and James Orchard Halliwell, eds. *Reliquiae Antiquae.* 2 volumes. London: William Pickering, 1841–43.

Yates, Frances A. *The Art of Memory.* Chicago: University of Chicago Press, 1966.

Yeager, Robert F. "British Library Additional MS 5141: An Unnoticed Chaucer Vita." *JMRS* 14 (1984): 261–81.

———. "Literary Theory at the Close of the Middle Ages: William Caxton and William Thynne." *SAC* 6 (1984): 135–64.

———. ed. *Fifteenth-Century Studies: Recent Essays.* Hamden: Archon Books, 1984.

Zumthor, Paul. *Essai de poétique médiévale.* Paris. Seuil, 1972.

———. "From (Hi)story to Poem, or the Paths of Pun: The Grands Rhétoriqueurs of Fifteenth-Century France." *New Literary History* 10 (1979): 231–63.

———. *Speaking of the Middle Ages.* Trans. Sarah White. Lincoln: University of Nebraska Press, 1986.